Information Technology for Intellectual Property Protection:

Interdisciplinary Advancements

Hideyasu Sasaki
Chinese University of Hong Kong, Hong Kong

Information Science
REFERENCE

Managing Director:	Lindsay Johnston
Senior Editorial Director:	Heather Probst
Book Production Manager:	Sean Woznicki
Development Manager:	Joel Gamon
Acquisitions Editor:	Erika Gallagher
Typesetters:	Adrienne Freeland
Print Coordinator:	Jamie Snavely
Cover Design:	Nick Newcomer

Published in the United States of America by
Information Science Reference (an imprint of IGI Global)
701 E. Chocolate Avenue
Hershey PA 17033
Tel: 717-533-8845
Fax: 717-533-8661
E-mail: cust@igi-global.com
Web site: http://www.igi-global.com

Library of Congress Cataloging-in-Publication Data

Information technology for intellectual property protection: interdisciplinary advancements / Hideyasu Sasaki, editor.
p. cm.
Includes bibliographical references and index.
Summary: "This book contains multidisciplinary knowledge and analysis by leading researchers and practitioners with technical backgrounds in information engineering and institutional experience in intellectual property practice"--Provided by publisher.
ISBN 978-1-61350-135-1 (hbk.) -- ISBN 978-1-61350-136-8 (ebook) -- ISBN 978-1-61350-137-5 (print & perpetual access) 1. Multimedia systems. 2. Information technology--Management. 3. Intellectual property. 4. Copyright infringement. I. Sasaki, Hideyasu.
QA76.575.I233 2012
364.16'62--dc23

2011031136

British Cataloguing in Publication Data
A Cataloguing in Publication record for this book is available from the British Library.

Table of Contents

Detailed Table of Contents

Section 1
Technologies

In this chapter, a robust watermarking technique based on distributive multiresolution transforms (DMT) and singular value decomposition is presented to improve the protection of the images. First, the watermark image is mapped to another form to get reference watermark which is secret and only known to the owner/creator. In order to map watermark image into reference form, chaotic maps are used. The core idea of the proposed technique is to decompose host image via DMT followed by reference watermark embedding in DMT coefficients by modifying the singular values. After embedding, inverse transform is performed to get watermarked image. Two new different distributive multiresolution transforms, namely distributive multiresolution Fourier and distributive multiresolution cosine transform, are explored and used. The feasibility of the proposed method and its robustness against different kind of attacks are verified by computer simulations, and superiority is carried out by the comparisons with the existing methods.

Many audio watermarking techniques, presented in the last years, make use of masking and psychological models derived from signal processing. Such a basic idea is winning because it guarantees a high level of robustness and bandwidth of the watermark as well as fidelity of the watermarked signal. This work first describes the relationship between Digital Right Management, Intellectual Property, and use of watermarking techniques. Then, the crossing use of watermarking and Masking Models is detailed, providing schemes, examples, and references. Finally, the authors present two strategies that make use of a Masking Model, applied to a classic watermarking technique. The joint use of classic frameworks and Masking Models seems to be one of the trends for the future of research in watermarking. Several tests on the proposed strategies with the state of the art are also offered to give an idea of how to assess the effectiveness of a watermarking technique.

The principal concern of this chapter is to provide those in the secure multimedia communication or content protection community with an overview of multimedia content encryption technology. Multimedia (image, audio or video) content encryption technologies are reviewed, from the background, brief history, and performance requirement, to research progress. Additionally, the general encryption algorithms are classified, and their performances are analyzed and compared. Furthermore, some special encryption algorithms are introduced. Finally, some open issues and potential research topics are presented, followed by some conclusions. The author hopes that the chapter will not only inform researchers of the progress of multimedia content encryption but also guide the design of practical applications in industry field.

In this chapter, we propose a new information hiding and extraction scheme for the application in digital watermarking, which does not embed any data to target content, by using non-linear feature extraction scheme trained on frequency domain. This is

In recent years impacts of information and communication technologies, market enclosures, and the opposing struggle to retain community and public goods have had significant impacts on the social interactions of communities. This chapter examines communities in the context of the knowledge commons – a space by which "a particular type of freedom" (Benkler, 2004) can be practised. It also provides an appropriate lexicon to the examination and discourse of communities and the ways they work. As Castells (2003) notes, self-knowledge "is always a construction no matter how much it feels like a discovery"–this construction is enabled when people work or associate themselves with each other. In particular, the chapter is concerned about the structure of open content licenses operating within such domains. The chapter first explores the concept of the knowledge commons to understand the types of intellectual property that are distinctive to communities (public, communal, and private). Thereafter, licenses as a structure are examined as they may apply within such contexts. A significant influence on the discussion is the contemporary media environment that communities operate in today, resulting in the breaking down of boundaries, the blurring of distinctions between an original and a copy, and shifting the nature of production in communities. These debates lead to a case for open content licenses as an appropriate structural mechanism for communities.

In this paper, the authors present a reference P2P architecture based on autonomous, self-emerging semantic communities of interest (CoIs) for collective intelligence creation and management. An approach for enabling knowledge organization and management at the level of a single peer is presented in the paper, as well as techniques for supporting a peer to participate to the construction of a shared community vocabulary, according to the terminological preferences automatically extracted from its personal knowledge. Furthermore, an application example in the e-health domain is presented in the framework of the iCoord system for P2P semantic coordination to show the use of a manifesto-based collective intelligence for enforcing effective collaboration in a real case study.

The emergence of Web 2.0 has brought along the trend of community. It is also the trend that contributes to socialization of the Internet. The essence of Web 2.0 is creation and sharing which give rise to social networking communities such as Blog, Wikipedia and Facebook. Through Wikipedia, Blogs, Facebook and other kinds of social networking websites, interactive relationship and bridge of knowledge sharing have been built up successfully. This paper attempts to propose an effective way to locate people with shared interests. By using Internet resources bookmarked by the users, the similarity of interests between them can be analyzed. Based on this relationship, people could build communities. Also, through community activities, the innovation and exchange of collective intelligence are accomplished.

Preface

Information technology for intellectual property protection is a hot issue on the globe in the twenty first century because the recent expansion of network connectivity to the Internet known as ubiquitous allows people to enjoy a number of contents and programs stored in the digital forms which are fragile to unauthorized electric duplication or copyright and patent infringement. Institutional protection against digital infringement of multimedia intellectual property has been practically supported by technical solutions which digitally maneuver multimedia contents and programs in the Internet. The advent of new solutions in the area of information technology will allow easy access to the tools for multimedia intellectual property infringement as a negative side effect of innovation.

Facing the digital infringement of intellectual property of contents and programs as operating software of those contents, those in the fields of multimedia information engineering and its institutional operations have been aware of a need of a complete reference of past, current, and future trends of multimedia intellectual property protection from technology to institutions. This book offers a first reference on information technology for intellectual property protection with multidisciplinary knowledge and analyses which are given by leading researchers and practitioners with technical backgrounds in information engineering and institutional experiences in intellectual property practice.

INTRODUCTION

The principal concern of this book is to provide those in the information technology and its institutional practice with a series of concise and thorough references on a variety of issues of intellectual property protection and its proper solutions from the technical aspects. We discuss both technical and institutional solutions to intellectual property protection.

We thoroughly discuss institutional and technical issues and provide their solutions on information technology for intellectual property protection. The goal of this book is to design a complete reference in the area of information technology for intellectual property protection. Already published books just discuss institutional analyses without interdisciplinary insights by technical experts. Meanwhile, technical references only talk about engineering solutions without the social impact to institutional protection. This book should fill in that gap to fulfill a great mission under which people in the field of information technology for intellectual property protection can discuss all the related issues and their solutions from both institutional and technical aspects.

CHALLENGES

The book brings in a first guidance or introductory reference to graduate students and students in professional schools, researchers, and practitioners in the areas of policy, engineering, and education, and provides them with mandatory knowledge bases on information technology for intellectual property protection. This kind of complete reference has not been available in the previous research publication. Its scholarly value is found in the brand new aspect of engineering solutions to intellectual property protection.

The content of the book is appealing to academia, in which those concerned about intellectual property management are eager to acquire sound techniques for intellectual property protection and fundamental knowledge on intellectual property rights in the frontiers of IT outbursts. Meanwhile, the book works as a technical milestone for research trends of intellectual property protection engineering in the target of the next ten years. Both practitioners with technical agendas and IT engineers of institutional agendas should appreciate this kind of interdisciplinary title.

ORGANIZATION

The book is organized into eleven chapters:

Chapter 1 discusses a robust watermarking technique which is based on distributed multi-resolution transforms (DMT) and singular value decomposition to improve the protection of images.

Chapter 2 discusses masking models and watermarking with two strategies for using a masking model in its application to a classic watermarking technique.

Chapter 3 discusses content encryption for secure communication and provides an overview of encryption technology from background, brief history, and requirement to research progress with general and special encryption algorithms.

Chapter 4 discusses damage-less watermark extraction for information hiding using non-linear feature extraction scheme trained on frequency domain.

Chapter 5 discusses user authentication in IP networks and introduces basic concepts of authentication and challenge-response frameworks.

Chapter 6 discusses query rewriting algorithms for access control to avoid resource-leakage in Semantic Web systems.

Chapter 7 discusses ticketing services using an auction system design for seat reservations at theaters.

Chapter 8 discusses legal protection of Web pages from the database perspective and refers to the World Intellectual Property Organization Copyright Treatments and European Directive 96/92/CE with its future trends.

Chapter 9 discusses a concept of knowledge commons and open content licenses from the perspective of communities.

Chapter 10 discusses a peer-to-peer architecture based on autonomous and self-emerging communities for managing collective knowledge.

Chapter 11 discusses a community creation using bookmarks as resources available in the Internet to make linkages between people of common interests.

GUIDELINE

The main target of prospective academic audience is graduate students who study computer science, information engineering, system engineering, information studies, management of information technology, and library science. Another target is students who are working towards professional degrees in business schools, management schools, MOT programs, public policy schools, law schools, or their equivalents. The other target is not a small number of practitioners including lawyers who counsel to IT companies as in-house counsels or at firms, chief information officers (CIOs), chief technology officers (CTOs), and chief risk management officers (CROs) in enterprises and the consultants in those related fields. Not the last but an important part of prospective audience is found in a large number of intellectual property related staff or administrators in universities and librarians.

The book is designed to offer a reference in the communities on information technology for intellectual property protection. The book has eleven chapters, which should be well allocated as assignments in class at Junior or Senior engineering of the undergraduate lectures, and master-level graduate schools.

Hideyasu Sasaki
Chinese University of Hong Kong, Hong Kong

Acknowledgment

The editor would like to thank all the authors who have submitted chapter proposals, and all authors and reviewers for their excellent contributions and insights, without which this book should not have been possible. Special thanks go to IGI Global for its great editorial assistance.

Hideyasu Sasaki
Chinese University of Hong Kong, Hong Kong
January 10, 2011

Section 1
Technologies

Chapter 1
Distributed Multiresolution Transform Based Framework for Watermarking

Gaurav Bhatnagar
University of Windsor, Canada

Jonathan Wu
University of Windsor, Canada

Balasubramanian Raman
Indian Institute of Technology Roorkee, India

ABSTRACT

In this chapter, a robust watermarking technique based on distributive multiresolution transforms (DMT) and singular value decomposition is presented to improve the protection of the images. First, the watermark image is mapped to another form to get reference watermark which is secret and only known to the owner/creator. In order to map watermark image into reference form, chaotic maps are used. The core idea of the proposed technique is to decompose host image via DMT followed by reference watermark embedding in DMT coefficients by modifying the singular values. After embedding, inverse transform is performed to get watermarked image.

DOI: 10.4018/978-1-61350-135-1.ch001

Two new different distributive multiresolution transforms, namely distributive multiresolution Fourier and distributive multiresolution cosine transform, are explored and used. The feasibility of the proposed method and its robustness against different kind of attacks are verified by computer simulations, and superiority is carried out by the comparisons with the existing methods.

INTRODUCTION

Nowadays, the substantial maturation of internet and web technologies have led to an environment in which some of very crucial issues for multimedia/digital media, particularly image, audio and video content, such as illegal copying, distribution, editing, copyright protection, authentication etc become very easy. This environment has led to an increasing demand for developing some standard solution to prevent these issues. As the possible solution, Cryptography (or encryption techniques) comes to our help. Cryptography is the art of secret (crypto) writing (graphy). It is the science of using mathematics to encrypt and decrypt data. Whilst the traditional cryptographic solutions can encrypt multimedia and transmit it across insecure channel so that it cannot be read by anyone except the authorized recipient. However they require the receiver to use a key to decrypt the data successfully. Moreover, such solutions do not prevent or track the content against illegitimate reproduction after it has been decrypted. It essentially provides end-to-end security while distributing digital media over a large variety of distributions systems. It is mainly concerned with the secured communication instead of ulterior copyright infraction and protecting the content of the message rather than their existence. As per their existence is concerned, a new terminology named steganography/data hiding comes into picture. Steganography (Katzenseisser & Petitcolas, 2000) is the art of covered (secret) writing (graphy). It enables hiding a message data into host multimedia such that there is no perceptual degradation in the host multimedia according to human perception. The composite multimedia is usually termed as the stego/marked multimedia. Unlike cryptography, steganography tries to conceal the existence of the messages. It typically relates only to covert point to point communication between two parties in other words it is a form of subliminal communication. The major drawback of steganographic techniques is the limited robustness against modification of the digital media, occurred during transmission, storage or file conversion. In order to take care of robustness problem, a new terminology named Digital Watermarking is identified as effective solution (Cox et al., 2001; Arnold et al., 2003). Thus, rather than steganography, digital watermarking is used wherever the intellectual property protection is concerned. The inserted/embedded message data is called watermark/signature/metadata whereas the multimedia to be protected is called cover-data (Muharemagic & Furht, 2004).

The word watermark is thought to have been derived from the German word "wassermarke" and is termed as the marks were thought to have resembled the effects of water on paper. Watermarking was first started by the Italians in the 13th century. Their watermark was wired patterns, created during paper production which left designs in the paper once it molded. The purpose is still unclear that watermarking was done due to decoration or some other purposes. However, the first possible purpose of ancient watermarking reflected from the eighteenth century where Europe and America have used watermarking technology in paper production to ensure trademarks, to track when the paper was created, indicate size of the sheets and prevent counterfeiting. From the basic imprints on paper, watermarks moved onto color where dyed ink was inserted into the paper during the molding process. Another possible advancement was to create a raise in the paper causing a slight bump on the surface like the slight bump commonly seen on nowadays paper currency. Therefore, it can be said that the ancient purpose of watermarking is to distinguish one paper manufacturer from other. Finally, the idea of digital watermarking appeared between in 1979, where Szepanski discussed a machine that could be used on documents which would place a pattern for anti-counterfeiting purposes (Szepanski, 1979). In 1988, Holt described a way of embedding an identification code in an audio signal and the term digital watermark first appeared (Holt *et al.*, 1988). However, for images the term digital watermarking was first coined in 1993 by Andrew Tirkel, in their paper "Electronic Water Mark" (Trikel *et al.*, 1993). But the digital watermarking has gained the attention of research community since about 1995. From then on, many papers were released discussing different ways for digital watermarks implementation and companies ranging from the music industry to business software began using this technique for security and protection. This fact is also justified by the number of publication, which was 13 until 1995, has jumped to 110 till 1998 and has become 1500 by the end of 2003. This trend points out that watermarking is a relatively growing field and its continuing progress is anticipated in both academic and industrial applications in the coming years.

The rest of chapter begins with the fundamental concept, requirements and application of digital watermarking followed by a more detailed discussion on different transform based watermarking techniques. Finally, a novel robust digital watermarking algorithm based on the distributive multiresolution transforms is also included in the chapter which should be of significant interest to experienced researchers as well as newcomers to the field.

DIGITAL WATERMARKING: PROBLEM FORMULATION

A general watermarking system or technique comprises of two main modules: (1) Watermark Embedding (2) Watermark Detection or Extraction. The watermark embedding module essentially combines the cover-data/host multimedia (C) with the watermark (W) and creates the watermarked/marked multimedia (C_W). The embedding is accomplished in two steps. In the first step, the original watermark is mapped into another form, called reference watermark $(\overline{W})$. This mapping is done with the help of a key K, which can be used to enforce security. This used key K could be either public or private or combination of these two. In the second step, $\overline{W}$ is added to C, to produce the marked data. Watermark detector/extractor either detects the existence of the metadata in marked data or it produces an estimate of metadata. The detection/extraction of the metadata is done with the help of the same key K, which is used in embedding. A typical watermarking system is shown in Figure 1. Mathematically, the embedding and detection/extraction process are defined as:

$$C_W = E(C, \overline{W}) \tag{1}$$

$$W_{ext} = D(C_w, C, K) \tag{2}$$

where $\overline{W} = \zeta(W,K)$, here ζ is a function that maps W into $\overline{W}$ with the help of key K. E is the encoder function that takes a cover-data and a watermark, and it generates a watermarked cover-data. Similarly, D is the decoder/extractor function that takes watermarked cover, original cover-data and a key K to generate the estimate of W. The extracted metadata W_{ext} will then be compared with the owner's original watermark W, considering a similarity function $S = sim(W, W_{ext})$ and is defined as:

$$S = sim(W, W_{ext}) \begin{cases} = 1 & if\ W = W_{ext} \\ < 1 & if\ W \neq W_{ext} \end{cases} \tag{3}$$

The value of S lies between [0, 1]. If the value of S is equal to 1 then the extracted watermark is just equal to the original one whereas if $S<1$ then the extracted watermark is having block artifacts and degradation. Usually, if S is greater than a predefined threshold then the detection/extraction is said to be successful.

Figure 1. Watermarking system (a) Watermark embedding; (b) Watermark detection/extraction

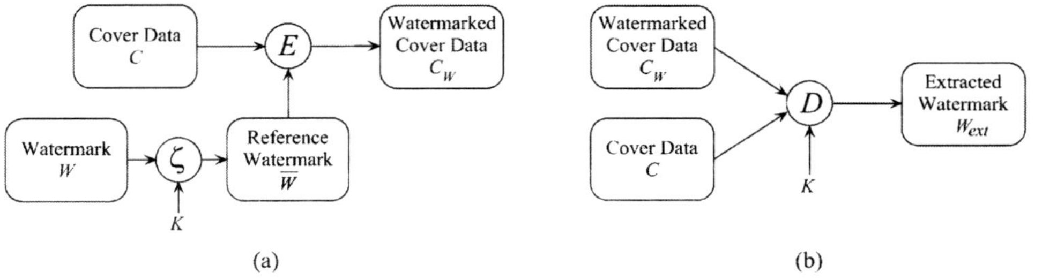

REQUIREMENTS FOR WATERMARKING SCHEMES

Depending on the problem formulation and purposes, watermarking schemes must satisfy five requirements. These requirements are transparency, robustness, security, capacity, and possibility of verification/detectability. Based on these requirements the watermarking can be evaluated. In general, if a specific watermarking scheme has adequate requirements and can be used for a certain application area. The meaning of these requirements is as follows:

- **Transparency/Imperceptibility** relates to the properties of the human visual system. A good watermarking scheme causes no artifacts or quality loss in the data.
- **Robustness** relates to the properties of the detection/extraction process. It usually describes whether the watermark can be reliably detected/extracted after intruder operations. In other words, it refers to the ability of the watermark to be preserved even after distortions introduced by standard or malicious data processing, which may be either intentionally or un-intentionally. These distortions are also known as watermarking attacks.
- **Security** describes whether the embedded watermarking information cannot be removed beyond reliable detection by targeted attacks based on a full knowledge of the embedding algorithm and the detector, except the key, and the knowledge of at least one watermarked data. The best way to improve security is the selection of secret key secretly and those who know the secret key can detect/extract the watermark.
- **Capacity** describes how much information can be embedded in the cover data. It addresses also the possibility of embedding more than one watermark in one cover data in parallel.
- **Detectability** intends to check whether the data is watermarked or not.

Figure 2. Possible tradeoff between these requirements

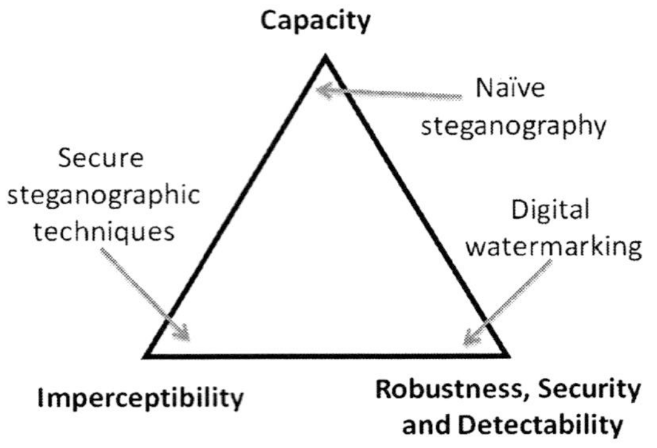

These five constraints are usually opposing each other and hence an application dependent trade-off must be found. A possible tradeoff is given in the Figure 2. Generally, the imperceptibility is the most important constraint because the artifacts introduced while watermarking process are not only annoying and un-desirable but also reduce or destroy its commercial value. Unfortunately, improving robustness often implies perceptual degradations, improving imperceptibility leads to less robustness, hiding more information (high capacity) leads to less robustness and conversely.

TYPES OF WATERMARKING

Digital watermarking can be classified according to many different criteria. For example, depending upon cover data, working domain, human perception and detection/extraction process. The complete classification of watermarking techniques is shown in the Table 1. Among these, categorizations by working domain and human perception have attracted main interest of the research community. Among spatial and frequency domain techniques, spatial domain techniques are less complex but not robust against various attacks. Frequency domain techniques are robust as compared to spatial domain techniques. This is due to the fact that when image is inverse transformed, watermark is distributed irregularly over the image, making the attacker difficult to read or modify. In visible watermarking, the embedded watermark appears visible to the viewers on a careful inspection. In invisible-robust watermarking, watermark is embedded in such a way that it cannot be perceptually noticed and it can be recovered only with appropriate decoding/extracting mechanism.

Table 1. Classification of watermarking techniques

Criterion (According to)	Category	Characteristic
Cover Data	Image	The watermark is embedded in an image.
	Audio	The watermark is embedded in an audio.
	Video	The watermark is embedded in a video. Since, the video can be regarded as the sequence of the correlated images. Therefore, one can do video watermarking either frame by frame or block wise (block of consecutive frames).
Working Domain	Spatial Domain	The watermark is embedded directly to the cover data coefficients.
	Frequency Domain	The watermark is embedded in the transform domain coefficients (e.g. DFT, DCT, DWT coefficients) of cover data. Embedding takes place either in a whole or blocks of coefficients.
Human Perception	Visible	If the watermark can be seen in watermarked cover data.
	Invisible	If the watermark cannot be seen in watermarked cover data, but can be detected/extracted algorithmically.
Detection/Extraction Process	Non-Blind	Watermarking that uses the original Cover data in the watermark detection/extraction process.
	Semi-Blind	Watermark detection/extraction that does not require the original Cover data but require side information.
	Blind	Watermark detection/extraction that does not require the original Cover data.

APPLICATIONS OF WATERMARKING

Digital watermarking is a flexible technology used in a broad range of applications (Cox et al., 2000; Mohanty, 1999). The earlier watermarking approaches were designed for owner authentication or copyright protection, where an owner or producer identification is embedded to prove ownership or source of the cover data. Gradually, different applications are explored and classified in a number of different ways. The best way to characterize applications of watermarking is based on the type of information conveyed by the watermark where each of the application has its own specific requirements with respect to robustness, capacity, imperceptibility, security and detectability to fulfill the desired goal. According to information conveyed the classification of watermarking applications are depicted in Figure 3 with their requirements. It is consequently obvious that there exists no watermarking scheme which would be optimal for every application.

Figure 3. Applications of watermarking with requirements

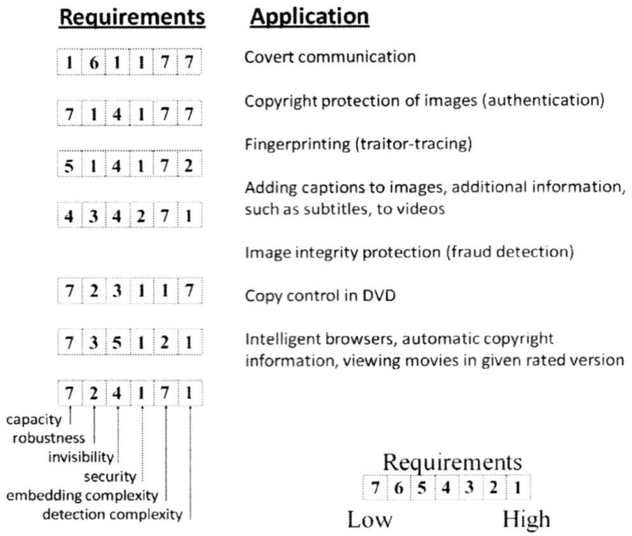

LITERATURE SURVEY FOR DIGITAL WATERMARKING

The existing literature includes several taxonomies for digital watermarking. Among these, the most common taxonomies are embedding in spatial and frequency domains. Spatial domain methods (Schyndle *et al.*, 1994; Hwang *et al.*, 1999) are less complex but not robust against various attacks as no transform is used in them. The basic idea behind spatial domain methods is the modification of pixel intensities while embedding watermark. Transform domain methods are robust as compared to spatial domain methods. This is due to the fact that when image is inverse transformed, watermark is distributed irregularly over the image, making the attacker difficult to read or modify. The basic idea behind transform domain methods is to transform the media by the means of *Fourier Transform* (FT) (Cox *et al.* (1997)), *Discrete Cosine Transform* (DCT) (Barni *et al.*, 1998), *Fractional Fourier Transform* (FrFT) (Djurovic *et al.*, 2001; Feng *et al.*, 2005; Yu *et al.*, 2006), *Wavelet Transform* (Xia *et al.*, 1997; Barni *et al.*, 2001; Meerwald & Uhl, 2001; Zhang *et al.*, 2003; Kundur & Hatzinakos, 2004; Wang & Lin, 2004) etc. Then, the transform domain coefficients are altered to embed the watermark and finally inverse transform is applied to obtain the watermarked digital media. Due to the superiority of frequency domain, we concentrate on existing frequency domain watermarking schemes.

Cox *et al.* (1997) have presented the most popular watermarking schemes based on the Spread Spectrum Communication. The watermark is embedded into the first *k* highest magnitude DFT/DCT coefficients of the image and extraction is done by comparing the DFT/DCT coefficients of the watermarked and the original image. Barni *et al.* (1998) have proposed a watermarking algorithm, which operates in the frequency domain, embeds a pseudo-random sequence of real numbers in a selected set of DCT coefficients. The watermark can be reliably extracted blindly by exploiting the statistical properties of the embedded sequence. Djurovic *et al.* (2001) have proposed fractional Fourier transform based watermarking scheme for the multimedia copyright protection. After decomposing image via FrFT, transformation coefficients are reordering in non-increasing sequence and the watermark is embedded in the middle coefficients. Feng *et al.* (2005) have proposed a blind watermarking algorithm in which multiple chirps are used as watermark and embedded in the spatial domain directly but detected in the FrFT domain. Yu *et al.* (2006) have used the same logic proposed by Feng *et al.* (2005), the only difference is that the embedding is done in FrFT domain where watermark position and the transform order are used as the encryption keys.

Xia *et al.* (1997) have added a pseudo-random sequence to the largest coefficients of the detail bands where perceptual considerations are taken into account by setting the amount of modification proportional to the strength of the coefficient itself. Watermark detection is achieved through comparison with the original un-watermarked image. Barni *et al.* (2001) proposed a method based on the characteristics of the human visual system operating in wavelet domain. Based on the texture and the luminance content of all image sub-bands, a mask is accomplished pixel by pixel. Kundur and Hatzinakos (2004) proposed the use of gray scale logo as watermark. They addressed a multiresolution fusion based watermarking method for embedding gray scale logos into wavelet transformed images via salience factor. Wang and Lin (2004) and Zhang *et al.* (2003) proposed a new watermarking algorithm based on wavelet tree quantization. Lin et al. (2006) have modified wavelet transform to distributed wavelet transform and applied it to enhance the security of images with improved operational efficiency when compared to existing scheme. The detailed survey on wavelet based watermarking techniques can be found in Meerwald and Uhl (2001).

Recently, a new transform, *singular value decomposition* (SVD)-based (Gorodetski *et al.*, 2001; Liu & Tan, 2002; Chandra, 2002; Ganic *et al.*, 2003) watermarking technique and its variants have been proposed. These approaches work on the simple concept of finding the SVD of a cover image or the SVD of each block of the cover image, and then modify the singular values to embed the watermark. Gorodestski *et al.* (2001) have proposed a scheme in which the host image is first segmented into blocks of size 4×4 and the largest singular value of each block is quantized to embed one bit of data. Liu and Tan (2002) have proposed an algorithm based on SVD. In this algorithm, authors find the singular values of the host image and then modify it by adding the watermark. SVD transform is again applied on the resultant matrix to find the modified singular values. These singular values are combined with the known component to get the watermarked image. Inverse process is used for the extraction of watermark. Chandra *et al.* (2002) have described a method for embedding singular values of the watermark into the singular values of entire image. Ganic *et al.* (2003) have proposed an optimal watermarking scheme. In which the embedding strength factor depends on the host and watermark image singular values. Recently, researchers have presented hybrid watermarking schemes in which they have combined SVD with other existing transforms (Ganic & Eskicioglu, 2005; Sverldov *et al.*, 2005; Li *et al.*, 2007; Chang *et al.*, 2005; Bhatnagar & Raman, 2009a; Bhatnagar & Raman, 2009b). SVD based scheme withstands a variety attacks but it is not resistant to geometric attacks like rotation, cropping etc. Hence, for improving the performance hybridization is needed. Ganic and Eskicioglu (2005) have presented hybrid-watermarking scheme based on DWT and SVD. After decomposing the cover image into four bands, SVD is applied on each band, and modify the singular values of each band with the singular values of the visual watermark. Sverldov *et al.* (2005) have used the same concept taking DCT and SVD. DCT coefficients are mapped into four quadrants via ZIG-ZAG scan and modify the singular values of each quadrant. Li *et al.* (2007) have proposed the same hybrid DWT-SVD domain watermarking scheme by exploiting the properties of human visual system. Chang *et al.* (2005) have proposed a new technique in which embedding is done in D and U components. Bhatnagar and Raman (2009a) have proposed a self reference watermarking scheme in wavelet domain where watermark is embedded in the reference image made according to human visual system. Further, Bhatnagar and Raman (2009b) have proposed another reference watermarking scheme in wavelet packet domain. For embedding, authors have extended the concept of SVD to bi-diagonal SVD and then watermark is inserted in the bi-diagonal singular values.

DISTRIBUTED MULTIRESOLUTION TRANSFORM (DMT)

The Fourier transform (Bracewell, 1965) is one of the most important mathematical tools used in physical optics, linear system theory, signal processing, and so on. The essence of the Fourier transform of a signal is to decompose or separate the signal into a sum of sinusoids of different frequencies. Fourier transform is the time-frequency representation of the signal. In time-frequency representation, normally a plane is used with two orthogonal axes corresponding to time and frequency. The conventional Fourier transform can be visualized as a change in representation of the signal corresponding to a counterclockwise rotation of the axis by an angle $\pi/2$.

Two successive rotations of the signal through $\pi/2$ will result in an inversion of the time axis. Let the 1D signal sequence with period N is $X = \{X(l): l = 0, 1, 2, \ldots, N-1\}$ and the discrete Fourier transformed signal sequence is denoted by $Y = \{Y(k): k = 0, 1, 2, \ldots, N-1\}$. Then by definition, each $Y(k)$ is given by:

$$Y(j) = \sum_{k=0}^{N-1} X(k)\, e^{-2\pi kj / N}, 0 \le j \le N-1 \tag{4}$$

Further, in order to reconstruct the original signal from transformed signal following inverse formula is used:

$$X(k) = \frac{1}{N} \sum_{j=0}^{N-1} Y(j)\, e^{2\pi kj / N}, 0 \le k \le N-1 \tag{5}$$

Due to separability of the transform, two dimensional discrete Fourier transform can be obtained by successively taking one dimensional discrete Fourier transform of rows and columns. One of the most appealing aspects of the DFT is the existence of an efficient procedure for calculating it, using $O(N \log N)$ complex operations, rather than $O(N^2)$ operations required for the naive algorithm. The most famous algorithm for calculating DFT, is known as the FFT (the Fast Fourier Transform) (Brigham, 2002). It takes advantage of symmetry properties of the complex roots of unity, and uses repeated clever partitioning of the input sequence into two equally long subsequences, each of which can be separately processed. Due to separability of the transforms, two dimensional transforms can be obtained by successively taking one dimensional transforms along both the axis. Besides lot of advantages, Fourier transform has some drawbacks. The main drawbacks of Fourier transform are as follows:

- It does not give any information about the occurrence of the frequency component at the particular time.
- Location information is stored in phases and difficult to extract. For example, consider discrete functions defined on an N-point grid with grid points $x_j = jh$, $j=0,1,\ldots,N-1$, where $h = 2\pi/N$. If host signal (X) is defined by

$$X(j) = \begin{cases} 1 & j = p \\ 0 & j \ne p \end{cases} \tag{6}$$

For some p, then DFT of X is given by

$$\overline{X}(k) = \frac{h}{\sqrt{2\pi}} e^{-ikj} \tag{7}$$

If the above equation will observed then we see that the Fourier coefficients all have the same magnitude, so the only way to tell from the Fourier transform that this function is concentrated at a single point in time space, and to determine the location of that point, is to examine the phase of the coefficients.

Because of this, it can be very difficult, if not impossible, to determine whether a signal includes a particular frequency at a particular point in time. This is especially difficult for a high frequency, in view of the sampling theorem, which states that a signal with N frequencies can be represented with complete accuracy using $2N$ samples per second. However, this sampling rate must be maintained for the entire duration of the signal, not just the interval of interest.

- The Fourier transform is very sensitive to changes in the function. In view of the previous example, a change of $O(\varepsilon)$ in one point of a discrete function can cause as much as $O(\varepsilon)$ change in every Fourier coefficient. Similarly, a change in any one Fourier coefficient can cause a change of similar magnitude at every point in time space.

These drawbacks of Fourier transform are rectified in wavelet transform. Wavelet transform (WT) is a *multiresolution decomposition* with high-energy compaction properties (Mallat, 1989; Mayer, 1989; Dabuchies, 1992). WT can be viewed as a block transform with overlapping basis functions of variable lengths. Using WT the time domain signal can be expanded in terms of a weighted sum of a set of basic functions, in a way similar to the Fourier transform where the basic functions are translations and dilations of a single fixed function called the mother wavelet instead of sinusoids of different frequency as used in Fourier transform. In general, wavelet transform decomposes the signal into different multiresolution bands where the lowest resolution band (approximation sub-band) is the smallest band in size and it includes high amplitude approximation coefficients. The high resolution bands (detail sub-bands) containing wavelet coefficients, have small magnitudes. But the problem with wavelet transform is its memory inefficiency, conceptually complex structure and non-perfect reconstruction. The meaning of the word memory inefficiency is that wavelet transform needs huge memory due to the use of filters. Hence, to overcome these drawbacks, concept of *Distributed Multiresolution Transform* (DMT) is proposed by Bhatnagar and Raman (2009c; 2010). Here, two distributed multiresolution transforms namely *Distributed Multiresolution Discrete Fourier Transform* (D-MR-DFT) and *Distributed Multiresolution Discrete Cosine Transform* (D-MR-DCT) are considered, which rectify the limitations of the traditional transforms. Without loss of generality, let us assume I represents a 2-D signal (image) having dimension $M \times N$ along both x- and y- direction. The D-MR-DFT and D-MR-DCT of I are implemented as follows:

Step 1. FFT/DCT is performed on image I, which is denoted by I_1.
Step 2. Perform horizontal process as:

$$I_2(:, x)=I_1(:, x)+I_1(:, x + N/2)$$

$$I_2(:, x+N/2)=I_1(:, x)-I_1(:, x + N/2) \tag{8}$$

Step 3. Perform vertical process as:

$$I_3(y,:)=I_2(y,:)+I_2(y + M/2,:)$$

$$I_3(y+M/2)=I_2(y,:)-I_2(y + M/2,:) \tag{9}$$

where I, I_1, I_2 and I_3 refer to original, FFT/DCT transformed, temporary and final D-MR-DFT/ D-MR-DCT signal respectively. Figure 4 shows the D-MR-DFT/ D-MR-DCT decomposition process of a block of size 4×4. Similarly, inverse D-MR-DFT/ D-MR-DCT is also implemented in three steps:

Step 1. Perform reverse vertical process as:

$$\begin{aligned} \bar{I}_1(y,:) &= I_3(y,:) + I_3(y + M/2,:) \\ \bar{I}_1(y + M/2,:) &= I_3(y,:) - I_3(y + M/2,:) \end{aligned} \tag{10}$$

Step 2. Perform reverse horizontal process as:

$$\begin{aligned} \bar{I}_2(:,x) &= \bar{I}_1(:,x) + \bar{I}_1(:,x + N/2) \\ \bar{I}_2(:,x + N/2) &= \bar{I}_1(:,x) - \bar{I}_1(:,x + N/2) \end{aligned} \tag{11}$$

Step 3. Inverse FFT/DCT is performed on image $\bar{I}_2$ to get reconstructed image, which is denoted by $\bar{I}$.

Figure 4. Process for distributed multiresolution transform

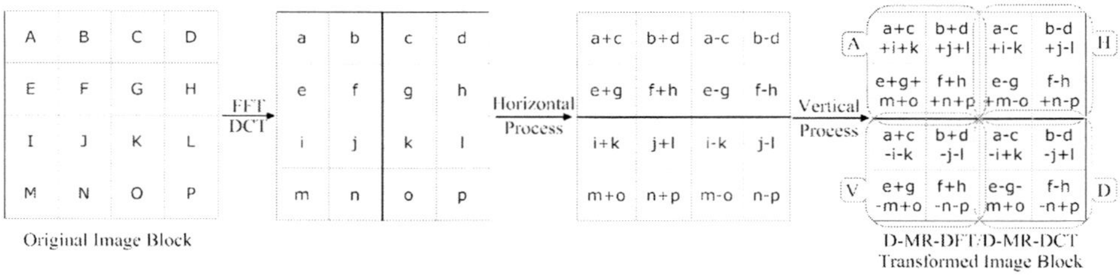

where $\bar{I}_1$, $\bar{I}_2$ and $\bar{I}$ refer to the reversed vertical, reconstructed FFT/DCT transformed and reconstructed signals. Since, D-MR-DFT/ D-MR-DCT are the extensions of DFT and DCT, all the properties of DFT (DCT) are present in the D-MR-DFT (D-MR-DCT).

CHAOTIC MAPS

Chaos is an aperiodic dynamic process having numerous excellent properties such as the ergodicity, sensitive dependence on initial conditions, random-like behaviors etc. (Lasota & Mackey, 1997; Devaney, 2003). Due to these properties, chaos theory is suitable and nowadays widely used in cryptography (Carroll *et al.*, 1992). Generally, chaos theory is represented by the chaotic system which is in the form of maps. The simplest maps are one-dimensional maps which have the advantages of high-level efficiency and implicit nature (Elnashaie & Abasha, 1995; Baptista, 1998). *Logistic map* is one of the examples of one-dimensional map which is being widely used now. The logistic map is a polynomial mapping (equivalently, recurrence relation) of degree 2, often cited as an archetypal example of how complex, chaotic behavior can arise from very simple non-linear dynamical equations. The map was popularized by the biologist Robert May by modifying logistic equation (the Verhulst model: a model of population growth) to a discrete quadratic recurrence relation. Mathematically, logistic map is described as

$$x_{i+1} = \tilde{F}(x_i, \mu) \Longrightarrow x_{i+1} = \mu\, x_i(1-x_i),\ i=0,1,2,\ldots \quad (12)$$

where $x_n \in (0,1)$, $\mu > 0$ is the parameter which control the chaotic nature of the map and x_0 is the initial condition for the map. Thus, given initial condition x_0 and parameter μ, one sequence $\{x_i\}_{i=0}^{\infty}$ is obtained and refers to the orbit of the map corresponding to (x_0, μ). In order to see the restrictions on μ, the bifurcation diagram

Figure 5. Bifurcation diagram of logistic map

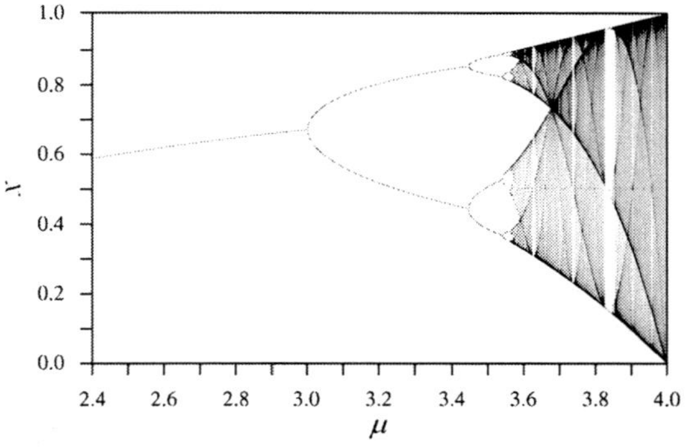

of logistic map is considered which is depicted in Figure 5. Bifurcation diagram is a plot shows the possible long-term values (equilibria/fixed points or periodic orbits) of a system as a function of a parameter (μ) in the system. For $\mu \epsilon [0,1]$, the trivial solution is the only fixed point where as a non-trivial fixed point is the solution when $\mu \epsilon (1,3]$. The map exhibits the phenomenon of periodic doubling for $\mu \epsilon (3,3.57]$ and the chaos appears when $\mu \epsilon (3.57,4]$. Therefore this range is said to be chaotic region for logistic map. Finally, for μ=4, the generated chaos values cover the whole range of (0,1). In order to show that Logistic map is sensitive to its initial condition and parameter, the orbits are calculated with slight change in these. Figure 6(a) shows the orbit after 10 iterations with slight change in initial condition whereas Figure 6(b) shows the orbit with slight change in μ. The change is made in such a manner that original and changed values are approximately same. From figure it is clear that slight change in any of these leads a huge change in orbit. Therefore, Logistic map is highly sensitive to its initial condition and parameter.

PROPOSED WATERMARKING FRAMEWORK

In this section, some of the motivating factors are discussed in design of our framework to watermarking. Distributed Multiresolution transforms and SVD is used for developing the framework. Let us consider F is the host image and W is the watermark. The host and watermark images are gray scale images of size $M \times N$ and $m \times n$ respectively. The block diagram of proposed algorithm is given in Figure 7.

Figure 6. Sensitivity of logistic map to its initial condition (x_0) and Parameter (μ): (a) 10 Iteration with slight change in x_0; (b) 10 Iteration with slight change in μ

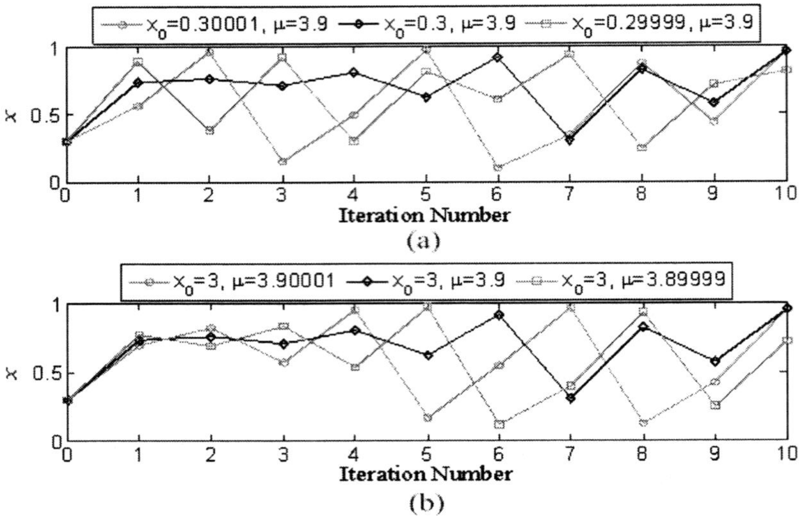

Figure 7. Proposed embedding and extraction process using distributed multiresolution transform

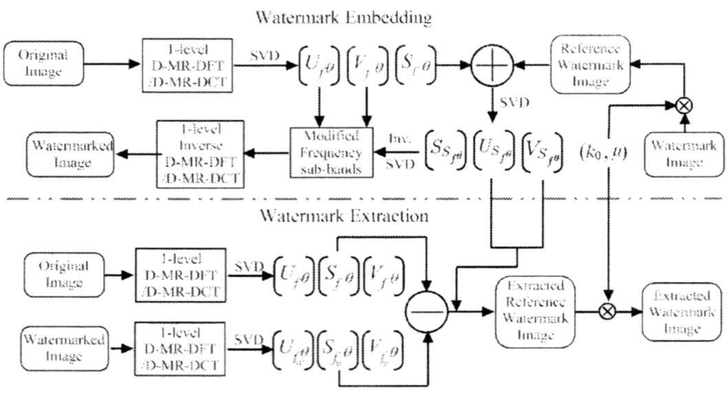

Embedding Process

The embedding process is given as follows.

Step 1. Perform DMT on the host image (F), which is denoted by f^{θ}, where $\theta \in \{A, H, V, D\}$.

Step 2. Perform SVD transform on each sub-bands f^{θ}

$$f^{\theta} = U_{f^{\theta}} S_{f^{\theta}} V_{f^{\theta}}^{T} \tag{13}$$

Adopting

Step 3. k_{0}, μ and $l(>m\times n)$ as keys, iterate logistic map l times, to generate a stochastic sequence, say κ

Step 4. Map κ into the stochastic integer sequence as

$$\kappa^{new} = \langle (1*\kappa) mod 255 \rangle \tag{14}$$

where $\langle \circ \rangle$ denotes the airthmetic rounding operation.

Step 5. Stack the last $m\times n$ values of stochastic integer sequence κ^{new} in an array, say $\mathcal{K}$.

Step 6. Obtain a reference watermark with the help of W and $\mathcal{K}$ as

$$W^{ref} = (W+\mathcal{K}) \text{ mod } 255 \tag{15}$$

Step 7. Modify the singular values of each sub-band of host image with the watermark as

$$S_{f^{\theta}}^{new} = S_{f^{\theta}} + \alpha_{\theta} W^{ref} \tag{16}$$

where α_{θ} gives the watermark strength for each orientation.

Step 8. Perform SVD transform on each sub-bands $S_{f^{\theta}}^{new}$

$$S_{f^{\theta}}^{new} = U_{S_{f^{\theta}}^{new}} S_{S_{f^{\theta}}^{new}} V_{S_{f^{\theta}}^{new}}^{T} \tag{17}$$

Step 9. Perform inverse SVD taking new singular values i.e..

$$f_{new}^{\theta} = U_{\theta} S_{S_{f^{\theta}}^{new}} V_{\theta}^{T} \tag{18}$$

Step 10. Perform inverse DMT to construct the watermarked image, denoted by F_{new}.

Extraction Process

The extraction process is given as follows.

Step 1. Perform DMT on the watermarked and host image, which are denoted by fw^θ and f^θ, where $\theta \in \{A, H, V, D\}$.

Step 2. Perform SVD transform on both fw^θ and f^θ,

$$fw^\theta = U_{fw^\theta} S_{fw^\theta} V^T_{fw^\theta} \tag{19}$$

$$f^\theta = U_{f^\theta} S_{f^\theta} V^T_{f^\theta} \tag{20}$$

Step 3. Extract the matrix that includes the watermark from each sub-band of watermarked image as

$$S^{new}_{fw^\theta} = U_{S^{new}_{f^\theta}} S_{fw^\theta} V^T_{S^{new}_{f^\theta}} \tag{21}$$

Step 4. Obtain the extracted reference watermark as

$$W^{ref}_{ext} = \frac{S^{new}_{fw^\theta} - S_{f^\theta}}{\alpha_\theta} \tag{22}$$

Step 5. Adopting k_0, μ and $l(>mn)$ as keys, the array $\mathcal{K}$ is obtained using Step 3-Step 5 of embedding process.

Step 6. Obtain the extracted watermark using W^{ref}_{ext} and $\mathcal{K}$ as follows

$$W_{ext} = (W^{ref}_{ext} - \mathcal{K}) \bmod 255 \tag{23}$$

RESULTS AND DISCUSSIONS

The watermarking framework discussed in the above section has been implemented in MATLAB for the gray scale Lena image considered as host image, which are of size 256×256. For watermark, 8-bit gray scale Circle logo of size 128×128 is used. We have implemented proposed framework for D-MR-DFT and D-MR-DCT followed by the comparison in order to judge which distributed transform is better

Figure 8. (a) Original Lena image; watermarked lena image using (b) DWT (c) D-MR-DFT (d) D-MR-DCT (e) Original Watermark (f) Reference Watermark; Extracted watermark from (g) DWT (h) D-MR-DFT (i) D-MR-DCT

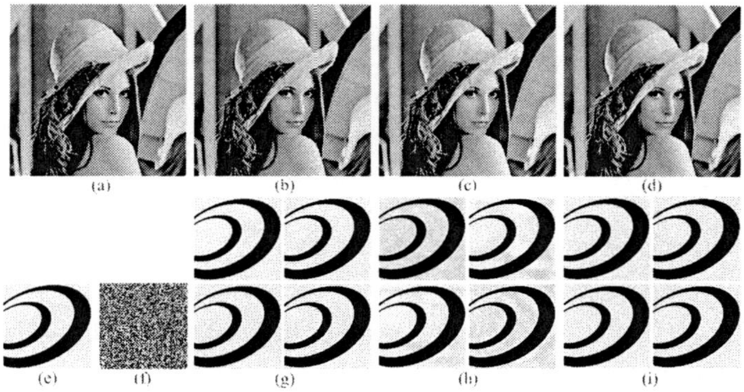

for watermarking. The host image, original watermark, watermarked images using both D-MR-DFT and D-MR-DCT along with extracted watermark images are shown in Figure 8. The watermarked image quality is measured using *Peak Signal to Noise Ratio* (PSNR). The PSNR indicates the similarity between two images. The higher the value of PSNR, the greater similarity in the images. Mathematically, PSNR is defined as

$$PSNR = 10\lg\frac{255^2}{RMSE^2} \tag{24}$$

where RMSE (root mean square error) is defined as

$$RMSE^2 = \frac{1}{MN}\sum_{i=1}^{M}\sum_{j=1}^{N}[x_{i,j} - y_{i,j}]^2 \tag{25}$$

where MN is the total number of pixels in the image, $x_{i,j}$ and $y_{i,j}$ are the values of the ij^{th} pixel in original and watermarked image. If original and the watermarked images are observed then no perceptual degradation is found according to human visual system (HVS). The values of PSNR, for watermarked Lena images using D-MR-DFT and D-MR-DCT come to be 41.6122 Db and 40.3014 Db respectively. Now, the watermarked image undergoes to different kind of intentional and un-intentional attacks followed by the watermark extraction. In order to verify the quality of extracted watermark, different measures can be used to show the similarity between the original and the extracted singular values. In the proposed algorithm, the correlation coefficient is used. Mathematically, the *correlation coefficient* between the original and extracted singular values is given by

$$\rho(w,\bar{w}) = \frac{\sum_{i=1}^{r}(w(i) - w_{mean})(\bar{w}(i) - \bar{w}_{mean})}{\sqrt{\sum_{i=1}^{r}(w(i) - w_{mean})^2}\sqrt{\sum_{i=1}^{r}(\bar{w}(i) - \bar{w}_{mean})^2}} \tag{26}$$

where w, $\bar{w}$, w_{mean} and $\bar{w}_{mean}$ are the original, extracted singular values, mean of original and extracted singular values and $r=min(M,N)$. The value of ρ lies between [-1, 1]. If the value of ρ is equal to 1 then the extracted singular values are just equal to original one whereas if the value of ρ is -1 then the difference is negative for the largest singular values. In this case, the lighter parts of the image become darker and darker parts become lighter i.e., constructed watermark looks like negative thin film. All the original, watermarked and extracted watermark images are depicted in Figure 8.

Since, the embedding is done in the singular values of the host image. Therefore, the magnitude of the singular values obtained in each transform domain i.e., D-MR-DFT, D-MR-DCT and DWT are first analyzed. To achieve desired goal, the largest singular value of the four sub bands, of the host image are computed for proposed and DWT domains. The comparison between getting maximum singular values for all the three methods are given in Figure 9. It is clear from the figure that the magnitude of the singular values is decreased as we go from A to D sub band. If the singular values are compared in D-MR-DFT, D-MR-DCT and DWT domain then we see that D-MR-DFT and D-MR-DCT domain contains higher magnitude of the singular values than DWT domain. If the singular value distribution is considered then one can see only approximate sub-band contains higher magnitude whereas detail parts contain very less magnitude of singular values. On the contrary, all sub-bands contain approximately same magnitude of singular values in distributed multiresolution transform. This shows another amiable ability of distribute energy of signal equally in all sub-bands. This is why these transforms are coined as Distributive Multiresolution transform.

We investigate the robustness of the algorithm by considering Gaussian Blur, Gaussian noise addition, JPEG compression, Symmetric Crop, Resize, Rotation, Histogram Equalization, Contrast Adjustment and Sharpening attacks. After these attacks on the watermarked image, extracted singular values of watermark are

Figure 9. Comparison among singular values of transformed Lena image in a) A (LL) b) H(HL) c) V(LH) d) (HH) sub-bands in DWT, D-MR-DFT and D-MR-DCT domain

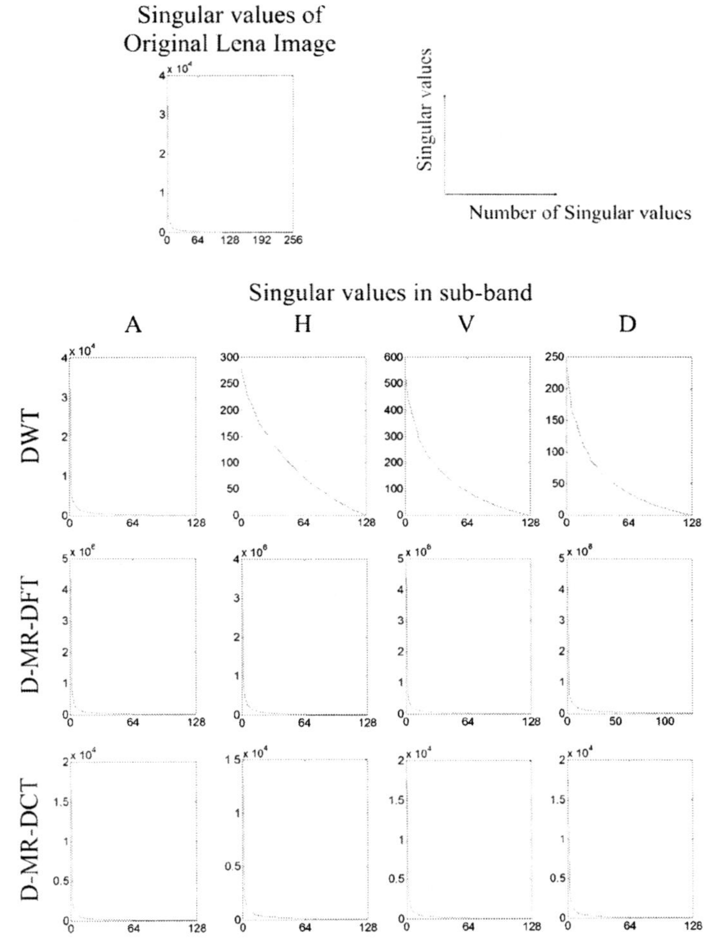

compared with the original one using Equation. 26. The watermarked Lena image after these attacks are depicted in Figure 10 whereas extracted watermarks after these attacks are given in Gigure 11 and the corresponding correlation coefficient values are given in Table 2. Table shows the improved performance in terms of imperceptibility and robustness against attacks.

The most common manipulation in digital image is blurring. Watermark is extracted after applying *Gaussian blurring* considering 5×5 window. To verify the robustness of the watermarking scheme, another measure is Noise addition. In real life, the degradation and distortion of the image come from noise addition. In our

Figure 10. Attacked watermarked Lena images

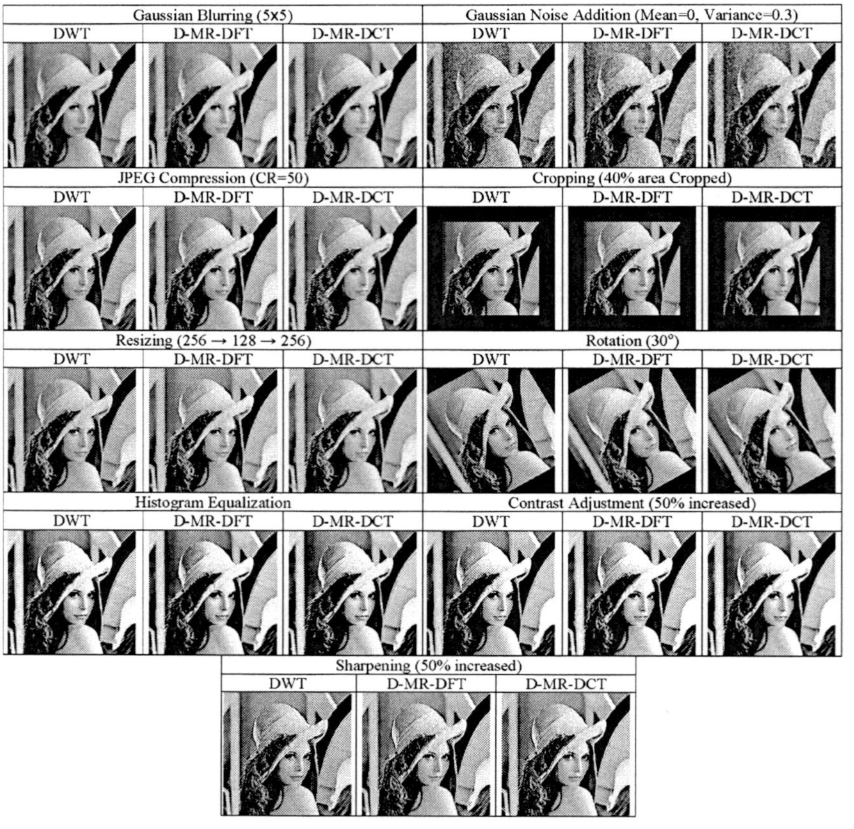

experiments, we have added P% additive *Gaussian noise* in the watermarked image. In our experiments, the watermark is extracted from 30% attacked watermarked image. In real life applications, storage and transmission of digital data, a lossy coding operation is often performed on the data to reduce the memory and increase efficiency. Hence, we have tested our algorithm for the *JPEG compression* (50:1). We have also tested our algorithm for resizing, rotation, cropping, Histogram Equalization, Contrast Adjustment and Sharpening attacks. For *resizing*, first we reduce the size of the image to 128×128 and again carried back to original size 256×256. For *rotation*, watermark image is extracted from 30° rotated image. For *Contrast Adjustment*, we increase the contrast of the watermarked image by 50%. Similarly, the *sharpness* is increased by 50% of the watermarked image.

In order to show the improved performance of the proposed watermarking algorithm, we compare our results from the DWT-SVD based method depicted in Ganic

Table 2. Correlation coefficients of the extracted watermark images

Attacks	Method	Correlation Coefficients (ρ)				
		A	H	V	D	Maximum
No Attack	DWT	1.0000	1.0000	1.0000	1.0000	1.0000 (All)
	D-MR-DFT	0.9997	0.9969	0.9973	0.9987	0.9997 (A)
	D-MR-DCT	1.0000	1.0000	0.9999	1.0000	1.0000(A,H,D)
Gaussian Blur (5×5)	DWT	0.0503	-0.4060	-0.4328	-0.6633	0.0503 (A)
	D-MR-DFT	0.8780	0.8564	0.8643	0.7746	0.8780 (A)
	D-MR-DCT	0.8735	0.7874	0.8690	0.8653	0.8735 (A)
Gaussian Noise Addition (30%)	DWT	0.4817	0.5351	0.5339	0.4946	0.5351 (H)
	D-MR-DFT	0.8392	0.8643	0.8702	0.8789	0.8789 (D)
	D-MR-DCT	0.8602	0.8860	0.8684	0.8687	0.8860 (H)
JPEG Compression (CR=50)	DWT	0.9935	0.9846	0.9824	0.9481	0.9935 (A)
	D-MR-DFT	0.9980	0.9953	0.9948	0.9966	0.9980 (A)
	D-MR-DCT	0.9983	0.9989	0.9988	0.9992	0.9992 (D)
Cropping (40% Area Cropped)	DWT	-0.9584	0.8912	0.6980	0.9737	0.9737 (D)
	D-MR-DFT	-0.9637	-0.8434	-0.9090	0.9951	0.9951 (D)
	D-MR-DCT	-0.7252	-0.8062	-0.9073	-0.9252	-0.7252 (A)
Resizing (256→128→256)	DWT	0.8903	-0.3606	-0.3679	-0.6610	0.8903 (A)
	D-MR-DFT	0.9768	0.9665	0.9665	0.9418	0.9768 (A)
	D-MR-DCT	0.9699	0.9455	0.9760	0.9753	0.9760 (V)
Rotation (30°)	DWT	-0.2883	0.7150	-0.6399	-0.7308	0.7150 (H)
	D-MR-DFT	-0.4968	0.8404	0.4935	0.9425	0.9425 (D)
	D-MR-DCT	0.8296	0.4711	0.5417	-0.2648	0.8296 (A)
Histogram Equalization	DWT	0.7789	0.8815	0.8578	0.9297	0.9297 (D)
	D-MR-DFT	0.7082	0.8746	0.8129	0.7775	0.8746 (H)
	D-MR-DCT	0.6731	0.7010	0.8503	0.7754	0.8503 (V)
Contrast Adjustment (50% Increased)	DWT	0.6459	0.8633	0.8307	0.9123	0.9123 (D)
	D-MR-DFT	0.8750	0.9652	0.9770	0.9044	0.9770 (V)
	D-MR-DCT	0.9665	0.8687	0.9371	0.9259	0.9665 (A)
Sharpen (50% Increased)	DWT	0.4755	0.9071	0.8499	0.9165	0.9165 (D)
	D-MR-DFT	0.9346	0.9355	0.9301	0.8564	0.9255 (H)
	D-MR-DCT	0.9248	0.8864	0.9343	0.9301	0.9343 (V)

Figure 11. Extracted watermark images

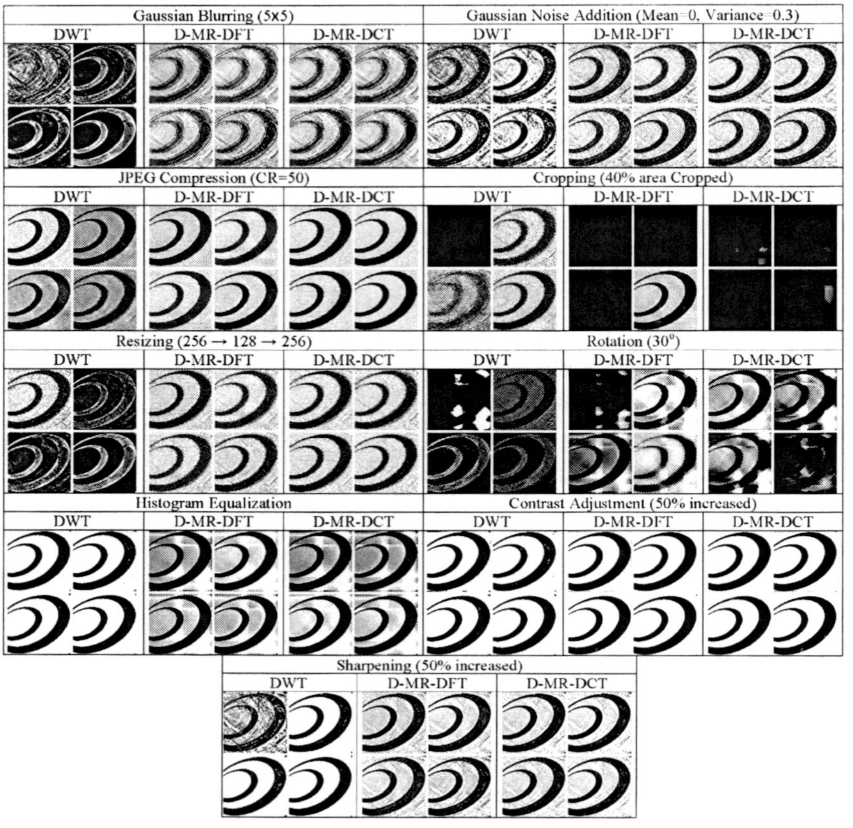

and Eskicioglu (2005). The visual results and correlation coefficients are depicted in Figure 11 and Table 2 respectively.

From figure and table, it is clear that the extracted watermark from all sub-bands is better than the extracted watermarks from DWT based method. The only exception comes in cropping, where watermark is extracted efficiently in DWT based method. In DWT based method, three pattern of watermarks are extracted from H, V and D sub-bands respectively whereas in D-MR-DFT based method only one pattern is extracted from D sub-bands but its quality is better than that of extracted from DWT. The D-MR-DCT fails to detect watermark from any of the sub-bands. Further, in all other cases, D-MR-DFT and D-MR-DCT perform very well. If we compare D-MR-DFT and D-MR-DCT based methods then one can find that D-MR-DCT performance is superior than D-MR-DFT. Moreover, the step of making reference watermark add more complexity in the extraction process because without knowing the keys of logistic map (i.e. k_0 and μ) but knowing the whole algorithm, one can extract only reference watermark which is in degraded form. Hence, in order to get perfect extraction, knowledge of keys used for logistic map and whole algorithm is necessary.

CONCLUSION

In this chapter, the distributive multiresolution transforms namely Distributed multiresolution discrete Fourier transform (D-MR-DFT) and Distributed multiresolution discrete Cosine transform (D-MR-DCT) (based on DFT and DCT respectively) are explored for images, which is localized in both time and frequency domain and improves the magnitude of singular values in all frequency sub-bands when compare to conventional wavelet transform. On the basis of distributive multiresolution transform and SVD, a robust watermarking scheme is proposed in which we exploit the advantages of all DFT, DWT and SVD, which make proposed scheme robust enough and superior than DWT-SVD based methods. The experimental results and comparison with existing schemes clearly demonstrate the improved performance in terms of imperceptibility and robustness against different kind of attacks.

REFERENCES

Arnold, M., Schmucker, M., & Wolthusen, S. D. (2003). *Techniques and applications of digital watermarking and content protection*. Norwood, MA: Artech House.

Baptista, M. S. (1998). Cryptography with chaos. *Physics Letters. [Part A]*, *240*(1-2), 50–54. doi:10.1016/S0375-9601(98)00086-3

Barni, M., Bartiloni, F., Cappellini, V., & Piva, A. (1998). A DCT domain system for robust image watermarking. *Signal Processing*, *66*(3), 357–372. doi:10.1016/S0165-1684(98)00015-2

Barni, M., Bartiloni, F., & Piva, A. (2001). Improved wavelet based watermarking through pixel wise masking. *IEEE Transactions on Image Processing*, *10*, 783–791. doi:10.1109/83.918570

Bhatnagar, G., & Raman, B. (2009a). A new robust reference watermarking scheme based on DWT-SVD. *Computer Standards & Interfaces*, *31*(5), 1002–1013. doi:10.1016/j.csi.2008.09.031

Bhatnagar, G., & Raman, B. (2009b). Robust reference watermarking scheme using wavelet packet transform and bidiagonal-singular value decomposition. *International Journal of Image and Graphics*, *9*(3), 449–477. doi:10.1142/S0219467809003538

Bhatnagar, G., & Raman, B. (2009c). Robust watermarking using distributed MR-DCT and SVD. In *Proc. Int. Conf. on Advances in Pattern Recognition* (pp. 21-24). Kolkatta, India: IEEE Press.

Bhatnagar, G., & Raman, B. (2010). Distributed multiresolution discrete Fourier transform and its application to watermarking. *International Journal of Wavelets, Multresolution, and Information Processing*, *8*(2), 225–241. doi:10.1142/S021969131000347X

Bochner, S., & Chandrasekharan, K. (1949). *Fourier transforms*. New York, NY: Princeton University Press.

Bracewell, R. (1965). *The Fourier transform and its applications*. New York, NY: McGraw-Hill.

Brigham, E. O. (2002). *The fast Fourier transform*. New York, NY: Prentice-Hall.

Carroll, J. M., Verhagen, J., & Wong, P. T. (1992). Chaos in cryptography: The escape from the strange attractor. *Cryptologia*, *16*(1), 52–72. doi:10.1080/0161-119291866766

Chandra, D. V. S. (2002). Digital image watermarking using singular value decomposition. In *Proc. Midwest Sym. on Circuits and Systems* (pp. 264–267). Tulsa, OK: IEEE Press.

Chang, C. C., Tsai, P., & Lin, C. C. (2005). SVD-based digital image watermarking scheme. *Pattern Recognition Letters*, *26*, 577–1586. doi:10.1016/j.patrec.2005.01.004

Cox, I. J., Killian, J., Leighton, F. T., & Shamoon, T. (1997). Secure spread spectrum watermarking for multimedia. *IEEE Transactions on Image Processing*, *6*(12), 1673–1687. doi:10.1109/83.650120

Cox, I. J., Miller, M. L., & Bloom, J. A. (2000). Watermarking applications and their properties. In *Proc. Int. Conf. on Information Technology* (pp. 1-5). Las Vegas, NV: IEEE Press.

Cox, I. J., Miller, M. L., & Bloom, J. A. (2001). *Digital watermarking*. San Francisco, CA: Morgan Kaufmann.

Daubechies, I. (1992). *Ten lectures notes on wavelet*. Philadelphia, PA: SIAM.

Devaney, R. L. (2003). *An introduction to chaotic dynamical systems*. Colorado, US: Westview Press.

Djurovic, I., Stankovic, S., & Pitas, I. (2001). Digital watermarking in the fractional fourier transformation domain. *Journal of Network and Computer Applications*, *24*(4), 167–173. doi:10.1006/jnca.2000.0128

Elnashaie, S. S. E. H., & Abasha, M. E. (1995). On the chaotic behaviour of forced fluidized bed catalytic reactors. *Chaos, Solitons, and Fractals*, *5*(5), 797–831. doi:10.1016/0960-0779(95)93891-F

Feng, Z., Xiaomin, M., & Shouyi, Y. (2005). Multiple-chirp typed blind watermarking algorithm based on fractional Fourier transform. In *Proc. Int. Sym. on Intelligent Signal Processing and Communication Systems* (pp. 141–144). Philadelphia, PA: IEEE Press. doi:10.1109/ISPACS.2005.1595366

Ganic, E., & Eskicioglu, A. M. (2005). Robust embedding of visual watermarks using DWT-SVD. *Journal of Electronic Imaging*, *14*, 043004. doi:10.1117/1.2137650

Ganic, E., Zubair, N., & Eskicioglu, A. M. (2003). An optimal watermarking scheme based on singular value decomposition. In *Proc. Int. Conf. on Communication, Network, and Information Security* (pp. 85-90). Uniondale, NY: Acta Press.

Gorodetski, V. I., Popyack, L. J., Samoilov, V., & Skormin, V. A. (2001). SVD-based approach to transparent embedding data into digital images. In *Proc. Int. Workshop on Mathematical Methods, Models and Architectures for Computer Network Security* (pp. 263-274). St. Petersburg, Russia: Springer.

Holt, L., Maufe, B. G., & Wiener, A. (1988). *Encoded marking of a recording signal*. UK Patent, GB 2196167A.

Hwang, M. S., Chang, C. C., & Hwang, K. F. (1999). A watermarking technique based on one-way hash functions. *IEEE Transactions on Consumer Electronics*, *45*(2), 286–294. doi:10.1109/30.793411

Katzenseisser, S., & Petitcolas, F. A. P. (2000). *Information hiding techniques for steganography and digital watermarking*. London, UK: Artech House.

Kundur, D., & Hatzinakos, D. (2004). Towards robust logo watermarking using multiresolution image fusion. *IEEE Transactions on Multimedia*, *6*, 185–197. doi:10.1109/TMM.2003.819747

Lasota, A., & Mackey, M. C. (1997). *Chaos, fractals, and noise-stochastic aspects of dynamics*. New York, NY: Springer.

Li, Q., Yuan, C., & Zong, Y. Z. (2007). Adaptive DWT-SVD domain image watermarking using human visual model. In *Proc. Int. Conf. Advanced Communication Technology* (pp. 1947-1951). Gangwon-Do, Korea: IEEE Press.

Lin, C. H., Jen, J. S., & Kuo, L. C. (2006). Distributed discrete wavelet transformation for copyright protection. In *Proc. Int. Workshop on Image Analysis for Multimedia Interactive Services* (pp. 53-56). Incheon, Korea: Springer.

Liu, R., & Tan, T. (2002). An SVD-based watermarking scheme for protecting rightful ownership. *IEEE Transactions on Multimedia, 4*(1), 121–128. doi:10.1109/6046.985560

Mallat, S. G. (1989). A theory for multiresolution signal decomposition: The wavelet representation. *IEEE Transactions on Pattern Analysis and Machine Intelligence, 11*, 674–693. doi:10.1109/34.192463

Meerwald, P., & Uhl, A. (2001). A survey of wavelet-domain watermarking algorithms. In *Proc. SPIE, Electronic Imaging, Security and Watermarking of Multimedia Contents III, 4314*. San Jose, CA: SPIE.

Meyer, Y. (1989). Orthonormal wavelets. In Combes, J. M. (Ed.), *Wavelets: Time-frequency methods and phase spaces (Lecture Notes on IPTI)* (pp. 21–37). New York, NY: Springer Verlag.

Mohanty, S. P. (1999). Digital watermarking: A tutorial review. In *Report on Dept. of Electrical Engineering*. Bangalore, India: Indian Institute of Science.

Muharemagic, E., & Furht, B. (2004). *Multimedia security: Watermarking techniques*. Chicago, IL: Comprehensive Report on Information Security, International Engineering Consortium.

Schyndle, R. G. V., Tirkel, A. Z., & Osbrone, C. F. (1994). A digital watermark. In *Proc. of Int. Conf. on Image Processing,* vol. 2 (pp. 86-90). Austin, TX: IEEE Press.

Sverldov, A., Dexter, S., & Eskicioglu, A. M. (2005). Robust DCT-SVD domain image watermarking for copyright protection: Embedding data in all frequencies. In *Proc. European Signal Processing Conference*. Antalya, Turkey: Curran Associates, Inc.

Szepanski, W. (1979) A signal theoretic method for creating forgery-proof documents for automatic verification. In *Proc. Carnahan Conf. on Crime Countermeasures* (pp. 101-109). Lexington, KY.

Trikel, A. Z., Rankin, G. A., Schyndel, R. M. V., Ho, W. H., Mee, N. R. A., & Osborne, C. F. (1993). Electronic water-mark. In *Proc. Digital Image Computing: Techniques and Applications* (pp. 666-672). Macquarie University, Sydney.

Wang, S. H., & Lin, Y. P. (2004). Wavelet tree quantization for copyright protection watermarking. *IEEE Transactions on Image Processing, 13*(2), 154–165. doi:10.1109/TIP.2004.823822

Xia, X., Boncelet, C. G., & Arce, G. R. (1997). A multiresolution watermark for digital images. In *Proc. Int. Conf. on Image Processing*, vol. 3 (pp. 548-551). Santa Barbara, CA: IEEE Press.

Yu, F. Q., Zhangi, Z. K., & Xu, M. H. (2006). A digital watermarking algorithm for image based on fractional Fourier transform. In *Proc. IEEE Conf. on Industrial Electronics and Applications* (pp. 1-5). Singapore: IEEE Press.

Zhang, X. D., Feng, J., & Lo, K. T. (2003). Image watermarking using tree-based spatial-frequency feature of wavelet transform. *Journal of Visual Communication and Image Representation, 14*, 474–491. doi:10.1016/S1047-3203(03)00047-6

Chapter 2
Masking Models and Watermarking:
A Discussion on Methods and Effectiveness

Mirko Luca Lobina
University of Cagliari, Italy

Daniele D. Giusto
University of Cagliari, Italy

Davide Mula
European University of Rome, Italy

ABSTRACT

Many audio watermarking techniques, presented in the last years, make use of masking and psychological models derived from signal processing. Such a basic idea is winning because it guarantees a high level of robustness and bandwidth of the watermark as well as fidelity of the watermarked signal. This work first describes the relationship between Digital Right Management, Intellectual Property, and use of watermarking techniques. Then, the crossing use of watermarking and Masking Models is detailed, providing schemes, examples, and references. Finally, the authors present two strategies that make use of a Masking Model, applied to a classic watermarking technique. The joint use of classic frameworks and Masking Models seems to be one of the trends for the future of research in watermarking. Several tests on the proposed strategies with the state of the art are also offered to give an idea of how to assess the effectiveness of a watermarking technique.

DOI: 10.4018/978-1-61350-135-1.ch002

INTRODUCTION

Ownership is the one's right to possess something and decide what is to be done with it. The concept of ownership is distinct from possession, intended as having something in one's custody. Such demarcation, very easy to understand and prove in case of a material good (e.g., as a house or a car), becomes particularly ephemeral in case of digital data. First of all, the diffusion and movement of a digital content cannot be practically traced: as an example a collection of songs can be published on a Website, a CD or a DVD, and once it is legally distributed for the first time there is no way to control its following circulation. Then, there are many ways to reproduce a digital content and obtain copies identical to the original. Starting from a copy, a malicious can alter or manipulate the original content, and present himself as the owner. This can result in a great damage for the rights' genuine owner, since an image, or a song, however in a digital format, are esteemed on the whole respect to their origin, which is a proof of quality, source and content integrity. From this introduction it seems, and it is definitely true, that the encountering problems in ownership for a digital content are the digital nature itself of the content: an image, printed on a photo-paper, can be copied more difficulty without the original matrix (e.g., the negative, in case of a photo; or the master registration in case of an audio sample) and, in every case, the copy can be easily distinguished from the original; furthermore, a photo-paper image could not be present on million of instances at the same time as happens to an image published on the Web. For all these reasons, different approaches have been developed for proving origin's copyright information of a digital content. On the whole, Digital Rights Management (i.e., DRM) is any of these technologies, when used to control access to digital data. DRM is not a Technical Protection Measures (i.e., TPM). Actually, such technology controls or restricts the use and access of digital media content on electronic devices with such technologies installed, acting as components of a DRM design (See Figure 1). The objective of this chapter is to provide a comprehensive explanation of the crossing use of masking threshold and watermarking, as one of the most effective DRM strategies.

This work is organized as follows. The first section provides an overview of DRM, discusses the distinction between cryptography and watermarking (explaining the relevant applicative fields in a DRM context of both solutions), describes watermarking in general and introduces the Masking Models. The second part is a description of the crossing use of the Masking Models and watermarking followed by two examples of use from the authors. The third part introduces what has been done in the very recent past in this field of research. Finally, some conclusions on the trade-off robustness/fidelity, and more generally on the use of Masking Models in watermark schemes, are drawn.

Figure 1. DRM and TPM

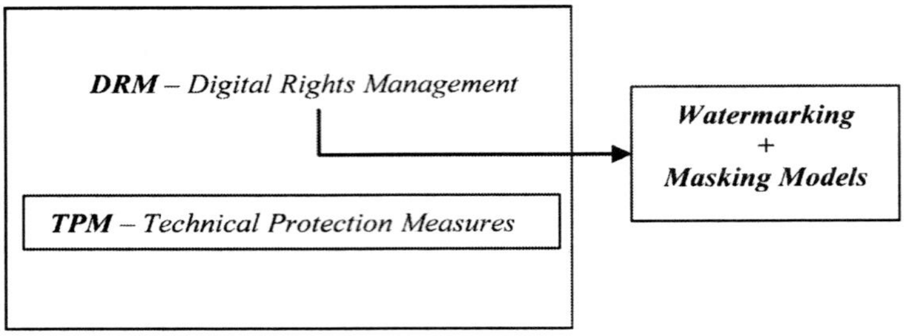

BACKGROUND

DRM (Digital Rights Management) and IP (Intellectual Property)

As already stated, Digital Rights Management (i.e., DRM) is any technology used to control access to digital data. Such term has been created to individuate the whole set of technical measures, where applied to digital media, or analog media released in digital format. The term "digital" is here repeated many times to underline that, while quality diminishes every copy with analog media, digital media may be copied an limitless number of times without degradation in the quality. That is, there is no difference in quality between the "master" and "copies". The last years have been characterized by a large pressure for legislation and regulation of DRM schemes' usage (specifically to publish the detailed functionalities of some of the most diffused DRM frameworks). An example of this will of regulation is the Digital Millennium Copyright Act (i.e., DMCA). That is, a United States copyright law which criminalizes creation and broadcasting of technology that can avoid measures taken to protect the owner's rights. An early example of DRM is the Content Scrambling System (i.e., CSS), based on a simple encryption algorithm (this last term is clearly explained when cryptography is introduced in the following). CSS is used in DVDs since 1996 and requires DVD device manufacturers to sign a license agreement restricting the inclusion of certain features in their players, which could be used to extract a high-quality digital copy disk. Approaching the problem of protecting the owner's rights from a legal point of view, we meet the term Intellectual Property (i.e., IP). IP defines how the holder of a legal entitlement (respect to ideas/information) can exercise his rights to the "subject matter" of the IP. Where, the term "subject matter" is used to reflect the idea that it is the product of the mind or the intellect. Thus, DRM and IP are complementary aspects of the same context (See Figure 2). DRM approaches the problem of protecting copyrights from a technical point of view. The legal basis of DRM are linked to IP and the underlying idea that the subject matter is the product of the mind or the intellect.

Figure 2. DRM and IP

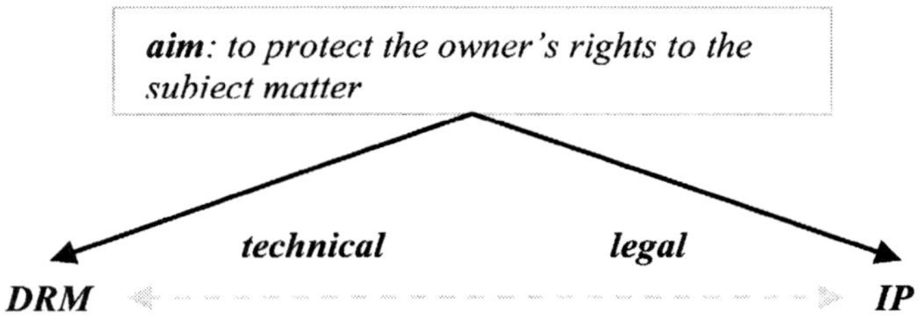

Cryptography and Watermarking

Cryptography and watermarking can be effective solutions for the distribution problem and rights management. In the following the featuring factors of both techniques will be analyzed and discussed. Cryptography is the study of converting information from its comprehensible form into an incomprehensible format, rendering it unreadable without a secret knowledge (i.e., usually a numeric key). The field of cryptography has mainly expanded in two ways. The first one comprises mechanisms for more than just keeping secrets, as schemes for digital signatures and digital cash. Cryptography finds a second application in secure protocols, used in infrastructure for computing and telecommunications. In many cases such protocols are applied without the users being aware of their presence. Cryptography is concerned more with this second field and it is used mainly in tenable communications. De facto, once digital data is widely distributed also via a protected channel (Macq, 1995), cryptography does not preclude for its further storage, and illegal actions as the copy. Digital watermarking, also referred to as simply watermarking, is an adaptation of the paper watermarks to the digital milieu. That is, a pattern of bits is inserted into a digital content, identifying the origin's copyright information. Like printed watermarks the purpose is to provide copyright protection for intellectual property in digital format. This implies robustness and capacity of the watermarking technique. Robustness measures the digital watermark ability to resist to intentional/unintentional attacks, while capacity reflects the ability of conveying a number of useful information embedded in the original signal. But, unlike printed watermarks, which are intended to be somewhat visible, digital watermarks are designed to be completely, or at most partially, inaudible/invisible. This feature is referred to as fidelity, that is a measure of the similarity (i.e., or of the antonym distance) between original and watermarked signal. Transparency implicitly means that fidelity has been attained.

Figure 3. Cryptography and watermarking

Strategy:	***Applied to:***	***Typology:***
Cryptography	*Content/Channel*	*Active*
Watermarking	*Content*	*Reactive*

Figure 4. Information hiding and watermarking

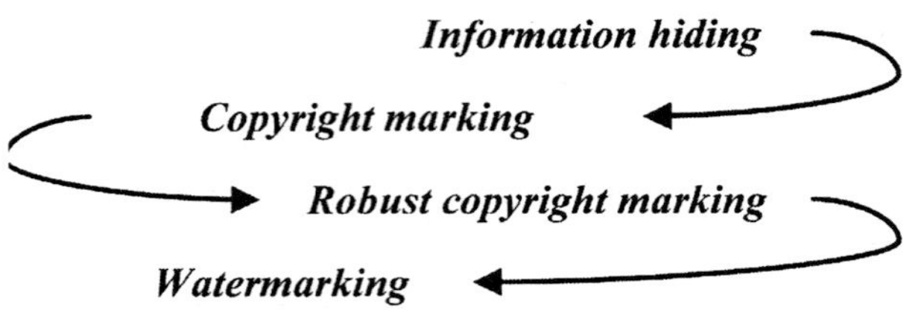

From what has been said, it is clear that cryptography and watermarking are complementary aspects and solve different classes of problems with unlike approaches. On one hand, there is cryptography that provides more than simple content encryption/decryption though (i.e., message/content confidential), but it is also involved in the distribution of a secret key in a secure manner to all the involved parties (i.e., secure channel). In this sense, cryptography provides the necessary protocols for communicating parties to steadily authenticating themselves with each other, and can be considered as an "active" solution to global security. In addition, the use of digital signatures and message authentication codes provides a means for verifying that the content has not been manipulated in any way (See Figure 3). While on the other hand, watermarking for copyright protection is useful for tracking illegally copied content, although this is a very "reactive" approach to content security.

Watermarking in Detail

The first aim of this part is to provide the reader a very general overview of what is watermarking. Petiticolas, Anderson and Kuhn in their survey (Petitcolas, 1999), published at the end of the nineties on information hiding, introduce watermarking as a sub-category of copyright marking (See Figure 4). This is a very important account, since with this classification they consider the robustness against possible attacks as one of the additional and mandatory requirements.

Figure 5. Watermarking features

Robustness: **measure of the digital watermark's ability to resist to intentional/unintentional attacks**
Capacity: **ability of conveying a number of useful information embedded in the original signal**
Fidelity: **distance between original and watermarked signals**
Transparency: **inaudibility/invisibility of the digital watermark**

Really, watermarking has three main means: monitoring (i.e., tracing of illegal copies), copyright protection (i.e., authentication of the copyright owner by the knowledge of the secret key to read the secret watermark), fingerprinting (i.e., during the phase of authentication to a secure network), information carrier and indication of content manipulation, that will be discussed in detail in the following. All these possible applications are included in two main possible watermarking schemes: secret and public. Secret watermarking is used as authentication and content integrity mechanisms. This implies that the watermark is readable/understandable only by authorized persons with the knowledge about the existence/position of the embedded secret. On the other hand, public watermarking means that the watermark is just an information carrier.

As it has been introduced before, watermarking is the insertion of a pattern of bits, identifying the origin's copyright information, into a signal. The righteousness of the watermarking technique is measured in terms of robustness, capacity, transparency and fidelity (See Figure 5).

A good watermarking technique should achieve these features as much as possible. Let see briefly in the following the implications of such attributes.

- The host signal should be non-degraded and the embedded data be minimally perceptible; that is the embedded data has to remain hidden to an observer of the watermarked signal;
- The host signal and the data to be embedded must be coherent in terms of embedding dominio. That is, the watermarking must be inserted taking into account for the features of the original signal (as compression or encoding). In this sense, it is very important to retrieve as much information as possible on the signal to be watermarked and on its use;
- The embedded data should be resistant to intentional/unintentional modifications. That is, the original signal is modified to try a removal of the watermarking. The possible modifications are wide and include: channel noise, filtering, resampling, cropping, encoding, lossy compressing, printing and scanning, digital-to-analog (D/A) conversion, and analog-to-digital (A/D)

Figure 6. Robustness vs. bandwidth

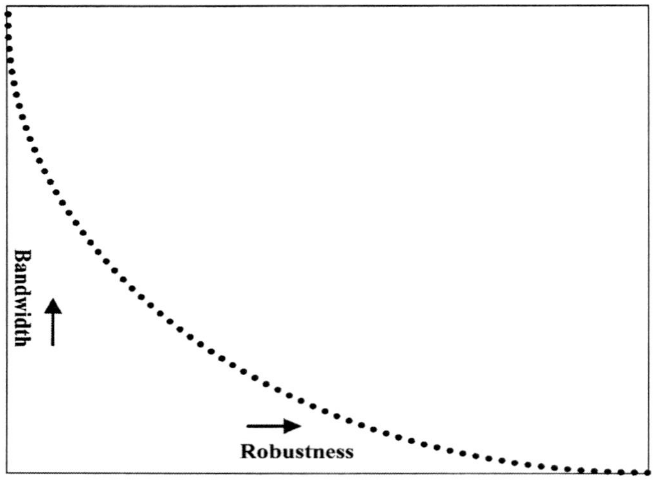

conversion, etc. Most of these will be described in detail when introducing the typologies of possible attacks.

Let analyze the problem of non-degrading the original signal. Obviously, trade-offs exist between almost three factors: total amount of data that can be embedded (i.e., "bandwidth"), transparency respect to the host signal, and robustness/resistence to modifications. A technique can be planned that, constraining the host signal degradation, tries to reach high embedding data, or high robustness. The two last factors are mutually divergent: as one increases, the other must decrease (See Figure 6).

The statement on the above cited three factors is true for every possible configuration of such parameters. For this reason, different kinds of technique have been developed for different applications and requirements (See Figure 7). That is, the application fixes the requirements, the three- factors' trade-offs and consequently the technique itself.

In (Bender, 1996) another classification of watermarking techniques is proposed, depending on the application in terms of the amount of information that is embedded in the host signal. In this sense, the simpler technique implies the embedded data are used to place an indication of ownership in the host signal, the position is the copyright indication itself. A second category is the tamper-proof, while the third is the feature-location. Tamper-proof frameworks can be effectively included in two categories as "fragile" or "semi-fragile", as proposed in (Kazakeviciute, 2005). Fragile means that watermarks act as a digital signature, allowing to detect any modifications of the content. Instead, semi-fragile frameworks allow to detect

Figure 7. Requirements and watermarking's trade-offs

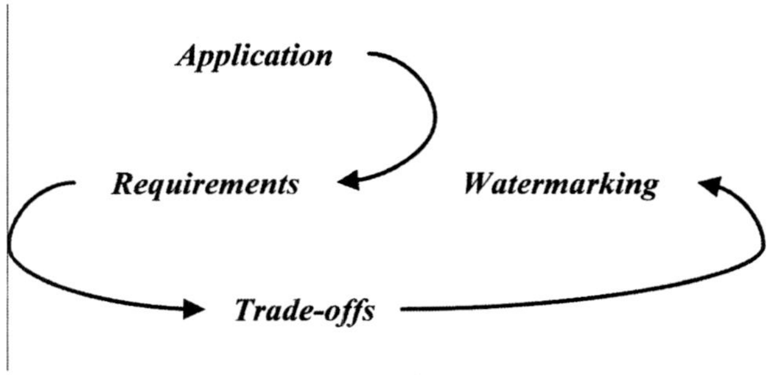

and localize any modification of the content changes. The second category is more effective respect to the set of functionalities from digital signature. In (Wu, 1998) a set of desired features for tamper-proof frameworks is presented as follows:

- Determination whether a host signal has been altered or not;
- Integration of authentication data with host signal rather than as a separate data file;
- Invisibility of the embedded authentication data under normal viewing/auditing conditions;
- Localization of the alteration which was made on the signal;
- Storage of the watermarked signal in lossy compression format.

Feature-location watermarks enable to identify individual content features, by introducing a certain degree of modification in the host signal. Generally, it requires a large amount of information respect to the other two previous techniques. Always referring to Figure 7, the "application" level includes also the case the signal to be marked is an audio, or an image, signal. The aim here is to exploit the main traits in the methods, considering both contexts (i.e., audio/image signals) and low/high bandwidths (always refer to Figure 7).

Blind audio watermarking (Eggers, 2000) techniques are firstly described in detail as follows. The term blind is here used to indicate that the watermarking scheme can detect and extract watermarks without non-watermarked/original audio signal. Obviously, the blind methods need an effective method for watermark's self-detection. Compared to non-blind techniques (which implies the original signal for comparing purposes), there is a saving of 50% for storage and bandwidth.

To give the reader a comprehensive and simple overview, five categories (See Figure 8) of frameworks are described. Of course, much more techniques are accessible (take also in account that a watermarking method must obligatory be published).

Figure 8. Blind-audio watermarking techniques

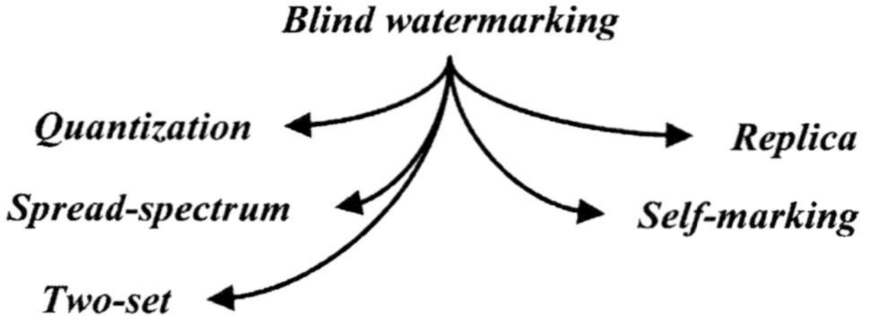

This section does not introduce methods based on psychological models since they will be described in detail in the following.

Wikipedia introduces the term quantization as the procedure of constraining something to a discrete set of values. In the specific field of audio signals, it is the process of approximating a continuous range of values (or a very large set of possible discrete values) by a relatively-small set of discrete symbols or integer values. Thus, a quantization method quantizes a value of the original signal (let say x) and assigns it a new value based on the quantized sample value D and function $q(x,D)$, in a way $y=q(x,D)\pm D$, where the signs ± depend on the value of the value of the binary watermark message $\{0,1\}$. This scheme is quite robust (Chen, 1999) and resistant to several types of attack. The detection method is exactly the inverse respect to the embedding process.

Spread spectrum was originally developed for military applications. Since its declassification, it has found civilian use, particularly in communications for cellular telephony. Spread-spectrum is one of the most diffused and discussed scheme in state of art (Cox, 1996; Kim, 2000; Cvejic, 2001). Several implementations have been proposed in the past, but in this work, the basic idea is presented. In spread spectrum, a narrowband signal (the message to be transmitted) is modulated by a broadband carrier signal, which spreads the original spectrum. Spread-spectrum is a correlation method which inserts a pseudo-random sequence into the original signal, in time or transform domain, and detects the watermark by calculating the correlation between the watermarked signal and the pseudo-random sequence. The carrier is the pseudo-random sequence (i.e., with statistical properties similar to a truly random signal) obtained with a random-number generator that has been initialized with a particular seed, known only to the owner. Thus, a generic binary message (the watermark) can be modulated by the pseudo-random sequence generated by means of the seed. Obviously, it is not possible to determine the watermark without the knowledge of the seed. Generally, such factor is the privileged information that the sender and an authorized receiver possess. Apart from the seed, spread-spectrum presents another element of robustness. That is, a large signal power is distributed over the entire frequency spectrum, so only a small amount of power is added at each frequency.

The two-set watermarking scheme marks two sets from the original signal differently. Thus, the presence of the difference itself between the two sets allows to understand if a signal is marked or not. Also in this case, the state of art has been very rich and purposeful (Arnold, 2000; Bender, 1996; Yeo, 2003). Many variations have been proposed. In this section we will deep in analysis a particular approach, i.e. the patchwork approach, as in the following section "Future Trend" the crossing use of the audio Masking Model and two-set patchwork approach is described. Original patchwork approach works in embedding phase in two steps using a statistical approach: first of all, two sets, or patches, of the original signal are chosen in time/transform domain; then, a small constant value (let say *d*) is added to one patch, and subtracted from the other. Obviously, the patch in is composed by more than one element, so that it is possible to evaluate the mean value of the elements composing each of the two patched sets (let say $\overline{\beta}^*$ and $\overline{\alpha}^*$). It is also possible to evaluate the mean value of the difference of the single mean values of the elements of the two patched sets (let say $E(\overline{\beta}^* - \overline{\alpha}^*)$ [1]), while the corresponding mean value of the difference of the single mean values of the elements of the two original sets can be indicated with $E(\overline{\beta} - \overline{\alpha})$. This change in $E(\overline{\beta}^* - \overline{\alpha}^*)$ and $E(\overline{\beta} - \overline{\alpha})$ is very useful in the detection phase as the value itself changes from the original value $\overline{x}$ to that corresponding to the patched situation $\overline{x} + 2d$. Also in this case the position, respect to the original signal, of the two sets is chosen by means of a random number generator with a seed. The presence of the watermark can be individuated only with the exact knowledge of the seed using the statistical approach previously described. Note that the statistical distribution of the values of the two patches does not change (because the same quantity is added and subtracted), it is the difference in the mean values that allows a detection (See Figure 9). The detection is performed by means of an hypothesis test. That is, given the null hypothesis (denoted H_0) against the alternative hypothesis (denoted H_1), the outcome of a hypothesis test is 'reject H_0' or 'do not reject H_0'. In this case the null hypothesis can be formulated as "the signal is not watermarked". Thus, the aim is to reject the null hypothesis. The performance of the patchwork scheme strongly depends on the distance between $E(\overline{\beta}^* - \overline{\alpha}^*)$ and $E(\overline{\beta} - \overline{\alpha})$, which is function of *d*. Obviously, a greater the factor *d* corresponds to a less probability of failure in the detection phase, but also to a minus transparency of the watermark in the original signal. Thus, also in this case the trade-off robustness vs. transparency must be carefully evaluated.

Figure 9. Comparison between watermarked and un-watermarked distributions of the mean differences

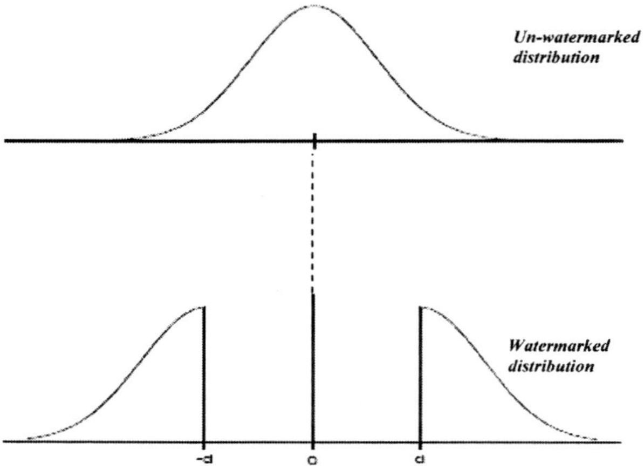

The idea behind Replica method is that the original signal itself can be used as a watermark. Echo hiding (Bender, 1996) is a good example of replica scheme. An echo is characterized by three factors: initial amplitude α, delay (offset) and decay rate (See Figure 10).

The echo is perceived as added tone respect the original signal (See Figure 11).

The detection phase can be considered as a decoding process, involving the evaluation of the cepstrum of the echoed signal. The "cepstrum" can be used to separate the excitation signal (which contains the pitch of an audio signal) and the transfer function (which contains the audio quality). Without deepening too much technical aspects (we remind to (Bender, 1996)) the basic idea behind detection in a replica scheme is to determine the spacing between the echoes.

Finally, self-marking method (Mansour, 2001; Wu, 2000) embeds a signal (a self-evident mark) in time/frequency domain in a way it is easily noticeable. In this work, we report specifically for time-scale modification strategy (Mansour, 2001), which basically is the process of compressing/expanding the time-scale of the audio signal between salient points. In (Mansour, 2001) such points are selected extrema of the wavelet decomposition and the length of the interval is chosen accordingly to the watermark to be embedded. In the last decade, the study of audio watermarking has been characterized by a huge improvement. This first part surveys the main five categories of audio watermarking apart from the use of masking and psychological models. A series of general thoughts can be expressed on such methods. Quantization approach is simple, but at the same time not very robust to several kinds of attack.

Figure 10. Replica method

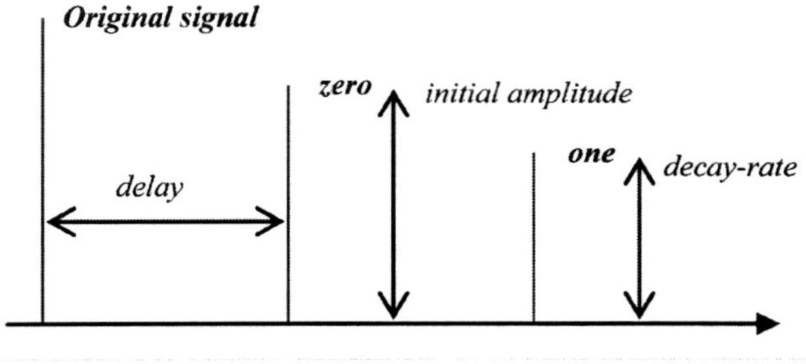

Figure 11. Outcome of the replica method

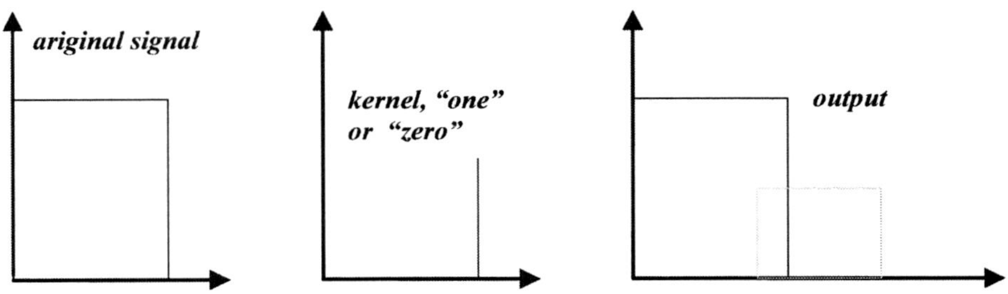

In this sense, it is better than echo-hiding which is more complex, but presents the same lacks in robustness. On the other hand we have robust schemes like the two-set (and specifically the patchwork strategy) and replica approaches. Finally, the spread-spectrum which is effective but can lead to serious modifications of the original signal. For this reason, it requires a psychological model for inaudible watermark embedding. But this last consideration can be also considered true for several of the proposed frameworks.

Most of the above described strategies are applied both for images and audio signals. As an example, the patchwork strategy, a low bandwidth strategy, is applied on the same way for image and audio. The difference is about the importance of the patch shape (See Figure 12) and its visibility within the image. The optimal choice of patch shape depends upon the expected image modifications, that is, if a JPEG image is considered, it is preferable to use a patch that embeds the energy in low frequencies. A comprehensive description of such relation is proposed in (Bender, 1996).

Figure 12. Patch shapes

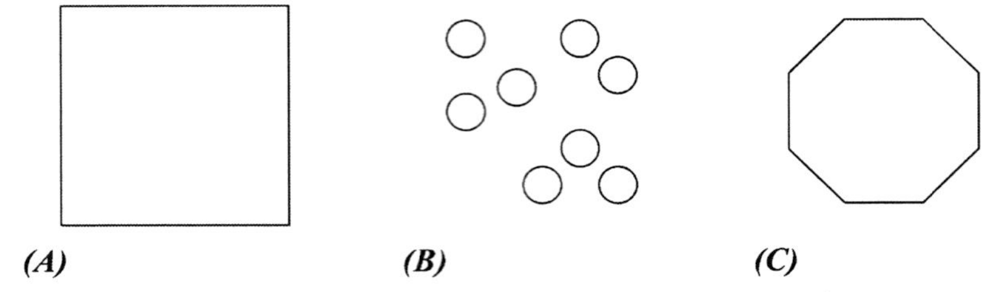

The patchwork strategy is obviously an example but the main differences between implementations of watermarking frameworks of image and audio signals are about two factors. That is, on one hand the Human Visual/Auditory Systems (i.e., HVS/HAS) and on the other the nature of the original signal itself. In the following a brief explanation of both such factors is proposed (Bender, 1996).

A still image (the original signal to be watermarked) is typically a 8-bit 200x200 pixels. Furthermore, it is also realistic to suppose that an image will be subject to many kinds of operations, as filtering, lossy compression and blurring. At the same time, the HVS presents sensitivity to contrast as a function of spatial frequency and the masking effect of edges (both in luminance and chrominance). The HVS is not very sensible to small changes in luminance. This is the first "hole" of the HVS. The second is the HVS's insensitivity to very low spatial frequencies such as continuous changes in brightness across an image. Many texts can be cited that propose a comprehensive description of human eye and visual system. In this work we quote for (Tovèe, 1996; Marr, 1982; Delaigle, 2002). High-quality audio is usually a 16-bit 44.1 KHz signal (as Windows Audio-Visual (WAV)). A compressed audio (i.e., from (ISO MPEG-AUDIO) perceptual encoding standard, originally described in (Brandenburg, 1992) presents statistics of the signal drastically changed respect to the original; while the characteristics that a listener perceives are the same. Many documents and information can be retrieved about audio standards and HAS, but for a base-knowledge the authors suggest a read on the original standard (Brandenburg, 1992; Pan, 1995), while the HAS will be described in the following sections.

Masking Models

Psychological and Masking Models are usually inherited from data compression mechanisms and are very difficult to understand and explain in detail. Thus, the idea of the authors is to provide the reader general key information and a some references to find detailed information. First of all, independently from the nature of the signal itself, a Masking Model determines the levels of intensity (as a function of time or frequency) of a signal, to be perceived in presence of another signal. The Masking Model is usually a function, or a set of data, called simply mask. The mask modulates the watermark to ensure its transparency, or to increase the watermark's energy for a given fidelity/transparency constraint. The main problem is specifically due to the fidelity feature; in fact, while concentrating on the increasing of the trade-off energy/fidelity, little attention has been paid to the potential vulnerability of the masked watermark to a malicious attack. The scope of this work is to provide the reader a comprehensive description of watermark methods based on Masking Models, evaluate their effectiveness respect to an intentional attack and draw some conclusions for future trends. The concept of mask, as employed in Masking Models, is used to signify a set of values (i.e., a matrix), which is computed on individual processing blocks (i.e., a block of 20 ms of an audio trace, or 8×8 pixel of an image) of the original signal. The original signal is defined as stationary, in its temporal and spectral features, in an individual block. This is quite important for the definition of a correct mask. The reading of the mask leads to understand in which regions of the transform domain a signal can be suitably inserted, in a way its energy remains lower than the energy-threshold fixed by the mask, and thus can be as inaudible as possible. That is, the mask shapes the message (i.e., the sequence of bits to be inserted in the original signal to prove its copyright) to obtain the watermark. The shaping could involve all, or a portion of the transform domain: the mask can be spread over the entire transform domain (i.e., an identity matrix, multiplied by a small constant), or can be selectively embedded in particular regions of the transform domain (i.e., a matrix with all null values expect from specific regions with no-zero coefficients). The retrieval of the mask differs from audio to image samples. Let consider first of all the audio context. The psychoacoustic model is based on many studies of human perception. These studies have shown how an average human respond to sound near in frequency and/or time. The main two properties of the human perception are: absolute threshold of hearing (i.e., ATH) and auditory masking.

ATH means that humans can hear frequencies in the range from 20 *Hz* to 20,000 *Hz*. However, this does not mean that all frequencies are heard in the same way. This consideration divides the range 20 *Hz* to 20,000 *Hz* in critical bands which are non-uniform, non-linear, and dependent on the heard sound. Signals within one critical bandwidth are hard to separate for a human observer. Without introducing the relationship between Hertz and Bark (for a deep investigation the authors quote (Smith, 1999), ATH has been defined as a function of frequency and represents the threshold of audibility of a sound at a certain frequency (See Figure13).

Figure 13. ATH, absolute threshold of hearing

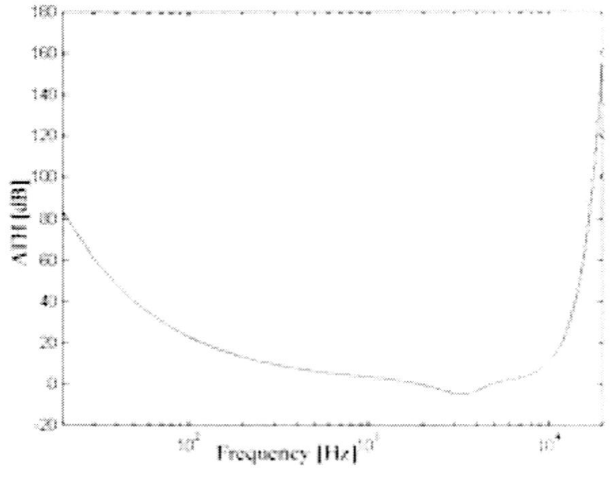

The second properties, auditory masking, means that humans do not have the ability to hear minute differences in frequency. This inability can be determined as function of three factors: tone and noise maskers, masking effect. A tone has a sharp peak in the frequency spectrum, which indicates that it is above the ambient noise of the signal. When a tone is very near to another in frequency, there is high probability that the first should mask the second (See Figure14).

Humans have difficulty discerning signals within a critical band, the noise found within each of the bands can be combined to form one mask. Thus, the idea is to take all frequency components within a critical band that do not fit within tone neighbourhoods, add them together, and place them at the geometric mean location within the critical band. Finally, the masking effect is related to the fact that the maskers, previously determined, affect not only the frequencies within a critical band, but also in surrounding bands: this results in a spreading of the effects of the masker (tone/noise). Apart from this straightforward introduction, if there are multiple noise and tone maskers, the overall effect is a little harder to determine. Several references can be quoted to provide the reader an idea of how the audio *Masking Models* and ATH work. First of all, the standard (ISO MPEG-AUDIO) and (Pan, 1995) which represents a good starting point also to non-specialized people. Then, to understand the anatomy and functionalities of the HAS: (Probst, 1993; Robinson, 1999). (Campbell, 1966; Pantle, 1969) presented masking effects in the visual domain in their works in late 60s, and later in (Tovèe, 1996). Such effects, selective for bands of spatial frequencies and orientations, are the basis for the HVS and, as for the audio context, result in visual masking (Ferweda, 1997). The reader can find an exhaustive description of the parameters for masking in (Legge, 1980). This last

Figure 14. Frequency masking

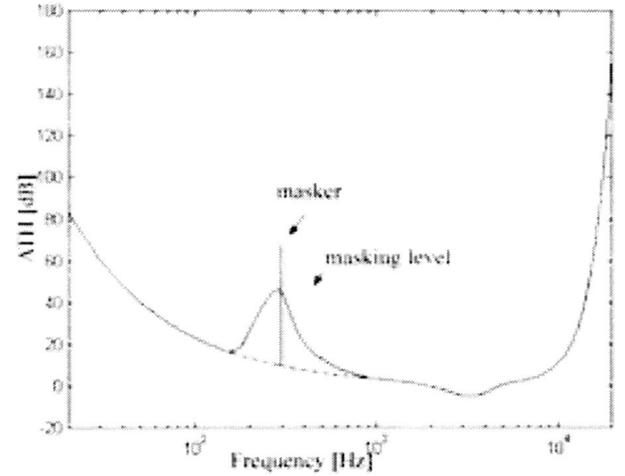

article is also the reference for many of the proposed image data hiding strategies presented in the last years. The authors also suggest: (Pennebaker, 1993; Lambrecht, 1996; Lubin, 1993) and an important study on appearance colour pattern (Poirson, 1993).

Watermarking Framework Based on Masking Models

A consistent number of watermark frameworks have been developed that control the trade-off between robustness and inaudibility by means of Masking Models. The approach is similar for audio and image watermarking. As an example, the audio Masking Model is here shortly presented as above stated, the spectral audio Masking Model is based on a very simple observation. Given a tone at a certain frequency, humans do not hear this tone, and all the others below/above it, if its intensity is below the energy-threshold fixed by the mask. The most widely-used audio Masking Model can be detailed as following: (1) divide the signal in 20 *ms* non-overlapping blocks; and for each block: (2) compute short-term power spectrum; (3) evaluate noise and pure-tones components; (4) remove all the masked components[2]; (5) compute the individual masking thresholds[3]; (6) compute the global masking thresholds. Usually the watermark is inserted 3-6 dB below the mask, to enhance its inaudibility. In the following, we briefly describe the strategy presented in (Mitchell, 1998), to give the reader an example of a well-projected *watermarking* framework based on Masking Models. The macro-steps of the embedding phase (for a block of fixed dimension from the audio signal) are:

- Compute the power spectrum of the audio segment;
- Compute the frequency mask of the power spectrum;
- Use the mask to create the shaped author-signature;
- Compute the inverse FFT (IFFT) of the frequency shaped noise;
- Compute the temporal mask;
- Use the temporal mask to further shape the frequency shaped noise creating the watermark of that audio segment;
- Create the watermarked block.

That is, the temporal/spectral Masking Models are applied (steps 2/5) to create a signal-shaped watermark. We have described this strategy also because it is probably the most representative and simple to be valued for non-specialized readers. The detection phase, without describing too much technical aspects that can be found in (Mitchell, 1998), is always based on a hypothesis test as described on a previous section. The basic idea at the base of detection phase is that, as the embedded watermark is noise-like, a pirate has insufficient knowledge to directly remove the watermark. The state of art is very prosperous of techniques based on Masking Models. In this work we quote several papers both for the novelty of the presented strategy and the results and comparisons. The reader should examine in particular: (Tovèe, 1996; Robert, 2005; Xing, 2005; Herkiloglu, 2004; Wang, 2005; Quan, 2004; Xie, 2005; Swanson, 1998). The reader can find better explanation of aspects related to the use of psychological (i.e., masking) models in watermarking in IBM Research CyberJournal (Craver, 1996; Craver, 1997).

In the following the authors present two examples of the crossing use of the Masking Models and watermarking. The first strategy is an adaptive approach of the patchwork algorithm (originally presented in (Bender, 1996) for image watermarking). While the second framework (named "Opportunity" strategy) is an improvement of the first in a aspect regarding the detection phase of the watermark.

Patchwork, Watermarking and Masking Models

A set of basic features for a reliable watermarking strategy was presented in (Arnold, 2000). Two characters are mostly significant, and, apparently contradicting: inaudibility and robustness to signal processing. Inaudibility means that the differences between the original and the watermarked signal should not be perceivable by the human ear. Secondly the watermark must be robust against intentional or unintentional attacks. One of the most impairing attack is the signal processing, and specifically the lossy compression. A possible defense against different forms of signal processing attack is the patchwork strategy and specifically the optimal shaping of the patch. The original implementation of this technique (for images) presents several limitations when applied to other media samples; and generally, quite a few adaptations have been proposed to improve considerably its performance (Arnold, 2000; Kim, 2003; Yeo, 2003; Bassia, 2001). However, from these studies, the work-dominion and the adaptive patch shaping appear as the key points for the applying of the original strategy to audio samples such as for its perfection.

The proposed strategy starts from these points and works on an assumption introduced in (Bender, 1996): treating patches of several points have the effect of shifting the noise to low frequencies, where there is lower probability to be filtered by lossy compression techniques. The problem is the dimension of the patch. Such factor is fixed by comparing the spectrum of watermarked signal to the minimum masking threshold, as obtained referring to the psychoacoustic model 2 (ISO MPEG-AUDIO). The patch shaping is performed in the Fourier dominion. The proposed technique is applied to audio samples and compared with the adaptive patchwork state of art, referring to the framework proposed in (Gordy, 2000). As previously described, the patchwork strategy is a two-set method, that is it makes different two sets from a host signal (Yeo, 2003). This difference is used to verify, or not, a hypothesis H_0 (e.g., the watermark is embedded).

The original strategy (Bender, 1996) is applied to sets with more than 5,000 elements. The samples of each subset are considered uniformly distributed and with equal mean values. The elements are modified by adding and subtracting the same quantity d. Thus, the detection of a watermark is related to the condition $E[A_{marked}-B_{marked}]=2d$. Several of these statements must be reassessed when working with audio samples (Arnold, 2000). In particular the distribution of the sample value is assumed as normal (See Figure15). Recent approaches modify the original strategy to better take into account the human ear sensibility to noise interferences. These methods can be classified in temporal and spectral approaches, depending on the domain where the watermark is embedded. In (Bassia, 2001) a technique is proposed, that is based on the transformation of time-domain data. A set of N samples, corresponding to 1*sec* of stereo audio signal, is modified by a watermark signal w(i). (Arnold, 2000; Kim, 2003; Yeo, 2003) propose spectral patchwork approaches. In particular, (Arnold, 2000) works with a dataset of $2N$ Fourier coefficients. The relationship between d and the elements of the dataset is multiplicative. The parameter d is adaptively chosen to prevent perceptual audibility, basing on the characteristics of the audio signal (i.e., it is introduced for the first time the concept of power density function in the hypothesis tests). In (Kim, 2003) the patchwork algorithm is applied to the coarsest wavelet coefficients, providing a fast synchronization between the watermark embedding and detection. While, in (Yeo, 2003) the Modified Patchwork Algorithm (i.e., MPA) is presented. Such approach is very robust due to three attributes: the factor d is evaluated adaptively and is based on sample mean and variance; the patch size in the transformed domain is very little: this guarantees good inaudibility; finally, a sign function is used to enhance the detection rate. These features are included in an embedding function so that the distance between the sample means of the two set bigger than a certain value d. The temporal approaches are easier to implement than the spectral ones; at the same time, they present several weaknesses against general signal processing modifications (Kim, 2003). The association between a watermarking algorithm and a noisy communication system is not new (Muntean, 2002). Actually, a watermarking strategy adds a mark (i.e., the noise) in a host signal (i.e., the communication channel). In this sense, the watermark embedding can be considered as an operation of channel coding: the watermark is adapted to the characteristics of the transmission channel (i.e., the host signal in which the watermark should be embedded). In case of audio contents, what it is usually considered as an impairment, the sensibility of the human ear, can be used as a way to spread and dimension the watermark. The human auditory system (HAS) is well known, that is it is sensible to specific frequencies (i.e., from $2KHz$ to $4KHz$) and reacts to specific events (i.e., frequency and temporal masking). Given a signal S, it is possible to recover its minimum masking threshold. The minimum masking threshold of audibility represents a limit between the audible and inaudible signals for S at different frequencies. Independently from S, it is also possible to recover the absolute threshold of hearing (i.e., ATH). Such curve (i.e., referred to as quiet curve (Cvejic, 2001) is different than the previous and defines the required intensity of a single sound expressed in unit of decibel (dB) to be heard in the absence of another sound (Zwicker, 1991). Several methods, outside the patchwork fashion, have been proposed that make use of psychoacoustic models to guarantee perceptual inaudibility of the mark (Boney, 1996; Cvejic, 2001; Arnold, 2002). Usually, the state of art methods shape the watermark referring mainly to the quiet. The filtered watermark signal is scaled in order to embed the watermark noise below the quiet curve (ISO,1993). In addition, other methods increase the noise energy of the watermark, referring undeniably to the minimum threshold of audibility. Such threshold can be recovered through a well defined psychoacoustic model. The MPEG/audio standard provides two example implementations of the psychoacoustic model. Psychoacoustic model 1 is less complex than psychoacoustic model 2 and has more compromises to simplify the calculations. Either model works for any of the layers of compression. However, only model 2 includes specific modifications to accommodate Layer III. In this paper, we refer to the model 2, differently from the past approaches.

As already stated, the proposed patchwork strategy modifies two set of N elements/coefficients from the original signal (i.e., signalUn-Marked). The signalMarked strongly belongs to the correspondent signalUn-Marked. The core of our strategy is the shaping of the frequency-response of the mark signal, using psychoacoustic model 2. The algorithm proposed in this work embeds the watermark in the fre-

Figure 15. Distribution of the mean difference of the samples in un-watermarked and watermarked signals

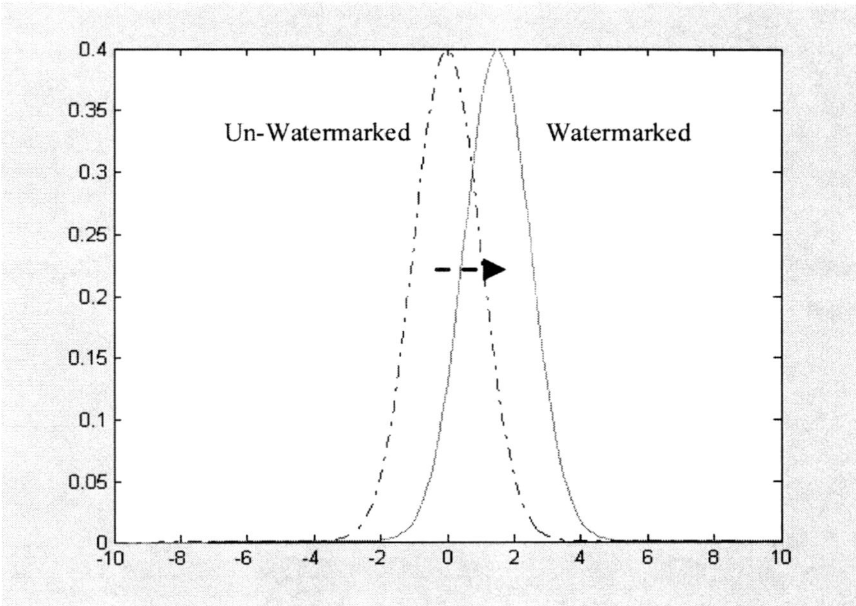

quency domain, by modifying 2N Fourier coefficients. The choice of this transform domain is justified by the use of the psychoacoustic model. The embedding steps (See Figure 16) can be summarized as follows:

1. Evaluate the threshold of minimum audibility for the signalUn-Marked, referring to psychoacoustic model 2.
2. Map the secret key and the watermark to the seed of a random number generator. Next, generate two N-points index sets $I_N^A = \{a_1, a_2, ..., a_N\}$ and $I_N^B = \{b_1, b_2, ..., b_N\}$.
3. Let $X=\{X_1,X_2,...,X_{2N}\}$ be 2N DFT coefficients of the signalUn-Marked, corresponding to the index sets I_N^A and I_N^B.
4. The original amplitude of the patch and the number of re-touched coefficients, starting from the generic elements of index a_i or b_i, have respectively standard values (δ,θ). Such values are modified iteratively to verify that the spectrum of the watermark signal is under the minimum audibility threshold (i.e., obtained from point 1). Iteratively means a constant referring to the block of model 2 from the block-shaping (See the dotted loop in Figure 16).

Figure 16. Steps (1-4) of the patchwork shaping algorithm

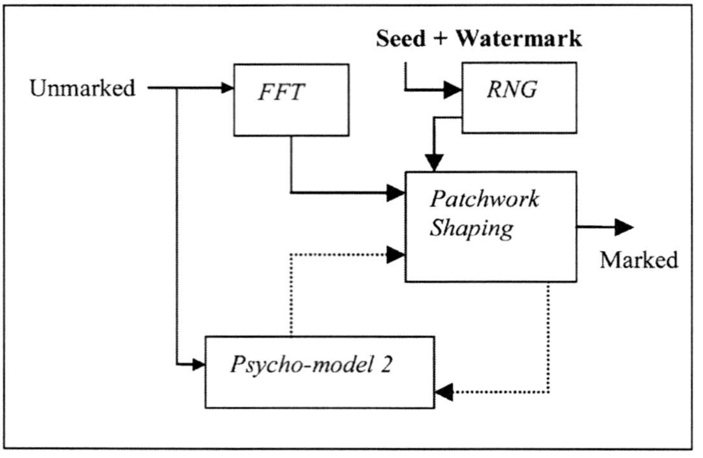

5. The time-domain representation of the output signal is found, applying an Inverse DFT to the signalMarked.

The phase of detection is as follows:

1. Define two test hypothesis: Ho (the watermark in not embedded) and H1 (the watermark is embedded).
2. Map the seed and the watermark to a Random Number Generator and generate two sets $I_N^{A'}$ and $I_N^{B'}$.
3. Fix a threshold Δ for the detection, and evaluate the mean value (i.e., $\bar{z} = E(\cdot)$) of the random variable $z = a_i^{'} - b_i^{'}$, for $a_i^{'} \in \{I_N^{A'}\}$ and $b_i^{'} \in \{I_N^{B'}\}$.
4. Decide for Ho, or H1, depending on $\bar{z} < \Delta$, or $\bar{z} \geq \Delta$.

We tested the proposed algorithm on 16-*bit* stereo audio signals, sampled at Fs = 44.1KHz. The size of the each patch (i.e., *N*) was fixed to 50 points; while the default values for (δ,θ) were set to (0,5,10). Higher values for θ were also tested only for robustness evaluation, regardless of quality aspects. The state of art proposes a framework for the evaluation of audio watermarking techniques (Gordy, 2000). In this work, we referred to this framework and considered, in particular, two key factors: quality of the watermarked signal and robustness to mp3 compression. The evaluation of quality is an essential part in testing our strategy, since the basic idea was to guarantee the maximum rate of inaudibility of the patch. The tests were performed using a subjective score (i.e., a *MOS*) and the *SNR* of the watermarked signal versus the host signal. The robustness of the proposed strategy was tested in two steps: at first, coding and decoding the watermarked signal with a commercial MP3 encoder at different rates (e.g., usually 128*Kbps*); secondly, trying the detection of the watermarked on the uncompressed signal. Quality and robustness cannot be evaluated separately. These factors are strongly correlated, that is: a decrease in quality causes an increase, in most cases significant, of robustness. All the performed tests showed good results. The idea of increasing the number of points of the patches reveals its successfulness. Good subjective quality appears since all the patches are below the audibility threshold for that signal ($SNR \leq 26$). At the same time, treating more points has the effect of shifting the patchwork-noise to low frequencies, where it has a lower probability to be filtered by the mp3 compression. Figure 17 shows different probability density functions (i.e., introduced as empirical *Pdf* (i.e., Probability Density Function) in (Bassia, 2001) of the random variable z, as described in the detection phase. The density function of z, before the mp3 compression, is compared with different behaviours (i.e., varying the dimension of the patch). This test shows clearly that higher dimensions of θ lead to lower alterations in the detection values. This results in a *Pdf* nearer to that of the uncompressed signal. We have also evaluated the error probability at different rates of compression (i.e., 128, 96 and 64 *Kbps*). Two kinds of errors can be individuated. The state of art refers to them is terms of Type I (Rejection of H_0, when H_0 is true) and Type II (Non-Rejection of H_0, when H_1 is true) (Yeo, 2003). Type II errors seem to be the most impairing (the watermark is inserted (i.e., quality degradation) but the ownership cannot be proven). Figure 18 presents the Type II errors for a test audio signal. Clearly, the probability of rejection of H_0, when H_1 is true, decreases correspondently with the mp3-rate of compression.

The "Opportunity" Framework

The above proposed strategy can be improved in two points: the modelling of the patch and the possibility of a wrong detection (that is, increasing the distance d, both the wrong detection and the inaudibility decrease). Actually these step are quite coarse. Further studies have been centred on more refined mathematical mechanisms of patch-shaping (i.e., such as the curve fitting) respect to the minimum masking threshold. The "Opportunity" strategy proposes a possible solution to the possibility of a wrong detection. The embedding steps are:

1. Choosing pseudo-randomly two sets from Ψ.
2. Defining a small quantity d.
3. Adding d to a set and subtracting the same value from the other set. Specifically, $x_i^* = x_i + d, y_i^* = y_i + d,$ where $x_i \in A, y_i \in B$ and $(A,B) \in \Psi$.

Figure 17. Probability density function of detection for the random variable z, varying the dimension of the patch with SNR = 26

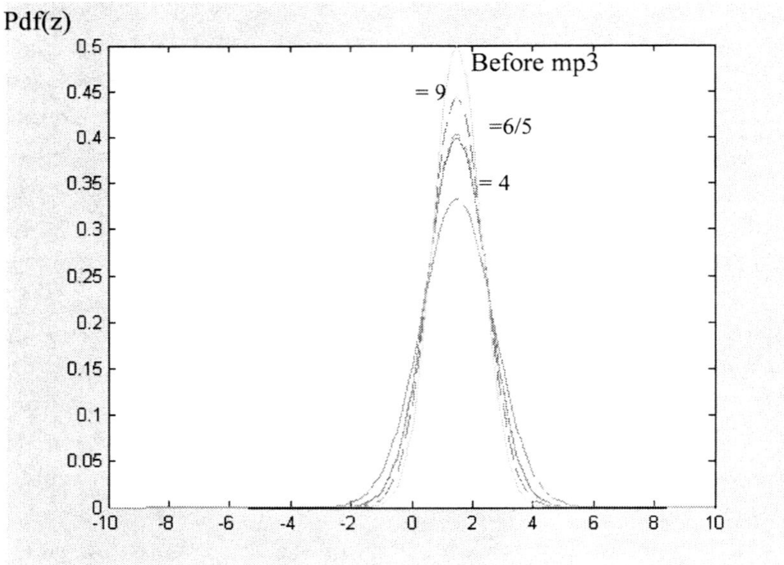

Figure 18. Error probabilities for lossy compression at different rates

Type II Errors(%)	
MPEG I Layer III (128Kbps)	0.1
MPEG I Layer III (96Kbps)	0.7
MPEG I Layer III (64Kbps)	1.6

The detection phase is based on a hypothesis testing, that is defined on a test statistic *z* and a test hypothesis *H*. The basic theory is as follows: let suppose the *pdf* of a random variable *z* (i.e., the test statistic) is a known function *f(Z,*θ*)* depending on the parameter θ. We wish to test the assumption $\theta=\theta_0$ against $\theta\neq\theta_0$. The assumption $\theta=\theta_0$ is denoted with the null hypothesis H_0, where $\theta\neq\theta_0$ is signified by the alternative hypothesis H_1 The purpose is to establish whether experimental evidence support the rejection of H_0 Referring to the watermarking context: (1) the test statistic *z* is defined as a function of elements from *A* and *B*: $z = \vec{x} - \vec{y}$; (2) the distribution of *z* (e.g., Φ(z)) is normal (Arnold, 2000), with an expected mean value $\overline{z} = 0$ in the unmarked and $\overline{z} = 2d$ in the marked case (i.e., in this case, $\Phi(z)=\Phi_m(z)$); (3) the test hypothesis (H_0, H_1) are defined and verified: H_0 (i.e., the watermark is not embedded) and H_1 (i.e., the watermark is embedded and $\Phi(z)=\Phi_m(z)$).

The main problem is the definition of *d*: the probability of a wrong decision remains, although the distribution in the watermarked case is shifted to the right (See Figure 15). A possible solution could be increasing the distance factor *d*, with the effect of having a lower probability of false rejection, but also a greater impairment on the audibility of the watermark in the host signal.

The literature tries to solve this problem in several ways. In this sense, the idea that seems to work better is the spectral patchwork (Arnold, 2000; Kim, 2003; Yeo, 2003), with a dataset of *2N* Fourier coefficients. The relationship between *d* and the elements of the dataset is multiplicative. The parameter *d* is adaptively chosen to prevent perceptual audibility, basing on the characteristics of the audio signal (i.e., it is introduced for the first time the concept of power density function in the hypothesis tests). In (Kim, 2003) the patchwork algorithm is applied to the coarsest wavelet coefficients, providing a fast synchronization between the watermark embedding and detection. While, in (Yeo, 2003) the Modified Patchwork Algorithm (i.e., MPA) is presented. Such approach is very robust due to three attributes: the factor *d* is evaluated adaptively and is based on sample mean and variance; the patch size in the transformed domain is very little: this guarantees good inaudibility; finally, a sign function is used to enhance the detection rate. It is stated that the watermark-embedding can be considered as an operation of channel coding (Muntean, 2002): the watermark should adapt to the characteristics of the transmission channel (i.e., the host signal in which the watermark should be embedded). In case of audio contents, what it is usually considered as an impairment, the sensibility of the human ear, can be used as a way to spread and dimension the watermark. Given a signal *S*, it is possible to recover its minimum masking threshold and use it to opportunely shaping the watermark-noise. Several methods, outside the patchwork fashion, have been proposed that make use of *psychoacoustic models* to guarantee perceptual inaudibility of the mark. Opportunity refers and applies this approach in a patchwork schema, maximizing a cost function that represents how much the watermark impairs the original signal. The minimum masking threshold is recovered using the *psychoacoustic model 2* (ISO MPEG-AUDIO). The proposed strategy works as follows (See Figure19): (1) the value of *d* is fixed *a priori* to minimize the possibility of false rejection; (2) given Ψ, its minimum masking threshold is recovered; (3) the secret key and the watermark are mapped to the seed of a Random Number Generator (i.e., *RNG*) to find a couple (a_i, b_i); (4) the patchwork approach is applied to the DFT coefficients of the host signal corresponding to (a_i, b_i) using the distance factor *d*; (5) a cost function $\Delta=\Delta(a_i, b_i)$ if defined, that represents the global distance between the minimum masking threshold and the amplitude of the patch (i.e., the condition $\Delta>0$ must be verified by default, otherwise a new set (a_i, b_i) is generated); (6) the process of generation of (a_i, b_i) (i.e., steps (3)-(5)) is iterated N' times to find the couple (a_{i_min}, b_{i_min}):$\Delta=\Delta\ (a_{i\_min}, b_{i\_min})=\Delta_{MAX}$; (8) the

Figure 19. "Opportunity" strategy

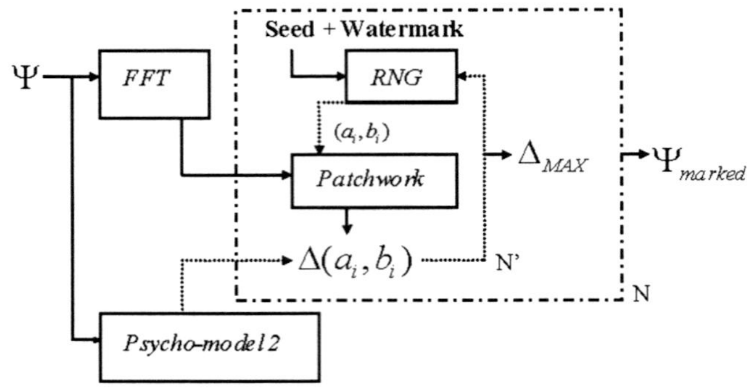

entire process is repeated to embed N couples of patches (i=1...N) and the watermarked signal Ψ_{marked} is obtained. The phase of detection is as follows:

1. Define H_0 (the watermark in not embedded) and H_1 (the watermark is embedded.
2. Map the seed and the watermark to a RNG and generate the two global sets $I_N^{A'}$ and $I_N^{B'}$ (e.g., containing the elements (a_i, b_i),i=1...N).
3. Fix a threshold Δ for the detection, and evaluate the mean value (i.e., $\bar{z} = E(\cdot)$) of the random variable $z = a_i^{'} - b_i^{'}$, for $a_i^{'} \in \{I_N^{A'}\}$ and $b_i^{'} \in \{I_N^{B'}\}$;
4. Decide for H_0, or H_1, depending on $\bar{z} < \Delta$, or $\bar{z} \geq \Delta$.

We tested the proposed algorithm on 16-bit stereo audio signals, sampled at Fs = 44.1KHz. The size of the patch (i.e., N) was fixed to 100 couple of points; while the default value for d was set to 0.25 (e.g., where the original algorithm (Bender, 1996) selected a fixed value 0.15 in the experiments). Higher values for d were also tested only for robustness evaluation, regardless of quality aspects, to test the rate of probability rejection. The performed investigations on the proposed strategy have the aim of showing *good audio quality* (e.g., inaudibility of the mark) of the watermarked signals and, at the same time *low probability of false rejection,* also when the audio signal is subjected to post-processing. In the following the results of such tests are presented. The evaluation of quality is an essential part in testing our strategy, since the basic idea was to guarantee the maximum rate of inaudibility of the patch. Good subjective quality appears since all the patches are below the audibility threshold for that signal (SNR≤26). We also compared the marked/unmarked signals, using the

Figure 20. PEAQ – MOS rating

Opportunity	4.77
MPA [YK03]	4.00
Arnold [A00]	3.23

PEAQ strategy (ITU-R BS.1387-1): Opportunity shows a better performance, respect to the other tested strategies with default parameters (See Figure 20). The second aim of the tests was to verify a decreasing in the probability of false rejection. Two kinds of errors can be individuated. The state of art refers to them in terms of Type I (Rejection of H_0, when H_0 is true) and Type II (Non-Rejection of H_0, when H_1 is true) (Yeo, 2003). Type II errors seem to be the most impairing (the watermark is inserted (i.e., quality degradation) but the ownership cannot be proven). Figure 21 presents the Type II error for a non-compressed test audio signal (test1.wav). We also prove the efficiency of Opportunity when compressing-decompressing (i.e., at different rates of compression (i.e., 128, 96 and 64 *Kbps*)) and re-synchronizing the same test signal (See Figure 22).

RECENT PAST AND PRESENT TRENDS

Many interesting works and new ideas, based on Masking Models and watermarking, have been proposed in the last years (between 2006 and late 2009). In the following, a significant part of them is presented in a chronological order.

In (Shetty, 2006) a method is presented that reduces the perceptibility of a robust *watermarking* scheme (a visual equalized-spectrum watermarking) using human visual models. The visual mask is generated using Watson's model, which is based on the block discrete cosine transform (DCT). The generated mask is applied to the watermarked image as a post-watermarking process. An adaptive watermarking method to improve both transparence and robustness of quantization index modulation (QIM) scheme is proposed by (Guoxi, 2006). A variable quantization step size, adapted to image content, is found balancing the robustness of extraction and the transparence of embedding. The modified steps are determined by the contrast masking thresholds of Watson's perceptual model. The method appears to be robust to several forms of attack (as an example: additive white Gaussian noise, salt & pepper noise, JPEG compression). In (Wei, 2007), it is proposed a novel approach that transforms the test signal to a perceptually uniform domain and then performs Bayesian hypothesis testing in that domain. Within a spread spectrum approach, the watermark signal is usually modulated by the just-noticeable difference (JND) of the

Figure 21. Error probabilities for non-compressed signal (test1.wav)

Type II Errors(%)	
Opportunity	0.1
MPA [YK03]	0.7
Arnold [A00]	1.6

Figure 22. Error probabilities for lossy compression at different rates (test1.wav)

Type II Errors(%) **-Opportunity-**	
MPEG I Layer III (128Kbps)	0.32
MPEG I Layer III (96Kbps)	0.68
MPEG I Layer III (64Kbps)	0.81

host image, characterized as a nonlinear function of local image features. The authors study the optimum detection scheme for such nonlinearly embedded watermarks and propose optimum detectors for arbitrary host signal distributions and arbitrary JND models. The optimality of the proposed detector is justified mathematically according to the Neyman-Pearson criterion. (Shuang-An, 2007) proposes watermark technique based on echo hiding. Similarly to what has been proposed in the "Opportunity" framework an interesting temporal masking technique is used to guarantee inaudibility. (Belkacem, 2007) presents a novel watermarking approach for applications in copy protection and digital archives based on perceptual masking. In the proposed scheme, local properties of the image and the features of the human visual system in discrete cosine transform (DCT) domain are taken into consideration in order to optimize the watermark strength. The luminance masking effect of the HVS is used in the masking image, since the human eye is less sensitive to change in regions with high brightness as well as in very dark regions compared to mid-grey regions, where the distortion is most noticeable. Another work based on the Watson's model is proposed in (Dong, 2008), with an adaptive spread-transform dither modulation (ASTDM) algorithm. The technique should be resistant both to the amplitude scaling and coefficient re-quantization attacks. In fact, the luminance masking is modified to be consistent with amplitude scaling without affecting the original parameters. Then, by incorporating the improved model with STDM algorithm, a maximum labeling strength and an appropriate quantization step-size shrinking with the local values of a host image are achieved. Proposed experiments demonstrate that with high embedding rate and transparence, ASTDM can greatly increase the robustness against the above cited factors. (Bouchakour, 2008) evaluates the usability of the

JND mask in the wavelet domain. This work is particularly interesting since the use of the mask in the DWT domain involves some approximations. The paper shows that the HVS decomposition and the wavelet decomposition do not perfectly fit altogether. The efficiency of the so obtained mask is tested both in terms of invisibility and robustness. In (Maha, 2008) an audio watermarking technique is proposed for protecting audio copyrights based on human psychoacoustic model (HPM), discrete wavelet transform (DWT), neural network (NN) and error correcting code. Such blind retrieval technique exploits frequency perceptual masking studied in HPM to guarantee that the embedded watermark is inaudible. A neural network is used to memorize the relationships between a Wavelet central sample and its neighbors, and the watermark is also refined by the Hamming error correcting code. The encoded mark is embedded as new watermark in the transformed audio signal. The authors suggest their audio watermarking algorithm is robust to common audio signal manipulations like MP3 compression, noise addition, silence addition, bit per sample conversion, noise reduction, dynamic changes and Notch filtering. (Tavakoli, 2008) presents a patchwork audio watermarking scheme with a psychoacoustic model of HAS in DFT domain, while another interesting approach, based on the entropy of motion information, is proposed for video in (Li, 2008). (Liu, 2009) proposes an approach similar to "Opportunity" which seems to be resistant to statistical attacks. This work is cited as a term of comparison with other similar techniques.

CONCLUSION

This work has presented an overview of the use of Masking Models in watermarking techniques, which is a well consolidated and interesting field of research. The aim of such techniques is to guarantee a high level of robustness and bandwidth of the watermark as well as fidelity of the watermarked signal. The general scheme for audio content has been presented both in embedding and detection phase. The approach is similar both for audio and image contents. To give also an idea on how to design, implement and verify techniques based on such an approach, two techniques on audio watermarking are proposed in the second section. Such strategies are both based on a two-set method, as presented in (Bender, 1996) for image watermarking, but combined with a Masking Model. It seems to be a trend for the future the development of new techniques jointly based on classic techniques and Masking Models. The strategies have been compared to others in terms of robustness and transparency of the watermark. The last section has presented a brief overview of new frameworks proposed in the last years (between 2006 and late 2009). This last section proves an enormous work of research has been done on Masking Models and watermarking. Each work, proposed in chronological order, is described with a short abstract of the core-technique.

REFERENCES

Arnold, M. (2000). Audio watermarking: features, applications and algorithms. *IEEE International Conf. Multimedia and Expo, 2*, 1013-1016.

Arnold, M., & Schiltz, K. (2002). Quality evaluation of watermarked audio tracks. *SPIE Electronic Imaging, 4675*, 91–101.

Bassia, P., Pitas, I., & Nicholaidis, N. (2001). Robust audio watermarking in the time domain. *IEEE Transactions on Multimedia, 3*, 232–241. doi:10.1109/6046.923822

Bender, W., Gruhl, D., Morimoto, N., & Lu, A. (1996). Techniques for data hiding. *IBM Systems Journal, 35*(3-4).

Boney, L., Twefik, A. H., & Hamdy, K. N. (1996). Digital watermarks for audio signal. *International Conference on Multimedia Computing and Systems*, (pp. 473-480).

Brandenburg, K., & Stoll, G. (1992). *The ISO/MPEG-audio codec: A generic standard for coding of high quality digital audio*. 92nd AES-Convention, preprint 3336.

Campbell, F. W., & Kulikowski, J. J. (1966). Orientation selectivity of the human visual system. *The Journal of Physiology, 187*, 437–445.

Chen, B., & Wornell, G. W. (1999). Dither modulation: A new approach to digital *watermarking* and information embedding. *Proceedings of the SPIE – Security and Watermarking of Multimedia Contents, 3657*, (pp. 342-353).

Cox, I. J., Kilian, J., Leigton, F. T., & Shamoon, T. (1996). Secure spread spectrum watermarking for multimedia. *IEEE Transactions on Image Processing, 6*, 1673–1687. doi:10.1109/83.650120

Craver, S., & Memon, N., & Yeo, B.-L., & Yeung, M. (1996). Can invisible watermarks resolve rightful ownerships? *IBM Research Technical Report RC 20509 IBM CyberJournal*.

Craver, S., Memon, N., Yeo, B.-L., & Yeung, M. (1997). Resolving rightful ownerships with invisible watermarking techniques: Limitations, attacks and implications. *IBM Research Technical Report RC 20755 IBM CyberJournal*.

Cvejic, N., Keskinarkaus, A., & Seppanen, T. (2001). *Audio watermarking using m-sequences and temporal masking* (pp. 227–230). IEEE Workshops on Applications of Signal Processing to Audio and Acoustics.

Delaigle, J. F., Devleeschouwer, C., Macq, B., & Langendijk, L. (2002). Human visual system features enabling watermarking. *Proceedings of Multimedia and Expo, ICME02*, 489–492.

Eggers, J. J., Su, J. K., & Girod, B. (2000). A blind *watermarking* scheme based on structured codebooks. *Secure Images and Image Authentication-IEE Colloquium*, 4/1-4/6.

Ferwerda, J. A., Pattanaik, S. N., Shirley, P., & Greenberg, D. P. (1997)... *Computer Graphics*, *31*, 143–152.

Gordy, J. D., & Bruton, L. T. (2000). Performance evaluation of digital audio watermarking algorithms. *Proceedings of the 43rd Midwest Symposium on Circuits and Systems*.

Herkiloglu, K., Sener, S., & Gunsel, B. (2004). Robust audio watermarking by adaptive psychoacoustic masking. *Proceedings of 12th IEEE Conference on Signal Processing and Communications Applications*, (pp. 29-32).

Huang, J., & Shi, Y. Q. (2002). Adaptive image watermarking scheme based on visual masking. *Electronics Letters*, *34*(8), 748–750. doi:10.1049/el:19980545

Kazakeviciute, G., Januskevicius, E., Rosenbaum, R., & Schumann, H. (2005). Tamper-proof image *watermarking*, based on existing public key infrastructure. *Informatica, 16*(1).

Kim, H. (2000). Stochastic model based audio watermark and whitening filter for improved detection. *IEEE International Conference on Acoustics, Speech, and Signal Processing, 4,* (pp. 1971-1974).

Kim, H. J. (2003). *Audio watermarking techniques*. Pacific Rim Workshop on Digital Steganography. ISO/IEC Joint Technical Committee 1. (1993). *Subcommittee 29 working group 11, information technology-coding of moving pictures and associated audio for digital storage media at up to about 1.5 Mbit/s, Part 3: Audio*. ISO/IEC 11172-3.

Kim, H. J., & Yeo, I. (2003). Modified patchwork algorithm: A novel audio watermarking scheme. *Transactions on Speech and Audio Processing, 11*(4), 381–386. doi:10.1109/TSA.2003.812145

Kim, H. O., Lee, B. K., & Lee, N. Y. (2001). *Wavelet-based audio watermarking techniques: Robustness and fast synchronization*. Research Report 01-11, Division of Applied Mathematics-Kaist.

Lambrecht, C., & Verscheure, O. (1996). Perceptual quality measure using a spatio-temporal model of the human visual system. *Proceedings of the Society for Photo-Instrumentation Engineers, 2668*, 450–461.

Legge, G. E., & Foley, J. M. (1980). Contrast masking in human vision. *Journal Optical Society, 70*, 1458–1470. doi:10.1364/JOSA.70.001458

Lubin, J. (1993). *The use of psychophysical data and models in the analysis of display system performance. Digital images and human vision* (pp. 163–178). A. B. Watson.

Macq, B., & Quisquater, J. (1995). Cryptology for digital TV broadcasting. *Proceedings of the IEEE, 83*, 944–957. doi:10.1109/5.387094

Mansour, M. F., & Tewfik, A. H. (2001). Audio watermarking by time-scale modification. *International Conference on Acoustics, Speech, and Signal Processing, 3,* (pp. 1353-1356).

Marr, D. (1982). *Vision: A computational investigation into the human representation and processing of visual information*. San Francisco, CA: W. H. Freeman.

Mitchell, D. S., Bin, Z., Tewfik, A. H., & Boney, L. (1998). Robust audio watermarking using perceptual masking. *IEEE Signal Processing, 66*(3), 337–355. doi:10.1016/S0165-1684(98)00014-0

Muntean, T., Grivel, E., Nafornita, I., & Najim, M. (2002). *Audio digital watermarking for copyright protection*. International Workshop on "Trends and Achievements in Information Technology.

Pan, D. (1995). A tutorial on MPEG/audio compression. *IEEE MultiMedia, 2*(2), 60–74. doi:10.1109/93.388209

Pantle, A., & Sekuler, R. W. (1969). Contrast response of human visual mechanisms sensitive to orientation and direction of motion. *Vision Research, 9*, 397–406. doi:10.1016/0042-6989(69)90087-X

Pennebaker, W. B., & Mitchell, J. L. (1993). *JPEG: Still image data compression standard.* Van Nostrand Reinhold.

Petitcolas, F. A. P., Anderson, R. J., & Kuhn, M. G. (1999). Information hiding – A survey. *Proceedings of the IEEE - Special Issue on Protection of Multimedia Content, 87*(7), 1062-1078.

Poirson, A., & Wandell, B. (1993). Appearance of colored patterns. *Journal of the Optical Society of America, 10*(12), 2458–2470. doi:10.1364/JOSAA.10.002458

Probst, R., Lonsbury-Martin, B. L., & Martin, G. K. (1991). A review of otoacoustic emissions. *Journal of Acoustic Society, 89*, 2027–2067. doi:10.1121/1.400897

Quan, X., & Zhang, H. (2004). Audio watermarking for copyright protection based on psychoacoustic model and adaptive wavelet packet decomposition. *Proceedings of 2004 International Symposium on Intelligent Multimedia, Video and Speech Processing*, (pp. 282–285).

Robert, A., & Picard, J. (2005). On the use of *masking models* for image and audio *watermarking. IEEE Transactions on Multimedia, 7*(4), 727–739. doi:10.1109/TMM.2005.846781

Robinson, D. J. M., & Hawksford, M. J. (1999). Time-domain auditory model for the assessment of high-quality coded audio. *107th Convention of the Audio Engineering Society* - preprint 5071.

Smith, J. O., & Abel, J. A. (1999). *Bark and ERB bilinear transforms.*

Swanson, M. D., Bin, Z., & Tewfik, A. H. (1998). Multiresolution scene-based video watermarking using perceptual models. *IEEE Journal on Selected Areas, 16*(4), 540–550. doi:10.1109/49.668976

Tilki, J. F., & Beex, A. A. (1996). Encoding a hidden digital signature onto an audio signal using psychoacoustic masking. *Proceedings 1996 7th International Conference on Signal Processing* (pp. 476-480).

Tovée, M. J. (1996). *An introduction to the visual system* (pp. 180–202). Cambridge University Press.

Trichili, H., Bouhlel, M.-S., Solaiman, B., & Kamoun, L. (2003). Exploitation of the HVS features for the enhancement of image watermarking techniques. *ISPA03, 2*, (pp. 1076–1081).

Wang, R. D., Xu, D. W., & Qian, L. (2005). Audio watermarking algorithm based on wavelet packet and psychoacoustic model. *PDCAT, 2005*, 812–814.

Wu, C. P., Su, P. C., & Kuo, C. C. J. (2000). Robust and efficient digital audio watermarking using audio content analysis. [SPIE]. *Security and Watermarking of Multimedia Contents, 3971*, 382–392.

Wu, M., & Liu, B. (1998). Watermarking for image authentication. *Proceedings of 1998 IEEE International Conference on Image Processing*, 2, (pp. 437-441).

Xie, G., & Shen, H. (2005). Toward improved wavelet-based watermarking using the pixel-wise Masking Model. *ICICP2005, 1*, (pp. 689-692).

Xing, H., & Scordilis, M. S. (2005). Improved spread spectrum digital audio watermarking based on a modified perceptual entropy psychoacoustic model. *Proceedings of IEEE Southeast Conference*, (pp. 283-286).

Yeo, I. K., & Kim, H. J. (2003). Modified patchwork algorithm: A novel audio watermarking scheme. *IEEE Transactions on Speech and Audio Processing, 11*(4).

Zwicker, E., & Zwicker, U. T. (1991). Audio engineering and psychoacoustics: Matching signals to the final receiver: The human auditory system. *Journal of the Audio Engineering Society. Audio Engineering Society, 39*(3), 115–126.

ADDITIONAL READING

Belkacem, S., Dibi, Z., & Bouridane, A. (2007) A Masking Model of HVS for Image Watermaking in the DCT Domain. *14th IEEE International Conference on Electronics, Circuits and Systems, 2007. ICECS 2007*, 330-334.

Bouchakour, M., Jeannic, G., & Autrusseau, F. (2008) JND mask adaptation for wavelet domain watermarking. *2008 IEEE International Conference on Multimedia and Expo*, 201-204.

Dong, Y., Lihong, M., Guoxi, W., & Hanqing, L. (2008) Adaptive spread-transform dither modulation using an improved luminance-masked threshold. *15th IEEE International Conference on Image Processing 2008*, 449-452.

Guoxi, W., Lihong, M., Kang, C., & Hanqing, L. (2006) Modified Quantization Index Modulation Watermarking Adaptive to Contrast Masking Thresholds. *First International Conference on Communications and Networking in China, ChinaCom '06*, 1-5.

Li, Z., & Chen, X. (2008) Self-Adaptive Video Watermarking Based on the Motion Characteristic Detection and the Model of Entropy. *International Conference on Intelligent Information Hiding and Multimedia Signal Processing, IIHMSP 2008*, 845-848.

Liu, X., Sun, S., Zhu, J., Jiang, M., & Xie, D. (2009) An Audio Watermarking Method of Resistance Statistics Attack Based on Psychoacoustic Model. *Fifth International Conference on Information Assurance and Security, 2009. IAS 2009*, 737-739.

Maha, C., Maher, E., & Chokri, B. A. (2008) A blind audio watermarking scheme based on neural network and psychoacoustic model with error correcting code in wavelet domain. *3rd International Symposium on Communications, Control and Signal Processing 2008*, 1138-1143.

Shetty, N. K., & Rodriguez, J. J. (2006). Equalized-spectrum Watermarking Using Perceptual Modeling. *2006 Southwest IEEE Symposium on Image Analysis and Interpretation*, 1-5.

Shuang-An, C., Shih-Fu, H., & Ko-Chiang, L. (2007) A Temporal Masking Technique and its Performace Analysis for Audio Watermarking. *2007 IEEE International Conference on Multimedia and Expo*, 1774-1777.

Tavakoli, E., & Tabandeh, M. (2008) A new method for using a psychoacoustic model with patchwork audio watermarking in DFT domain. *34th Annual Conference of IEEE on Industrial Electronics, IECON 2008*, 1822-1827.

Wei, L., Lina, D., & Wenjun, Z. (2007). Optimum Detection for Spread-Spectrum Watermarking That Employs Self-Masking. *IEEE Transactions on Information Forensics and Security*, *2*(4), 645–654. doi:10.1109/TIFS.2007.908226

ENDNOTES

1 The expression E(∘) indicates the operation of mean value in statistics.

2 Including components below the absolute hearing threshold, or components too much close to others to be heard.

3 This step involves the human auditory system.

Chapter 3
Multimedia Content Encryption for Secure Multimedia Communication

Shiguo Lian
France Telecom (Orange Labs) Beijing, China

ABSTRACT

The principal concern of this chapter is to provide those in the secure multimedia communication or content protection community with an overview of multimedia content encryption technology. Multimedia (image, audio or video) content encryption technologies are reviewed, from the background, brief history, and performance requirement, to research progress. Additionally, the general encryption algorithms are classified, and their performances are analyzed and compared. Furthermore, some special encryption algorithms are introduced. Finally, some open issues and potential research topics are presented, followed by some conclusions. The author hopes that the chapter will not only inform researchers of the progress of multimedia content encryption but also guide the design of practical applications in industry field.

INTRODUCTION

With the development of computer technology and Internet technology, multimedia data (images, videos, audios, etc.) are used more and more widely, such as video-on-demand, video conferencing, broadcasting, and so on. Now, multimedia communication is in close relation with daily life, such as education, commerce,

DOI: 10.4018/978-1-61350-135-1.ch003

politics, military, etc. In order to keep privacy or security, some sensitive data need to be protected before transmission or distribution. Originally, access right control method is used, which controls media data's access by authenticating the users. For example, in video-on-demand, the pair of user name and password is used to control the browsing or downloading operations. However, in this method, multimedia data themselves are not protected, and may be stolen in transmission process. Thus, to realize secure multimedia communication, multimedia data should be encrypted before transmission or distribution.

Till now, various encryption algorithms have been proposed and widely used, such as DES, RSA or IDEA (Mollin, 2006), most of which are used in text or binary data. It is difficult to use them directly in multimedia data, for multimedia data (Furht, 1999) are often of high redundancy, of large-volumes and require real-time operations, such as displaying, cutting, copying, bit-rate conversion, etc. For example, the image Figure 1(a) is encrypted into Figure 1(b) by DES algorithm directly. As can be seen, Figure 1(b) is still intelligible in some extent. This is because the adjacent pixels in an image are of close relation which cannot be removed by DES algorithm. Besides security issue, encrypting images or videos with these ciphers directly is time cost and not suitable for real time applications. Therefore, for multimedia data, some new encryption algorithms need to be studied.

During the past decades, various multimedia encryption algorithms have been studied. In the following content, the basic knowledge, brief history and Intellectual Property investigation are introduced. Additionally, the general requirement, general encryption schemes and special encryption schemes are analyzed and compared in detail. Finally, some open issues are presented, and conclusions are drawn.

THE BASIC OF MULTIMEDIA CONTENT ENCRYPTION

Multimedia content encryption refers to adopt cryptographic techniques to protect multimedia content. Thus, the basic includes both cryptographic techniques and multimedia techniques.

Cryptography

In cryptography, cryptosystem design and cryptanalysis are two close-related topics. Cryptosystem includes traditional ciphers and some new ciphers. Traditional ciphers are often based on the computing difficulty of attack operations. For example, RSA is based on the difficulty to factor a large prime number, Ellipse Curve Cipher is based on the difficulty to solve a discrete logarithm, and such block ciphers as DES and AES are based on the computing complexity caused by iterated confusion and

Figure 1. The image is encrypted by DES directly: (a) original image, and (b) encrypted image

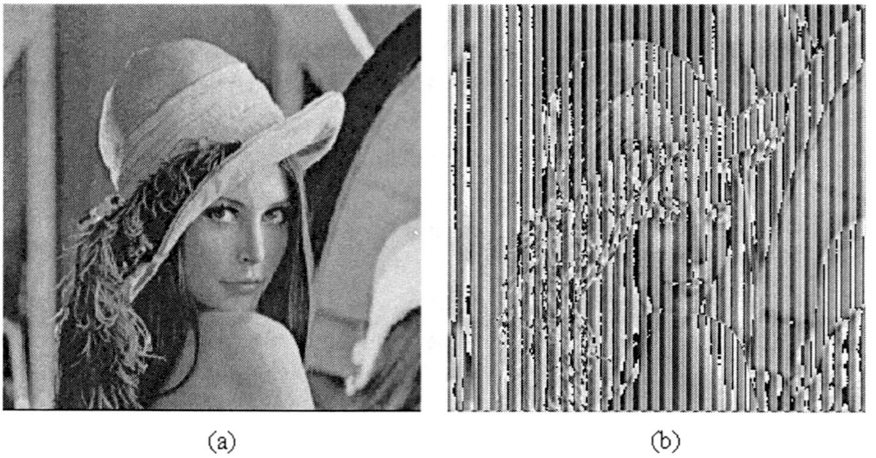

diffusion operations. Besides traditional ciphers, some new ciphers have being studied in the past decade. The typical one is chaotic cipher (Fridrich, 1997; Dachselt & Wolfgang, 2001), which uses chaotic dynamic systems to construct stream ciphers or block ciphers. Cryptanalysis (Mollin, 2006) is the inverse process of cryptosystem design, that is, to break a cryptosystem. Generally, the security of a cryptosystem depends on the key. For a secure cryptosystem, it is should survive such attacks as brute-force attack, statistical attack, differential attack, linear analysis, etc.

Multimedia Technology

Multimedia technology (Furht, 1999) includes multimedia compression, transmission, retrieve, analysis and so on. Here, multimedia compression is focused. Generally, multimedia data are transformed into frequency domain, which benefits the compression operation. Based on the transformation, multimedia compression codecs can be classified into several types: FFT (Fast Fourier Transformation) based codec, DCT (Discrete Cosine Transformation) based codec and wavelet based codec. For example, MP3 (MPEG Layer 3) is the codec based on FFT, DCT based codec includes JPEG (Pennebaker & Mitchell, 1993), MPEG1/2/4, H.263/4, etc., and wavelet based codec includes EZW (Shapiro, 1993), SPIHT (Said, 1996), JPEG2000, etc.

BRIEF HISTORY OF MULTIMEDIA CONTENT ENCRYPTION

Multimedia encryption technology is firstly reported in 1980s (Matias & Shamir, 1987), and becomes a hot research topic in the second half of 1990s. According to the development, it can be partitioned into three phases, e.g., raw data encryption, compressed data encryption, and partial encryption.

Before 1990s, few multimedia encoding methods are standardized. More of multimedia data, such as image or video, are stored or transmitted in the raw form. In this period, multimedia encryption is mostly based on pixel scrambling or permutation. That is, the image or video is permuted so that the result one is unintelligible. For example, Space Filling Curves (Matias & Shamir, 1987) are used to permute image or video data, which confuse the relation between adjacent image pixels or video pixels. European TV network adopts Eurocrypt standard to encrypt TV signals, which permutes each TV field line by line. These methods are of low computing complexity and low cost. However, the permutation operation changes the relation between adjacent pixels, which will make the followed compression operation out of work. Thus, these encryption algorithms are only suitable for the applications that need no compression.

In the first half of 1990s, with the development of multimedia technology, some image, audio or video encoding standards are formed, such as JPEG, MPEG1/2, etc. Generally, multimedia data are compressed before being stored or transmitted. Thus, the permutation algorithms for raw data encryption are not suitable for these applications. Alternatively, novel algorithms that encrypt the compressed data directly are preferred. For example, Qiao et al (Qiao & Nahrstedt, 1997) proposed the VEA algorithm that uses DES algorithm to encrypt video data, Romeo et al (Romeo, et al., 1999) proposed the RPK algorithm that combines a stream cipher and a block cipher. These algorithms focus on the system security. However, for they encrypt all the compressed data, the computing cost is high, which makes it difficult for large volume data. Additionally, the file format is changed by the encryption algorithm, which makes the encrypted data can not be played or browsed directly. Thus, these algorithms are more suitable for secure multimedia storing than for real time transmission.

Since the second half of 1990s, with the development of Internet technology, multimedia applications put more requirements to real time operation and interaction. By encrypting only parts of the media data, the encrypted data volumes can be greatly reduced, which improves the encryption efficiency. For example, Cheng et al (Cheng & Li, 2000) proposed the algorithm that encrypts only parts of the data stream in wavelet transformed images or videos, Lian et al (Lian, et al., 2005) proposed the algorithm that encrypts only parts of the parameters in Advance Video Coding, Servetti et al (Servetti, et al., 2005) proposed the algorithm that encrypts only the bit allocation parameters in MP3 files. These algorithms encrypt few parts that are significant in human perception, while leaving the other parts unchanged. Thus, the real time requirement can be met. Additionally, the file format can be kept unchanged, which benefits the transmission process.

INTELLECTUAL PROPERTY INVESTIGATION

As a hot topic, multimedia content encryption has attracts many researchers. In some well-known international academic conferences, it is an important topic, such as ICIP (IEEE International Conference on Image Processing), ICME (IEEE International Conference on Multimedia & Expro), ICASSP (IEEE International Conference on Audio, Speech and Signal Processing), CMS (IFIP Conference on Communications and Multimedia Security), SPIE International Conference on Security and Watermarking of Multimedia Contents, etc. Some well-known international journals also publish the research results on multimedia content encryption, such as IEEE Transaction on Multimedia, IEEE Transaction on Circuits and Systems for Video Technology, IEEE Transaction on Consumer Electronics, etc.

The paper and patent publications in the past decades are listed in Figure 2. The papers are indexed by Compendex database, and the patent publications are indexed by European Patent Office. The research topics include image encryption, audio encryption and video encryption, etc. The applications include TV program encryption, digital video encryption, broadcast encryption, satellite encryption, speech signal encryption, music encryption, color image encryption, etc.

GENERAL REQUIREMENTS OF MULTIMEDIA CONTENT ENCRYPTION

Multimedia data are often of high redundancy, large volumes, real time operations, and the compressed data are of certain format. All these properties require that multimedia encryption algorithms should satisfy some requirements.

Security

Security is the basic requirement of multimedia content encryption. Generally, for multimedia encryption, an encryption algorithm is regarded as secure if the cost for breaking it is no smaller than the one paid for the authorization of multimedia content. This is different from traditional cipher for text/binary data encryption. For example, in broadcasting, the news may be of no value after an hour. Thus, if the

Figure 2. Statistics of published papers and patents on multimedia content encryption

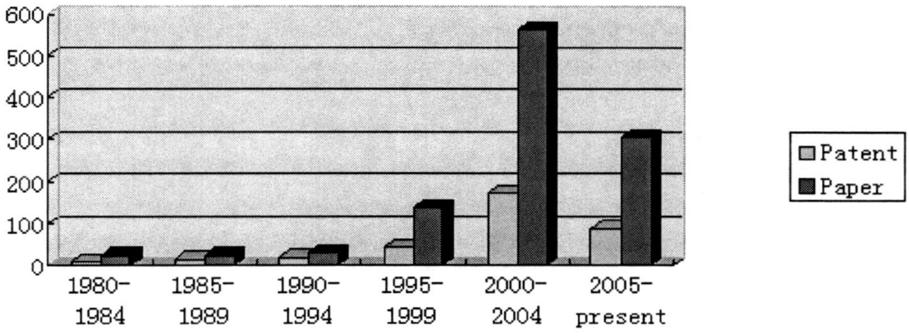

attacker cannot break the encryption algorithm during an hour, then the encryption algorithm may be regarded as secure in this application. Different from text/binary encryption, multimedia encryption requires both cryptographic security and perception security. The former one refers to the security against cryptographic attacks (Mollin, 2006), and the latter one means that the encrypted multimedia content is unintelligible to human perception. According to perception security, knowing only parts of the multimedia data may do little help to understand multimedia content. Thus, encrypting parts of the multimedia data may be reasonable if the cryptographic security is satisfied.

Efficiency

Since real time transmission or access is often required by multimedia applications, multimedia encryption algorithms should be efficient so that they don't delay the transmission or access operations. Generally, two kinds of method can be adopted: the first one is to reduce the encrypted data volumes, and the other one is to adopt lightweight encryption algorithms.

Compression Ratio

Multimedia data are compressed in order to reduce the storage space or transmission bandwidth. In this case, multimedia encryption algorithms should not change compression ratio or at least keep the changes in a small range. This is especially important in wireless or mobile applications, in which, the channel bandwidth is limited.

Format Compliance

Multimedia data are often encoded or compressed before transmission, which produces the data streams with some format information, such as file header, time tamp, file tail, etc. The format information will be used by the decoders to recover the multimedia data successfully. For example, the format information can be used as the synchronization information in multimedia communication. Encrypting the data except the format information will keep the encrypted data stream format-compliant. This will support the decoding operations and improve the error robustness in some extent.

Direct Operations

In some applications, it will save some cost to operate directly on the encrypted multimedia data, but not to do the triple operations of decryption-operation-encryption. For example, the encrypted multimedia data can be recompressed, the bit-rate of the encrypted multimedia data can be controlled, the image block or frame can be cut, copied or inserted, etc. If the encrypted multimedia data can be operated by certain operations, then the corresponding encryption algorithm supports the corresponding operations.

GENERAL ENCRYPTION SCHEMES

Till now, many multimedia encryption algorithms have been proposed. According to the encryption manner, they are classified into three types: direct encryption, partial encryption, and compression-combined encryption. In the following content, they are summarized, analyzed and compared, respectively.

Direct Encryption

Direct encryption algorithm, as shown in Figure 3, encrypts raw data or compressed data directly with traditional or novel ciphers under the control of an encryption key. The decryption process is symmetric to the encryption process. The performances of the encryption system depend on the adopted cipher and the relation between encryption and compression. Generally, direct encryption algorithm is classified into two types: raw data encryption and compressed data encryption.

Figure 3. Architecture of direct encryption

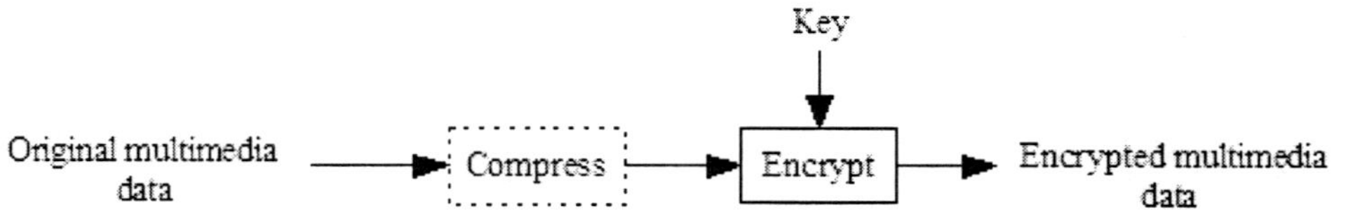

Raw Data Encryption

Raw data encryption algorithm encrypts raw data directly, which does not consider the compression process. Generally two kinds of method are often used: permutation algorithm and permutation-diffusion algorithm.

Permutation algorithms permute the uncompressed multimedia data with the control of an encryption key. For example, pay-per-view TV program is scrambled by the permutation algorithm based on pseudorandom number. This algorithm permutes the TV field line by line, and assigns each field a unique key. Alternatively, Pseudorandom Space Filling Curves are used to change the scanning order of image or video pixels (Matias & Shamir, 1987), which reduces the intelligibility of image or video. In the algorithm, the scanning order is controlled by an encryption key that determines the space filling curves' shape. Additionally, chaotic maps are used to permute images or videos (Scharinger, 1998; Pichler & Scharinger, 1996). Taking the image or video pixels' coordinates as the initial value of a chaotic map, the coordinates are changed into another one by iterating the chaotic map. The control parameters of the chaotic map act as the encryption or decryption key. Furthermore, some mathematical transforms are used to permute image or audio data, such as the magic cube (Ye, et al., 2003) or Fibonacci transform (Qi, et al., 2000), which change the pixels' position in the order controlled by the key. These permutation algorithms are of low cost in computing cost or power cost, and often make the permuted images unintelligible, as shown in Figure 4. However, they are not secure enough in cryptographic view point, e.g., they are not secure against select-plaintext attacks (Li, et al., 2004).

Permutation-diffusion algorithms not only permute the pixels of multimedia data but also change the amplitudes of the pixels. For example, the block ciphers based on chaotic maps (Fridrich, 1997; Mao, et al., 2004) firstly permute the pixel's position and then change the pixel's amplitude by diffusing the changes from one pixel to another adjacent one. These algorithms are often of higher security than permutation algorithms, while of lower efficiency than permutation algorithms.

In general, these raw data encryption algorithms decrease multimedia data's understandability through changing the adjacent relation among image pixels. They

Figure 4. Examples of some permutation algorithms: (a) original image, (b) line permutation, (c) SFC permutation, (d) chaotic map permutation and (e) Fabonacci permutation

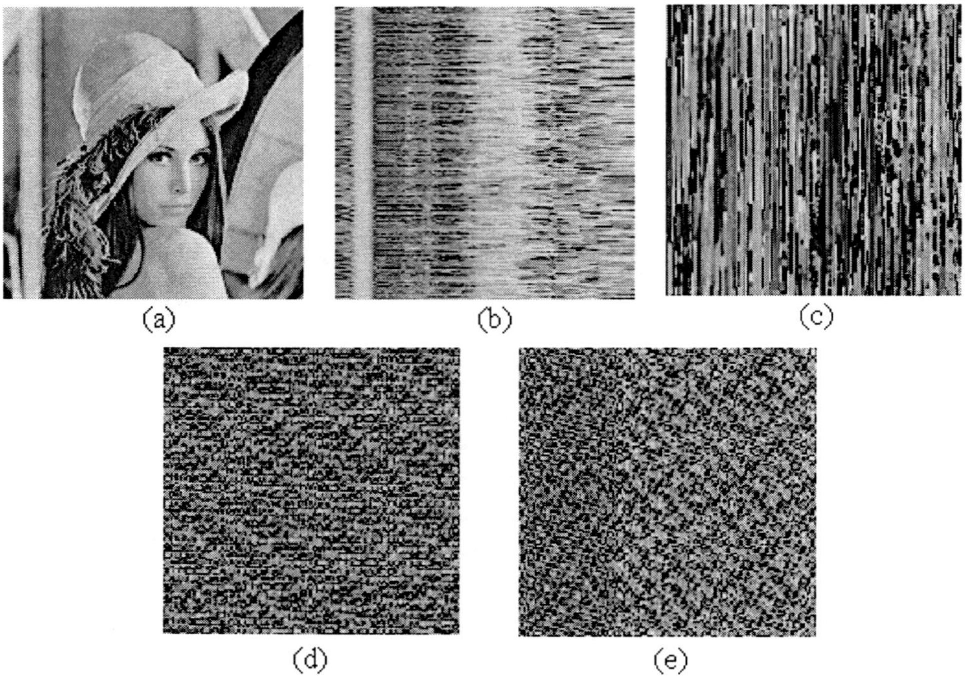

are of low cost in computing or power. However, they often change the statistic properties of multimedia data, which will affect the following compression operation. Therefore, these algorithms are often used to encrypt the multimedia data that need no compression, such as TV signal, BMP image, audio broadcasting, etc.

Compressed Data Encryption

Compressed data encryption algorithm, as shown in Figure 3, encrypts the compressed data stream directly. The existing algorithms can be classified into two types: data stream permutation algorithm and data stream encryption algorithm.

Data stream permutation algorithms permute the compressed data stream directly. For example, Qiao et al (Qiao & Nahrstedt, 2000) proposed that MPEG1/2 video stream can be permuted with a byte as a unit because of three reasons: firstly, it is convenience, secondly, a byte is meaningless, and thirdly, it is random. In this algorithm, the video stream is often partitioned into segments, and then permuted segment by segment. The segment size determines the security level. That is, the bigger the segment is, the higher the security is, otherwise, on the contrary. This kind of algorithm is of low cost, while also of low security. Thus, it is more suitable for the applications that require real time operation and low security.

Data stream encryption algorithms encrypt the compressed data stream with modified or novel ciphers. For example, Qiao et al (Qiao & Nahrstedt, 1997) proposed VEA (Video Encryption Algorithm) that encrypts only the even half of plaintext with DES and obtains the odd half through XOR-operation on the even half and the odd half. Thus, the encryption time is reduced to nearly 46% compared with DES. Tosun et al (Tosun & Feng, 2001) extended the algorithm by partitioned the even half into two halves again, and decreased the encryption time to nearly a quarter. Agi et al (Agi & Gong, 1996) proposed the video encryption algorithm that uses the key stream produced by DES algorithm to modulate the video stream bit by bit. Romeo et al (Romeo, et al., 1999) proposed RPK algorithm that combines a stream cipher with a block cipher. Wee (Wee & Apostolopoulos, 2001) proposed the algorithm that encrypts the progressive data stream with a stream cipher layer by layer. These algorithms are often of high security that benefits from the adopted traditional ciphers. However, they change the file format, which makes the encrypted data cannot be operated without decryption. Additionally, since all the compressed data are encrypted, the efficiency is not high enough.

Partial Encryption

Partial encryption algorithm, as shown in Figure 5, encrypts only a part of the multimedia data with the control of an encryption key while leaves the other part unchanged. The performances of the encryption system depend on the encrypted data part and the adopted cipher. For efficiency, the smaller the encrypted data part is, the lower the cost is. To obtain high security, three points are required: firstly, the encrypted data part should be independent from the unencrypted part, secondly, the encrypted data part should be significant to human perception, and thirdly, the adopted cipher should be of high security. According to the type of multimedia data, the existing partial encryption algorithms can be classified into audio encryption, image encryption and video encryption.

Audio Encryption

Audio data are often encoded before being transmitted in order to save transmission bandwidth. Thus, audio encryption is often applied to the encoded data. For example, the speech data are encrypted by encrypting only the parameters of Fast Fourier Transformation during speech encoding process (Sridharan, et al., 1991).

Figure 5. Architecture of partial encryption algorithm

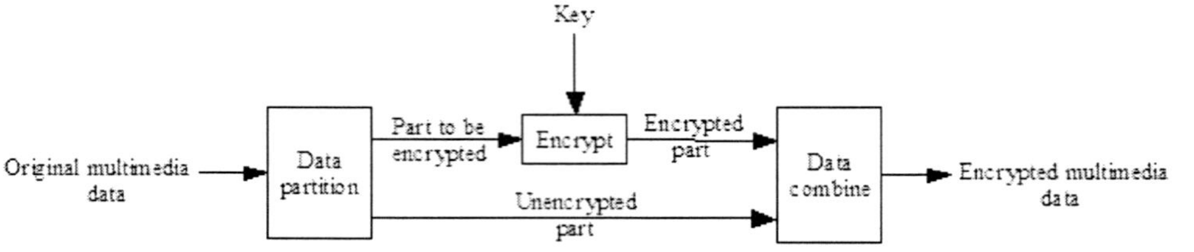

In decryption, the right parameters are used to recover the encrypted data. For MP3 (Gang, et al., 2001) music, only the sensitive parameters of MP3 stream are encrypted, such as the bit allocation information. For encrypting only few data, this kind of encryption algorithm is often of high efficiency.

Image Encryption

A straightforward partial encryption algorithm for images is bit-plane encryption (Podesser, et al., 2002). That is, in an image, only several significant bit-planes are encrypted, while the other bit-planes are left unchanged. By reducing the encrypted bit-planes, the encryption efficiency can be improved. However, the security cannot be confirmed, especially against replacement attacks. In replacement attacks, the encrypted data part is replaced by other data, which may make the encrypted image intelligible. For example, two most significant bit-planes of an image are encrypted, as shown in Figure 6(a) and (b), and the image (c) can be recovered from (b) by replacing the most significant bit-plane with zeros.

For compressed images, the algorithms based on DCT and wavelet codecs attract more researchers, such as JPEG or JPEG2000. In JPEG, an image is partitioned into blocks, and each block is transformed by DCT followed by quantization, run-length code, entropy code, etc. The algorithm proposed in (Pfarrhofer & Uhl, 2005) encrypts only some significant bit-planes of DCT coefficients, which obtains high perception security and encryption efficiency. In JPEG2000, an image is transformed by wavelet transformation and partitioned into blocks, and then, each block is quantized, encoded by run-length code, entropy code, etc. The algorithms proposed in (Norcen & Uhl, 2003; Fukuhara, et al., 2002) encrypts only the significant streams in the encoded data stream, which is selected according to the progressiveness in space or frequency. Generally, no more than 20% of the data stream is encrypted, which obtains high efficiency. Another algorithm (Lian, et al., 2004a) encrypts different number of significant bit-planes of wavelet coefficients in different frequency bands, which obtains high security in human perception and keeps secure against replacement attacks.

Figure 6. Examples of bit-plane encryption and replacement attack: (a) original image, (b) encrypted image, and (c) replacement attack

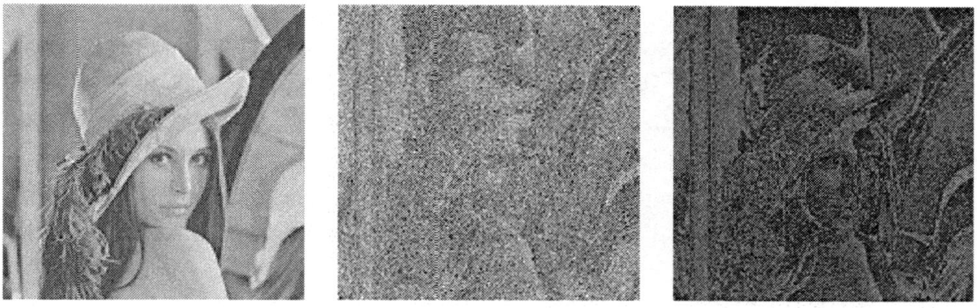

(a) (b) (c)

Video Encryption

Since video data are of larger volumes compared with image or audio data, video data are often compressed in order to reduce the bandwidth. Generally, the compressed video data stream is composed of such parts as format information, texture information or motion information. Taking MPEG1/2/4 for example, texture information refers to DCT coefficients. Thus, according to the data parts, video partial encryption algorithms are classified into several types: format information encryption, frame encryption, motion vector encryption, texture encryption, and both motion vector and texture encryption.

Format Information Encryption

Since format information helps the decoder to recover the multimedia data, encrypting the format information will make the decoder out of work (Agi & Gong, 1996; Ho & Hsu, 2005). However, it is not secure in cryptographic view point to encrypt only format information. This is because the format information is often in certain grammar, which can be broken by statistical attacks (Agi & Gong, 1996). These algorithms change the format information and thus make the encrypted multimedia data cannot be displayed or browsed by a normal browser.

Frame Encryption

In such video codec as MPEG1/2/4, the frame is often classified into three types: I-frame, P-frame and B-frame. I-frame is often encoded directly with DCT transformation, while P/B-frame is often encoded by referencing to adjacent I/P-frame.

Thus, I-frame is the referenced frame of P/B-frame. Intuitively, encrypting only I-frame will make P/B-frame unintelligible. However, experiments (Agi & Gong, 1996) show that this is not secure enough. The reason is that some macroblocks encoded with DCT transformation in P/B-frame are left unencrypted. For some videos with smart motion, the number of such macroblock is high enough to make the encrypted video intelligible. As an improved method, SECMPEG algorithm (Tang, 1996) encrypts all the macroblocks encoded with DCT transformation in I/P/B-frame. In these algorithms, the motion information is left unencrypted, which makes the motion track still intelligible.

Texture Encryption

The coefficients in DCT or wavelet transformation determine the intelligibility of the multimedia data. Encrypting the coefficients can protect the confidentiality of the texture information. For example, Shi et al (Shi & Bhargava, 1998) proposed the algorithm that encrypts the signs of DCT coefficients. If the coefficient is positive, then the sign bit is "1", otherwise, the sign bit is "0". The sign bits are encrypted with a cipher and then returned to the corresponding coefficients. In AVC codec, the intra-prediction mode of each block is permuted with the control of the key (Ahn, et al., 2004), which makes the video data degraded greatly. These algorithms are efficient in computing, but not secure enough. Firstly, the motion information is left unencrypted, which makes the motion track still intelligible. Secondly, the video can be recovered in some extent by replacement attacks (Lian, et al., 2005). For example, the encrypted intra-prediction mode in the scheme (Ahn, et al., 2004) can be replaced by certain one, and thus, the decoded video is intelligible, as shown in Figure 7.

Motion Vector Encryption

In most video codecs, motion vector represents the motion information. Thus, encrypting motion vector will make the motion track unintelligible. For example, Yen et al (Yen & Guo, 1999) proposed the algorithm that encrypts motion vectors in MPEG1/2 stream with the pseudorandom sequence generated by a chaotic map. However, if there is little motion in a video, then few motion vectors are encrypted, and thus, the video is still intelligible. Therefore, encrypting only motion vector is not secure enough.

Figure 7. Examples of replacement attacks on texture encryption: (a) original video, (b) encrypted AVC video, and (c) replacement attack

Both Motion Vector and Texture Encryption

To keep secure, it is necessary to encrypt both DCT/wavelet coefficient and motion vector. Considering that these two kinds of information occupy many percents in the whole video stream, they should be encrypted partially or selectively. Generally, two kinds of partial encryption method are often used, e.g., coefficient permutation and sign encryption. For example, in the algorithm proposed by Shi et al (Shi, et al., 1999), both the coefficient's sign and motion vector's sign are encrypted with DES or RSA [1]. Zeng et al (Zeng & Lei, 2003) proposed the algorithm that permutes coefficients or encrypts the signs of coefficients and motion vectors in DCT or wavelet transformation. Lian et al (Lian, et al., 2005; Lian, et al., 2006a) proposed the algorithm that encrypts the DCT coefficients and motion vectors in AVC codec with sign encryption. These algorithms encrypt both the texture information and motion information, and thus, obtain high security in human perception, as shown in Figure 8. Additionally, the partial encryption operation, such as coefficient permutation or sign encryption, is often of low cost, which makes the encryption

Figure 8. Examples of both coefficient and motion vector encryption: (a) original video, (b) encrypted MPEG2 video, and (c) encrypted AVC video (Lian, et al., 2006a)

schemes of high efficiency. Furthermore, these partial encryption algorithms keep the file format unchanged.

Compression-Combined Encryption

Compression-combined encryption, as shown in Figure 9, combines encryption operation and compression operation, and implemented encryption and compression simultaneously. According to the compression operations, the existing algorithms can be classified into several types: entropy code based algorithm, and coefficient encryption algorithm.

Entropy Code Based Algorithm

Entropy code based algorithm combines encryption operation with entropy encoding and realizes secure entropy encoding. For example, Wen et al (Wen, et al., 2001) proposed the algorithm based on Fixed Length Code and Variable Length Code.

Figure 9. Architecture of compression-combined encryption algorithm

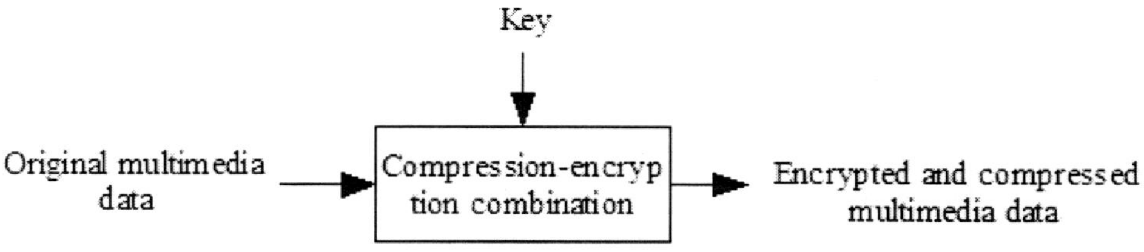

This algorithm permutes the codeword table or encrypts the index of the codeword. Tosun et al (Tosun & Feng, 2001) proposed the algorithm based on Forward Error Correction code. This algorithm makes the encrypted data stream have the ability of error correction. Wu et al (Wu & Kuo, 2000; Wu & Kuo, 2001) proposed Multi-Huffman Tree algorithm and Multi-State Index algorithm based on Huffman encoding and arithmetic encoding, respectively. These two algorithms realize secure Huffman encoding and arithmetic encoding by changing the codeword or the index randomly. These algorithms often obtain high security by losing some compression efficiency because some redundancy should be introduced into the original codec in order to confirm enough brute-force space.

Coefficient Encryption Algorithm

During image/video compression, DCT or wavelet transformation is often applied, which produces the coefficients in frequency domain. These coefficients are then quantized, scanned and encoded. By changing the scanning manner or coefficient sign, the decoded data become unintelligible. For example, Uehara (Uehara, 2001) proposed the algorithm that combines compression and encryption. In this algorithm, the wavelet coefficients of the transformed image are permuted in different frequency bands, which produce the images with different quality. This algorithm is of low cost, and supports such direct operations as displaying, recompression, or bit-rate conversion. However, the algorithm is not secure against replacement attack and changes compression efficiency greatly. As an improvement, Lian et al (Lian, et al., 2004b) proposed the algorithm based on SPIHT codec, which reduces the effect on compression efficiency by permuting the coefficients in trees. The examples of these encryption algorithms are shown in Figure 10. For DCT based codec, Tang et al (Tang, 1996) proposed the algorithm that permutes DCT coefficients completely in each block. Tosun et al (Tosun & Feng, 2000) improved the algorithm by partitioning each block into three segments and permuting DCT coefficients in each segment. Furthermore, Lian et al (Lian, et al., 2004c; Lian, et al., 2004d) improved

Figure 10. Examples of coefficient encryption in wavelet domain: (a) original image, (b) frequency band permutation, and (c) tree permutation

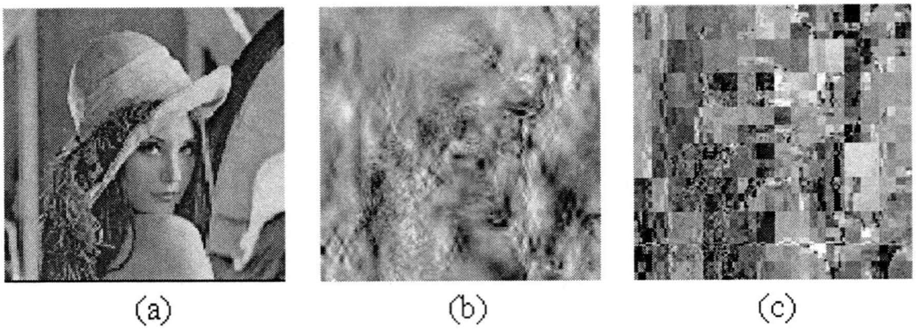

Figure 11. Examples of coefficient encryption in DCT domain: (a) original video, (b) complete permutation, (c) segment permutation, and (d) inter/intra-block permutation

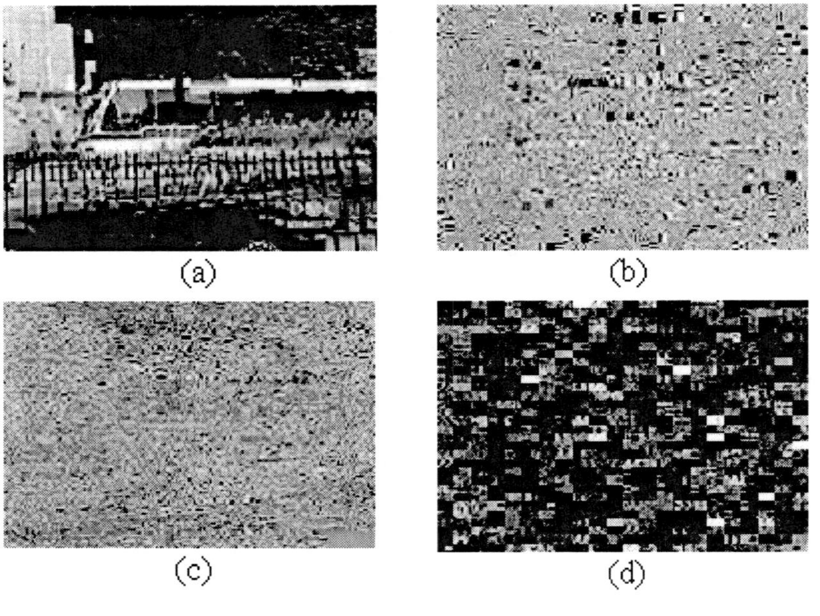

the algorithm by introducing sign encryption and intra-block permutation. The examples of these algorithms are shown in Figure 11. These coefficient encryption algorithms are often of low cost, produce unintelligible data, and support such direct operations as displaying, recompression, or bit-rate conversion. However, the compression efficiency is often changed, and the cryptographic security is to be studied. Compression-combined encryption algorithms are of low cost, keep file

Figure 12. Performance comparison between different direct encryption algorithms

The algorithms		Security		Efficiency (high, middle or low)	Compression ratio (no change, slight change or great change)	Format compliance (Yes or No)	Direct operations (Enabled or Disabled)			Some applications
		Cryptographic security (high, middle or low)	Perception security (high, middle or low)				Display, browse	Bitrate change	Recompression	
Direct encryption	Raw data permutation [22,23,29-32]	Low	Middle or high	High	No change	No	Enabled	Disabled	Disabled	Broadcast encryption, TV program encryption
	Permutation-diffusion [34-36]	Middle	High	Middle	No change	No	Enabled	Disabled	Disabled	Secure image transmission
	Data stream permutation [37]	Low	High	High	No change	No	Disabled	Disabled	Disabled	Not secure
	Data stream encryption [24,25,38,39]	High	High	Low	No change	No	Disabled	Disabled	Disabled	Secure storage

format unchanged and support some direct operations. Thus, they are more suitable for such real time application as mobile or wireless multimedia communication.

Performance Comparison

Comparisons between the proposed three types of encryption algorithms are done to show the security (cryptographic security and perception security), compression ratio, efficiency, format compliance and direct operations (displaying, browsing, bit-rate conversion, recompression, etc.). As shown in Figure 12, Figure 13 and Figure 14, several typical algorithms in each type are analyzed and compared. Generally, direct encryption algorithms are independent on file format, partial encryption algorithms often obtain a tradeoff between security, efficiency and format compliance, and compression-combined encryption algorithms often support more direct operations than other algorithms. Thus, direct encryption algorithms are more suitable for data encryption without considering of the file format, partial encryption algorithms are more suitable for real time transmission, and compression-combined encryption algorithms are more suitable for mobile or wireless multimedia transmission.

Figure 13. Performance comparison between different partial encryption algorithms

The algorithms		Security		Efficiency (high, middle or low)	Compression ratio (no change, slight change or great change)	Format compliance (Yes or No)	Direct operations (Enabled or Disabled)			Some applications
		Cryptographic security (high, middle or low)	Perception security (high, middle or low)				Display, browse	Bit-rate change	Recompression	
Partial encryption	Significant audio parameter encryption [28,43]	Middle	High	High	No change	Yes	Enabled	Disabled	Disabled	Real time Music or speech encryption
	Significant image stream encryption [46-51]	High	High	High	No change	Yes	Enabled	Partially enabled	Disabled	Internet or mobile image encryption
	Format encryption [52]	Low	High	High	No change	Yes	Disabled	Disabled	Disabled	Not secure
	Texture encryption [54,55]	Low	Low	High	No change	Yes	Enabled	Disabled	Disabled	Not secure
	Motion encryption [56]	Low	Low	High	No change	Yes	Enabled	Disabled	Disabled	Not secure
	Texture + motion encryption [57-59]	High	High	Middle or high	No change	Yes	Enabled	Disabled	Disabled	Wireless multimedia encryption

SPECIAL ENCRYPTION SCHEMES

Besides the general encryption schemes that aim at multimedia confidentiality protection, some special encryption schemes (Lian, 2008a; Lian, 2009a; Lian & Zhang, 2009a; Lian, et al., 2009a) are also reported, which aim at special applications, such as secure multimedia preview, scalable transmission, secret communication or secure content distribution, etc.

Perceptual Encryption

In some applications, multimedia data's quality may be reduced before being used for free preview. If the customer is interested in the data, he will pay for the copy of high quality. To reduce the quality, perceptual encryption algorithm is used, which is

Figure 14. Performance comparison between different compression-combined algorithms

The algorithms		Security		Efficiency (high, middle or low)	Compression ratio (no change, slight change or great change)	Format compliance (Yes or No)	Direct operations (Enabled or Disabled)			Some applications
		Cryptographic security (high, middle or low)	Perception security (high, middle or low)				Display, browse	Bit-rate change	Recompression	
Compression-combined encryption	FEC based encryption [61]	Middle	High	Middle	Slight change	Yes	Disabled	Disabled	Disabled	Secure mobile multimedia
	FLC/VLC based encryption [60,62,63]	Middle	High	Middle	Slight change	Yes	Disabled	Disabled	Disabled	Real time communication
	Coefficient permutation [53,64,66]	Low	High	High	Great change	Yes	Enabled	Enabled	Enabled	Not secure
	Coefficient permutation + sign encryption [65,67,68]	Middle	High	High	Slight change	Yes	Enabled	Enabled	Enabled	Secure mobile or wireless communication

firstly reported by Torrubia et al (Torrubia & Mora, 2003; Torrubia & Mora, 2002). In the proposed perceptual encryption algorithms, two parameters are used to control the encryption or decryption operation, e.g., the key K and the quality factor Q. Here, K is the encryption key, and Q controls the quality of the encrypted multimedia data. Generally, the bigger Q is, the higher the quality is, while the smaller the encryption strength is, otherwise, on the contrary. To control the quality of JPEG image and MP3 music, variable number of coefficient in each data block are encrypted. However, for the proposed algorithms encrypt the compressed data stream, they do not support such direct operation as bit-rate control or recompression. Alternatively, Lian et al (Lian, et al., 2004b; Lian, et al., 2004c; Lian, et al., 2004e) proposed the algorithms combined with JPEG/MPEG2, JPEG2000 and SPIHT encoding. These perceptual encryption algorithms permute certain number of coefficients in certain frequency band and encrypt certain number of coefficient sign under the control of both the key and the quality factor. The examples based on JPEG and JPEG2000 are shown in Figure 15, where (a), (b), (c) and (d) are JPEG images, (e), (f), (g) and (h) are JPEG2000 images. For the encryption operations are implemented during compression operations, they realize encryption and compression simultaneously, keep file format unchanged, and support such direct operations as bit-rate control

Figure 15. Perceptual encryption of JPEG or JPEG2000 images: (a), (b), (c) and (d) are JPEG images, (e), (f), (g) and (h) are JPEG2000 images. (a) Q=100, (b) Q=90, (c) Q=50, (d) Q=30, (e) Q=100, (f) Q=80, (g) Q=60, and (h) Q=30.

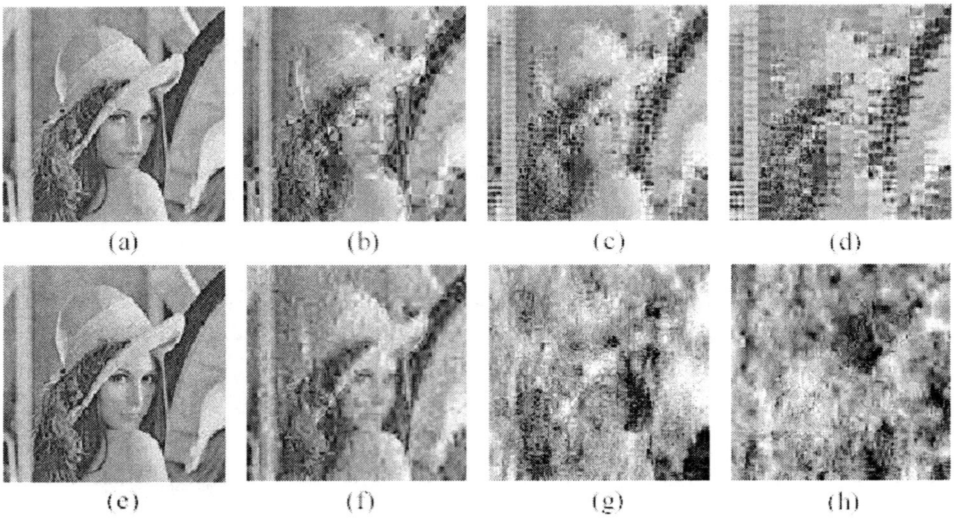

or recompression. Thus, they are suitable for secure multimedia preview in wireless or mobile environment.

Scalable Encryption

Scalable video codecs often generate scalable data stream that is composed of a base layer and several enhancement layers. The data stream is more suitable for time-varying channels. For example, if the channel bandwidth becomes smaller, then the data stream can be cut short directly in order to adapt the channel. In this case, special encryption methods are expected, which are named scalable encryption methods here. Till now, several scalable encryption algorithms have been proposed. Tosun el al (Tosun & Feng, 2000) proposed the algorithm that encrypts only the base layer and middle layer in the three layers (base layer, middle layer and enhancement layer) of a MPEG video stream. In this algorithm, the enhancement layer is left unencrypted, which can be cut off directly. Yu et al (Yu & Yu, 2003) proposed the algorithm that encrypts the pixel's bits from the most significant one to the least significant one selectively. Kunkelmann et al (Kunkelmann & Reineman, 1997) proposed the algorithms that encrypt a particular subset of important DCT coefficients in scalable MPEG video streams. Wee et al (Wee & Apostolopoulos, 2001; Wee & Apostolopoulos, 2003) proposed the algorithms for secure scalable streaming enabling transcoding without decryption. In these algorithms, the scalable stream is partitioned into segments, and then encrypted segment by segment. To change the bit-rate, some segments at the end of the stream are cut off directly. Grosbois et al (Grosbois, et al., 2001) proposed the encryption algorithm for JPEG2000 images, which supports the scalable property of the data stream. Yuan et al (Yuan, et al., 2003) proposed the encryption algorithms for MEPG-4 FGS (Fine Granularity Scalability) that encrypt the base layer and also the sign bits of DCT coefficients in the enhancement layer to enable full scalability for the encrypted video.

Based on scalable encryption, some typical digital rights management system or conditional access system can be constructed. For example, in (Lian & Zhang, 2009b), a secure mobile TV access system is presented, which transmits the encrypted TV content through a broadcasting channel while distributing the access rights over the personal mobile terminal channel. This system is extended to support the adaptation between home TV and mobile TV in (Lian, 2010a; Lian, et al., 2009b). Furthermore, the conditional access system for three-screen TV (home TV, Internet TV and mobile TV) is constructed in (Lian, 2009d; Lian, 2010b), which supports the scalable switch between various access modes and the corresponding business models. Additionally, the digital rights management system (Lian, 2008e) is constructed to realize the right transfer between mobile TV and home TV. Thus, it is available for the user to watch home TV by paying only once through his mobile phone.

Joint Decryption and Fingerprint Embedding

Joint decryption and fingerprint embedding is a technique to embed such fingerprint information as user ID (Identification) into multimedia data during data decryption, which produces different copies to different users. By detecting the fingerprint in an illegal copy, the illegal distributor can be traced. Thus, this technology is often used for secure multimedia content distribution. Till now, some algorithms have been proposed. For example, the multicast media distribution method (Parnes & Parviainen, 2001) is constructed based on the broadcast encryption scheme (Macq & Quisquater, 1995). In this method, different watermark is embedded into the two cipher-segments before encryption, and the decryption process selects different cipher-segment randomly, which produces the copy contains a unique watermark sequence. The main disadvantage of this method is that double copies need to be transmitted, which wastes the bandwidth. Anderson et al (Anderson & Manifavas, 1997) proposed the Chamloen method based on a stream cipher, which encrypts multimedia data with a stream cipher and embeds different watermarks into the least significant bits (LSB) by changing the decryption key slightly. This scheme is efficient, while cannot survive such signal processing as recompression, adding noise, A/D conversion, etc. Kundur et al (Kundur & Karthik, 2004) proposed the Joint

Fingerprint embedding and Decryption (JFD) method based on partial encryption, which confuses the sign bit of the DCT coefficients in encryption and decrypts only part of the sign bits in decryption. This scheme can survive some signal processing operations. However, the encrypted media data are still intelligible (perception security is not high enough), and the decrypted media data's quality is reduced greatly by sign encryption. Lian et al (Lian, et al., 2006b) proposed the watermarking based algorithm that encrypts the multimedia data by increasing the embedding strength and decrypts them by reducing the embedding strength under the control of both the key and the fingerprint. This algorithm is time efficient, and keeps the decoded multimedia data of high quality. But the method's security needs to be confirmed.

The JFD schemes are suitable for secure multimedia content distribution because of realizing two important functionalities, i.e., confidentiality protection, and copy identification. The two functionalities depend on the encryption operation and digital fingerprinting operation, respectively, which have been analyzed in (Lian, 2008c). Three cases should be considered in order to construct a good JFD scheme: the encryption operation's security, the fingerprinting operation's tracing ability, and the secure combination of encryption and fingerprinting. Firstly, the encryption operation should be designed carefully, which has been mentioned in the previous sections. Secondly, for the fingerprinting operation, the ability of traitor tracing (Lian, 2008d) is the most important concern. Thirdly, the encryption operation and fingerprinting operation should be combined carefully in order to avoid security flaws. For example, in some JFD schemes, there are apparent flaws between the encryption operation and fingerprinting operation (Lian, et al., 2010; Lian, et al, 2008a; Lian, et al., 2008b), which make the schemes fragile to attacks. Of course, it is available to find new ways to combine the encryption and fingerprinting operations. For example, in (Lian & Wang, 2008), the encryption operation and fingerprinting operation are both based on the modulation operation, which can overcome the security flaws caused by unsuitable combinations.

Commutative Watermarking and Encryption (CWE)

In some cases, it is benefit if the watermarking operation and encryption operation can be commutative (Lian, 2008b). Thus, two cases may happen. In the first case, the watermark is firstly embedded into the multimedia content, then the marked content is encrypted. And from the encrypted content, the watermark is still detectable. In the second case, the media content is firstly encrypted, then the watermark is embedded into the encrypted content. After decryption, the watermark is still detectable. As can be seen, both the cases support the watermarking operation in the encrypted domain. This property can be extended to data processing in encrypted domain. Till now, two solutions have been reported, e.g., partial encryption and watermarking, and homomorphic encryption and watermarking. In the first solution (Lian, et al., 2007), the media content is partitioned into two independent parts, i.e., the first one is encrypted, while the second one is watermarked. Since the two parts are independent, the watermark operation and encryption operation may be independent, and can be selected freely. For these kind of solution, the potential security flaw is the replacement attack that replaces the watermarked part with another one. In the second solution (Lian, 2009c), the encryption operation and watermarking operation are homomorphic, e.g., the module addition based stream cipher and the additive watermarking, and thus, can be commutative. Generally, the difficulty is how to find homomorphic encryption and watermarking operations. The commutative watermarking and encryption (CWE) scheme has been applied to secure video distribution. For example, in (Lian 2009b), the video content is partitioned into several parts, among which, the most significant part is encrypted, and another important part is watermarked. After these operations are done before video content distribution, which reduces the server's workloads greatly.

Visual Cryptography

Visual cryptography is based on secret sharing (Blakley, 1979; Shamir, 1979). Secret sharing refers to the method for distributing a secret among a group of participants. Each participant is allocated a share of the secret, and the secret can only be reconstructed when the shares are combined together. Visual cryptography refers to share a secret image by partitioning it into image shares. The secret image can be recovered only when all the image shares are combined together. Since each image share is meaningless in this case, they can be transmitted secretly. The first visual cryptographic algorithm is proposed by Naor and Shamir (Naor & Shamir, 1994). In this algorithm, a secret halftone image is partitioned into random halftone images printed on transparencies, each of which is meaningless. In decryption, the image is recovered by superimposing the proper transparencies. Nakajima et al (Nakajima & Yamaguchi, 2004) proposed a visual cryptographic algorithm that partitions a secret image into image shares, each of which is a pre-specified image instead of a random noise. To make each image share meaningful, more redundancy is added, which makes reduces the quality of the recovered secret image. Fu et al (Fu & Au, 2004) proposed the algorithm combining visual cryptography and watermarking. In this algorithm, each image share is embedded into a carrier image with watermarking technology, which produces a new image share. The secret image is visible when all the new image shares are combined together.

OPEN ISSUES

During the past decades, multimedia content protection has been studied in deep, and some means have been reported, which satisfy various applications. However, for multimedia technology itself is in development, multimedia content protection is still not mature. In this field, there still some open issues.

Security Analysis

Due to the difference between multimedia encryption and traditional encryption, the security analysis methods may also be different. Taking partial encryption for example, not only such cryptographic attacks as brute-force attack, differential attack and statistical attack but also some other attacks should be considered, such as replacement attacks (Lian, et al., 2005) and other unknown attacks. Till now, it is still difficult to get a suitable metric on the intelligibility of multimedia content, which increases the difficulty to analyze a partial encryption algorithm.

Communication-Compliant Encryption

In practice, it is difficult to avoid transmission error or delay in multimedia communication. Thus, making the encrypted data robust to transmission error is necessary. Till now, few solutions have been reported. Lian et al (Lian, et al., 2006a) proposed the solution based on segment encryption. In this algorithm, the data stream is partitioned into segments, and then encrypted segment by segment, with each segment independently encrypted. However, it is difficult to determine the size of the segment because segment size often contradicts the security.

Format Independence or Format Compliance

In order to keep format compliance, the encryption algorithm often varies with the compression codec. In some cases, format independence is more attractive. Taking Digital Rights Management (DRM) for example, it is required that all the content encoded with various codecs should be protected equally. Thus, there is a contradiction between format compliance and format independence.

Key Management

Key management is important in multimedia encryption systems. For example, to improve the security, multimedia data are often partitioned into blocks, and each block is encrypted with a sub-key. In this case, the generation and storage of the sub-keys are problems. Generally, the tradeoff between the security and the computing cost should be determined. In another case, key synchronization in transmission delay or transmission error is a challenging topic.

Combining Encryption and Watermarking

Encryption and watermarking realize different functionality in multimedia content protection. Combining them together may bring some conveniences, such as saving time cost or increasing the security. Although it is a challenging field, some prior works have been done, i.e. the commutative encryption and watermarking (Lian, et al., 2006c) and joint fingerprint embedding and decryption (Kundur & Karthik, 2004).

Special Operation Supported Encryption Method

In some applications, it is benefit to operate on the encrypted multimedia content directly because of the large data volumes, such as multimedia database index, information retrieval or data mining in patent search. In these applications, the partial encryption methods suitable for the special requirements should be designed. For example, in multimedia database encryption, the key field is left for indexing while the other fields in a record are encrypted. In patent encryption, the patent file is encrypted word by word according to a secret dictionary, and the patent file is indexed by translating the keywords. Generally, according to different applications, the corresponding encryption methods can be designed, while the performances, such as security, efficiency or compliance need also to be evaluated.

CONCLUSION

In this chapter, the history and research progress of multimedia content protection are reviewed, which is the key for secure multimedia communication, and the existing schemes are classified, analyzed and compared. Additionally, some special encryption algorithms are presented, and some open issues are given. According to the urgent demand of secure multimedia communication, multimedia content encryption will be still a hot research topic.

ACKNOWLEDGMENT

The author wants to thank Prof. Wang for his great help and the reviewers for their valuable advices.

REFERENCES

Agi, I., & Gong, L. (1996). An empirical study of MPEG video transmissions. In *Proceedings of the Internet Society Symposium on Network and Distributed System Security*, San Diego, CA, (pp. 137-144).

Ahn, J., Shim, H., Jeon, B., & Choi, I. (2004). Digital video scrambling method using intra prediction mode. *PCM2004. Springer LNCS, 3333*, 386–393.

Anderson, R., & Manifavas, C. (1997). Chamleon – A new kind of stream cipher. In *Lecture Notes in Computer Science, Fast Software Encryption*, (pp. 107-113P. Springer-Verlag. Blakley, G. R. (1979). Safeguarding cryptographic keys. In. *Proceedings of the National Computer Conference, 48*, 313–317.

Cheng, H., & Li, X. (2000). Partial encryption of compressed images and videos. *IEEE Transactions on Signal Processing, 48*(8), 2439–2451. doi:10.1109/78.852023

Dachselt, F., & Wolfgang, S. (2001). Chaos and cryptography. *IEEE Trans. Circuits Syst. I, 48*(12), 1498–1509. doi:10.1109/TCSI.2001.972857

Fridrich, J. (1997). *Secure image ciphering based on chaos*. Final Technical Report RL-TR-97-155, Rome Laboratory, New York.

Fu, M. S., & Au, A. C. (2004). Joint visual cryptography and watermarking. *Proceedings of the International Conference on Multimedia and Expro (ICME2004)*, (pp. 975-978).

Fukuhara, T., Ando, K., Watanabe, O., & Kiya, H. (2002). *Partial-scrambling of JPEG2000 images for security applications*. ISO/IEC JTC 1/SC29/WG1, N2430.

Furht, B. (1999). *Handbook of internet and multimedia systems and applications*. CRC Press.

Gang, L., Akansu, A. N., Ramkumar, M., & Xie, X. (2001). Online music protection and mp3 compression. In *Proc. of Int. Symposium on Intelligent Multimedia, Video and Speech Processing*, Hong Kong, China, May, 13-16.

Grosbois, R., Gerbelot, P., & Ebrahimi, T. (2001). Authentication and access control in the JPEG 2000 compressed domain. *Proc. of SPIE 46th Annual Meeting, Applications of Digital Image Processing XXIV, vol. 4472*, (pp. 95-104). San Diego, July 29th-August 3rd, 2001.

Ho, C., & Hsu, W. (2005). *Image protection system and method*. US Patent: US2005114669.

Kundur, D., & Karthik, K. (2004). Video fingerprinting and encryption principles for digital rights management. *Proceedings of the IEEE, 92*(6), 918–932. doi:10.1109/JPROC.2004.827356

Kunkelmann, T., & Reineman, R. (1997). A scalable security architecture for multimedia communication standards. *Proceedings of the 4th IEEE International Conference on Multimedia Computing and Systems*. Darinstadt Univ. of Technology, IT0. D-64283 Darmstadt, Germany, (pp. 660-663).

Li, S., Li, C., Chen, G., & Bourbakis, N. G. (2004). *A general cryptanalysis of permutation-only multimedia encryption algorithms*. IACR's Cryptology ePrint Archive: Report 2004/374.

Lian, S. (2008a). *Multimedia content encryption: techniques and applications*. Auerbach Publication, Taylor & Francis Group, September 2008.

Lian, S. (2008b). Multimedia encryption and watermarking in wireless environment. In Zhang, Y., Zheng, J., & Ma, M. (Eds.), *Handbook of research on wireless security*. Hershey, PA: IGI Global. doi:10.4018/978-1-59904-899-4.ch016

Lian, S. (2008c). Secure multimedia content distribution scheme based on watermarking technology. In Li, C.-T. (Ed.), *Multimedia forensics and security*. Hershey, PA: IGI Global. doi:10.4018/978-1-59904-869-7.ch002

Lian, S. (2008d). Traitor tracing in mobile multimedia communication. In Khalil Ibrahim, I. (Ed.), *Handbook of research on mobile multimedia* (2nd ed.). Hershey, PA: IGI Global. doi:10.4018/978-1-60566-046-2.ch030

Lian, S. (2008e). Digital rights management for the home TV based on scalable video coding. *IEEE Transactions on Consumer Electronics, 54*(3), 1287–1293. doi:10.1109/TCE.2008.4637619

Lian, S. (2009a). *Multimedia communication security: Recent advances*. Nova Publishers, April 2009.

Lian, S. (2009b). Secure video distribution scheme based on partial encryption. [Wiley-Blackwell Publisher]. *International Journal of Imaging Systems and Technology, 19*(3), 227–235. doi:10.1002/ima.20199

Lian, S. (2009c). Quasi-commutative watermarking and encryption for secure media content distribution. [Springer.]. *Multimedia Tools and Applications, 43*(1), 91–107. doi:10.1007/s11042-008-0258-4

Lian, S. (2009d). Secure multimedia transcoding for scalable video streams. In Ahmad, A. M. A., & Khalil Ibrahim, I. (Eds.), *Multimedia transcoding in mobile and wireless networks*. Hershey, PA: IGI Global.

Lian, S. (2010a). *Content and service protection for the ubiquitous TV based on convergent networks*. Wireless Personal Communication. Springer. DOI 10.1007/s11277-009-9783-3

Lian, S. (2010b). *Secure service convergence based on scalable content and service protection*. Telecommunications System. Springer. DOI 10.1007/s11235-009-9233-2

Lian, S., Chen, X., Dong, Y., & Wang, H. (2010). *On the secure multimedia distribution scheme based on partial encryption*. IEEE ICC 2010.

Lian, S., Dong, Y., & Wang, H. (2009b). *A secure solution for ubiquitous multimedia broadcasting*. 2009 IEEE International Conference on Communications (ICC 2009), Dresden, Germany, 13-18 June, 2009.

Lian, S., Kanellopoulos, D., & Ruffo, G. (2009a). Recent advances in multimedia information system security. *Informatica. Slovenian Society Informatika*, *33*(1), 3–24.

Lian, S., Liu, Z., Dong, Y., & Wang, H. (2008a). On the security of the delay-based fingerprint embedding scheme. *Proceedings of 2008 International Conference on Communication in China* (ChinaCom2008), IEEE Publisher, Aug. 25-27, 2008, Hangzhou, China, (pp. 699–703).

Lian, S., Liu, Z., Dong, Y., & Wang, H. (2008b). On the joint audio fingerprinting and decryption scheme. *Proceedings of 2008 IEEE International Conference on Multimedia and Expo* (ICME2008), IEEE Publisher, June 23-26, 2008, Hannover, Germany, (pp. 261-264).

Lian, S., Liu, Z., Ren, Z., & Wang, H. (2006a). Secure advanced video coding based on selective encryption algorithms. *IEEE Transactions on Consumer Electronics*, *52*(2), 621–629. doi:10.1109/TCE.2006.1649688

Lian, S., Liu, Z., Ren, Z., & Wang, H. (2006b). *Secure distribution scheme for compressed data streams*. Accepted by 2006 IEEE Conference on Image Processing (ICIP 2006).

Lian, S., Liu, Z., Ren, Z., & Wang, H. (2006c). Commutative watermarking and encryption for media data. *International Journal of Optical Engineering*, *45*(8), 0805101–0805103.

Lian, S., Liu, Z., Ren, Z., & Wang, H. (2007). Commutative encryption and watermarking in compressed video data. *IEEE Transactions on Circuits and Systems for Video Technology, 17*(6), 774–778. doi:10.1109/TCSVT.2007.896635

Lian, S., Liu, Z., Ren, Z., & Wang, Z. (2005). Selective video encryption based on advanced video coding. In *Proceedings of 2005 Pacific-Rim Conference on Multimedia (PCM2005), Part II, Springer LNCS, 3768*, (pp. 281-290).

Lian, S., Sun, J., & Wang, Z. (2004b). Perceptual cryptography on SPIHT compressed images or videos. *Proceedings of IEEE International Conference on Multimedia and Expro (I)* (ICME 2004), Taiwan, China, June 2004, 3, (pp. 2195-2198).

Lian, S., Sun, J., & Wang, Z. (2004d). A novel image encryption scheme based-on JPEG encoding. In *Proceedings of the Eighth International Conference on Information Visualization* (IV04), London, UK, July, (pp. 217-220).

Lian, S., Sun, J., & Wang, Z. (2004e). Perceptual cryptography on JPEG2000 encoded images or videos. *Proceedings of International Conference on Computer and Information Technology*, (pp. 78-83).

Lian, S., Sun, J., Zhang, D., & Wang, Z. (2004a). A selective image encryption scheme based on JPEG2000 codec. *2004 Pacific-Rim Conference on Multimedia (PCM2004), Springer LNCS, 3332*, (pp. 65-72).

Lian, S., & Wang, Z. (2008). Collusion-traceable secure multimedia distribution based on controllable modulation. *IEEE Transactions on Circuits and Systems for Video Technology, 18*(1), 1462–1467. doi:10.1109/TCSVT.2008.2002829

Lian, S., Wang, Z., & Sun, J. (2004c). A fast video encryption scheme suitable for network applications. *Proceedings of International Conference on Communications, Circuits and Systems*, Chengdu, China, 1, (pp. 566-570).

Lian, S., & Zhang, Y. (2009a). *Handbook of research on secure multimedia distribution*. Hershey, PA: IGI Global. doi:10.4018/978-1-60566-262-6

Lian, S., & Zhang, Y. (2009b). Protecting mobile TV multimedia content in DVB/GPRS heterogeneous wireless networks. *Journal of Universal Computer Science, 15*(5), 1023–1041.

Macq, B. M., & Quisquater, J. J. (1995). Cryptology for digital TV broadcasting. *Proceedings of the IEEE, 83*(6), 944–957. doi:10.1109/5.387094

Mao, Y. B., Chen, G. R., & Lian, S. G. (2004). A novel fast image encryption scheme based on the 3D chaotic baker map. *International Journal of Bifurcation and Chaos in Applied Sciences and Engineering, 14*(10), 3613–3624. doi:10.1142/S021812740401151X

Matias, Y., & Shamir, A. (1987). A video scrambling technique based on space filling curves. *Proceedings of Advances in Cryptology-CRYPTO'87* [Springer.]. *LNCS, 293*, 398–417.

Mollin, R. A. (2006). *An introduction to cryptography*. CRC Press.

Nakajima, N., & Yamaguchi, Y. (2004). Enhancing registration tolerance of extended visual cryptography for natural images. *Journal of Electronic Imaging, 13*(3), 654–662. doi:10.1117/1.1758729

Naor, M., & Shamir, A. (1994). Visual cryptography. In De Santis, A. (Ed.), *Advances in Cryptology-Eurocrypt '94, Lecture Notes in Computer Science, Springer-Verlag, 950* (pp. 1–12). Berlin.

Norcen, R., & Uhl, A. (2003). Selective encryption of the JPEG2000 bitstream. *IFIP International Federation for Information Processing. Springer LNCS, 2828*, 194–204.

Parnes, R., & Parviainen, R. (2001). Large scale distributed watermarking of multicast media through encryption. In *Proc. IFIP Int. Conf. Communications and Multimedia Security, Issues of the New Century*, Darmstadt, Germany, (pp. 21-22).

Pennebaker, W. B., & Mitchell, J. L. (1993). *JPEG still image compression standard*. New York, NY: Van Nostrand Reinhold.

Pfarrhofer, R., & Uhl, A. (2005). Selective image encryption using JBIG. *Communications and Multimedia Security, 2005*, 98–107. doi:10.1007/11552055_10

Pichler, F., & Scharinger, J. (1996). Finite dimensional generalized Baker dynamical systems for cryptographic applications. *Lecture Notes in Computer Science, 1030*, 465–476. doi:10.1007/BFb0034782

Podesser, M., Schmidt, H. P., & Uhl, A. (2002). Selective bitplane encryption for secure transmission of image data in mobile environments. In CD-ROM *Proceedings of the 5th IEEE Nordic Signal Processing Symposium (NORSIG 2002)*, Tromso-Trondheim, Norway, October.

Qi, D., Zou, J., & Han, X. (2000). A new class of scrambling transformation and its application in the image information covering. [English Edition]. *Science in China - Series E, 43*(3), 304–312. doi:10.1007/BF02916835

Qiao, L., & Nahrstedt, K. (1997). A new algorithm for MPEG video encryption. In *Proceeding of the First International Conference on Imaging Science, Systems and Technology (CISST'97)*, Las Vegas, Nevada, July, (pp. 21-29).

Qiao, L., & Nahrstedt, K. (2000). Comparison of MPEG encryption algorithm. *International Journal on Computers and Graphics*, *22*(4), 437–448. doi:10.1016/S0097-8493(98)00033-8

Romeo, A., Romdotti, G., Mattavelli, M., & Mlynek, D. (1999). Cryptosystem architectures for very high throughput multimedia encryption: The RPK solution. *Proceedings of the 6th IEEE International Conference on Electronics, Circuits and Systems*, 1, 5-8 Sept., (pp. 261-264).

Said, A. (1996). A new fast and efficient image codec based on set partitioning in hierarchical trees. *IEEE Transactions on Circuits and Systems for Video Technology*, *6*(3), 243–250. doi:10.1109/76.499834

Scharinger, J. (1998). Kolmogorov systems: Internal time, irreversibity and cryptographic applications. In D. Dubois, (Ed.), *Proceedings of the AIP Conference on Computing Anticipatory Systems, 437*. Woodbury, NY: Amer. Inst. of Phys.

Servetti, A., Testa, C., Carlos, J., & Martin, D. (2003). Frequency-selective partial encryption of compressed audio. Paper presented at the *International Conference on Audio, Speech and Signal Processing*, Hong Kong, April 5, (pp. 668-671).

Shamir, A. (1979). How to share a secret. *Communications of the ACM*, *22*(1), 612–613. doi:10.1145/359168.359176

Shapiro, J. M. (1993). Embedded image coding using zerotrees of wavelet coding. *IEEE Transactions on Signal Processing*, *41*(12), 3445–3462. doi:10.1109/78.258085

Shi, C., & Bhargava, B. (1998). A fast MPEG video encryption algorithm. In *Proceedings of the 6th ACM International Multimedia Conference*, Bristol, UK, September, (pp. 81-88).

Shi, C., Wang, S., & Bhargava, B. (1999). MPEG video encryption in real-time using secret key cryptography. In *Proc. of PDPTA'99*, Las Vegas, Nevada, Computer Science Research, Education and Application Press, (pp. 2822-2828).

Sridharan, S., Dawson, E., & Goldburg, B. (1991). Fast Fourier transform based speech encryption system. *IEE Proceedings of Communications. Speech and Vision*, *138*(3), 215–223. doi:10.1049/ip-i-2.1991.0029

Tang, L. (1996). Methods for encrypting and decrypting MPEG video data efficiently. In *Proceedings of the Fourth ACM International Multimedia Conference (ACM Multimedia'96)*. Boston, MA, November 1996, (pp. 219-230).

Torrubia, A., & Mora, F. (2002). Perceptual cryptography on MPEG Layer III bit-streams. *IEEE Transactions on Consumer Electronics*, *48*(4), 1046–1050. doi:10.1109/TCE.2003.1196437

Torrubia, A., & Mora, F. (2003). Perceptual cryptography of JPEG compressed images on the JFIF bit-stream domain. *Proceedings of the IEEE International Symposium on Consumer Electronics*, ISCE, 17-19 June 2003, (pp. 58-59).

Tosun, A. S., & Feng, W. C. (2000). Efficient multi-layer coding and encryption of MPEG video streams. *Proceedings of IEEE International Conference on Multimedia and Expo.*, *1*, 119–122.

Tosun, A. S., & Feng, W. C. (2001). Lightweight security mechanisms for wireless video transmission. *Proceedings International Conference on Information Technology: Coding and Computing, 2-4*(April), 157–161. doi:10.1109/ITCC.2001.918783

Tosun, A. S., & Feng, W. C. (2001). On error preserving encryption algorithms for wireless video transmission. *Proceedings of the ACM International Multimedia Conference and Exhibition*, IV, Ottawa, Ont, (pp. 302-308).

Uehara, T. (2001). *Combined encryption and source coding*. Retrieved from http://www.uow.edu.au/~tu01/CESC.html.

Wee, S. J., & Apostolopoulos, J. G. (2001). Secure scalable video streaming for wireless networks. In *Proceedings of the IEEE International Conference on Acoustics, Speech, and Signal Processing*. Salt Lake City UT, May 4, (pp. 2049-2052).

Wee, S. J., & Apostolopoulos, J. G. (2003). Secure scalable streaming and secure transcoding with JPEG-2000. *Proceedings of IEEE International Conference on Image Processing, 1,* (pp. 205-208). Sept. 14-17.

Wen, J., Sevra, M., Luttrell, M., & Jin, W. (2001). A format-compliant configurable encryption framework for access control of multimedia. In *Pro. IEEE Workshop on Multimedia Signal Proc*. Cannes, France, Oct., (pp. 435-440).

Wu, C., & Kuo, C. C. (2000). Fast encryption methods for audiovisual data confidentiality. In *SPIE International Symposia on Information Technologies 2000, Proceedings of SPIE, 4209*, Boston, MA, USA, Nov. 2000, (pp. 284-295).

Wu, C., & Kuo, C. C. (2001). Efficient multimedia encryption via entropy codec design. In *SPIE International Symposium on Electronic Imaging 200, Proceedings of SPIE, 4314,* San Jose, CA, USA, Jan. 2001, (pp. 128-138).

Ye, Y., Yang, Q., & Wang, Y. (2003). Magic cube encryption for digital image using chaotic sequence. *Journal of Zhejiang University of Technology, 31*(2), 173–176.

Yen, J. C., & Guo, J. I. (1999). A new MPEG encryption system and its VLSI architecture. *IEEE Workshop on Signal Processing Systems*, Taipei, (pp. 430-437).

Yu, H., & Yu, X. (2003). Progressive and scalable encryption for multimedia content access control. *Proceeding of IEEE International Conference on Communications*, (pp. 547-550).

Yuan, C., Zhu, B., Wang, Y., Li, S., & Zhong, Y. (2003). Efficient and fully scalable encryption for MPEG-4 FGS. *IEEE Int. Symp. Circuits and Systems*, May, (pp. 620-623).

Zeng, W., & Lei, S. (2003). Efficient frequency domain selective scrambling of digital video. *IEEE Transactions on Multimedia, 5*(1), 118–129. doi:10.1109/TMM.2003.808817

Chapter 4
Advancement on Damage-Less Watermark Extraction Using Non-Linear Feature Extraction Scheme Trained on Frequency Domain

Kensuke Naoe
Keio University, Japan

Yoshiyasu Takefuji
Keio University, Japan

ABSTRACT

In this chapter, we propose a new information hiding and extraction scheme for the application in digital watermarking, which does not embed any data to target content, by using non-linear feature extraction scheme trained on frequency domain. This is done by processing the selected coefficients from the selected feature sub-blocks as an input vector to the trained neural network and observing output signal from the neural network. This output signal is used as watermark signal which distinguishes its image from other images. This model trains an artificial neural network to assign predefined secret code for corresponding input feature vector of an image and use this trained artificial neural network weight and the coordinates of the selected feature sub-blocks as a key to extract the predefined secrete code.

DOI: 10.4018/978-1-61350-135-1.ch004

The proposed method contributes to secure image digital watermarking for content identification without damaging or losing any detailed data of visual images. The features of our proposed method employ an application to authenticate multimedia, similarity comparison, verification of image integrity and copyright protection of multimedia contents.

INTRODUCTION

In this chapter, a new model of digital watermarking is proposed, which do not embed any data into the image but are able to extract meaningful data from the image. This is done by processing the coefficients of the selected feature sub blocks to the trained neural network. This model trains artificial neural network to assign predefined secret code and use the artificial neural network weight and the coordinates of the selected feature sub blocks as a key to extract the predefined code. This means that it would not damage the content at all.

Our method consists of three layers for information hiding and retrieval method. First, the proposed method of key generation is to extract certain type of bit patterns in the forms of visual features out of visual objects or data as training data set for machine learning of watermark signal. Second, the proposed method of watermark extraction is processed by presenting visual features of the target visual image into extraction key or herein is a classifier generated in advance by the training approach of machine learning technology. Third, the training approach is to generate the extraction key which is conditioned to generate watermark signal patterns only if proper visual features are presented to the classifier. In our proposed method, this classifier which is generated by the machine learning process is used as watermark extraction key. The discussed watermark extraction key and feature extraction key identify the related or associated hidden bit patterns which is the watermark signal values for proper digital watermark embedding and extraction procedure as shown in Figure 1 and 2.

The proposed method is to hide or relate bit patterns of visual information as training data set for machine learning and to generate classifiers as watermark extraction key. These hidden bit patterns are prepared in advance to the training of classifiers which will eventually generates the associated visual information as watermark signals. This trained classifier acts as watermark extraction key. The feature extraction keys generate the feature values necessary for generation of watermark extraction keys. The feature extraction keys contain visual information including feature coordinates and regions of frequency coefficients. Machine learning also generates classifiers as watermark extraction keys. The discussed watermark extraction key and feature extraction key identify the secure and unique hidden bit

Figure 1. Overview of key generation procedure in the proposed method

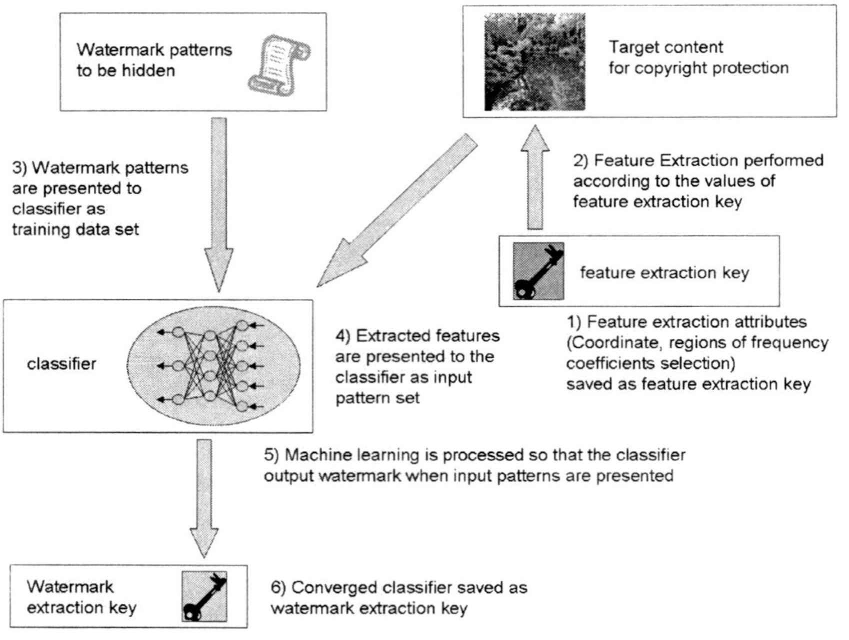

patterns for proper digital watermarking procedure. The proposed method is to contribute to secure information hiding and retrieval without losing any detailed data of visual information.

These hidden patterns can be used as the feature values which illustrate the characteristic of the image. Hash functions are frequently called message digest functions. Their purpose is to extract short binary string from a large digital message. A key feature of traditional cryptographic hash algorithms is sensitiveness to the manipulation of the original message. Even with the alteration of one bit of the original content will result in the alteration of the binary string generated by hash functions. However, multimedia content such as digital static visual images undergo various manipulations like compression and graphical alteration by filters and etc. A robust information hiding method should instead take into account the changes in the visual domain and produce information based on the images' visual appearance. Such method would facilitate comparisons and searches in large image databases. Therefore, our proposed method can employ for content protection, content authentication, image identification and image similarity comparison.

The proposed method is to contribute to secure visual digital watermarking without losing any detailed data of visual objects or any additional resources of hiding visual

Figure 2. Overview of watermark extraction procedure in the proposed method

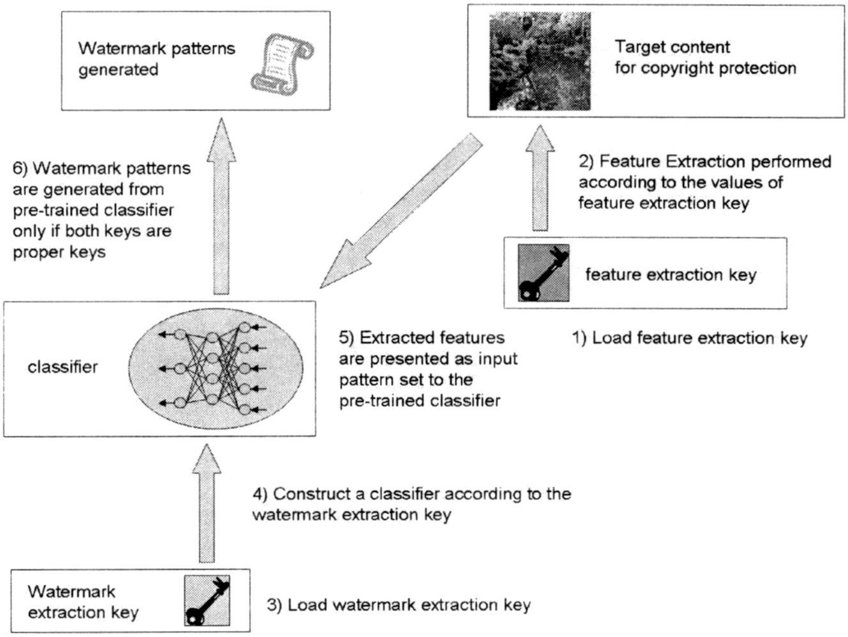

objects as molds to embed hidden visual objects. The proposed method has used neural network for its training approach not limited but open in its applications to other machine learning approaches including fuzzy, Bayesian network and others. In this chapter, the target content is a static visual data which are constructed with discrete data set and we have demonstrated the feasibility of solving this problem by using neural network model. We would enhance our method by using those other approaches, such as fuzzy for dynamic visual data like video stream data and Bayesian network for continuous data structures.

In Section 2, we discuss the background surrounding digital watermarking, frequency transformation and neural networks. We demonstrate the characteristics and discuss what techniques are useful for the implementations to digital watermarking. In Section 3, we propose the method of damage-less information hiding and retrieval scheme for still images. In Section 4, we provide an experiment results for testing its robustness and fragileness. In Section 5 and 6, we conclude with discussion of the proposed method and indicate some future works of the proposed method. Finally, we will outline this chapter.

BACKGROUND

In this section, we discuss the background surrounding digital watermarking. And we go deeply to the backgrounds and researches in frequency transformation and neural networks, which consist of important modules for the proposed method.

General Background Surrounding Digital Watermarking

Recently, with the rapid progress of information technologies and the emergence of the internet, digital multimedia contents are easily distributed on the network. This circumstance helped to open digital contents to the public without difficulty, even for ordinary computer users, but also helped illegal distribution and copying of contents. Due to the characteristics of digital contents, digital contents are easy to make an exact copy and to alter the content itself. This became main concerns for author, publisher and legitimate owners of the contents. Therefore, digital watermark became key technology for protecting the copyrights. Digital watermark protects unauthorized change of the contents and assures legal user for its copyright.

There are several ways to protect digital content. One example is to encrypt the content and to share decryption key between the author and the observer. But this method prevents other observers without a decryption key from accessing the content. This feature avoids a free distribution and circulation of the content through the network, which most of the time, not desirable to the author of the content. While digital watermark only embeds data to the content and this feature do not avoid the distribution of the content.

Watermarking techniques are one technique of information hiding techniques (Katzenbeisser & Petitcolas, 2000). The research in information hiding has a history (Kahn, 1996) and namely the researches in digital watermark and steganography have been active. Both are very similar but its applications are different (Reither & Rubin, 1998). Digital watermark can be classified in several ways. First classification is by the perceptibility of the watermark signal to human. Perceptible watermark has various usages but because it limits the utility of the content, most of the research in this area has focused on imperceptible watermarking techniques. Digital watermark is often embedded imperceptibly to human receptors to avoid contaminating the content. For imperceptible images, human visual system (HVS) model is often used. There are many still image watermark researches which make use of HVS model (Westen, et al., 1996; Swanson, et al., 1996; Delaigle, et al., 1998; Kim, et al, 2002). For imperceptible audio, psychoacoustic model is often used. Basic idea of psychoacoustic model is that human ears are insensitive to the change in phase and amplitude, but very sensitive to the change in the time domain. Also human has limitation to high frequency domain and low frequency domain (Cox et al., 2002). There are many researches for audio watermark and many of them use psychoacoustic model for implementations (Boney et al., 1996; Baumgarte, et al., 1995; Wolfe & Godsill, 2000; Gruhl, et al., 1996).

Most of imperceptible still image watermark method uses HVS model in order to embed data into frequency domains after the frequency transformation of multimedia content, such as DFT, DCT and DWT. Perceptible watermark are sometimes used, but it limits the use of the images. Therefore main concern in this research area has focused on imperceptible watermark. In general, digital watermark is a technique to conceal a code imperceptibly to the content to anybody who observes it, and is also difficult to remove the code from the content to protect its intellectual property rights.

Second classification of watermark technique is based on whether the original content data is used during the watermark extraction process. Watermark method which needs original content to extract a watermark from embedded content is called non-blind detection watermark. Watermark method which does not need original content and only need the embedded content to extract a watermark is called blind detection watermark.

Third classification of watermark is based on its robustness to the attacks. Robust watermark is normally strong against illegal alteration of the content and it is difficult to remove watermark data from the content. Even if the attacker was able to remove the watermark data, the damage to the content is very intense. Therefore, robust watermark are often used for copyright protection. A watermark method using spread spectrum is widely known for its robustness (Cox et al., 1997). Spread spectrum has been deployed in many researches to strengthen the robustness of the watermark. There are many researches of robust watermarking techniques (Bender et al., 1995; ORuanaidh & Pun, 1998) and watermark for other media such as motion picture (Echizen et al., 1999) and text data (Brassil et al., 1994; Brassil & O'Gorman, 1996).

To the contrary, a method called fragile watermark is a watermark method which is usually weak to alteration of the content. The watermark data will be broken or diminished when the content data is damaged. Therefore, fragile watermark is often used for integrity check of the content. Another watermark known as semi-fragile watermark has a characteristics of both robust and fragile watermark.

Recently, watermark method using neural network has been spreading widely. Commonly seen methods in this area are the one which uses either DCT or DWT for decomposition of the image and backpropagation neural network are used for embedding of the watermark (Davis & Najarian, 2001; Zhang et al., 2002; Lou et al., 2003; Hong et al., 2004). Beside from that, watermark method which uses generalized Hebb (Pu et al., 2004), RBF neural network (Zhang et al., 2003; Liu & Jiang, 2005), full counterpropagation neural network (Chang & Su, 2005), Hopfield neural network (Zhang, F. & Zhang, H., 2004; Zhang, X. & Zhang, F., 2005) and many more are introduced. The use of neural network can be used to achieve both robust and fragile watermarking method.

But many of the methods which use neural network, embeds watermark into the content data, which will alter the quality of data. Our method does not embed any data to the target content, which does not damage the content data at all. This characteristic is the biggest difference between the conventional methods.

Background for Frequency Transformation

In the research area of information hiding, including digital watermarking, orthogonal transformation is used for embedding process to embed watermark signal into frequency domain of the image. Embedding in the frequency domain is commonly used because this method is able to limit the damage to the content than embedding signal to the image directly. Frequency analysis is useful tool because with the analysis, it is able to understand which range of frequency band is the important frame of the image and which is not. According to Human Visual System (HVS), human are sensitive to the changes in the low frequency domain and insensitive to the changes in the high frequency domain. Consequently, watermark signals are embedded to the higher frequency domain to achieve imperceptible watermarking. But embedding watermark signal to the high frequency band has a risk of data loss in case of image compression that uses the feature of HVS systems, like JPEG compression.

There are several methods to transform an image to frequency domain, such as Discrete Fourier Transform (DFT), Discrete Cosine Transform (DCT) and Discrete Wavelet Transform (DWT). In our proposed method, DCT is used, so we will discuss it in more detail.

Discrete Cosine Transform is one method of orthogonal transformation. The image compression using DCT, orthogonally transforms the small blocks in the image. Compression using Discrete Cosine Transform is known to be very effective, and is employed in MPEG format and JPEG format.

Discrete Cosine Transform divides an image into N*N pixel small blocks. The transformation will be processed independently to the individual N*N blocks. When expressing the coefficients after the Discrete Cosine Transform as $F(u,v)$, the Discrete Cosine Transform function and Inverse Discrete Cosine Transform function to the N*N block of two dimensional image signal $f(x,y)$ is as following.

DCT function of N*N two dimensional image:

$$F(u,v) = \frac{2}{N} c(u)c(v) \sum_{x=0}^{N-1}\sum_{y=0}^{N-1} f(x,y)\cos\left\{\frac{(2x+1)u}{2N}\right\}\cos\left\{\frac{(2y+1)v}{2N}\pi\right\}$$

if u=0 then c(u)= $\frac{1}{\sqrt{2}}$ if v=0 then c(v) = $\frac{1}{\sqrt{2}}$

if u≠0 then c(u) = 1 if v≠0 then c(v) =1

Inverse discrete cosine transformation function of N*N two dimensional image:

$$f(x,y) = \frac{2}{N} \sum_{x=0}^{N-1}\sum_{y=0}^{N-1} c(u)c(v)\, F(u,v)\cos\left\{\frac{(2x+1)u}{2N}\right\}\cos\left\{\frac{(2y+1)v}{2N}\pi\right\}$$

When the size of N is the bigger, the less inferior the image will be but the calculation cost will increase proportional to N^2 and ideal number of N is known to be 8. When the image is 512*512 pixels in size, the amount of 8*8 blocks will be 64*64, total of 4096 of 8*8 sub blocks. Generalized Discrete Cosine Transform function of N=8 is:

$$S(u,v) = \frac{1}{4}\, \mathrm{C(u)C(v)} \sum_{m=0}^{7}\sum_{n=0}^{7} \mathrm{P(m,n)}\cos\frac{(2m+1)u\pi}{16}\cos\frac{(2m+1)v\pi}{16}$$

$$C(u)C(v)\begin{cases} if\ \frac{1}{\sqrt{2}} & then\ u,v = 0 \\ if\ 1 & then\ u,v \neq 0 \end{cases}$$

$(u,v=0,1,2,\ldots,7)$

Background for Neural Network

Neuron is a nervous cell and brain consists of many nervous cells. Neuron itself only has simple function of input and output of electric signal. But when these neurons organically connected to form a network, the network is capable of complex processing. Mathematical models of these networks are called neural network, and processing these artificial neural networks on computers are called neural computing. Neural computing is a classic research topic and neural network are known to be capable of solving various kinds of problems by changing the characteristics of neuron, synaptic linking and formation of the network.

Binary model (Hopfield & Tank, 1985), sigmoid model (McCulloch & Pitts, 1943), radial basis function model (Moody & Darken, 1989; Poggio & Girosi, 1990) and competitive neuron model (Kohonen, 1982; Kohonen, 1995; Takefuji et al., 1992) are some of the models classified by the model of neuron units itself. Neural network can also be classified by its network formation. Recurrent model is a model which neurons are connected mutually. Feed forward model is a model which neurons are connected in a layer and signals are transmitted simply from input layer to output layer, whereas feedback model is a model similar to feed forward model but it has a backward or recursive synaptic link. Both feed forward and feedback model sometime has a bias synaptic link.

Proposed method uses a multi-layered perceptron model as network model which has a feedforward synaptic link. Multi-layered perceptron model was introduced by Rosenblatt (Rosenblatt, 1985). Two layer perceptron can classify data linearly but can not classify data non-linearly. Multi-layered percptron with more than three layers are known to have an approximation ability of a non-linear function if properly trained, but then there was no ideal learning method for this kind of training. This model became popular when training method called back propagation learning, which uses generalized delta rule, was introduced by Rummelhart (Rummelhart et al., 1986). Since then, this neural network model is often used to solve non-linear classification problems. Other popular neural network models are RBF network model (Broomhead & Lowe, 1988), pulsed neural network model (Eckhorn et al., 1990; Johnson, 1994), second order neural network model (Maxwell et al., 1986), chaotic neural network model (Aihara, 1990), Elman network model (Elman, 1994) and many others.

Background for Multi-Layered Perceptron Model

Multi-layered perceptron basically has a synaptic link structure with neurons between the layers but no synaptic link among the layer itself. Signal given to the input layer will propagate forwardly according to the synaptic weight of the neurons connected and reaches to the output layer as shown in figure 3.

For each neuron, input values are accumulated from former layer and outputs a signal value according to a certain function, normally sigmoid function is used. Sigmoid function has a graph like Figure 4 and this function is expressed as:

$$y = \frac{1}{1 + \exp(-x)}$$

Figure 3. Example of multi-layered perceptron model

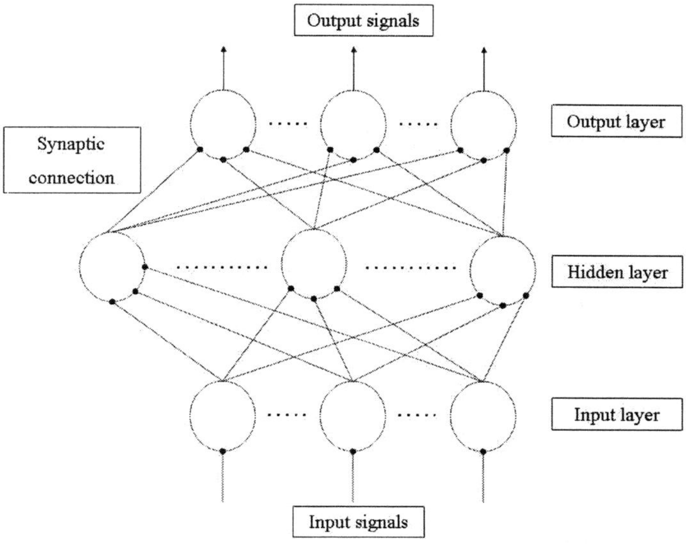

Figure 4. Graph of sigmoid function

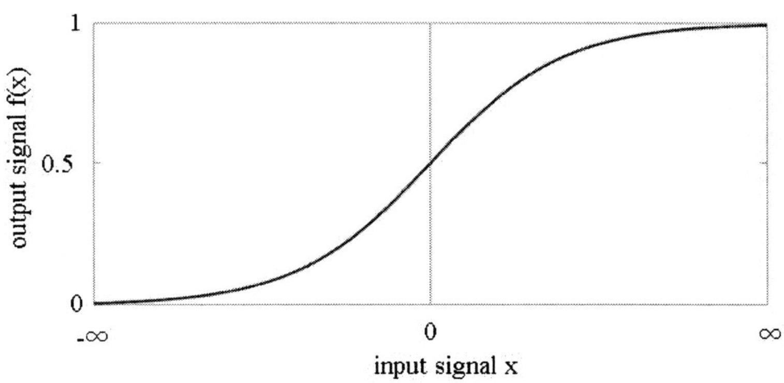

Each network connection has a network weight. The network weight from unit i to unit j is expressed as Wij. The output value from the former layer is multiplied with this value. These output values of the former layer are summed and connected to the upper layer. Therefore, the output values for the output layer are determined by the network weight of the neural network as shown in Figure 5.. Consequently, to change the output value to a desired value, adjustment of these network weights are needed. Learning of the network is a process of conditioning the network weight with the corresponding teacher values.

Figure 5. Input values and network weights determinate the output value

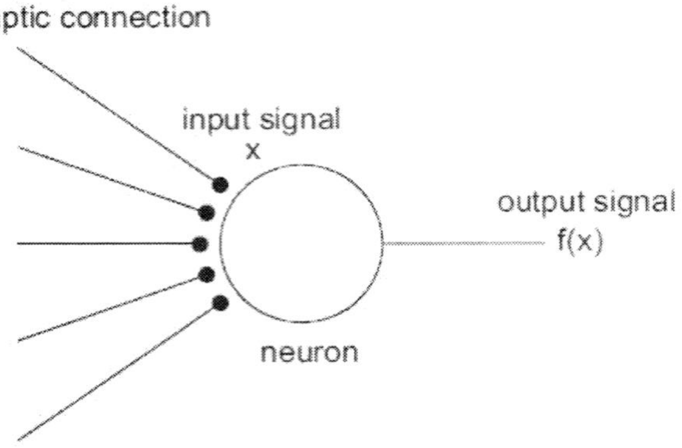

Background for Back Propagation Learning

Back propagation learning is the process of adjusting the network weights to output a value close to the values of the teacher signal values. Back propagation learning is a supervised learning. In back propagation learning, teacher signal values are presented to the network. This training tries to lower the difference between the teacher signal values and the output values by changing the network weight. This learning is called back propagation because the changes of the network weight according to the difference in the upper layer propagate backward to the lower layer. This difference between the teacher signal values are called as error and often expressed as delta (δ).

When teacher signal t_j is given to the unit j of output layer, the error δ_j will be the product of the differential for sigmoid function of output unit y_j and difference between the teacher signal t_j and output value of unit y_j. So the function for calculating the error value for the output unit is:

$$\delta_j = (t_j - y_j)f'(y_j) = (t_j - y_j)1 - y_j)y_j$$

On the other hand, calculation of error value for the hidden neurons is more complicated. This is because the error value of the output unit affects the error value for the hidden neuron. The error value for the hidden unit varies with the network weight between the hidden layer and output layer. In order to calculate the error value δ_i for hidden unit, error value δ_j of the output unit is used. So the function to calculate the error value δ_i for hidden unit i is:

$$\delta_j = f'(y_i)\sum_{j=1} W_{ij}\ \delta_j = (1-y_i)y_i \sum_{j=1} W_{ij}\delta_j$$

After calculating the error values for all units in all layers, then network can change its network weight. The network weight is changed by using the function:

$$\Delta W_{ij} = \eta\delta_j y_i$$

η in this function is called learning rate. Learning rate normally has a value between 0 and 1 and generally represents the speed of learning process. The lower the learning rate is the more gradual the learning process will be and the bigger the learning rate is more acute the learning process will be. Sometimes this parameter must be tuned for stable learning.

PROPOSED METHOD

In this section, we present the hidden bit patterns embedding method to the neural network using the selected feature values from the image and extraction method using the network weight from the trained network with the selected feature values. With this algorithm, we are able to implement a function of digital watermark with no embedding of data into the content data. No embedding into the content implies no damage to the content data.

To accomplish our goals, we use values of certain area in the frequency domain as input data to the neural network and teach the network with classification set of data. The classification data set will be the identification information which acts as a watermark data. Trained neural network will have a network weights, and are used as the extraction keys for the output data that is trained to approximate the watermark signal. With this model, the attacker can not reproduce a watermark signal if he has only one of the input data set or network weights. The extractor must have both proper input data and network weights to induce a watermark signal from neural network.

With proposed embedding method, we must decide the structure of neural network. The amount of neurons for input layer is decided by the number of pixels selected as feature values from the content data. Proposed method uses the diagonal values of the frequency domain from the selected feature sub block of the content data. For example, if the image is 512*512 pixels in size and the frequency transform is done by 8*8 DCT, then there will be 4096 sub blocks being produced and the neurons in the input layer will be 8. We select unique feature sub block in obedience to the teacher signal. Diagonal 8 pixels of the selected sub block will be taken as input values for the neural network. Our proposed method, one bias neuron is added for better approximation also. Therefore, we will have nine neurons in the input layer for proposed method.

The output layer will be trained to output 1 or 0 as an output value. The amount of neurons for output layer is decided by the number of identification values or patterns to be embedded into the network. In case where 32 unique identification values are to be embedded into the network, five set of network with one output neuron must be prepared in order to embed five bits of data. This is because each network represents for each digit of the binary watermark signal respectively and 5 binary digits are sufficient to represent 32 different values.

The adequate amount of neurons in the hidden layer necessary for an approximation, in general, is not known. So the number of neurons in the hidden layer will be taken at will. For better approximation, bias neuron like in input layer can be introduced for the hidden layer too. After the neural network structure is decided, the process is move on to back propagation learning procedure.

This learning process uses watermark signal data as teacher signal, which is either 1 or 0 corresponding to the digit of the watermark. After the learning process, the network weights are converged to certain values. We use this network weights and the coordinates of selected feature sub blocks as the extraction keys of the embedded watermark data.

For extraction process, we'll take the same neural network structure with the network weights generated in the embedding process. Only with the proper input values of the selected feature sub blocks will output the proper watermark signal. Proper input values are induced only when you know the proper coordinates of the sub blocks for the corresponding watermark signal.

Key Generation and Watermark Extraction Process in the Proposed Method

Here, we present a method of key generation for damage-less digital watermarking using neural network model as its exemplary approach for non-linear feature extraction method. We describe both key generation procedure and watermark extraction procedure in detail in the following sections. Key generation procedure includes the generation of feature extraction key and watermark extraction key. Information extraction procedure is also explained in detail.

Key generation process consists of following procedures:

1. Feature extraction by frequency transformation of target image
2. Selection of the feature regions according to the feature extraction attributes and saved as feature extraction key

Figure 6. RGB color space image constructed with R, G and B color space

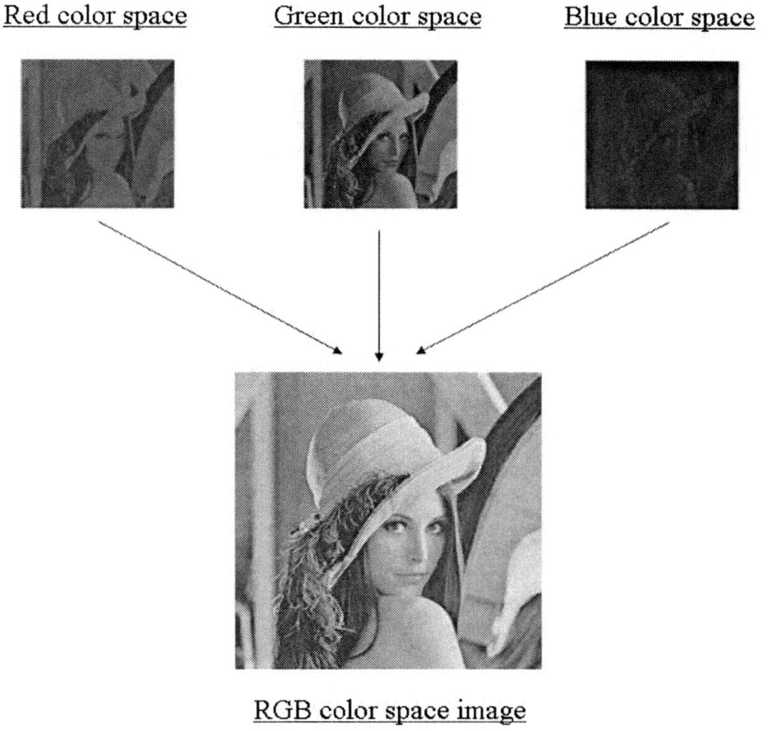

3. Prepare watermark signal patterns to be related to the target image
4. Generation of extraction key to output watermark signal patterns by back propagation learning of neural network using feature extraction key
5. Save the converged neural network classifier as watermark extraction key

In the first procedure for key generation, feature extraction of target image in RGB color space is performed. Since the colors red, green, and blue are additive primaries, every color can be specified as a weighted sum of a red, green, and a blue component as shown in Figure 6. A vector in RGB space describes the intensities of these components.

Then, YCbCr values are calculated and the conversion from RGB to YCbCr is calculated using the following equation:

- $Y = 0.299R + 0.587G + 0.114B$
- $Cb = -0.169R - 0.322G + 0.500B$
- $Cr = 0.500R - 0.419G - 0.081B$

Figure 7. Focusing on the divided sub-block after DCT

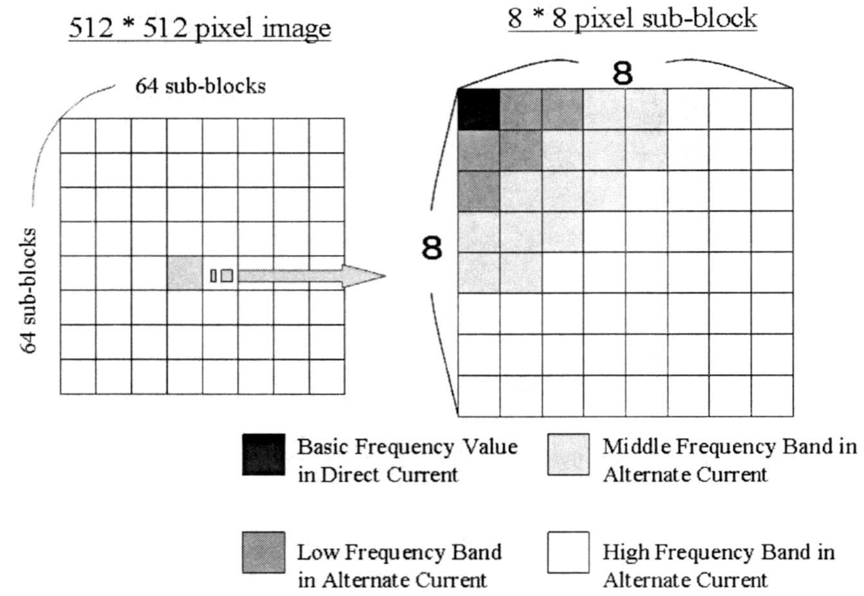

Then, frequency transformation is performed. In our proposed method, *8 * 8* DCT is used for the frequency transformation. The original image is divided into *8 * 8* pixel sub-blocks. As shown in Figure 7, each of divided sub-blocks is transformed to DCT coefficients of DC value and AC values.

In the second procedure, we select the coordinates of feature sub-blocks and this information is saved and used as attribute in feature extraction key. Also, the region of the feature sub-blocks used for the learning is decided. In our proposed method, we use the 8 diagonal pixels of the DCT coefficients in the selected sub-blocks. For example, in the case of condition of Table 1, the allocation of the feature sub-blocks is shown in Figure 8. This feature coordinates is selected randomly in our proposed method.

Then, the diagonal DCT coefficients from selected sub-blocks are used as input vector in the learning process.

In the third procedure, we prepare watermark signal patterns to be concealed to the target image. Again, example of watermark signal patterns to be prepared for each sub-block is shown in Table 1 as teacher signal.

In the fourth procedure, learning process of the neural networks is performed using the input vector and teacher signals generated in the previous process. Since the output values for the neural network is in the range of 0 to 1, we will arrange a threshold in order to determine the output value to be a binary value of 1 or 0. In our

Figure 8. 32 sub-blocks chosen from original image

proposed method, threshold of 0.5 is used for the learning process and generation of watermark signal value (see Figure 9).

In the fifth procedure, the converged neural network weights are saved as watermark extraction key.

Here, we describe the information extraction process. Extraction process consists of following procedures:

1. Obtain feature extraction key and watermark extraction key
2. Feature extraction of target image using the feature extraction key
3. Construct a neural network model using watermark extraction key
4. Observe the output patterns from neural network

In the first procedure, we must obtain both feature extraction key and watermark extraction key.

In the second procedure, feature extraction of the target image is done according to the values of feature extraction key. With proper feature extraction key, we will have the proper input vectors for the trained neural networks from proper selected feature sub-blocks.

Table 1. Examples of the coordinates and the teacher signal for all 32 patterns

	x-axis	y-axis	coordinate	teacher signal
Pattern 1	22	37	(22,37)	00000
Pattern 2	16	27	(16,27)	00001
Pattern 3	64	13	(64,13)	00010
Pattern 4	58	33	(58,33)	00011
Pattern 5	23	46	(23,46)	00100
Pattern 6	18	56	(18,56)	00101
Pattern 7	6	48	(6,48)	00110
Pattern 8	16	64	(16,64)	00111
Pattern 9	58	56	(58,56)	01000
Pattern 10	21	32	(21,32)	01001
Pattern 11	37	58	(37,58)	01010
Pattern 12	12	2	(12,2)	01011
Pattern 13	48	41	(48,41)	01100
Pattern 14	8	61	(8,61)	01101
Pattern 15	25	3	(25,3)	01110
Pattern 16	56	19	(56,19)	01111
Pattern 17	55	44	(55,44)	10000
Pattern 18	53	38	(53,38)	10001
Pattern 19	16	5	(16,5)	10010
Pattern 20	58	57	(58,57)	10011
Pattern 21	39	32	(39,32)	10100
Pattern 22	9	58	(9,58)	10101
Pattern 23	11	49	(11,49)	10110
Pattern 24	57	42	(57,42)	10111
Pattern 25	63	63	(63,63)	11000
Pattern 26	39	11	(39,11)	11001
Pattern 27	24	9	(24,9)	11010
Pattern 28	15	49	(15,49)	11011
Pattern 29	29	21	(29,21)	11100
Pattern 30	42	30	(42,30)	11101
Pattern 31	16	22	(16,22)	11110
Pattern 32	30	1	(30,1)	11111

Figure 9. System structure of neural network for learning and extraction

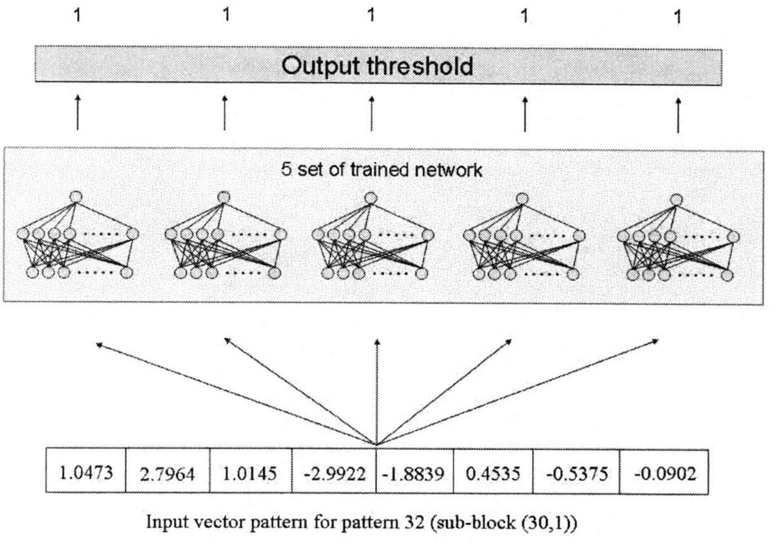

In the third procedure, we will construct a neural network classifier according to the values of watermark extraction key. With the proper watermark extraction key, we will have the proper neural network structure necessary for the proper signal values to be generated.

In the fourth procedure, we will observe the output signals generated by the constructed neural network with the output threshold value configured in the previous process.

EXPERIMENTS AND FUTURE WORKS

Experiment 1

In this experiment, we will examine if we can retrieve the watermark signal patterns from both original image and graphically changed image. For the latter, we choose high pass filter and JPEG compressed image as the alteration method.

Figure 10. Original Lenna image

Experimental Conditions and Results in Experiment 1

In this experiment, we used TIFF format Lenna image, which are 512*512 pixels in size, as target content data. Original and high pass filtered Lenna image is shown in Figure 10 and 11.

We embedded 32 different patterns as hidden signals as shown in Table 2. Five neural networks are used for classification of 32 patterns. Each network output value represents the binary digits of watermark signal patterns. In this experiment, network 1 represents the largest binary bit and network 5 represents the smallest binary bit. The number of hidden layer units was set to 11 including one bias unit. Learning process is repeated until the output values converge to a learning threshold of 0.1. Also, the output threshold in this experiment is set to 0.5. This means that if output value is larger than 0.5, output signal is set to 1, and if it is less than 0.5, output signal is set to 0. For example, output signals in binary bit pattern for pattern 1 is [00000], output signals for pattern 11 is [01010] as shown in Table 2.

Figure 11. Filtered Lenna image

Experimental Results in Experiment 1

Here, we will discuss about the experimental results in the limitation discussed above for Lenna. The output signals retrieved from high pass filtered image are shown to be slightly different compared to the output signals for the original image and also the output signals retrieved from JPEG compressed image is damaged more than of filtered image, but with the same output threshold of 0.5, we were able to retrieve same hidden information patterns for all 32 set from high pass filtered image and JPEG compressed image. These results showed the robustness to high pass filtering and JPEG compression alteration for both two different static visual images. The results of this experiment, output signals for original image, high pass filtered image and JPEG compressed image of Lenna are shown in Figure 12, 13, 14, 15 and 16 for each neural network.

Conclusions in Experiment 1

In this experiment, we have shown that our proposed method were able to generate the proper watermark signal patterns from the target content. Also, we were able to generate the proper watermark signal patterns from graphically altered image, herein

Table 2. Teacher signals for experiment 1

	network 1	network 2	network 3	network 4	network 5
Pattern 1	0	0	0	0	0
Pattern 2	0	0	0	0	1
Pattern 3	0	0	0	1	0
Pattern 4	0	0	0	1	1
Pattern 5	0	0	1	0	0
Pattern 6	0	0	1	0	1
Pattern 7	0	0	1	1	0
Pattern 8	0	0	1	1	1
Pattern 9	0	1	0	0	0
Pattern 10	0	1	0	0	1
Pattern 11	0	1	0	1	0
Pattern 12	0	1	0	1	1
Pattern 13	0	1	1	0	0
Pattern 14	0	1	1	0	1
Pattern 15	0	1	1	1	0
Pattern 16	0	1	1	1	1
Pattern 17	1	0	0	0	0
Pattern 18	1	0	0	0	1
Pattern 19	1	0	0	1	0
Pattern 20	1	0	0	1	1
Pattern 21	1	0	1	0	0
Pattern 22	1	0	1	0	1
Pattern 23	1	0	1	1	0
Pattern 24	1	0	1	1	1
Pattern 25	1	1	0	0	0
Pattern 26	1	1	0	0	1
Pattern 27	1	1	0	1	0
Pattern 28	1	1	0	1	1
Pattern 29	1	1	1	0	0
Pattern 30	1	1	1	0	1
Pattern 31	1	1	1	1	0
Pattern 32	1	1	1	1	1

Figure 12. Observed signal values for network 1 (Lenna)

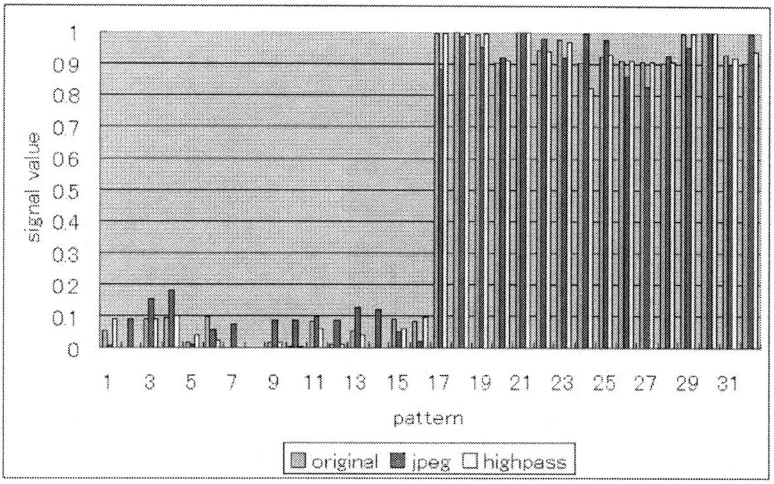

Figure 13. Observed signal values for network 2 (Lenna)

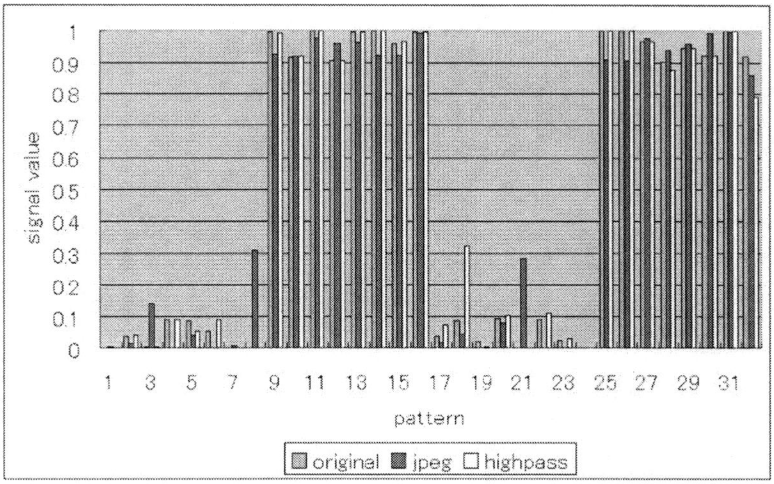

is a high pass filtered image of an original image and JPEG compressed image of an original image when using 0.5 as output threshold value. This implies that our proposed method has robustness against graphically altered images.

Figure 14. Observed signal values for network 3 (Lenna)

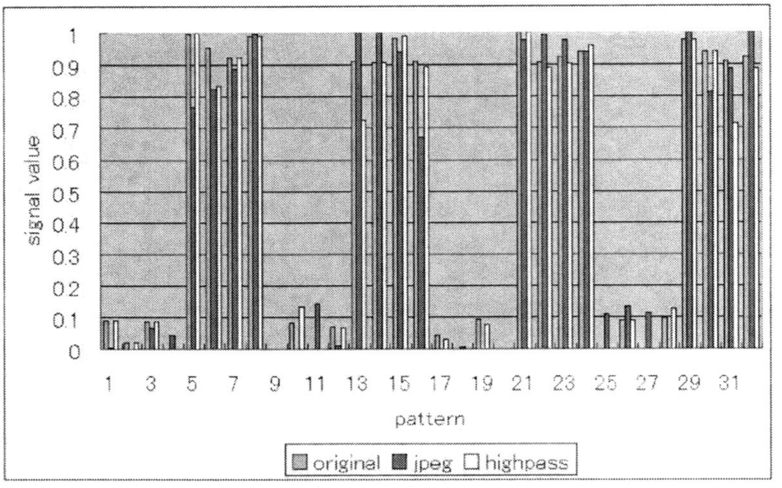

Figure 15. Observed signal values for network 4 (Lenna)

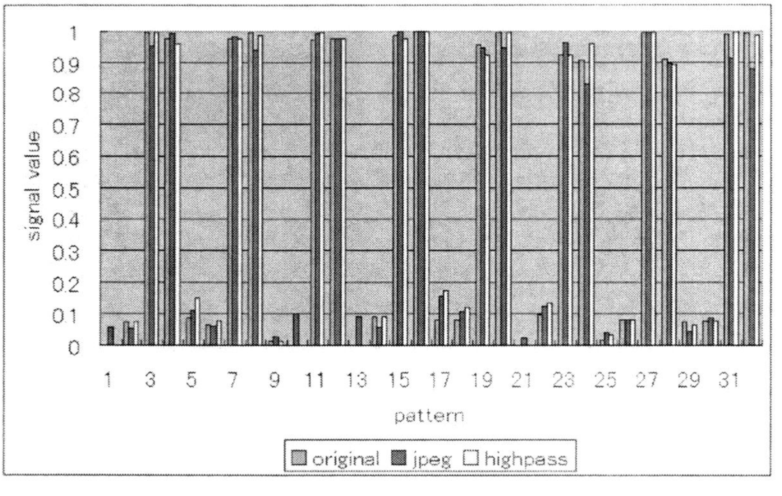

Experiment 2

In this experiment, we will examine the output of each network for all patterns from original image and format transformed images. We used Lenna as the test image and original format to be in BMP format. We performed watermark extraction for JPEG2000 format with no compression, JPEG2000 with compression to 25 percent

Figure 16. Observed signal values for network 5 (Lenna)

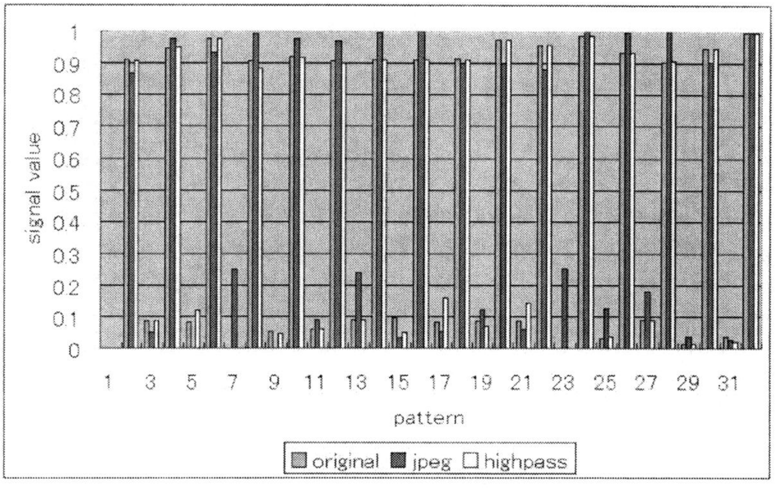

Figure 17. JPEG2000 with compression to 25 percent and JPEG2000 with compression to 1 percent

and JPEG2000 format with compression to 1 percent. In this experiment, we used BMP format Lenna which is 512*512 pixels in size, as original image (see Figure 17).

Experimental Results in Experiment 2

The observed signal values for all 5 networks are shown in Figure 18, 19, 20, 21 and 22.

Figure 18. Observed signal values for network 1

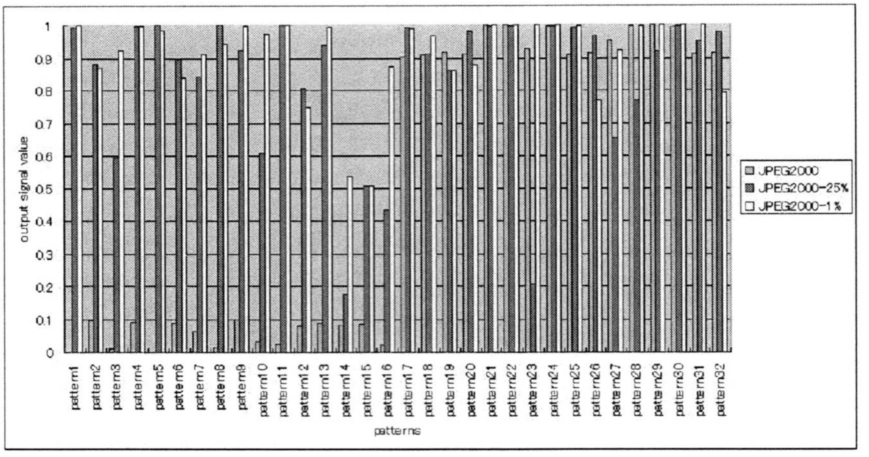

Figure 19. Observed signal values for network 2

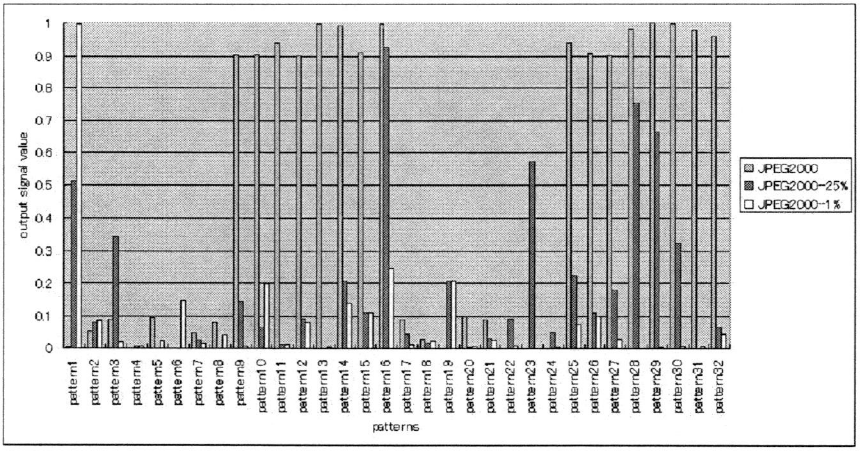

Conclusions in Experiment 2

In this experiment, we have shown that we can retrieve proper watermark signal patterns from JPEG2000 with no compression. JPEG2000 compression with large magnitude has very different output signals compared uncompressed images. Those compressed images have a distinct degradation of the image. Our proposed method was able to determine the large alteration in the image and was robust against normal image format transformation.

Figure 20. Observed signal values for network 3

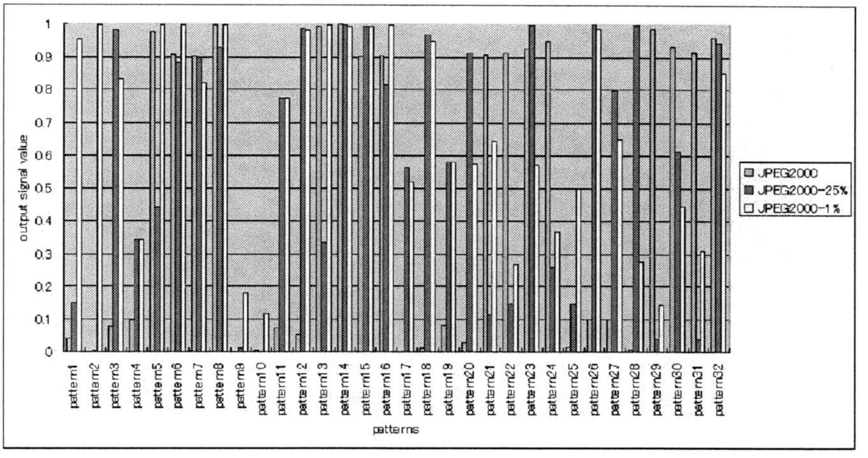

Figure 21. Observed signal values for network 4

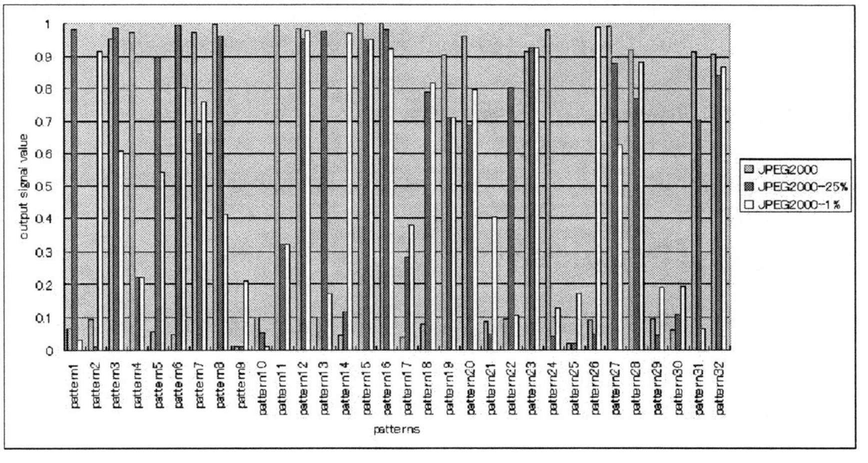

Experiment 3

In this experiment, we will directly alter the DCT coefficients values of the pixels after the frequency transform is being processed. We change the value of DCT coefficients to 0 for the values lower than the boundary value that increase from 0 to 2 with the step of 0.1. In this experiment, we examined the percentage of proper signal values for the neural network with three different parameter settings as the boundary changes:

Figure 22. Observed signal values for network 5

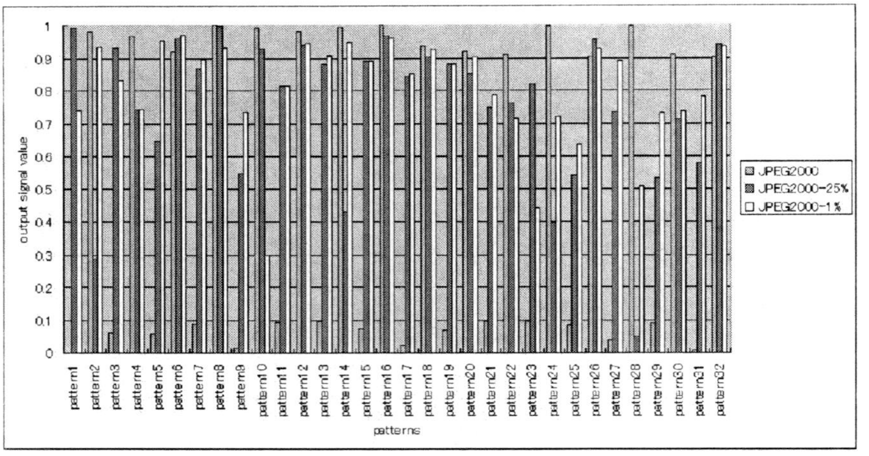

1. Number of hidden neurons = 10 and value of learning threshold = 0.05
2. Number of hidden neurons = 10 and value of learning threshold = 0.1
3. Number of hidden neurons = 20 and value of learning threshold = 0.1

Experimental Results in Experiment 3

The experimental results for case (a), (b) and (c) are shown in Figure 23, 24 and 25.

Conclusions in Experiment 3

There were not much notable difference in the result for (a), (b) and (c), so we can say that the learning threshold and the number of neurons in hidden layer does not affect vastly to the output signals. However, the calculation cost and the convergence time was higher when more hidden layer neurons used and lower the learning threshold was predefined.

When we look at the results of this experiment more in detail, we found that once some patterns failed to output the proper watermark signals, some of those patterns succeeded to output proper watermark signals as the alteration process advanced. This characteristic implies, in some cases, that complex connectivity of neural network and other supplement neurons make up for the damaged input neuron to output the proper signals. In Table 3, we show the transition of output signals values as boundary values increase by 0.2 for all 32 patterns. You can observe a recovery of output signals in patterns 16, 24, 26 and 28 in this experiment.

Figure 23. (a) Percentage of output units correctly outputting signals after the alteration of image data (when learning threshold is 0.05 and number of hidden neuron=10)

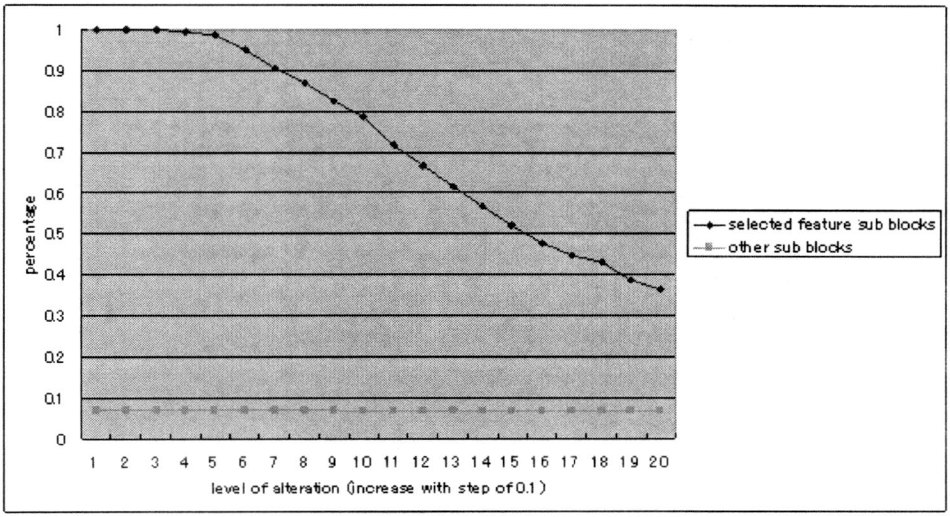

Figure 24. (b) Percentage of output units correctly outputting signals after the alteration of image data (when learning threshold is 0.1 and number of hidden neuron=10)

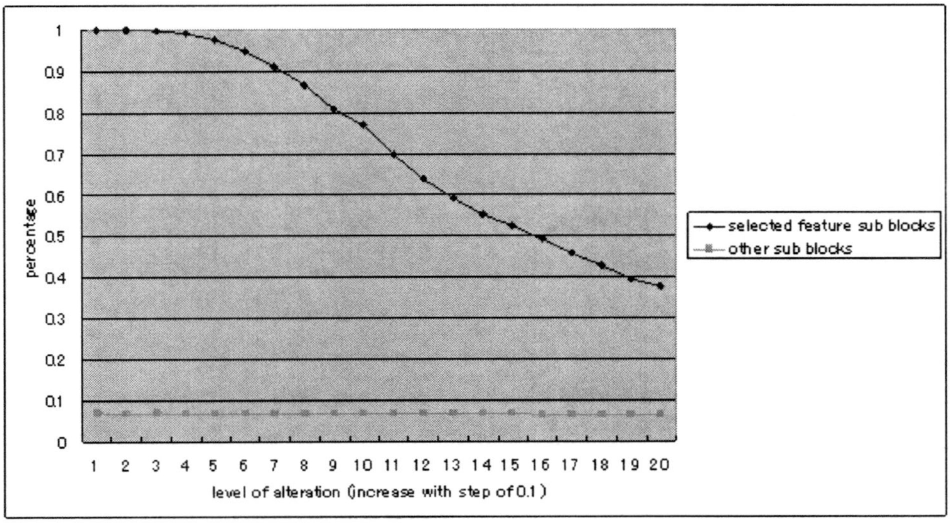

Figure 25. (c) Percentage of output units correctly outputting signals after the alteration of image data (when learning threshold is 0.1 and number of hidden neuron=20)

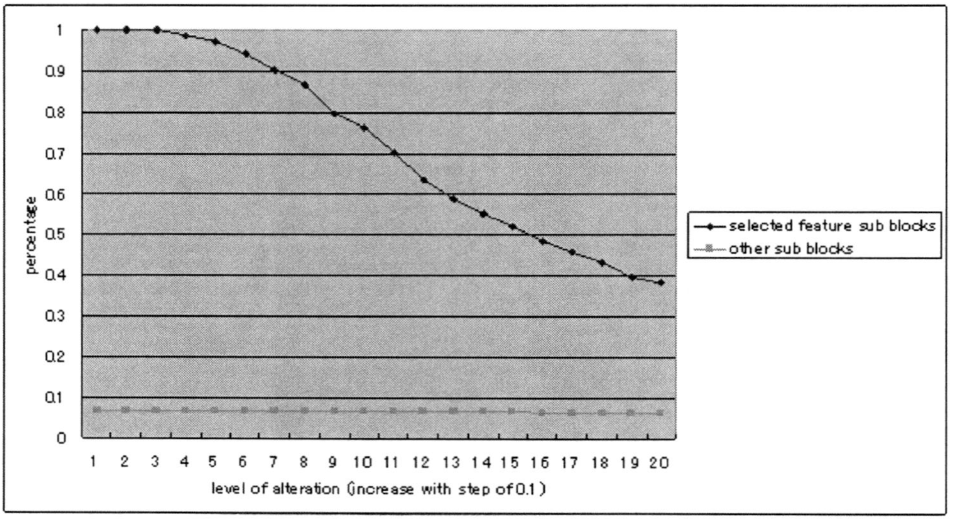

DISCUSSION AND FUTURE WORKS

In this section, we discuss the contribution and limitations of the proposed method.

We have shown the basic idea of key generation scheme for damage-less watermarking. This framework uses original image to generate watermark extraction key. Also, this framework must prepare feature extraction key which holds the information about the coordinates of selected feature sub-blocks and the regions of the DCT frequency domain used in the machine learning process.

Proposed method has shown the possibility of information hiding scheme without embedding any data into the target content. With the perspective of information security, this method showed the possibility for the applications for digital watermark and steganography. Using proposed method for digital watermark, it has both characteristics of robust and fragile watermark. This characteristic is determined by the quality of preprocessing for retrieving of the input values and parameter adjustments for learning process. Meanwhile, because proposed watermark extraction method relies on the position of the feature sub blocks, it is weak to geometric attacks like shrinking, expanding and rotation of the image. This problem will be considered as future works of this proposed method. In experiments 1 and 2 shown in previous section, we have shown the possibility of a robust watermarking without embedding any data into the target content. We have proved that our proposed method has robustness against simple image alteration method like high-pass filtering. However,

Table 3. Output values for all 32 patterns

	0.2	0.4	0.6	0.8	1.0	1.2	1.4	1.6	1.8	2.0
Pattern 1	1	1	1	1	1	1	1	1	1	1
Pattern 2	2	2	2	2	2	2	2	2	2	2
Pattern 3	3	3	3	3	11	11	11	11	11	11
Pattern 4	10	10	10	10	10	10	10	9	9	9
Pattern 5	5	5	5	5	9	9	13	13	13	26
Pattern 6	6	6	6	6	6	6	6	6	6	6
Pattern 7	7	7	7	7	7	7	7	7	7	7
Pattern 8	8	8	8	20	20	20	20	27	27	27
Pattern 9	9	9	9	9	9	9	9	9	5	5
Pattern 10	10	10	10	10	10	10	10	9	9	9
Pattern 11	11	11	11	11	11	11	3	3	3	3
Pattern 12	12	12	12	12	12	12	12	12	12	12
Pattern 13	13	13	13	13	13	13	13	13	13	14
Pattern 14	14	14	14	14	14	14	14	14	14	14
Pattern 15	15	15	15	15	15	15	15	15	15	11
Pattern 16	16	16	16	16	16	16	32	16	16	16
Pattern 17	17	17	17	17	17	17	17	17	17	17
Pattern 18	18	18	18	18	20	20	20	20	8	8
Pattern 19	19	19	19	19	19	19	27	27	27	27
Pattern 20	20	20	20	20	20	20	16	16	16	32
Pattern 21	21	21	21	21	21	21	21	21	21	21
Pattern 22	22	22	22	22	22	22	22	22	22	22
Pattern 23	23	23	23	23	23	7	7	16	16	16
Pattern 24	24	24	24	24	24	24	24	24	24	24
Pattern 25	25	25	25	25	25	25	25	25	25	25
Pattern 26	26	26	26	26	26	26	26	26	26	26
Pattern 27	27	27	27	27	27	27	27	27	27	27
Pattern 28	28	28	28	28	4	3	12	12	28	28
Pattern 29	29	29	29	29	29	29	29	29	29	29
Pattern 30	30	30	30	30	30	30	30	30	30	27
Pattern 31	31	31	31	31	31	31	31	31	31	27
Pattern 32	32	32	32	32	32	32	32	32	24	24

with distinct alteration and high compression, the watermark signal patterns in our proposed method will be destroyed, but not completely. In experiment 3, notice that the percentage of output signals by sub blocks other than the selected feature sub blocks are stable. The understanding of this feature will be also considered as future work.

One of the issues to be addressed is to determine the right parameters to output proper watermark signal patterns for certain graphical alteration and format transformation with high compression. Also, in our proposed method, we have not shown any solutions for robustness against images with geometrical alteration like rotation and resizing.

CONCLUSION

In this chapter, we have proposed an information hiding technique without embedding any data into the target content being employed. This characteristic is useful when the user does not want to damage the content but wishes to protect the intellectual property rights.

The proposed method uses multi-layered neural network model for classifying the input visual feature patterns to corresponding watermark signal patterns. For input visual feature values, we used DCT coefficients on YCbCr domain. The proposed method does not limit to DCT as frequency transformation method only, one can use DFT and DWT otherwise. Also, machine learning method can be replaced with others such as Bayesian network and fuzzy. In the experiment, we showed that our proposed method is robust to high pass filtering and image format transformation. Also, because propose method does not alter the target content, it is applicable to steganography. Meanwhile, because the proposed method relies on the position of the feature sub-blocks, it is weak to geometric attacks like shrinking or rotation of the image. This must take into consideration for future work.

In the experiment, we showed the robustness of this scheme to a high pass filter alteration, JPEG compressions and JPEG2000 with no compression. Also, for the experiment with direct change of DCT coefficients, watermark signals were not completely lost, but as the degree of alteration becomes stronger, watermark signals have failed to output proper signals and some have recovered. This implies, this scheme has both robust and fragile characteristics and can be conditioned with the parameter adjustments. Proposed method cultivated the damage-less watermark scheme and we hope more researches being accelerated in the areas of information hiding and information security.

REFERENCES

Aihara, K. (1990). Chaotic neural networks. In Kawakami, H. (Ed.), *Bifurcation phenomena in nonlinear system and theory of dynamical systems* (*Vol. 8*, pp. 143–161). Advanced Series on Dynamical Systems.

Baumgarte, F., Ferekidis, C., & Fuchs, H. (1995). *A nonlinear psychoacoustic model applied to the ISO MPEG layer 3 coder*. Preprint 4087, 99th AES Convention.

Bender, W., Gruhl, D., & Morimoto, H. (1995). Techniques for data hiding. *Proceedings of the Society for Photo-Instrumentation Engineers*, *2020*, 2420–2440.

Boney, L., Tewfik, A. H., & Hamdy, K. N. (1996). Digital watermarks for audio signals. *IEEE Proceedings of the International Conference on Multimedia Computing and Systems*, (pp. 473-480).

Brassil, J., Low, S., Maxemchuk, N. F., & O'Gorman, L. (1994). Electric marking and identification techniques to discourage document copying. *Proceedings of IEEE INFOCOM'94*, vol. 3 (pp. 1278-1287).

Brassil, J., & O'Gorman, L. (1996). Watermarking document images with bounding box expansion. *Proceedings of the First International Information Hiding Workshop*, vol. 1174 (pp. 227-235).

Broomhead, D., & Lowe, D. (1988). Multivariable functional interpolation and adaptive networks. *Complex Systems*, *2*, 321–355.

Chang, C. Y., & Su, S. J. (2005). Apply the counterpropagation neural network to digital image copyright authentication. *2005 9th International Workshop on Cellular Neural Networks and Their Applications IEEE* (pp. 110-113).

Cox, I. J., Kilian, J., Leightont, T., & Shamoon, T. (1997). Secure spread spectrum watermarking for images, audio and video. *IEEE Transactions on Image Processing*, *6*(2), 1673–1687. doi:10.1109/83.650120

Cox, I. J., Miller, M. L., & Muttoo, S. K. (2002). *Digital watermarking*. Morgan Kaufmann Pub.

Davis, K. J., & Najarian, K. (2001). Maximizing strength of digital watermarks using neural networks. *IEEE Proceedings of International Joint Conference on Neural Neworks*, vol. 4 (pp. 2893-2898).

Delaigle, J. F., De Vleeschouwer, C., & Macq, B. (1998). Watermarking algorithm based on a human visual model. *Signal Processing*, *66*, 319–335. doi:10.1016/S0165-1684(98)00013-9

Echizen, I., Yoshiura, H., Arai, T., Himura, H., & Takeuchi, T. (1999). General quality maintenance module for motion picture watermarking. *IEEE Transactions on Consumer Electronics*, *45*, 1150–1158. doi:10.1109/30.809196

Eckhorn, R., Reitboeck, H. J., Arndt, M., & Dicke, P. (1990). Feature linking via synchronization among distributed assemblies: Simulations of results from cat visual cortex. *Neural Computation*, *2*, 293–307. doi:10.1162/neco.1990.2.3.293

Elman, J. (1994). Finding structure in time. *Cognitive Science*, *14*, 179–211. doi:10.1207/s15516709cog1402_1

Gruhl, D., Lu, A., & Bender, W. (1996). Echo hiding. *Proceedings of the First International Information Hiding Workshop*, vol. 1174 (pp.295-316).

Hong, F., Shi, L., & Luo, T. (2004). A semi-fragile watermarking scheme based on neural network. *IEEE Proceedings of the Third International Conference on Machine Learning and Cybernetics*, vol. 6 (pp. 3536-3541).

Hopfield, J. J., & Tank, D. W. (1985). Neural computation of decisions in optimization problems. *Biological Cybernetics*, *52*, 141–152.

Johnson, J. L. (1994). Pulse-coupled neural nets: Translation, rotation, scale, distortion and intensity signal invariances for images. *Applied Optics*, *33*(26), 6239–6253. doi:10.1364/AO.33.006239

Kahn, D. (1996). The history of steganography. [Information Hiding, Springer-Verlag.]. *Lecture Notes in Computer Science*, *1174*, 1–5.

Katzenbeisser, S., & Petitcolas, F. A. P. (2000). *Information hiding techniques for steganography and digital watermarking*. Artech House.

Kim, Y. C., Byeong, C., & Choi, C. (2002). Two-step detection algorithm in a HVS-based blind watermarking on still images. *Revised Papers of Digital Watermarking First International Workshop IWDW 2002*, vol. 2613 (pp. 235-248).

Kohonen, T. (1982). Self-organized formation of topologically correct feature maps. *Biological Cybernetics*, *43*, 59–63. doi:10.1007/BF00337288

Kohonen, T. (1995). *Self-organizing maps*. Springer-Verlag.

Liu, Q., & Jiang, X. (2005). Design and realization of a meaningful digital watermarking algorithm based on RBF neural network. *IEEE International Conference on Neural Networks and Brain*, vol. 1 (pp. 214-218).

Lou, D. C., Liu, J. L., & Hu, M. C. (2003). Adaptive digital watermarking using neural network technique. *Proceedings of IEEE 37th Annual 2003 International Carnahan Conference on Security Technology*, (pp.325-332).

Maxwell, T., Giles, C., Lee, T. C., & Chen, H. H. (1986). Nonlinear dynamics of artificial neural systems. *AIP Conference Proceedings*, *151*, 299–304. doi:10.1063/1.36227

McCulloch, W. S., & Pitts, W. H. (1943). A logical calculus of the ideas immanent in nervous activity. *The Bulletin of Mathematical Biophysics*, *5*, 115–133. doi:10.1007/BF02478259

Moody, J. E., & Darken, C. (1989). Fast learning in networks of locally-tuned processing units. *Neural Computation*, *1*, 281–294. doi:10.1162/neco.1989.1.2.281

ORuanaidh, J. J. K., & Pun, T. (1998). Rotation, scale and translation invariant spread spectrum digital image watermarking. *Signal Processing*, *66*, 303–317. doi:10.1016/S0165-1684(98)00012-7

Poggio, T., & Girosi, F. (1990). Regularization algorithms for learning that are equivalent to multilayer networks. *Science*, *247*(4945), 978–982. doi:10.1126/science.247.4945.978

Pu, Y., Liao, K., Zhou, J., & Zhang, N. (2004). A public adaptive watermark algorithm for color images based on principal component analysis of generalized Hebb. *IEEE Proceedings of International Conference on Information Acquisition*, (pp. 484-488).

Reither, M. K., & Rubin, A. D. (1998). Crowds anonymity for Web transactions. *ACM Transactions on Information and System Security*, *1*(1), 66–92. doi:10.1145/290163.290168

Rosenblatt, F. (1985). The Perceptron: Probabilistic model for information storage and organization in the brain. *Psychological Review*, *65*, 386–408. doi:10.1037/h0042519

Rummelhart, D. E., & McClelland, J. L.PDP Research Group. (1986). *Parallel Distributed Processing* (*Vol. 1*). The MIT Press.

Swanson, M. D., Zhu, B., & Tewfil, A. H. (1996). Transparent robust image watermarking. *Proceedings of International Conference on Image Processing*, *3*, 211–214.

Takefuji, Y., Lee, K., & Aiso, H. (1992). An artificial maximum neural network: A winner-take-all neuron model forcing the state of the system in a solution domain. *Biological Cybernetics*, *67*, 243–251. doi:10.1007/BF00204397

Westen, S. J. P., Lagendijk, R. L., & Biemond, J. (1996). Optimization of JPEG color image coding using a human visual system model. *Proceedings of the Society for Photo-Instrumentation Engineers, 2657*, 370–381.

Wolfe, P. J., & Godsill, S. J. (2000). Towards a perceptually optimal spectral amplitude estimator for audio signal enhancement. *Proceedings of the IEEE International Conference on Acoustics, Speech, and Signal Processing, 2*, 821–824.

Zhang, F., & Zhang, H. (2004). Applications of neural network to watermarking capacity. *IEEE International Symposium on Communications and Information Technology 2004*, vol. 1 (pp. 340-343).

Zhang, J., Wang, N. C., & Xiong, F. (2002). Hiding a logo watermark into the multiwavelet domain using neural networks. *Proceedings of 14th IEEE International Conference on Tools with Artificial Intelligence*, (pp. 477-482).

Zhang, X., & Zhang, F. (2005). A blind watermarking algorithm based on neural network. *ICNN&B '05 International Conference on Neural Networks and Brain IEEE,* vol. 2 (pp. 1073-1076).

Zhang, Z. M., Li, R. Y., & Wang, L. (2003). Adaptive watermark scheme with RBF neural networks. *Proceedings of the 2003 International Conference on Neural Networks and Signal Processing IEEE,* vol. 2 (pp. 1517-1520).

Chapter 5
Property Protection and User Authentication in IP Networks through Challenge-Response Mechanisms:
Present, Past and Future Trends

Giaime Ginesu
University of Cagliari, Italy

Mirko Luca Lobina
University of Cagliari, Italy

Daniele D. Giusto
University of Cagliari, Italy

ABSTRACT

Authentication is the way of identifying an individual. The techniques used to accomplish such practice strongly depend on the involved parties, their interconnection, and the required level of security. In all cases, authentication is used to enforce property protection, and may be specifically intended for the copyright protection of digital contents published on the Internet. This work introduces the basic concepts of authentication explaining their relationship with property protection. The basic functionalities of Challenge-Response frameworks are presented, together with several applications and the future trends.

DOI: 10.4018/978-1-61350-135-1.ch005

INTRODUCTION

Authentication (Greek: αυθεντικός, from 'authentes' = 'one acting on one's own authority') is the process of identifying an individual, merely ensuring that the individual is who he/she claims to be. Such practice is essential in networking and distributed systems, where a party has not always the opportunity of verifying *ad personam* the identity of the other/s involved. The parties may be users, hosts or processes and they are generally referred to as *principals* in the authentication literature. During the authentication phase, the principals exchange messages and use the received ones to make decisions on how to act. Obviously, to prevent from malicious interferences, all the messages exchanged between principals are usually ciphered. The complete sequence of ciphered messages exchanged between principals is an authentication protocol (AP). The AP can perform a mutual authentication, *i.e.*, two-way authentication, when two principals are able to suitably authenticate each other, or a one-way authentication, when only one principal is authenticated. As an example, mutual authentication refers to a client authenticating itself to a server and that server authenticating itself to the client in such a way that both parties are assured of the others' identity. Typically, this is done for a client process and a server process without any physical interaction. Challenge-Response (*CR*) is a common AP, where a principal is prompted (the *challenge*) to provide some private information (the *response*) in order to access a service. Basically, given two principals sharing private information, *i.e.*, a secret key, CR is a one-way authentication (client-to-server) system that ensures the private information will be never sent uncrypted. However, many evolutions have been brought to the original idea. Thus, CR is a black-box, whose features strongly depend on what a principal is, has and knows. Independently from prior considerations and specifically in IP networks, *i.e.*, using the Internet Protocol, such as Internet, an AP is intended for property protection purposes, avoiding anything in the networked/distributed system from being considered public domain and taken without permission from the creator/owner of its copyright. The objectives of this work are:

1. To provide essential information and strategies of existing CR frameworks, including basic hashing/encrypting techniques;
2. To focus on one of the seemingly most prolific field related to AP: biometry applied to authentication;
3. To present a general and high-level overview of mutual image-based authentication, *i.e.*, IBA applied to this *milieu*.

BACKGROUND

This section defines the role of authentication, referring to the differences with Identification, its role in the AAA (Authentication, Authorization and Accounting) hierarchy, its main properties and protocols and its relationship with intellectual property protection. Specifically, the protocols are described both with common hashing/encrypting approaches and biometric features to focus on the different branches of security functions developed in the last years.

Authentication and Identification

The processes of identification and authentication are not the same practice, referring to implementation, protocols, and performances, even though the user may perceive them mistakenly as synonyms. Identification is the procedure where a unique piece of information is associated with a particular identity. It is performed by acquiring an identifier, that is, a piece of information that defines or indicates an entity, or a group of entities. Then, the process of identification is a one-to-many match test. On the other hand, authentication is the process of validating that the owning entity is really using the owned identity during interaction. Authentication is a one-to-one comparison and could be addressed to as an identification subroutine (Figure1). A user generally claims only his credentials to be identified. Without his identity the system searches (one-to-many search) for the profile matching with the presented credentials among a determined group of profiles and optionally performs authentication, inquiring for any other required information, *i.e.*, the couple (identity, credentials). Usually, the identity is defined by the username, and the credentials are a set of values to prove the user is the one he pretends to be. Reasonably, the complete framework of identification and authentication is more secure than identification alone, thanks to the two factors process.

Authentication, Authorization and Accounting (AAA)

The security functions of a generic system are usually divided into authentication, authorization and accounting (AAA). AAA constitutes a complete framework to control the access to resources and to audit the users' activities. As indicated in Figure 2, the three steps are consecutive. First, two principals must recognize each other (authentication) and subsequently establish a reciprocal relationship (authorization). Finally, they can monitor several parameters related to their communication (accounting). These steps are described more deeply in the following. The Authentication provides the techniques to identify a user by means of a unique set of criteria through his identity and credentials. After logging in, the user must be authorized

Figure 1. Authentication and identification

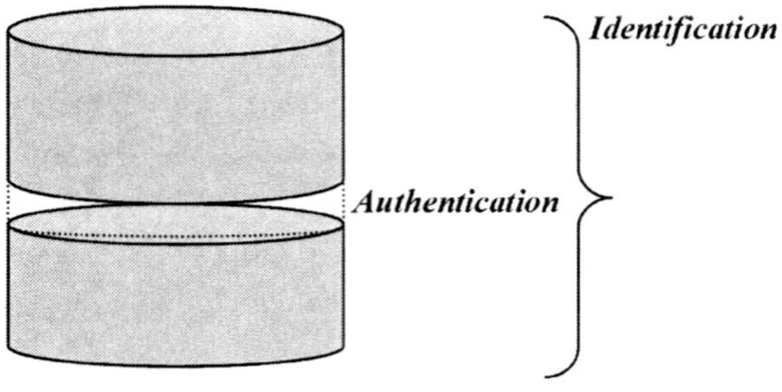

Figure 2. Authentication, authorization and accounting

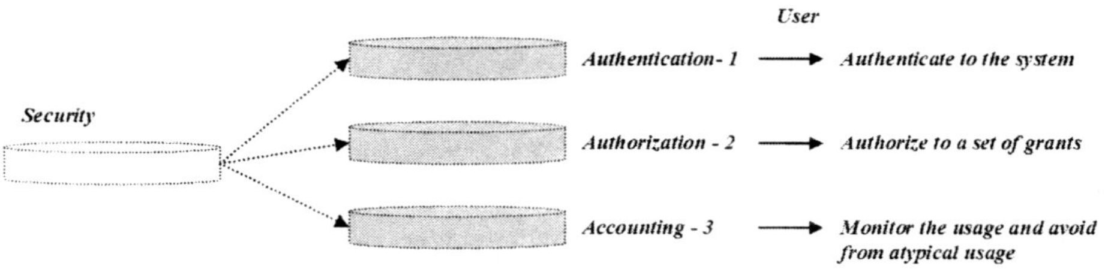

to perform some classes of activities, or services. Thus, the security system has to state what type of actions the trustfully authenticated user has the right to perform. Authorization is essentially an enforcing of the security system. After authentication and authorization, the security system should monitor the resources employed by the user. This is the last step of accounting, whose main purpose is the protection from intrusion of atypical profiles within the system.

Authentication Features

Authentication can be categorized on the basis of the location of the involved parties, the typology of the communication session and the type of interaction. In the following these attributes are explained in detail.

Local and Remote

First of all we must define the context in which the terms local and remote are defined in respect to authentication. Local authentication consists in authenticating a principal who tries to gain access to another principal's resources that reside on the same environment, such as the same server or the same trusted network. The authenticating principal is often considered to be reliable, since it is held under local control. Clearly, this situation is simpler than the classic remote authentication scheme, where the system cannot trust directly an alien authenticating principal. Remote authentication consists in authenticating a principal who tries to gain access to another principal's resources from a separate environment. It presents stronger security issues and still represents a great challenge for security experts. Any authentication protocol should be designed to avoid from malicious external intrusion.

Static, Rigid or Continuous

These features refer to the nature of the communication session, after the authentication phase. Static authentication describes the situation where the message exchange between principals takes place in clear, *i.e.*, without ciphering of the messages, once a party is authenticated to another. Inversely, rigid authentication implies a secured channel and is typically employed for the transmission of sensible data. Finally, continuous authentication entails an ad-hoc memoryless transmission channel. In this case the two communicating principals have to perform reciprocal authentication at each step of conversation. That is, each process/host/party never trusts the other involved in the authentication phase, without evidence of identification being previously provided. In this case, authentication takes place every time the parties want to trade a message.

Let us consider, for example, that a user wishes to trade stocks through an online brokerage house. If the brokerage perceives a business benefit to tracking the user's actions on the site, continuous mode may be useful. In continuous mode the brokerage would authenticate the user at the first attempt to access the site and then track the user continuously during the length of time they spend there.

On-Line and Off-Line

On-line authentication implies the interaction with a live party. In this case, the system is more robust against any kind of attacks that use old credentials. On the other hand, the authenticating party is exposed to a great variety of attacks, which may be somewhat related to the use of an unsecured channel, *e.g.*, sniffing. As an alternative or supplement to on-line authentication, various techniques have been employed to verify that the authenticating principal is trustful. For example, anticounterfeiting techniques involve the employ of unique or difficult characteristics of credentials that can be sensed to verify their authenticity. Private personal identification data has also been used along with coding techniques. When such techniques serve as the sole basis of certification (without on-line checking), the verification is gener-

Figure 3. Challenge-response scheme

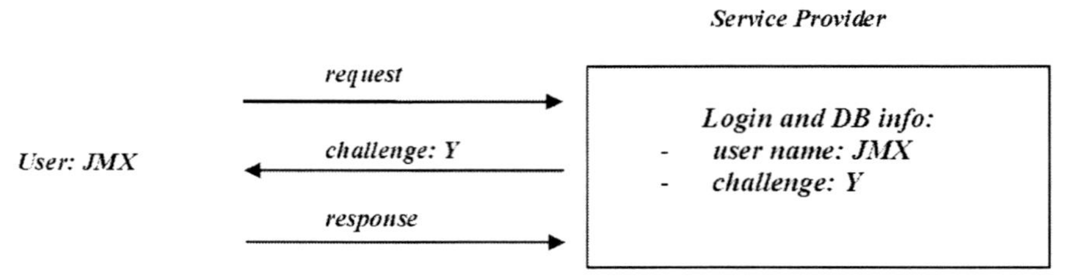

ally called "off-line" authentication. Off-line authentication avoids the risks related to continuous message exchange, but is less realistic when considering hosts connected remotely via the Internet. It is generally adopted in case of personal ID-based authentication, such as smart card or printed documents.

Authentication Protocols

This section provides the reader with a specific overview of the cryptographic designs applied in CR frameworks during the response phase. The reader can refer to (Mitchell, 1989) and (Omura, 1990) for an exhaustive coverage of the characteristics and limitations of the original schemes. As an example, Figure 3 proposes a typical CR framework.

Let us suppose that the user JMX requests a resource from a service provider. The provider knows JMX since the login name is found among the profiles stored in the internal DB, and sends him a challenge. The user replies with a response that depends on up to three factors: the challenge itself, a private information whose knowledge is shared by user and system, and the method that allows obtaining the correct response starting from challenge and private information, again shared by the two principals.

Kerberos, EAP (Extensible Authentication Protocol), NTLM and PAP (Password Authentication Protocol) are typical examples of authentication protocols. Kerberos relies on the fundamental basis that the two principals (user and service) implicitly trust the Kerberos authentication server (AS), which serves as a mediator. In order for this to work, both the user and the service must have a shared secret key registered with the AS. Such keys are generally referred to as long-term keys, since they last for weeks or months. The main steps are as follows. First, the user sends a request (typically the service name) to the AS, asking it to authenticate him to the service (step 1 in Figure 4). In the second step, the AS introduces the user and the service to each other; a new random secret key is generated to be shared only by the user and the service. The AS sends the user a two-part message: one part contains the

Figure 4. Kerberos scheme

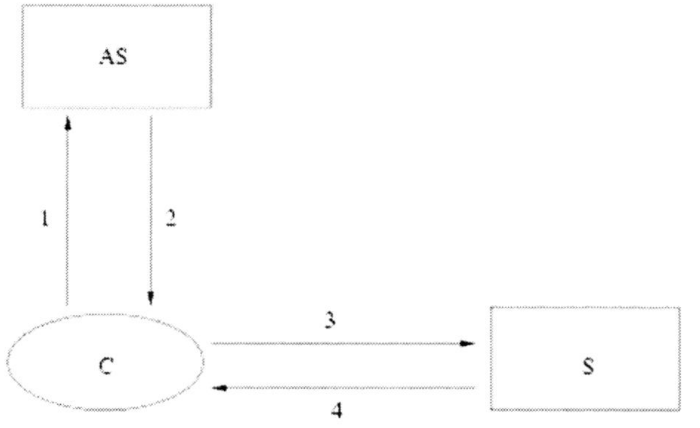

random key along with the service name, encrypted with the user's long-term key, while the other part contains that same random key along with the user's name, encrypted with the service long-term key (step 2 in Figure 4). In Kerberos, the former message is often called the *user's credentials*, the latter message is called the *ticket*, and the random key is called the *session key*. Only the user knows the session key, thus he generates a new message (the authenticator) and encrypts it with the session key. He sends the authenticator, along with the ticket, to the service (step 3 in Figure 4). The service decrypts the ticket with its long-term key and retrieves the session key. Since the service trusts the AS, it knows that only the legitimate user could have created such an authenticator. This completes the user authentication to the service (step 4 in Figure 4).

EAP is a universal authentication framework frequently used in wireless/wired networks and Point-to-Point connections. It is defined as an Internet Standard by RFC 3748. EAP is not a specific authentication mechanism, but an authentication framework. In this sense, it provides some common functions and a negotiation of the desired authentication mechanism. Such mechanisms are called EAP methods. Currently, there are about 40 different methods, such as EAP-MD5. One of the most interesting applications is the generation of a PMK (Pairwise Master Key) for authenticating clients in a wireless environment. A detailed description of the framework is presented in the above cited RFC.

NTLM is a suite of authentication and session security protocols used in various Microsoft network protocol implementations. It is probably best recognized as part of the "Integrated Windows Authentication" stack for HTTP authentication; however, it is also used in Microsoft implementations of SMTP, POP3, IMAP, Telnet, SIP, and possibly others. It consists of three sequential messages, commonly referred to as Type 1 (negotiation), Type 2 (challenge) and Type 3 (authentication). The client

Figure 5. MD5

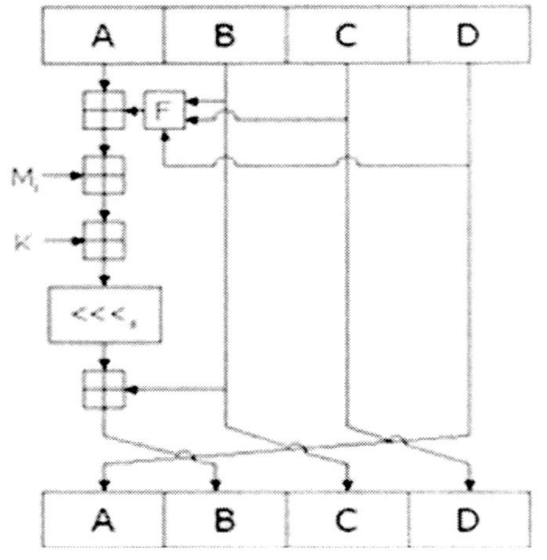

sends a Type 1 message to the server, which responds with a Type 2 message. This contains a challenge generated by the server. The client replies to the challenge with a Type 3 message. This holds several pieces of information about the client, including the client's domain and adopted username. The responses in the Type 3 message are the most critical piece of the overall authentication session, as they prove to the server that the client has knowledge of the account password.

Finally, the Password Authentication Protocol (PAP) provides a simple method for the peer to establish its identity using a 2-way handshake. PAP is not a strong authentication method. Passwords are sent over the circuit in text format, and there is no protection against sniffing. An exhaustive description and discussion on the PAP flaws is presented in (Ma, 2006).

Cryptographic Techniques

Any information exchanged during authentication obviously constitutes a sensible data and its privacy is fundamental for the security of the overall authentication system. This is particularly true when considering the response phase, which implies the submission of passwords, authentication keys or identity clues. Therefore, such information should not travel in clear. During the authentication phase, the CR framework uses common cryptographic schemes as hash or encryption in order to prevent an eavesdropper from deducing the response by means of brute force attack, or dictionary attack (Schneier, 1995). The hash value is created by applying a hash function and a seed, consisting in a sting obtained as the combination of the given password and usually other values, *e.g.*, pseudo-random data.

MD5 (Message-Digest algorithm 5) and SHA-1 (Secure Hash Algorithm) are frequently used as cryptographic hash functions. MD5 was designed by Ronald Rivest in 1991 to replace an earlier hash function, MD4, and is defined as an Internet standard in RFC 1321. The core of MD5 works with a 128 bit hash function that processes a variable length message into a fixed-length output of 128 bit. This sequence is divided into four 32-bit words, denoted A, B, C and D (Figure 5). The processing of a message block consists of four similar stages, also called *rounds*; each round is composed of 16 similar operations based on a non-linear function F, modular addition, and left rotation. The input message is divided in 512-bit message blocks (a sequence of bits is added to the original message to make its length multiple of 512: this operation is known as "padding") and the 128 bit hash function is performed on every block of 128 bits.

SHA-1 (RFC 3174) was designed by the National Security Agency (NSA) and published as a US government standard. It is part of the SHA family, officially published in 1993. Other than SHA-1, SHA-224, SHA-256, SHA-384, and SHA-512 (sometimes collectively referred to as SHA-2) have been issued. SHA-1 works as the MD5, with words of 32 bit and blocks of 512 bit. The difference resides on the output size, *i.e.*, *the digest*, which is of 160 bits, and is the core of SHA-1 operating on a sequence of five different words (A, B, C, D and E).

A different solution consists in the encryption of a public key. Let us focus on DES and RSA frameworks. DES (Data Encryption System) is an official Federal Information Processing Standard (FIPS) for the United States in 1976. At present, it is considered insecure for many applications, since its 56 bit keys have been broken in less than 24 hours. The detailed description of the DES strategy can be found in (Burr). The RSA was publicly described in 1977 (Rivest, 1998) by Ron Rivest, Adi Shamir and Len Adleman at MIT. RSA framework uses two keys: public and private. The public key is visible by anyone and is used to encrypt or verity the messages. On the other side, messages can only be signed or decrypted by means of the private key. In other words, anybody can encrypt a message, but only the holder of a private key can actually decrypt the message and read it. The complete sequence of steps for encryption/decryption and signature/verification is described in Figure 6.

When used in real systems, RSA must be combined with other strategies to avoid several problems. The first is the length/structure of the message to be encoded: this can lead definitely to a security reduction. The operative solution is the aforementioned padding of the message prior to RSA encryption. The PKCS (Public Key Cryptography Standards), described in RFC 3447, has been specifically designed for this aim. Early versions of the PKCS standard used ad-hoc schemes, which were later found vulnerable to several kinds of attacks. Modern approaches use secure

Figure 6. RSA algorithm

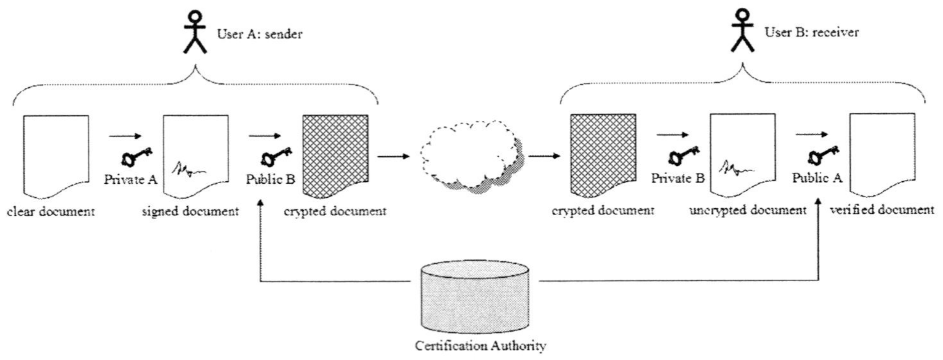

techniques such as OAEP (Optimal Asymmetric Encryption Padding) (Bellare, 1995) to protect messages from these attacks. Several standards among those previously cited have no practical use in modern communications due to their complexity, time-consumption and problems related to the distribution of personal keys. Furthermore, Wireless IP networking is generally limited by small computational capability, hardware incompatibilities and poor handiness of user terminals. In other words, the necessity of implementing very effective and simple solutions prevails on sophisticated techniques. From a commercial point of view, authentication in such context is mainly based on the WEP protocol (based on the RC4 stream cipher), traditionally used for WLAN protection (IEEE 802.11). This protocol can be attacked and broken relatively easily, allowing hackers to gain unauthorized access to digital data. The weakness of WEP has been partly solved by WPA (Wi-Fi Protected Access) and WAP2, both presented by the Wi-Fi Alliance in the IEEE 802.11i.

Cryptographic System in Network Devices

The first goal for network administrators is to secure the whole network infrastructure from malicious users. This can be accomplished in several ways using hardening and access control features. Despite the complexity of the network infrastructure, the first step is always the protection of login to a network device, *i.e.*, via console, vty lines or aux ports. This section briefly introduces some notes regarding this aspect. The simplest form of protection is through passwords. This is the easiest, but also the weakest approach as password-only logins are very vulnerable to brute-force attacks. A higher level of security can be achieved with user-id and password systems saved in a local or remote database, such as a Radius server or TACACS. In case of configuration with a local database, many operative systems, such as Cisco IOS or Juniper Junos, provide an additional level of security by locally encrypting the couple user-id and password with MD5. Large frameworks of network devices usually employ remote database. Related technologies TACACS/Radius are quite different in several features. TACACS main features are: TCP based (port 49), encryption of the entire packet, bi-directional authentication. Conversely, Radius is UDP based (port 1645 or 1812 for authentication and UDP port 1646 or 1813 for accounting) and provides the encryption of the password through unidirectional authentication. The choice between TACACS or RADIUS depends on the specific needs: RADIUS supports detailed accounting required for billing users and is particularly useful in large networks, *e.g.*, as an ISP, while a smaller organization with various user groups might select TACACS because it is well suited with per-user/per-group policies.

Authentication and Intellectual Property Protection

Intellectual property (IP) may be thought of as any intangible proprietary information. It can be anything from a particular manufacturing process to the plans for a product commercialization, a chemical formula or an algorithm. The World Intellectual Property Organization formally defines it as the creations of the mind - inventions, literary and artistic works, symbols, names, images, and designs used in commerce. From a legal standpoint, there are four types of intellectual property: patents, trademarks, copyright and trade secrets. IP protection is then an essential task for the proper exploitation of all results deriving from any creative process. Unfortunately, such practice is as well understood as hard to achieve and reports estimate that intellectual property theft costs U.S. companies about $300 billion each year. The simplest approach to perform IP protection is to restrict the access to the contents only to granted subjects. The selective right to use digital contents, as offered by the basic CR frameworks, is one of the first attempts to achieve such result in the digital era. Obviously, different access types can lead to different levels of authorization, *e.g.*, visualization only, local copy, modification, etc. In this sense, the subject of this chapter, CR frameworks, offers the first level of abstraction in order to solve the IP protection problem, presenting solutions of different complexity in case of different IP circumstances. Encryption, hashing, watermarking and transaction tracking are just few examples of techniques to be implemented in or used together with CR frameworks, in order to finalize a digital IP protection system.

Authentication Based on Biometric Features

Among the pieces of information that may be used for challenge-response authentication, biometric features (Jain, 1999; Kung, 2004) have a relatively long history,

Figure 7. General scheme for biometric authentication

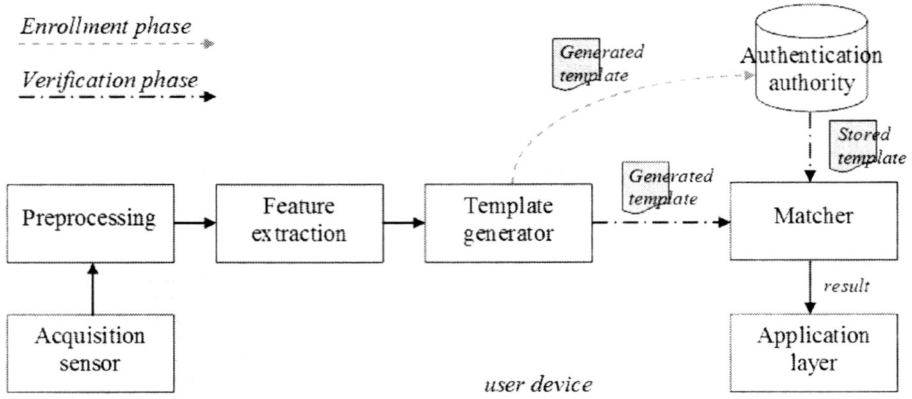

ranging back to the theory of fingerprint identification in 1880. By definition, biometric authentication is the verification of a user's identity by means of a physical trait or behavioral characteristic that cannot be easily changed. Since the discovery of fingerprint identification, a multitude of different biometric features have been considered and many processing systems and techniques have been developed accordingly. The basic idea behind biometric authentication is to recognize the user by something he is, instead of something he knows, *e.g.*, password, or has, *e.g.*, hardware key. As a result, such authentication systems are very straight, since the user must not remember any piece of information nor possess any physical key, and have been widely regarded as the most foolproof, provided the biometric feature is well-defined and unique. On the other hand, issues arise from their physical intrusiveness, the reliability of the considered feature and the cost of the technology/ system. Moreover, the collection of personal physical information might raise ethic and legal issues.

We represent a general block diagram for a biometric authentication system in Figure 7, regardless of what biometric feature is adopted. The enrollment phase refers to the first time an individual uses the biometric system. In this phase the biometric information is sampled and stored. The first functional block consists of a sensor to physically sample each specific biometrics, a preprocessing stage, feature extraction and template generation algorithms, and is often embedded into the user device. The matching is generally performed by an authentication authority, which compares the generated template with those previously acquired and stored. Depending on a distance metric result, *e.g.*, Hamming distance, and the accepted confidence level, a positive or negative match is produced and is further processed by the specific application.

For the purpose of this work, we briefly illustrate two examples of biometric authentication. The first, fingerprint recognition (Uchida, 2005; Maltoni, 2009), is the most mature and acknowledged biometric feature for identification. On the other hand the latter, facial identification (Samal, 1992; Chelappa, 1995; Zhao, 2003; Phillips, 1997; Li, 2005; Introna, 2009; Phillips, 2005), has been receiving considerable interest and constitutes one of the most lively research area in the field of biometrics.

Fingerprint-based identification may be achieved through two different approaches. The minutiae-based matching consists in analyzing the local ridge patterns, *i.e.*, minutiae, (Figure8). A complete fingerprint consists of about 100 minutiae points on average, while measured fingerprint area consists of about 30-60 minutiae points on average, depending on both the finger and the sensor. The minutiae points are represented by a dots distribution in a coordinate system. Such method is robust to fingerprint rotation and translation, but the extraction of minutiae can be negatively affected by noise and low average quality of the acquired image. The correlation-based approach is based on global pattern matching. The reference and test images are first aligned and checked for correspondence. This method is less robust against image distortions, which are unavoidable since fingers are not rigid. Current fingerprint identification systems may achieve a false accept rate (FAR) of 1/100,000, with a false reject rate (FRR) of 1% and matching speed of a few hundreds of msec.

The face is one of the most natural biometric features for identity authentication, also thanks to the fact that a face image can be easily acquired using an off-the-shelf desktop camera. The environment surrounding a face recognition application plays a fundamental role in the complexity of the method. A controlled environment generally comprises the acquisition of frontal and/or profile photographs, with uniform background and identical poses among the participants (*mug shots*). Given the complexity of a general setting, such approach is generally preferred to the uncontrolled one. Consequently, an application system typically restricts one of many aspects, including the environment (fixed location, fixed lighting, uniform background, single face, etc.), the allowable face change (neutral expression, negligible aging, etc.), the number of individuals to be matched against, and the viewing condition (front view, no occlusion, etc.). According to the FRVT2006 report (Phillips 2007), the performance of face recognition systems has been constantly improving in the past years. In fact, a gradual decrease in FRR is reported from 0.79 in 1993 to 0.01 in 2006, given a fixed FAR of 0.001, for a selection of milestone implementations.

Figure 8. Minutiae-based fingerprint matching

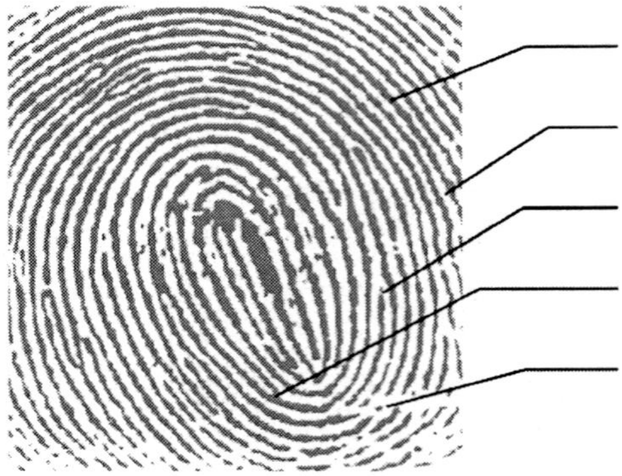

A wide variety of approaches to machine recognition of faces has been developed in the literature. Their categorization depends on different criteria. In terms of the sensing modality, a system can take 2D or 3D images, color or infra-red images, or any combination. In terms of viewing angle, a system may be designed for frontal, profile or general views, or any combination. In terms of temporal component, a system can take a static image or time-varying image sequences as input. In terms of computational tools, a system can use programmed knowledge rules, statistical decision rules, neural networks, genetic algorithms, or others.

Similarly to fingerprint recognition, the approaches used to perform face recognition may be categorized into two groups: holistic or global approaches and feature-based approaches. Global approaches use a single feature vector that represents the whole face image as input to a classifier. Several classifiers have been proposed in the literature, *e.g.*, minimum distance classification in the eigenspace, Fisher's discriminant analysis, and neural networks. Global techniques work well for frontal face views, but they are not robust against pose and environment changes in general.

Feature-based approaches rely on the identification and matching of several representative features, such as inter-ocular distance, distance between the lips and the nose, distance between the nose tip and the eyes, distance between the lips and the line joining the two eyes, eccentricity of the face, ratio of the dimensions of the bounding box of the face, width of the lips, etc. Feature-based methods are robust against geometric transforms, but are critical in the identification of features (Figure 9).

In Table 1 (Yun, 2002) a comparison of several biometric methods is reported on the basis of the features used for identification. Universality describes how common a biometric is found in each individual. Uniqueness is how well the biometric separates two individuals. Permanence measures how well a biometric resists aging. Collectability explains how easy it is to acquire the bio-metric. Performance indicates

Figure 9. Examples of facial recognition methods: local features (left) and eigenfaces (right)

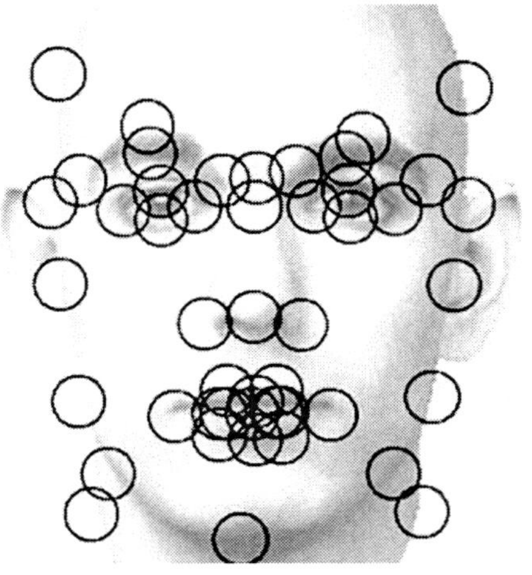

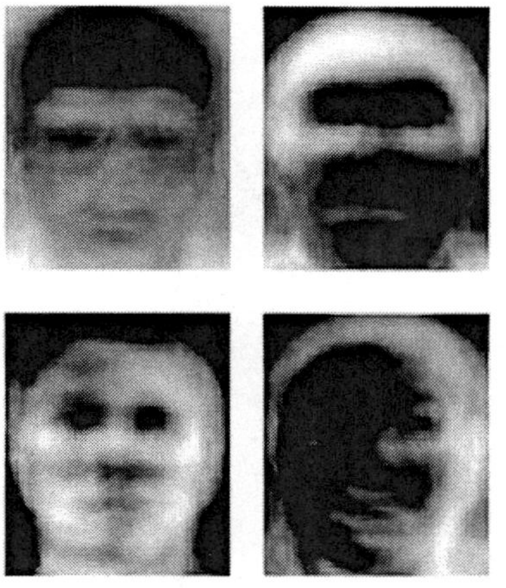

the accuracy, speed, and robustness of the system capturing the biometric. Acceptability indicates the degree of approval of a technology by the public in everyday life. Finally, circumvention is how easy it is to fool the authentication system. Rankings range from low (L) to high (H). Unfortunately, reliability and acceptability are often inversely proportional. For instance, while signature recognition has a high collectability and acceptability but low reliability and accuracy performance, DNA-based authentication offers high reliability but is poor on acceptability.

Another good example of trade-off between reliability and intrusiveness are the cases of retina scan and facial recognition. A retina scan requires the user to stare firmly at an acquisition system for 15 seconds, which may result in annoying interaction. On the other hand, the reliability of facial recognition methods greatly depends on application, demographic aspects such as sex, age, and time-delay, environment conditions, such as lighting and orientation.

A very promising area is represented by multiple features authentication. In this case, several biometric features are collected and analyzed simultaneously, *e.g.*, hand and fingerprint. The approaches that follow such architecture generally offer a high level of accuracy and security at the expense of simplicity and cost and are therefore indicated in critical applications. It must be noticed that multiple features authentication may be achieved also by the combination of a biometric feature and a traditional one, such as iris scan plus ID card identification.

Table 1. Biometric authentication

Method	*Universality*	*Uniqueness*	*Permanence*	*Collectability*	*Performance*	*Acceptability*	*Circumvention*
Face (Zhao, 2003)	H	L	M	H	L	H	L
Fingerprint (Driscoll, 1994)	M	H	H	M	H	M	H
Hand geometry (Hashemi, 2005; Faundez-Zanuy, 2005; Sanchez-Reillo, 2000)	M	M	M	H	M	M	M
Keystroke dynamics (Monrose, 2000)	L	L	L	M	L	M	M
Hand vein (Tanaka, 2004; Yuhang, 2005)	M	M	M	M	M	M	H
Iris (Daugman, 1994)	H	H	H	M	H	L	H
Retina (Simon, 1935)	H	H	M	L	H	L	H
Signature (Leclerc, 1994)	L	L	L	H	L	H	L
Voice (Atal, 1976; Campbell, 1997; Gish, 1994)	M	L	L	M	L	H	L
Facial Thermogram (Proloski, 1997)	H	H	L	H	M	H	H
DNA (Rudin, 2001)	H	H	H	L	H	L	L

Biometric authentication represents a very lively sector for research and development. In fact, thanks to its wide adoption at all security levels, ranging from personal computer login apparatus to high-security military applications, the future trend points to a very fast and consistent evolution of such authentication mechanisms. While the current biometric market is dominated by fingerprint authentication (44%) (Biometrics Market and Industry Report, 2006-2010), and will most probably be the main revenue contributor up to 2012 and even beyond (The Global Biometrics Market), other methods, such as face recognition or multiple features authentication are promising.

From the last cited report we find that fingerprint alone was worth $1.3 billion in 2007, and is forecast to grow to $2.7 billion by 2012, a CAGR (Compound Annual Growth Rate) of 16.3% over the next five years, while face recognition follows with $459 million in 2007 and is expected to rise to $1.3 billion by 2012, a CAGR of 23.8%. According to the report, the third player is hand biometry, while remaining biometric segments together constitute $729 million in 2007, with estimated to grow to $2.3 billion by 2012, a CAGR of 26%. The global market for biometrics increased from $1.95 billion in 2006 to an estimated $2.7 billion by the end of 2007 and it should reach $7.1 billion by 2012, a CAGR of 21.3%. Finally, Europe is leading the biometrics market due to higher user acceptance and the introduction of biometric passports in the majority of European countries, while the highest potential lies in the Asian regions. Such figures well represent the great interest that biometric authentication is raising in the industry and consumer world.

FUTURE WORKS

Given the extension of the object of this work, a full-spectrum discussion of future trends would be either too generic or extended. Rather, we want to concentrate the attention on a few aspects of challenge-response mechanisms that present particular interest and are object of current research and development. The first argument, strong password authentication, is principally about the evolution of common CR schemes, used for message exchange, as described in the background section. Mobile authentication deals with the evolution of the authentication technology towards the mobile framework and constitutes the second argument. The last argument, image-based authentication, is mostly related to the type of information used in the challenge-response exchange. The aspects related to mutual authentication through graphical passwords and the role of image scrambling and cryptography are discussed.

Strong Password Authentication

Strong password authentication embodies the challenge of CR frameworks against eavesdropping attacks, with particular interest for novel environments such as wireless networks. A strong password is characterized by extremely high entropy in a way it cannot be easily deduced. Many strong password strategies have been proposed in the last decade. In this sub-section we provide the reader with a comprehensive description of the state of art, discussing the advantages and disadvantages of each strategy.

One of the first effective strategies against eavesdropping has been proposed by Haller (1994) and it is known as S/KEY (Haller, 1994). S/KEY is a one-time password authentication system: any given password may be used exactly one time only, after which it is no longer valid. The system requires that both principals share one secret key, *w*, which is never transmitted except than during registration. Then, a secure hash function (a function that is easy to compute in forward direction, but computationally infeasible to reverse) is used for generating the one-time passwords by taking *w* as seed. Specifically, S/KEY uses the MD4 as hash function, taking 8 bytes of input and producing 8 bytes output, so that one-time passwords are 64 bits (8 bytes) long. The plural "passwords" has been used on purpose, since the output of the algorithm is a sequence of passwords to be used consecutively. Then, the core of the devised strategy is the transmission the personal passwords which are again used for verifying the user's authenticity at the server side. An eavesdropper, having monitored the authentication data exchange, would not be able to retrieve the personal key because of the use of an unknown hash function (far too complex to invert). Furthermore, the passwords are related in a way it would be computationally impractical to deduce any password from the preceding sequence.

The state of art in strong password authentication starts back in 1990 with the SAS strategy, proposed by Sandirigama et al. (Sandirigama, 2000). This algorithm has been found vulnerable to replay attacks (a form of network attack in which a valid data transmission is maliciously or fraudulently repeated or delayed, and carried out either by the originator or by an adversary who intercepts the data and retransmits it) and denial-of service attacks (an offensive action where the adversary could use some method upon the server so that the access requests issued by the legitimate user will be denied by the server) by Lin et al. (Lin, 2001) in 1991. Lin also proposed a solution with the OSPA (Optimal Strong-Password Authentication) protocol and its enhancement (Lin, 2003), which is robust against stolen-verifier (actually, in many schemes the verifiers of the passwords are stored by the server to enhance the passwords' security) and man-in-the-middle attacks (an attacker is able to read, insert and modify at will, messages between two parties without either party knowing that the link between them has been compromised.). Most recent strategies can be found in (Chang, 2004) and (Goyal, 2005). Both seem to be robust against online replay, dictionary and denial-of-service attacks.

Strong password authentication finds a key application field in wireless networks, whose diffusion and evolution is proceeding rapidly. In such environment, both authentication and data transfer are performed through the wireless link. Then, this scenario is particularly critical in terms of security. For this reason, new forms of hash functions and authentication methods are continuously proposed in the state of art literature. Usually, the process of producing novel frameworks is a trial-and-error procedure, which continuously leads to finding and fixing new security issues. Most novel methods are aimed at strong mutual authentication, in order to maintain a safe synchronous data communication between two principals during each authentication phase. Moreover, authentication in a wireless environment seems to be very sensitive, among all cited forms of attack, to the stolen-verifier attack, in which the attacker steals the user's verifier and impersonates the user. At present, several variants of the proposed techniques, in particular of the SAS strategy, try to solve this problem. The last desired feature for strong password authentication strategies will be lightness, to be implemented in low spec machines, as mobile phones. (Me, 2006) proposes a solution which combines a Web/mobile authentication system: a challenge/response process and an OTP, *i.e.*, One Time Password. In the first step a challenge is issued from an authentication server and a mobile device has to be authenticated. Then, the authentication with the web site or application is accomplished using a temporary OTP. The reader is suggested to have a read of (Weragama, 2007): a good review of their SAS-3 (simple and Secure) strong password authentication protocol. (Nallusamy, 2009) proposes a strong authentication mechanism for authenticating a mobile device using a digital certificate and Device ID along with the conventional User ID. The approach seems to be more advanced in respect to other proposed in the past. A different approach is provided in (Do Van Thanh, 2009) where the mobile phone is seen as an authentication token towards service providers on the Internet. A general overview of this approach is proposed with different authentication solutions with mobile devices. All these solutions are also discussed for complexity, strength and user-friendliness.

Mobile Authentication

Following the broad diffusion and constant development of mobile devices and services, the authentication technology has been undergoing an evolution to fully exploit the new possibilities of the mobile platform. SMS OTP authentication, mobile PKI and OOBA are briefly discussed in the following.

SMS-based OTP adopts short message service to deliver a one-time password upon request. Before the complete authentication, the user goes to the application website and requests the OTP. The one-time password is sent through SMS. By typing the OTP into the authentication form the user gains complete access to its private contents on the application website. As with similar systems, the OTP can be used only once, which provides much better security as compared to traditional passwords. SMS-based OTP are relatively insecure, primarily because of the relative insecurity of the SMS protocol. This solution is convenient for the casual retail consumer, but may result in scarce usability for enterprise users who authenticate frequently during the day and therefore must wait for the SMS delivery of the OTP each time.

Each GSM/UMTS mobile phone requires a SIM card, a standardized smartcard that is issued to the user by the IT operator and is primarily used to authenticate the user on the mobile network. The SIM card also allows for secure storage of digital keys that can be used for online authentication and digital signatures. This is referred to as Wireless PKI and Mobile PKI. Mobile PKI employs encrypted SMS text messages that are used to represent authentication or digital signature. The user is asked to express consent by entering a PIN code that secures the private key and which typically needs to be entered for each transaction separately. Comparing to other secure means of authentication, mobile PKI relies on well established standards, supported on all mobile phones. As a result, no additional authentication device is required, and there is no need for the user to install additional software on either the phone or on other client devices. Neither is there a need to manually enter codes, except for the PIN code itself. The advantages are then related to user-friendliness and robustness against malware and viruses. Mobile PKI is a very secure solution because it involves a hardware token that meets stringent requirements. Still, a man in the middle attack by a malevolent application provider is possible and the theft of the SIM card may allow others to conduct transactions while posing as the user, provided the attackers know the user's PIN code (PIN guessing is unlikely, since the system only allows for a few trials).

Out-of-Band Authentication (OOBA) requires that separate information channels are used for authentication and access. As an example, OOBA may require the application server to contact the user through a phone call. The proofing can come simply from the user's call back or from the input of a numerical string, but it can also include further verification, such as the biometric recognition of its voice print. Of the authentication options described in this section, OOBA provides the greatest security, primarily in terms of protection against man-in-the-middle attacks. As with SMS-based OTPs, usability could be an issue for enterprise users.

Image-Based Authentication

Image-based authentication (IBA) represents a relatively novel idea in the field of authentication systems. All systems based on the exchange or selection of some graphical information fall within such classification, while the justification for such systems resides in three main aspects: user friendliness, ease of memorization and the technical evolution of user terminals and connection capability (Suo, 2005).

The evolution of IBA methods may be chronologically arranged into two stages. An initial stage ranges from 1995 to 2000 with the works of (Blonder, 2005), who introduced the concept of graphical password. The project developed at Lucent Technologies labs comprises a relatively simple password selection scheme, consisting in the identification of a number of image areas, tap regions, in a given order. Authorization takes place upon recognition of the correct details sequence. The system allows for a certain region tolerance, depending on the required security level. Other methods include the systems by Naor, Shamir and Pinkas (Naor, 1995/1997), Jermyn (Jermyn, 1999), Dhamija and Perrig (Dhamija, 2000).

An evolution stage ranges from 2001 until present. Some works are Visual Password (VisualPass), Server authentication (Epshtein, 2002), Graphical Password (Sobrado, 2002), ImagePassword (Wei, 2002), A wase-E (Takada, 2003), Passfaces System (PassfacesTM), Viskey (Viskey), Picture Password (Jansen, 2003), Passpic (PassfacesTM), PicturePIN (Pointsec), Visual Security for Wireless Handheld Devices (Duncan, 2004), Associative memory scheme (Weinshall, 2004), Application-Scalable Image-based Authentication Framework with JPEG2000 (Ginesu, 2005) and IBA with Sign-In Seal (Nitin, 2008). All previous methods try to develop the idea of image based authentication while optimizing the aspects related to security, ease of memorization, computational complexity and user-friendliness. An optimal system has not yet been produced, and all solutions represent a compromise among the aforementioned requirements.

A typical image-based authentication method consists in the exchange of some graphical information between final user and authentication server. All systems are founded on the ground truth that "pictures speak louder than words" from several points of view. In this case, the memorization process is more effective with visual information rather than complex alphanumeric sequences (Pierce, 2003). In the example of Figure 10 top (PassfacesTM), the user is asked to iteratively recognize a sequence of pass-faces, *i.e.*, the face images that were selected during registration, while in Figure 10 bottom (Onali, 2006), the user is first asked to recognize his pass-image, *i.e.*, the image that was selected during registration, and continues by iteratively identifying one portion of the selected image.

The main concerns related to these methods depend on three factors: ease of memorization/recalling, data transfer and security. While the first factor can be

Figure 10. Example of IBA methods

1st passface selection 2nd passface selection 3rd passface selection

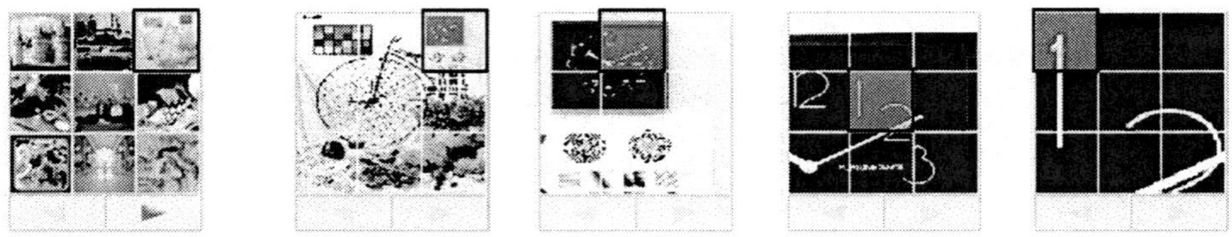

Pass-image selection 1st zoom level 2nd zoom level 3rd zoom level 4th zoom level

measured through extended subjective testing only, the other two strictly depend on the developed system and can be esteemed exactly. Data transfer performance is especially critical in mobile or portable applications, when the exchange of large volumes of data is either technically unfeasible or too expensive. Such aspect can be optimized with the adoption of image compressing routines and the accurate design and minimization of the system information flow. Security depends on a multitude of factors, such as possible input combinations, security of the communication link, usage environment and others. As an example, we show the performance estimation from (Ginesu, 2006) in Figure11. The proposed method (MIBA) is compared with three other graphical authentication systems on the basis of data transfer and level of security for different numbers of authentication steps.

Other graphical authentication systems are based on slightly different approaches. DAS (Draw A Secret) (Jermyn, 1999), for instance, asks the user to draw his secret image on a reference grid (Figure 12 left). The password is constituted by both the shape and the way it was generated. Password recognition is then achieved by evaluating the similarity between drawn and stored image and the similarity between executed and stored path progress. In Graphical Password (Sobrado, 2002), the user must recognize a particular geometrical configuration given by several pass-objects among a pseudo-random objects distribution (Figure 12 right). Au-

Figure 11. Security against data transfer performance from (Ginesu, 2006)

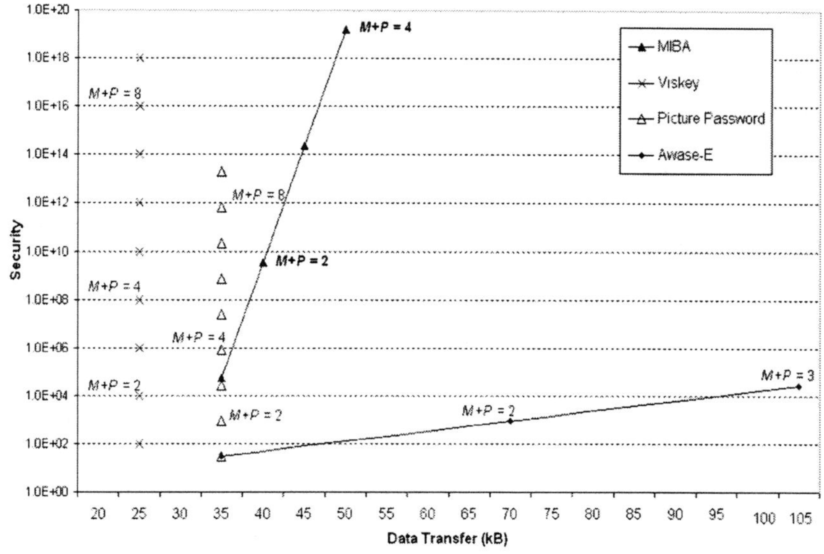

Figure 12. Other graphical authentication systems: DAS and graphical password

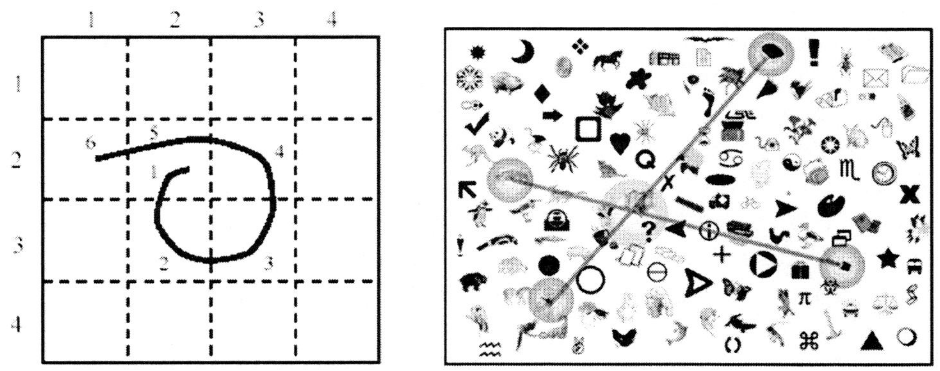

thentication is then based on the correct selection of a particular region, *e.g.*, the cross intersection in the given example.

Image watermarking, scrambling and encryption (Furht, 2004; Lee, 2001; Rey, 2002), play an important role in visual authentication methods, providing for additional protection from the illegal manipulation and acquisition of visual data. Some visual login systems based on encryption algorithms have been proposed in

Figure 13. Message exchange scheme for the registration and authentication phases of (Ginesu, 2006)

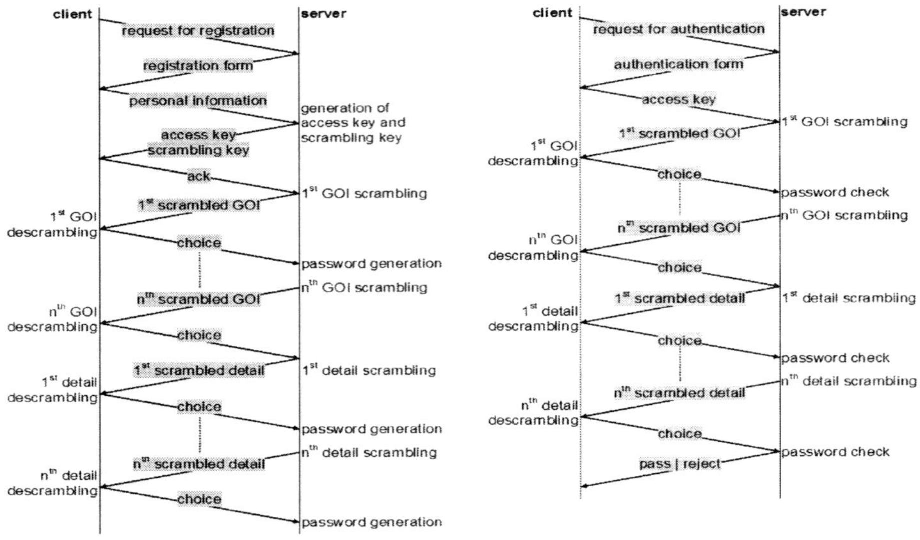

Registration　　　　Authentication

the literature. An example of visual cryptography (Naor, 1995/1997) provides each user with a transparency, *i.e.*, a portion of visual information, which reveals a secret when combined with another sent by the server during authentication. Steganography may be used together with visual cryptography (Kharrazi, 2004). The most widely known technique consists in replacing the last bit of each image pixel with a bit of secret information. These systems rely only on the secret keys exchange. In (Ginesu, 2006), an image scrambling technique is proposed explicitly for mutual image-based authentication. The system requires the server and client to share a scrambling key, which is used for scrambling/descrambling the visual data. During the authentication process, each time an interaction requires a piece of visual information, its encrypted version with the scrambling key is provided. Then, the client must descramble the visual information in order to make its content understandable and usable, *e.g.*, selection of the graphical password (Figure 13).

One last interesting application of images to authentication is provided in (Datta, 2009). This work provides an extensive study on the reliability and security of existing CAPTCHAs in respect of several systematic image distortions and proposes a novel method. CAPTCHA (Completely Automated Public Turing test to tell Computers and Humans Apart) is a particular type of challenge-response test used to ensure that the response is not generated by a computer. The process is generally used in addition to providing the authentication credentials, in order to reduce the risk of password guessing bots.

Also favored by the rapid growth and diffusion of personal mobile devices, the research on IBA methods is bound to continue producing interesting and practical results for the consumer market. We may conclude that the success of visual authentication methods will strongly depend upon their effective usability and low complexity.

CONCLUSION

This chapter has proposed an overview of Challenge-Response mechanisms for property protection. Both standard methods and state of art were presented. Although the area of authentication presents several consolidated points, researchers are continuously at work for verifying the robustness of existing techniques, refining the state of art algorithms and propose novel strategies or parts of them. Three different aspects can be identified as principal targets of innovation: the complete structure of authentication frameworks, the underlying algorithms for performing security function, such as ciphering, hashing, etc., and the typologies of information used as personal identification. Each of these aspects constitutes itself an entire applied research field. Transverse to these fields is the need and request for optimization in terms of computational complexity, user friendliness and robustness. Thus, innovation is moving towards these four research areas and is bound to achieve significant results, also thanks to the growing need for security in mobile devices. This last feature seems to be the most prolific field of research of the last years. Many interesting approaches have been presented about strong authentication password strategies, spacing from improved traditional methods to new frameworks such as the usage of the mobile device as an authentication token.

REFERENCES

Atal, B. S. (1976). Automatic recognition of speakers from their voices. *Proceedings of the IEEE, 64*, 460–475. doi:10.1109/PROC.1976.10155

Bellare, M., & Rogaway, P. (1995). Optimal asymmetric encryption - How to encrypt with RSA. *Extended abstract in Advances in Cryptology - Eurocrypt 94 Proceedings* [Springer-Verlag.]. *Lecture Notes in Computer Science*, 950.

Blonder, G. E. (2005). *Graphical password.* US Patent 5559961, Lucent Technologies Inc., Murray Hill, NJ.

Burr, W. E. (2000). Data encryption standard. In NIST (Ed.), *A century of excellence in measurements, standards, and technology: A chronicle of selected NBS/NIST publications, 1901-2000.* Retrieved from http://nvl.nist.gov/pub/nistpubs/sp958-lide/250-253.pdf

Campbell, J. P. (1997). Speaker recognition: A tutorial. *Proceedings of the IEEE, 85*(9), 1437–1462. doi:10.1109/5.628714

Chang, Y.-F., & Chang, C.-C. (2004). A secure and efficient strong-password authentication protocol. *ACM SIGOPS Operating Systems Review, 38*(3), 79–90. doi:10.1145/1035834.1035844

Chellappa, R., Wilson, C. L., & Sirohey, S. (1995). Human and machine recognition of faces: A survey. *Proceedings of the IEEE, 83*, 705–740. doi:10.1109/5.381842

Datta, R., Li, J., & Wang, J. Z. (2009). Exploiting the human-machine gap in image recognition for designing Captchas. *IEEE Transactions on Information Forensics and Security, 4*(3), 504–518. doi:10.1109/TIFS.2009.2022709

Daugman, J. G. (1994). *United States Patent No. 5,291,560: Biometric personal identification system based on iris analysis.* Washington DC: U.S. Government Printing Office.

Dhamija, R. (2000). *Hash visualization in user authentication.* Computer Human Interaction Conference.

Dhamija, R., & Perrig, A. (2000). *Déjà vu: A user study using images for authentication.* 9th Usenix Security Symposium.

Do van. T., Jorstad, I., Jonvik, T., & Do van, T. (2009). Strong authentication with mobile phone as security token. *International Conference on Mobile Adhoc and Sensor Systems*, (pp. 777-782).

Driscoll, D. (1994). Fingerprint ID systems. *Advanced Imaging (Woodbury, N.Y.), 9*(20).

Duncan, M. V., Akhtari, M. S., & Bradford, P. G. (2004). Visual security for wireless handheld devices. *The Journal of Science & Health at the University of Alabama, 2.* Retrieved from http://www.bama.ua.edu/~joshua/archive/may04/Duncan%20et%20al.pdf

Epshtein, D., & Krawczyk, H. (2002). *Image-based authentication of public keys and applications to SSH. Project report.* Technion – Dept. of Electrical Engineering, Technion.

Faundez-Zanuy, M. (2005). Biometric verification of humans by means of hand geometry. *39th Int. Carnahan Conf. on Security Technology CCST 2005*, (pp. 61-67).

Furht, B., & Kirovski, F. (2004). *Multimedia security handbook*. CRC Press.

Ginesu, G., Giusto, D. D., & Onali, T. (2005). *Application-scalable image-based authentication framework with JPEG2000*. IEEE International Workshop on Multimedia Signal Processing MMSP05.

Ginesu, G., Giusto, D. D., & Onali, T. (2006). Mutual image-based authentication framework with JPEG2000 in wireless environment. *EURASIP Journal on Wireless Communications and Networking.*

Gish, H., & Schmidt, M. (1994). Text-independent speaker identification. *IEEE Signal Processing Magazine*, *11*(4), 18–32. doi:10.1109/79.317924

Goyal, V., Kumar, V., Singh, M., Abraham, A., & Sanyal, S. (2005). CompChall: Addressing password guessing attacks. *ITCC05, 1*, (pp. 739-744).

Haller, N. M. (1994). The S/KEY (TM) one-time password system. *Proceedings of Internet Society Symposium on Network and Distributed System Security*, (pp. 151-158).

Hashemi, J., & Fatemizadeh, E. (2005). Biometric identification through hand geometry. *International Conference on Computer as a Tool EUROCON 2005, 2*, (pp. 1011-1014).

International Biometric Group. (2006). *Biometrics market and industry report 2006-2010*. Retrieved from http://www.biometricgroup.com/reports/public/market_report.html

Introna, L. D., & Nissenbaum, H. (2009). *Facial recognition technology: A survey of policy and implementation issues*. Center for Catastrophe Preparedness and Response. New York University, July, 22, 2009.

Jain, A. K., Bolle, R., & Pankanti, S. (1999). *Biometrics: Personal identification in networked society*. Kluwer Academic Publishers.

Jansen, W., Gavrila, S., Korolev, V., Ayers, R., & Swanstrom, R. (2003). *Picture password: A visual login technique for mobile devices*. NIST IR 7030.

Jermyn, I., May, A., Monrose, F., Riter, M., & Rubin, A. (1999). *The design and analysis of graphical passwords*. 8th USENIX Security Symposium.

Jermyn, I., May, A., Monrose, F., Riter, M., & Rubin, A. (1999). The design and analysis of graphical passwords. *Proceedings of 8th USENIX Security Symposium*.

Kharrazi, M., Sencar, H. T., & Memon, N. (2004). *Image steganography: Concepts and practice*. Lecture Note Series, Institute for Mathematical Sciences, National University of Singapore, April 2004.

Kung, S. Y., Mak, M. W., & Lin, S. H. (2004). *Biometric authentication: A machine learning approach*. Prentice Hall.

Leclerc, F., & Plamondon, R. (1994). Automatic signature verification: The state of the art - 1989-1993. *International Journal of Pattern Recognition and Artificial Intelligence*, *8*(3), 643–660. doi:10.1142/S0218001494000346

Lee, J., & Jung, S. (2001). A survey of watermarking techniques applied to multimedia. *Proceedings 2001 IEEE International Symposium on Industrial Electronics (ISIE2001), 1,* (pp. 272-277).

Li, S. Z., & Jain, A. K. (2005). *Handbook of face recognition*. Springer.

Lin, C. L., Sun, H. M., & Hwang, T. (2001). Attacks and solutions on strong-password authentication. *IEICE Transactions on Communications . E (Norwalk, Conn.)*, *84-B*(9), 2622–2627.

Lin, C.-W., Shen, J.-J., & Hwang, M.-S. (2003). Security enhancement for optimal strong-password authentication protocol. *ACM Operating System Review*, *37*(3), 12–16. doi:10.1145/881783.881785

Ma, X., McCrindle, R., & Cheng, X. (2006). *Verifying and fixing password authentication protocol*. SNPD'06.

Maltoni, D., Maio, D., Jain, A. K., & Prabhakar, S. (2009). *Handbook of fingerprint recognition* (2nd ed.). Springer. doi:10.1007/978-1-84882-254-2

Me, G., Pirro, D., & Sarrecchia, R. (2006). *A mobile based approach to strong authentication on Web* (p. 67). International Multi-Conference on Computing in the Global Information Technology.

Mitchell, C. (1989). Limitations of challenge-response entity authentication. *IEEE Electronic Letters*, *25*(17), 1195–1196. doi:10.1049/el:19890801

Monrose, F., & Rubin, A. D. (2000). Keystroke dynamics as a biometric for authentication. *Future Generation Computer Systems*, *16*(4), 351–359. doi:10.1016/S0167-739X(99)00059-X

Nallusamy, R., & Paul, S. (2009). Strong authentication for secure content access in converged networks. *International Symposium on Advanced Networks and Telecommunication Systems*, 2009, (pp. 1-3).

Naor, M., & Pinkas, B. (1997). Visual authentication and identification . In Kaliski, B. (Ed.), *Advances in Cryptology – Crypto '97, 1294* (pp. 322–336).

Naor, M., & Shamir, A. (1995). Visual cryptography . In De Santis, A. (Ed.), *Advances in Cryptology - EuroCrypt '94, 950* (pp. 1–12). doi:10.1007/BFb0053419

Nitin Sehgal, V. K., Chauhan, D. S., Sood, M., & Hastir, V. (2008). Image based authentication system with sign-in seal. *Proc. of the World Congress on Engineering and Computer Science 2008, WCECS 2008*, October 22 - 24, 2008, San Francisco, USA.

Omura, J. K. (1990). Novel applications of cryptography in digital communications. *IEEE Communications Magazine, 28*(5), 21–29. doi:10.1109/35.54344

Onali, T., & Ginesu, G. (2006). Transmission-efficient image-based authentication for mobile devices. *Lecture Notes in Computer Science*, 3893.

Passfaces, T. M. (n.d.). *Website*. Retrieved from http://www.realuser.com

PassPicc. (n.d.). *Website*. Retrieved from http://www.authord.com/PassPic/

Perrig, A., & Song, D. (1999). *Hash visualization: A new technique to improve real-world security.* International Workshop on Cryptographic Techniques and E-Commerce CrypTEC '99.

Phillips, P. J., Flynn, P. J., Scruggs, T., Bowyer, K. W., Chang, J., & Hoffman, K. … Worek, W. (2005). Overview of the face recognition grand challenge. *Proceedings of the 2005 IEEE Computer Society Conference on Computer Vision and Pattern Recognition* (CVPR'05), volume 1.

Phillips, P. J., Moon, H., Rauss, P., & Rizvi, S. (1997). The FERET evaluation methodology for face-recognition algorithms. *Proceedings IEEE Conference Computer Vision and Pattern Recognition CVPR, 97*, 137–143. doi:10.1109/CVPR.1997.609311

Phillips, P. J., Scruggs, T., O'Toole, A. J., Flynn, P. J., Bowyer, K. W., Schott, C. L., & Sharpe, M. (2007). *FRVT 2006 and ICE 2006 large-scale results.* National Institute of Standards and Technology, March 2007.

Pierce, J. D., Warren, M. J., Mackay, D. R., & Wells, J. G. (2004). Graphical authentication: Justifications and objectives, *Proceedings of the 2nd Australian Information Security Management Conference, Securing the Future* (AISM 2004), (pp. 49-63).

Pointsec Mobile Technologies. (n.d.). *Home*. Retrieved from http://www.pointsec.com

Prokoski, F. J. (1997). *Security and non-diagnostic medical uses for thermal imaging.* American Academy of Thermology 1997 Annual Meeting, Pittsburgh.

BCC Research. (2007). *The global biometrics market.*

Rey, C., & Dugelay, J. (2002). A survey of watermarking algorithms for image authentication. *EURASIP Journal on Applied Signal Processing, 6*, 613–621. doi:10.1155/S1110865702204047

Rivest, R., Shamir, A., & Adleman, L. (1998). A method for obtaining digital signatures and public-key cryptosystems. *Communications of the ACM, 21*(2), 120–126. doi:10.1145/359340.359342

Rudin, N., & Inman, K. (2001). *An introduction to forensic DNA analysis* (2nd ed.). CRC Press. doi:10.1201/9781420058505

Samal, A., & Lyengar, P. A. (1992). Automatic recognition and analysis of human faces and facial expressions: A survey. *Pattern Recognition, 25*, 65–77. doi:10.1016/0031-3203(92)90007-6

Sanchez-Reillo, R., Sanchez-Avila, C., & Gonzalez-Marcos, A. (2000). Biometric identification through hand geometry measurements. *IEEE Transactions on Pattern Analysis and Machine Intelligence, 22*(10), 1168–1171. doi:10.1109/34.879796

Sandirigama, M., Shimizu, A., & Noda, M. T. (2000). Simple and secure password authentication protocol (SAS). *IEICE Transactions on Communications . E (Norwalk, Conn.), 83-B*(6), 1363–1365.

Schneier, B. (1995). *Applied cryptography* (2nd ed.). Wiley.

Simon, C., & Goldstein, I. (1935). A new scientific method of identification. *New York State Journal of Medicine, 35*(18), 901–906.

Sobrado, L., & Birget, J. C. (2002). Graphical passwords. *The Rutgers Scholar, 4.*

Suo, X., Zhu, Y., & Owen, G. S. (2005). *Graphical passwords: A survey.* 21st Annual Computer Security Applications Conference (ACSAC 2005), Tucson AZ.

Takada, T., & Koike, H. (2003). Awase-E: Image-based authentication for mobile phones using user's favorite images. *Proceedings of 5th International Symposium, Mobile HCI 2003*, (pp. 347-351). Springer.

Tanaka, T., & Kubo, N. (2004). Biometric authentication by hand vein patterns. *SICE 2004 Annual Conference, 1,* (pp. 249-253).

Uchida, K. (2005). Fingerprint identification. *NEC Journal of Advanced Technology, 2*(1).

Viskey. (n.d.). *Home*. Retrieved from http://www.viskey.com

VisualPass. (n.d.). *Home*. Retrieved from http://penguin.poly.edu/seminars/visualpass/visualpasswords.ppt

Wei, L. (2002). *Password.* Retrieved from http://wlu-share.tripod.com/ImgPasswd.htm

Weinshall, D. (2004). *Secure authentication schemes suitable for an associative memory*. Leibniz Center for Research in Computer Science, Technical Report 2004-00.

Weragama, N. S., & Sandirigama, M. (2007). SAS-3: A polynomial based strong password authentication protocol. *International Conference on Industrial and Information Systems, 2007,* (pp. 41-46).

Yuhang, D., Dayan, Z., & Kejun, W. (2005). A study of hand vein recognition method. *IEEE International Conference Mechatronics and Automation, 4*, (pp. 2106-2110).

Yun, Y. W. (2002). The "123" of biometric technology. *Synthesis Journal, 2002.*

Zhao, W., Chellappa, R., Rosenfeld, A., & Phillips, P. J. (2003). Face recognition: A literature survey. *ACM Computing Surveys*, 399–458. doi:10.1145/954339.954342

Chapter 6
Access Control on Semantic Web Data Using Query Rewriting

Jian Li
Hong Kong Baptist University, China

William K. Cheung
Hong Kong Baptist University, China

ABSTRACT

Semantic Web technologies allow on-line resources to be semantically annotated to support more effective and intelligent online services. However, ontologies sometimes may contain sensitive information. Providing access to them requires proper control to ensure the data protection requirement. Yet, the protection should not be too restrictive to make the access management inflexible. While there has been recent work on policy-based access control, in this paper, the authors present a policy representation specifically for access control on ontology-based data and explain how issues like policy propagation and policy conflict resolution are addressed. The authors present bucket-based query rewriting algorithms for realizing the access control policies to avoid sensitive resources leakage in the context of the Semantic Web. The authors validate the correctness of the proposed mechanisms by going through some illustrative examples in detail.

DOI: 10.4018/978-1-61350-135-1.ch006

1. INTRODUCTION

The recent proliferation of the Semantic Web technologies has resulted in an increasing amount of on-line resources being semantically annotated to support more effective and intelligent online services, including customized search, autonomous information integration, etc. We here call such kind of semantically annotations of resources *semantic web data,* where domain ontologies are needed as some background knowledge for support semantic interpretation of various types. In the literature, projects on developing semantic web data management systems are abundant (Broekstra, et al., 2002; Wilkinson, et al., 2003; Heflin, et al., 1999) and related software tools have been available in the market for quite a while. By specifying the user retrieval requirements on the data as some semantic web queries which involve entities defined in some domain ontologies, relevant data can readily be retrieved. However, allowing better search on such distributed on-line resources also implies that more complicated access control is needed, especially for applications where data containing sensitive and private information (e.g., business, healthcare, national defense, etc.) could be found in the query results. In addition, if the queries are for supporting intelligent on-line services, the on-demand requirement will require the access control system to be not only secure but also flexible, or it will not be operationally viable. The conventional role-based access control model does allow some form of access control to be enforced, but rather restricted (e.g., context specific access control mechanisms are hard to be supported). In recent years, enforcing access control based on some declarative policies is gaining attention (Kagal, et al., 2003), and has been considered to be especially suitable for the dynamic characteristic of semantic web data (Bonatti, et al., 2006). One intuitive idea to implement the policy-based approach is to rewrite queries by adding some restrictions on them so that the rewritten queries will result only the data which can be accessed according to the access control policies. In this paper, we argue that proper use of ontology can allow more flexible access control on semantic web data to be supported. Also, we present a particular policy-based approach to demonstrate the viability of controlling query-based access to the semantic web data.

The main contributions of this paper include (1) an in-depth study of an ontological approach to specify access control policies as permission or forbiddance to access resources; and (2) algorithms for automatically rewriting queries which is made possible due to the unambiguous semantics of the proposed access control policies. For the latter, in particular, we propose algorithms that, given an ontology-based conjunctive query for web resources, can (a) select the policies which are relevant to the query, (b) extract the restrictions expression from the policies, and (c) rewrite the queries accordingly.

Figure 1. An ontology for the domain of weapon

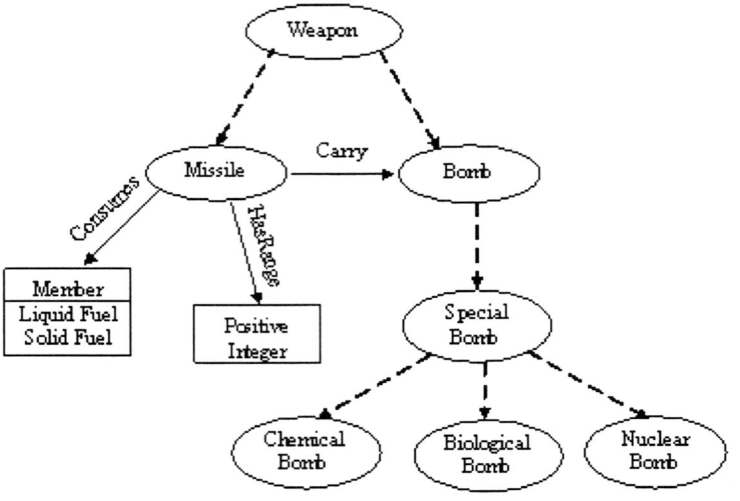

2. A BRIEF OVERVIEW ON SEMANTIC WEB

The vision of the Semantic Web (Berners-Lee, et al., 2001) is to have on-line resources expressed in a machine understandable format so that they can be interpreted and used by software agents. The ultimate goal is to enable Web users to find, share, integrate and thus reason on distributed information or knowledge more effectively. In the Semantic Web, ontology is one of the key concepts where entities and relationships intended to be modeled within some domains are described or posited as a form of knowledge. "Concept" and "role" are the two common terms used to refer to the two modeling elements in ontologies. Concepts (also called classes) refer to the abstract definitions of entities within the domain, whereas roles express the relationships between entities. On-line resources annotated with the labels of concepts are generally termed as *instances* of these concepts. Figure 1 shows a simple ontology about the domain of weapons, where concepts (e.g., "Weapon" and "Missile") are annotated using ellipses, "subclass" roles and other user defined roles (e.g., "HasRange") are annotated using dashed and solid lines respectively, and individual values are annotated using rectangles (e.g., "Liquid Fuel" and "Solid Fuel"). Resources about missiles can then be described accordingly using instances of concepts defined in this ontology.

Several markup languages, e.g., Resource Description Framework - RDF (Brickley & Guha, 2004) and Web Ontology Language - OWL (McGuinness & van Harmelen, 2004), have been proposed for describing ontologies and semantic web data. To retrieve semantic web data described in RDF and OWL, SPARQL

(Prud'hommeaux & Seaborne, 2008) and SPARQL-DL (Sirin & Parsia, 2007) are two examples of the query language proposed for that. In general, a retrieval requirement should first be expressed as a query Q using terms defined in some ontologies. For example, applying the query "$Q(x) \leftarrow Missile(x)$" to the semantic data described using the ontology in Figure 1 will result in all the instance resources under the concept of "Missile".

3. ACCESS CONTROL MODELS FOR SEMANTIC WEB

In this paper, we study how access control models can be applied to safeguard semantic web data when being queried. We propose the use of access authorization policies which specifies the rights of different subjects (e.g., users or other on-line services which can initiate access requests) to gain access to the data.

3.1. Policies for Access Control

Here we first give the formal definition of access control model for semantic web data and the corresponding policies being adopted in this paper.

- **Definition 1.** An access control model for semantic web data can be defined as a tuple $<O, R, S, P>$, where O is an ontology of the concerned domain; R is the set of instance resources annotated using entities in O; S is the set of subjects which can be entities like on-line services requesting to gain access to resources, which can be defined in O as well; and P is the set of policies specifying when some s in S can gain access to some r in R.
- **Definition 2.** Given an access control model $<O, R, S, P>$, a policy p ($p \in$P) is denoted as $<s, v, sign>$, where $s \in$S is a subject requesting to gain access to some resources, v is a **view** that defines a set of tuples with instance resources relevant to p,given as

  $$v(x_1,\ldots,x_n) \leftarrow c_i(x_i),\ldots,c_j(x_j),r_k(x_{k1}, x_{k2}),\ldots,r_m(x_{m1}, x_{m2}), aps$$

  with commas between predicates denoting conjunctive relationships, $c_i,\ldots,c_j$ and $r_k,\ldots,r_m$ denoting some concepts and roles in O, $c_i(x_i)$ referring to concept c_i's instances to be bound with variable x_i, $r_k(x_{k1}, x_{k2})$ referring to relation r_k between variables x_{k1} and x_{k2}, and aps denoting a conjunctive expression that consists of additional predicates such as "=", "<", ">", and $sign \in \{+,-\}$ defines an authorization that grants (for "+") or deny (for "-") subject s access right to the resources as defined by v.

In addition, we define "$c_i(x_i),\ldots,c_j(x_j),r_k(x_{k1}, x_{k2}),\ldots,r_m(x_{m1}, x_{m2})$, *aps*" to be the body expression of *v*, denoted as *body(v)*, and the variables $\{x_1,\ldots, x_n\}$ appearing in *v*'s head as *head_variable(v)*. The variables $\{x_1,\ldots,x_n\}$ in the head of *v* indicate the particular resources allowed for viewing per turple. The body of *v* governs the set of tuples which can be accessed. In particular, $c_i(x_i)$ implies that x_i is restricted to match with only instances of concept c_i and $r_k(x_{k1}, x_{k2})$, with x_i being either x_{k1} or x_{k2}, posts an additional restriction on x_i that it needs to satisfy as well the relation r_k with some other instances which in turn can be restricted as well. Also, the range of x_i can also be constrainted if specified in *aps*. We call *v* a safe view if the variables in *head_variable(v)* also appear in *body(v)*. There also exist cases where a subject is only granted access to some of the variables defined in *body(v)*. By allowing this variation in describing views, more flexible authorization rights can be described. To illustrate the flexibility, the following are some policy examples derived based on Definition 2 and the weapon ontology presented in Figure 1:

p_1: <s, v_1, +>, $v_1(x) \leftarrow$ *Missile(x), Carry(x,y), BiologicalBomb(y)*

p_2: <s, v_2, +>, $v_2(x,y) \leftarrow$ *Missile(x), Carry(x,y), BiologicalBomb(y)*

p_3: <s, v_3, ->, $v_3(x) \leftarrow$ *Missile(x), Carry(x,y), SpecialBomb(y), HasRange(x,z), z>3000*

Policy p_1 depicts the authorization which grants subject *s* the permission to gain access to the resources described as missiles that carry biological bombs as their warheads. Although the variable *y* (for binding with biological bomb instances) appears in the view's body, it does not appear in the view's head and thus the policy does not grant the permission to gain access to the resources of biological bombs. So, while the instances of missiles carrying biological bombs can be retrieved by *s*, the information about what particular biological bombs being carried is not accessible based p_1. Policy p_2 distinguishes from p_1 by retaining variable *y* in the head of its view so that instances of the biological bombs become accessible. Policy p_3 specifies the denial of subject *s* to gain access to the resources about missiles carrying special bombs with their range over 3000 miles.

3.2. Policy Propagation

As it is common for concepts and roles in the subject ontology and domain ontology to possess hierarchical relationships (e.g., "rdf:type" or "rdf:subClassOf" in RDF/RDFS), the authorization defined in a policy for subject *s* to have access to some resources could also be propagated to other subjects and/or resources accordingly (Javanmardi, et al., 2006).

Given a policy <*s*,*v*,*sign*> and the condition that *s'* is an instance or subclass of *s* (later on denoted as $s' \leq s$), a new policy <*s'*,*v*,*sign*> should also be valid. In other words, the authorization right assigned to *s* as defined by *v* should also be propagated and applied to *s'*. When compared with some existing policy propagation mechanisms (Javanmardi et al., 2006), the propagation of the type of policies we proposed is more complicated as the authorizations are here associated with sets of instance resources defined via views instead of explicitly specified individual instances. In addition, one view can be a "constrained" (to be more formally defined later) version of another one. Also, we can have views containing instances in common. How to propagate policies among such "overlapping" views is non-trivial due to the potential policy conflicts and thus the need to resolve the conflicts. In the remaining part of this subsection, we define formally the notion of constrained views. In the next section, we describe how the detection and resolution of conflicting policies caused by "overlapping" views can be handled.

- **Definition 3.** Given views *v* and *v'*, *v'* is a constrained view of *v*, denoted as $v' \preceq v$, if and only if the set of tuples defined by *v'*
  1. is equivalent to that defined by *v*, or
  2. is a subset of that defined by *v*, and/or the element set of each tuple in *v'* is a subset of the counterpart in *v*.

- **Lemma 1.** Given views *v* and *v'*, $v' \preceq v$ if one of the following holds:
  1. *body(v') = body(v)* and *head_variable(v')* ⊆ head_variable(v)
  2. *head_variable(v') = head_variable(v)*, all members in *body(v)* also appear in *body(v')*, and *body(v')* contains additional constraint expressions which do not appear in *body(v)*.
  3. *head_variable(v') = head_variable(v)*, members in *body(v')* and *body(v)* are equivalent except that there exists either (1) one concept $c'(x)$ in *body(v')* which is a subclass of its counterpart in *body(v)*, or (2) one role $r'(x,y)$ in *body(v')* which is a subproperty of its counterpart in *body(v)*.

- *Proof.* Let *R* be the set of tuples defined by *v*. For condition (1) where *body(v') = body(v)* and *head_variable(v')* ⊆ head_variable(v), the set of tuples defined by view *v'* will become $R' = \pi_{head\_variable(v')}(R)$ where π denotes a project operation. Then, it is easy to show that the element set of tuples in *R'* is a subset of that in *R*, and thus $v' \preceq v$ (by definition). For condition (2) where *body(v')* contains more constraints than *body(v)*, *R'* will be a subset of *R* and thus $v' \preceq v$ (by definition). For condition (3) with *body(v')*containing $c'(x) \subseteq c(x)$ or $r'(x,y) \subseteq r(x,y)$, again *R'* will be a subset of *R* which completes the proof. ∎

- **Lemma 2.**"$\preceq$" is a transitive relation, i.e., $v'' \preceq v$ if $v' \preceq v$ and $v'' \preceq v'$ hold.

- *Proof.* Let the sets of tuples defined by v, v' and v'' be R, R' and R'' respectively. If $v' \preceq v$ and $v'' \preceq v'$ hold, one can derive that $R' = \pi\sigma(R)$ and $R'' = \pi'\sigma'(R')$ where π and π' correspond to some project operations and σ, σ' corresponding to some select operations. Then, it can easily be shown that $R'' = \pi'\sigma'(\pi\sigma(R)) = \pi''\sigma''(R)$ for some π'' and σ'', which completes the proof. ■

As the resources associated with view v' are always associated with view v if $v' \preceq v$, the authority of subject s on view v can be propagated to s as its authority on view v'. So the authority propagation for our policies can be refined as: Given a policy $<s,v,sign>$, a new policy $<s,v',sign>$ can be derived if $v' \preceq v$.

The followings are some view examples derived based on the weapon ontology as depicted in Figure 1:

$v_4(x) \leftarrow Missile(x), Carry(x,y), SpecialBomb(y)$

$v_5(x,y) \leftarrow Missile(x), Carry(x,y), SpecialBomb(y)$

$v_6(x,y) \leftarrow Missile(x), Carry(x,y), BiologicalBomb(y)$

$v_7(x,y) \leftarrow Missile(x), Carry(x,y), BiologicalBomb\ (y), HasRange(x,z), z>3000$

Based on Lemma 1, one can easily derive that $v_4 \preceq v_5$, $v_6 \preceq v_5$ and $v_7 \preceq v_6$. Also, one can also derive that $v_7 \preceq v_5$ based on Lemma 2. In addition, given a policy $<s,v_5,sign>$, new policies $<s,v_4,sign>$, $<s,v_6,sign>$ and $<s,v_7,sign>$ can be derived. The only difference between v_4 and v_5 is the absence of variable y in the head of v_4. As $<s,v_5,sign>$ grants/denies subject s the permission to both instance variables x and y in v_5, same authorization rights should be granted to s for variable x in v_4 too.

3.3. Policy Conflict Resolution

Policy conflicts arise when there are policies which assert conflicting authorizations (permission and denial) for a subject to have access to identical resources at the same time.

- **Definition 4.** Two policies are conflicting if one grants and the other denies permission for a subject s to have access to some resource u.

Figure 2. Policy conflicts are caused when a positively and negatively authorized policies overlap

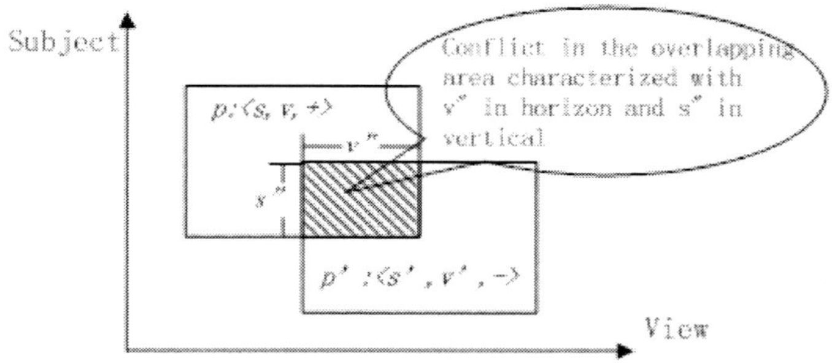

- **Lemma 3.** Policies *p* (<*s*,*v*,+>) and *p'* (<*s'*,*v'*,->) are conflicting if there exist subject *s"* and non-empty view *v"* such that *s"*≤ *s*, *v"* ⪯v and *s"*≤ *s'*, *v"* ⪯v' . (see Figure 2 for an illustration)

- *Proof.* If *s"*≤ *s*, *v"* ⪯v, all instances of *s"* are also instances of *s* and the tuple set defined by *v"* is the subset defined by *v*. So, policy *p* (<*s*,*v*,+>) should be propagated to *s"* for granting it access to resources of *v"*. By the same argument, *p'*(<*s'*,*v'*,->) will deny subject *s"* to gain access to resource of *v"*. So, two policies *p*(<*s*,*v*,+>) and *p'*(<*s'*,*v'*, ->) are conflicting.

For instance, according to the previously described example, policy p_2 grants subject *s* the permission to gain access to resources about missiles carrying biological bombs. Meanwhile, policy p_3 denies subject *s* to have access to resources about missiles carrying special bombs with their range over 3000 miles. Via propagation of p_3, subject *s* should be denied to have access to resources about the missiles carrying biological bombs (a subclass of special bombs) with their range over 3000 miles.

To resolve policy conflicts, some meta-policy rules based on priority or additional knowledge are normally required so as to determine which one prevails in the overlapped area. Then, the prevailing policy is reserved for the authority definition of the overlapped area, and the non-overlapping areas should be "split" and covered by several new policies revised from the originally conflicting ones. Consider the two aforementioned conflicting policies p_2 and p_3. If p_2 is chosen to grant subject *s* permission to gain access to the resources about missiles carrying biological bombs with their range over 3000 miles, p_3 should be revised and split into two policies with the help of policy propagation as follows:

p_3': <s, v_3, ->, $v_3(x) \leftarrow$ *Missile(x), Carry(x,y), ChemicalBomb(y), HasRange(x,z), z>3000*

p_3'': <s, v_3, ->, $v_3(x) \leftarrow$ *Missile(x), Carry(x,y), NuclearBomb(y), HasRange(x,z), z>3000*

Policies p_3' and p_3'' cover the range of policy p_3 except the overlapping range of p_2 and p_3 as the concept "Special Bomb" in Figure 1 is a union of the concepts "Chemical Bomb", "Biological Bomb" and "Nuclear Bomb". Alternatively, if p_3 is chosen to deny subject s to have access to the overlapping area, policy p_2 should be revised to a new policy p_2', given as:

p_2': <s, v_2, +>, $v_2(x,y) \leftarrow$ *Missile(x), Carry(x,y), BiologicalBomb(y), HasRange(x,z), z≤3000.*

It restricts the permission of subject s to have access to resources about missiles whose ranges are *within* 3000 miles to avoid conflicts with policy p_3.

3.4. Access Decision for Policies

Even after we have propagated policy authorizations and resolved policy conflicts, there still exists the possibility that access rights of some subjects on some resources are neither declared as permitted nor denied according to the policies. Jajodia et al. (2001) mentioned two well-known decision mechanisms called "Open" and "Close". Regarding whether subject s can gain access to resource u, we consider a policy <s',v,$\pm$> to be *applicable* if u is included in the resources that can be found in view v and $s \leq s'$. *Open and close decisions* can then be defined as follow:

- **Open Decision:** The access of subject s to resource u is denied only if a negatively authorized policy <s',v,-> is applicable, or allowed otherwise.
- **Close Decision**: The access of subject s to resource u is allowed only if a positively authorized policy <s',v,+> is applicable, or denied otherwise.

Without any policy conflict, the difference between Open and Close decision mechanisms lies on the access rights of subject s to resource u which is neither allowed nor denied by any positive or negative authorization policies. For Open (Close) decision, all the unspecified will be granted (denied) access. In other words, positive (negative) authorization policies need not be taken into consideration for access control under Open (Close) decision mechanism as shown in Figure 3. The

Figure 3. The scopes of access permitted or denied under different decision mechanisms. The access requests falling in the shaded areas are permitted, or denied otherwise.

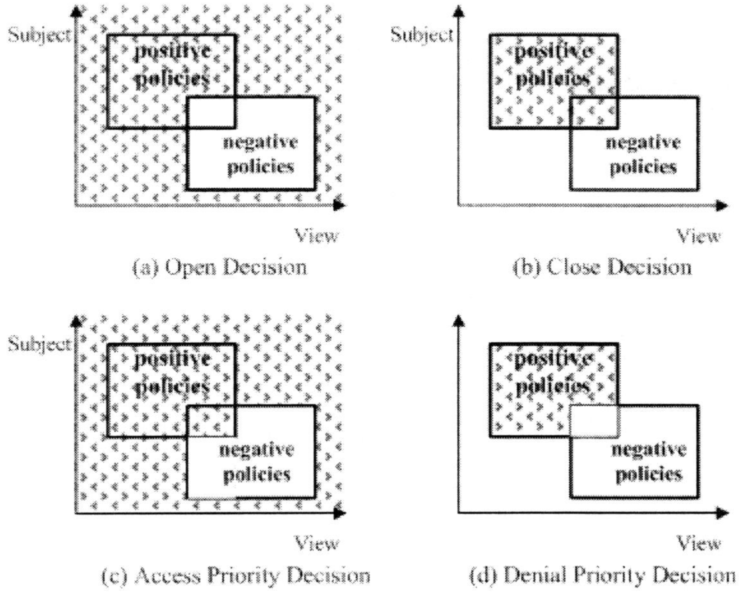

access is denied (allowed) only when a negative (positive) authorization policy can be applied.

Different from open decision and close decision, there also exist some possibilities for making access decisions where both positively authorized policies and negatively authorized policies are considered together. For example, we can have:

- **Access Priority Decision:** *If* a positively authorized policy <*s'*,*v*,+> is applicable *then* the access of subject *s* to resource *u* is allowed, *else if* a negatively authorized policy <*s'*,*v*,-> is applicable *then* this access is denied, *else* this access is allowed.
- **Deny Priority Decision: If** a negatively authorized policy <*s'*,*v*,-> is applicable *then* the access of subject *s* to resource *u* is denied, *else if* a positively authorized policy <*s'*,*v*,+> is applicable *then* this access is allowed, *else* this access is denied.

As the access is allowed by default for access priority decision when there exist no policies applicable, it can be derived that access priority decision will become the same as open decision. By a similar argument, deny priority decision will become equivalent to close decision. This, however, is only true if there exist no conflicts among the policies. If the policy conflicts are not resolved and the access falls onto the area of policy conflicts, the positively authorized policy prevails to allow it under access priority decision while it is denied under open decision; and the negatively authorized policy prevails to deny it under deny priority decision while it is allowed in close decision.

4. QUERY REWRITING FOR ACCESS CONTROL

Based on the declarative access control policies introduced in the previous section, we propose algorithms for rewriting queries on semantic web data so that sensitive information can be protected from unauthorized access via online services.

- **Definition 5.** A semantic web data query Q for retrieving some targeted instance resources takes a similar form as a view (defined in Definition 2), and is defined as:

  $$Q(x_1, \ldots, x_n) \leftarrow c_i(x_i), \ldots, c_j(x_j), r_k(x_{k1}, x_{k2}), \ldots, r_m(x_{m1}, x_{m2}), aps$$

  where $c_i, \ldots, c_j$ and $r_k, \ldots, r_m$ are some concepts and roles defined in the underlying ontology, $c_i(x_i)$ restricts variable x_i to be assigned with only instances of concept c_i, and $r_k(x_{k1}, x_{k2})$ restricts that there should exist an r_k relation between instances of the variables x_{k1}, x_{k2}, and *aps* is a conjunction expression consists of additional predicates such as "=", "<", ">".

The retrieval results based on a query take the form of an n-tuple, and each of the tuples contains instances which satisfies the relationships specified in the body (i.e., the right hand side of the arrow sign) of the query. Figure 4 illustrates w tuples returned (indicated using a box with solid line borders) given a query Q, where each tuple contains n instances corresponding to the variables $x_1, \ldots, x_n$ in the head of Q. If access to the tuples t_1, t_2 and t_w in this result set should be denied except for those indicated using the box with dashed line, say, according to some policy(ies), Q is then expected to be rewritten to a new Q' so as to reflect that. As previously described, the proposed policy representation also allows restriction to be imposed on variables. According to Figure 4, if x_1 and x_2 are restricted according to some policies, the resulting set of tuples will be shrunk as the box with pointed line and Q is then expected to be rewritten as Q'' to reflect that.

Figure 4. An illustration of some rewritten queries

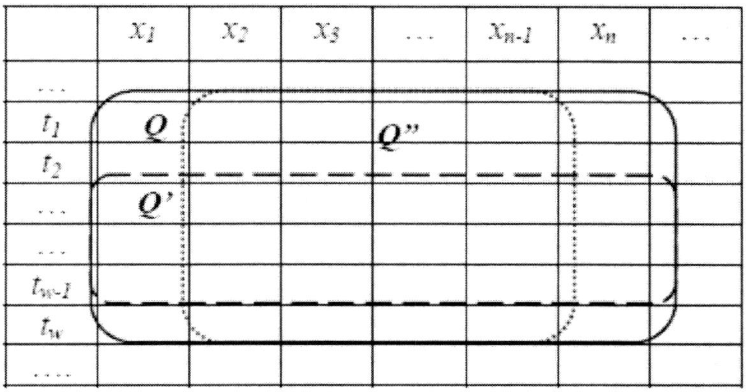

Box 1. Example 1

> **Example 1** (Access Control: Close Decision)
> Query from *s*: $Q_1(x) \leftarrow Missile(x)$
> Policies: e_{11}: $<s,v_1,+>$, $v_1(x) \leftarrow Missile(x), HasRange(x,z), z<3000$

- **Definition 6.** A query Q_1 is said to be **contained** by a query Q_2, denoted by $Q_1 \trianglelefteq Q_2$, if, for all resources, the tuples computed for Q_1 are tuples or reduced tuples (without some members) contained in those for Q_2'. "$\trianglelefteq$" **is a t**ransitive relation.

It can be derived from this definition that $Q_1 \cup Q_2$ are also contained by query Q denoted by $Q_1 \cup Q_2 \trianglelefteq Q$ if $Q_1 \trianglelefteq Q$ and $Q_2 \trianglelefteq Q$.

The query rewriting algorithms to be discussed in the following are to rewrite query Q' of query Q such that the retrieval results respect but only the query but also the access control policies, and thus the relationship $Q' \trianglelefteq Q$ should be hold.

4.1. Query Rewriting Algorithm under Close Decision

Under the close decision mechanism, only positive authorization policies are needed to be considered for access control (see Box 1).

As the decision for access control is close, it can be deduced from the policy e_{11} that subject *s* only has access to the resources about missiles whose ranges are within 3000 miles. Thus, only part of Q_1's results that meets policy e_{11} are allowed

Box 2. Example 2

Example 2 (Access Control: Close Decision)
Query from s: $Q_2(x,y) \leftarrow Missile(x), Carry(x,y), SpecialBomb(y)$
Policies: e_{21}: $<s, v_2, +>$, $v_2(x) \leftarrow Missile(x), HasRange(x,z), z<3000$

Box 3. Example 3

Example 3 (Access Control: Close Decision)
Query from s: $Q_3(x,y) \leftarrow Missile(x), Carry(x,y), SpecialBomb(y)$
Policies: e_{31}: $<s, v_{31}, +>$, $v_{31}(x) \leftarrow Missile(x), HasRange(x,z), z<3000$
e_{32}: $<s, v_{32}, +>$, $v_{32}(y) \leftarrow BiologicalBomb(y)$

to be returned to s. One obvious solution is to add the expression "HasRange(x,z), z<3000" to Q_1's body to form Q'_1:

$$Q'_1(x) \leftarrow \text{Missile}(x), \text{HasRange}(x,z), z<3000,$$

where $Q'_1 \trianglelefteq Q_1$, meaning that Q'_1 will return a subset of Q_1's result (see Box 2).

Compared with Example 1, query Q_2 is for (i) retrieving missile instances which are equipped with special bombs as well as (ii) retrieving the associated special bombs. As there is no policy allowing access to any special bomb (and thus nothing can be matched to the variable y), the result of Q_2 is an empty set. If we change $Q_2(x,y)$ *to* $Q_2(x)$, policy e_{21} becomes applicable and the variable x can be matched with the values such that "HasRange(x,z), z<3000" as that in Example 1:

$$Q'_2(x) \leftarrow \text{Missile}(x), \text{Carry}(x,y), \text{SpecialBomb}(y), \text{HasRange}(x,z), z<3000$$

This kind of variable reduction is useful when one only wants to hide the value of some sensitive variables (see Box 3).

Query Q_3 in Example 3 is to retrieve missile instances which are equipped with "SpecialBomb". There are two positive authorization policies e_{31} and e_{32} governing the query. Policy e_{31} allows only missiles with their ranges within 3000 miles to be accessed (allowed instances for x). Policy e_{32} allows only information related to biological bombs to be accessed (allowed instances for y). With both variables x and y governed by their corresponding positive authorization policies, the query Q_3 can thus be rewritten as:

$$Q'_3(x,y) \leftarrow \text{Missile}(x), \text{Carry}(x,y), \text{BiologicalBomb}(y), \text{HasRange}(x,z), z<3000.$$

Box 4. Example 4

> **Example 4** (Access Control: Close Decision)
> Query from s: $Q_4(x,y) \leftarrow Missile(x), Consume(x,z), Carry(x,y), SpecialBomb(y), z=Liquid\ Fuel;$
> Policies:
> e_{41}: $<s,v_{41},+>$, $v_{41}(x,y) \leftarrow Missile(x), HasRange(x,w), Carry(x,y), NuclearBomb(y), w<3000;$
> e_{42}: $<s,v_{42},+>$, $v_{42}(x) \leftarrow Missile(x), Consume(x,z), HasRange(x,w), w<3000, z = Liquid\ Fuel;$
> e_{43}: $<s,v_{43},+>$, $v_{43}(x) \leftarrow Missile(x), Consume(x,z), z = Solid\ Fuel;$
> e_{44}: $<s,v_{44},+>$, $v_{44}(y) \leftarrow ChemicalBomb(y);$

If the subject s is further restricted to access information associated with the variable x or y, Q_3 could also be rewritten as Q'_{31} and Q'_{32}, given as:

$Q'_{31}(x) \leftarrow$ Missile(x),Carry(x,y),SpecialBomb(y), HasRange(x,z), z<3000

$Q'_{32}(y) \leftarrow$ Missile(x),Carry(x,y),BiologicalBomb(y).

Example 4 (see Box 4) gives another illustration with a query being governed by four positive authorization policies. Applicable policies include e_{41}, e_{42} and e_{44}. Policy e_{43} is not applicable as it conflicts with Q_4 in the sense that it is only related to missiles consuming "Solid Fuel" which is disjointed with "Liquid Fuel" as put in the body of Q_4. The query can thus be rewritten as the union of the following two:

$Q'_{41}(x,y) \leftarrow$ Missile(x), Consume(x,z), Carry(x,y), NuclearBomb(y), HasRange(x,w), z =Liquid Fuel, w<3000;

$Q'_{42}(x,y) \leftarrow$ Missile(x), Consume(x,z), Carry(x,y), ChemicalBomb(y), HasRange(x,w), z =Liquid Fuel, w<3000;

$Q'_{41}(x,y)$ is derived by adding the restrictions described in policy e_{41} to Q. In particular, policy e_{41} restricts variable y to match with not all the instances of "SpecialBomb" but only those of its sub-concept "NuclearBomb", and at the same time with the additional restriction "HasRange(x,w), w<3000" satisfied. Similarly, $Q'_{42}(x,y)$ is derived by adding the restrictions in policies e_{42} and e_{44} to Q. In particular, the concept "SpecialBomb" is restricted to "ChemicalBomb" and additional restriction "HasRange(x,w), w<3000" is added.

The query rewriting process illustrated can be computationally formulated. Three main steps are needed for the rewriting. First, policies which are applicable to the query have to be identified. Then, for each applicable policy, their restriction expressions to be added to the query are computed by comparing the policy's view bodies and the query body. Lastly, different combinations of the restriction expressions are computed (with details to be provided afterwards) so that all the variables in Q's head can be covered and the query can be rewritten accordingly.

The detailed query rewriting algorithm based on the close decision mechanism is presented as follows:

Algorithm 1: Query Rewriting Algorithm under Close Decision

Input

Query form s: $Q(x_1,\ldots,x_n) \leftarrow c_i(x_i),\ldots,c_j(x_j),r_k(x_{k1}, x_{k2}),\ldots,r_m(x_{m1}, x_{m2}),aps$;
Policy set: P
Ontology: O

Output

Rewritten query: $Q'(x_{1'},\ldots,x_{n'}) \leftarrow c_{i'}(x_{i'}),\ldots,c_{j'}(x_{j'}),r_{k'}(x_{k1'},x_{k2'}),\ldots,r_{m'}(x_{m1'},x_{m2'}),aps$;

Process

1. **Create buckets for storing restrictions of applicable policies to the query.** For each variable in Q's head, create a bucket for storing (1) the concepts in the body of the query that the variables are associated, and (2) the restriction expressions of the applicable policies' views.[1]
2. **Identify applicable policies with respect to Q.** For each variable x in Q's head, identify its associate concepts by either locating the concept $c(x)$ directly in Q's body or locating x in one of the roles $r(x_{k1}, x_{k2})$ from which the concept of x can be deduced based on the ontological description in O. Also, apply the same concept identification step to the variables defined in the view's head of each positive authorization policy p (<s', v, +>) in P where $s \leq s'$. Then, try to establish a semantic match between each variable, say x, in Q and those in v, and replace the label of the corresponding variable in v by x. Let this kind of semantic match between variables be Θ. In addition, ensure that there is no conflict found between the bodies of Q and the view of p so that p is identified as an applicable policy for Q; or p will be not applicable and can be ignored. With all the previous checking passed, add v to the "Views" slot of x's bucket created in Step 1 to prepare for restriction expression extraction. In the sequel, the view's body after the variable replacement is denoted as Θ(body(v))).
3. **Derive restriction expressions from the applicable policies and fill up the corresponding buckets.** For each applicable policy identified in Step 2, compare Θ(body(v)) with Q's body to derive the following two types of restrictions on Q and then add the restriction expressions to its corresponding buckets:

a. **Subsumption Restriction:** The scope of each c_i (r_k) in Q should be further restricted if some sub-concept $c_{i'}$ (sub-role $r_{k'}$) is found to appear in Θ(body(v)). Once identified, add the annotation "$c_i \rightarrow c_{i'}$"(or "$r_k \rightarrow r_{k'}$") in "Subsumption Restriction" column of the bucket(s) of v.

b. **Additional Restriction:** After the subsumption restrictions are handled, locate the remaining expressions in Θ(body(v)) that have not been matched and add them to the "Additional Restriction" column of the bucket(s) of v.

4. **Collect appropriate restriction expressions from the buckets and rewrite the query by adding them to the query body.** In the buckets, find a minimal set of views $\{v_1,\ldots,v_u\}$ such that all variables in Q's head are covered[2]. If there exists any conflict among the restrictions covered by the minimal view, the view should be ignored and the next minimal set of views will be checked again until it is conflict-free. Then, extract all subsumption restrictions and additional restrictions from these views' buckets and rewrite Q as follow:

a. Replace c_i or r_k in Q's body with the greatest lower bound[3] of $c_{i'}$ or $r_{k'}$ among all subsumption restrictions "$c_i \rightarrow c_{i'}$" or "$r_k \rightarrow r_{k'}$" in the buckets of the minimal view set.

b. Add all the "Additional Restriction" expressions in the buckets of this view set to Q's body to give Q'.

Repeat this step with different minimal sets of views to get all possible Q', and return $Q' = \cup Q'$ as the output.

5. **If Step 4 fails, check if Q can be rewritten with a reduced variable set so that some results can still be obtained.** If it is impossible to find a view set that can cover all variables in Q's head according to the buckets created, the query rewriting will not be possible. There is an option that the query system can be designed to identify some rewritten version of Q with some column(s) of the returned tuple removed. Assume that $\{x_1,\ldots,x_w\}$ is a maximal subset of variables in Q's head where a minimal view set $\{v_1,\ldots,v_u\}$ can be found to cover them, try to construct the body of rewriting query Q' for reduced variable set $\{x_1,\ldots,x_w\}$ in Q's head as in Step 4.

Repeat this step to find all such Q', and return $Q' = \cup Q'$ as the output.

6. **If Step 5 still fails after all the variables being removed from Q's head, return Φ.** According to Example 4, Q_4's head contains two variables x and y. v_{41}, v_{42} and v_{43} are related to the variable x indicating that the resources to match with are under the concept of "Missile", and v_{41} and v_{44} are related to the variable y indicating the resources to match with are under the concept of "SpecialBomb" (as shown in the second column of Table 1). v_{41} is then added to variable x's bucket with the subsumption restriction "SpecialBomb → NuclearBomb" and the additional restriction "HasRange(x,w), w<3000"

Table 1. The buckets created for rewriting Q_4 in Example 4

	Concept	Views		
			Subsumption Restriction	**Additional Restriction**
x	Missile	v_{41}	SpecialBomb → NuclearBomb	HasRange(x,w), w<3000
		v_{42}		HasRange(x,w), w<3000
y	SpecialBomb	v_{41}	SpecialBomb → NuclearBomb	HasRange(x,w), w<3000
		v_{44}	SpecialBomb → ChemicalBomb	

inserted. There is no need to add v_{43} as "z = Solid Fuel" in v_{43} and "z = Liquid Fuel" in Q_2 conflicts with each other. View v_{41} covers also the variable y and is inserted to its buckets. In a similar manner, as v_{42} covers x and v_{44} covers y, the subsumption and additional restrictions are added to the corresponding buckets, as shown in Table 1. For this example, there are two minimal sets of views, including $\{v_{41}\}$ and $\{v_{42}, v_{44}\}$. Rewriting Q_4 according to the restrictions from corresponding buckets of the two minimal sets of views gives Q'_{41} and Q'_{42} respectively as previously presented. The query $Q_4' = Q'_{41} \cup Q'_{42}$ is then the final output.

It is to be noticed that the idea of this algorithm comes from the bucket algorithm in the area of answering queries with views for databases surveyed by Halevy, (2001). Different from the bucket algorithm, the rewriting queries are not composed of authorized views but are obtained by adding some restrictions to the original ones according to the policies. Also, ontology specific features which are different from those of database schema, such as the "is-a" relation between concepts, are required to be considered in our algorithm.

4.2. Query Rewriting under Open Decision

In contrary to close decision, only negative authorization policies are needed to be considered for access control with open decision mechanism adopted. Query rewriting with negative authorization policies is different from that with positively authorized policies. To illustrate the differences, two more examples are presented in Box 5.

In Example 5, policy e_{51} denies subject s to have access to missiles with their ranges over 3000 miles. Access to the missiles with their ranges within 3000 miles is thus permitted under open decision mechanism. So, Q_5 should be rewritten as follows:

$Q'_5(x) \leftarrow Missile(x), HasRange(x,z), z<3000$

Box 5. Example 5

Example 5. (Access Control: Open Decision) Query from *s*: $Q_5(x) \leftarrow Missile(x)$ Policies: e_{51}: $<s,v_{51},->$, $v_{51}(x) \leftarrow Missile(x), HasRange(x,z), z>=3000$

Box 6. Example 6

Example 6. (Access Control: Open Decision) Query from *s*: $Q_6(x,y) \leftarrow Missile(x), Carry(x,y), SpecialBomb(y);$ Policies: e_{61}: $<s,v_{61},->$, $v_{61}(x,y) \leftarrow Missile(x), Consume(x,z), Carry(x,y), SpecialBomb(y), z = Liquid\ Fuel;$ e_{62}: $<s,v_{62},->$, $v_{62}(x) \leftarrow Missile(x), HasRange(x,w), w>3000;$ e_{63}: $<s,v_{63},->$, $v_{63}(y) \leftarrow NuclearBomb(y);$

In Example 6 (see Box 6), all policies e_{61}, e_{62} and e_{63} are applicable and should be considered in rewriting Q_6. Based on policy e_{61}, information related to missiles carrying special bombs and consuming "Liquid Fuel" is NOT ALLOWED for access. Based on policy e_{62}, information related to missiles with their range larger than 3000 miles are NOT ALLOWED for access. Also, based on policy e_{63}, missiles carrying nuclear bombs are NOT ALLOWED. The overall set of instances whose access is NOT ALLOWED can be specified by the disjunction of the three "NOT ALLOWED" conditions. For providing access control to the query, the constraints to be directly added should be specifying the *allowable* range of instances. For this open decision case, the allowable range is formed by taking the conjunction of the negation of the restrictions derived from the negative policies. Referring to Example 6, the restriction expressions to be added to the query should be the conjunction of "missiles carrying special bombs and NOT consuming Liquid Fuel", "missiles with their range within 3000 miles", and "missiles carrying special bombs which are NOT nuclear bombs".

As "NOT nuclear bombs" can result in either "BiologicalBomb" or "ChemicalBomb" based on the ontology *O*, Q_6 can thus be rewritten as the union of the following:

$Q'_{61}(x,y) \leftarrow Missile(x), Carry(x,y), Consume(x,z), HasRange(x,w), BiologicalBomb(y), z \neq Liquid\ fuel; w \leq 3000;$

$Q'_{62}(x,y) \leftarrow Missile(x), Carry(x,y), Consume(x,z), HasRange(x,w), ChemicalBomb(y), z \neq Liquid\ fuel; w \leq 3000;$

In case no results can be obtained by the union of $Q'_{61}(x,y)$ and $Q'_{62}(x,y)$, the query can be rewritten with further restriction on the variable set in Q_6's head as follow:

$Q'_{63}(x) \leftarrow Missile(x), Carry(x,y), Consume(x,z), HasRange(x,w), SpecialBomb(y), z \neq Liquid\ Fuel; w \leq 3000;$

$Q'_{64}(y) \leftarrow Missile(x), Carry(x,y), BiologicalBomb(y);$

$Q'_{65}(y) \leftarrow Missile(x), Carry(x,y), ChemicalBomb(y);$

To summarize, the query rewriting process involves three main steps for the rewriting. First, policies which are applicable to the query have to be identified. Then, for each applicable policy, compare the policies' view bodies and the query body and extract the policies' their restriction expressions which match with the query. Compute the conjunction of the negations of the restrictions, obtained based on *O*, for rewriting the query.

Algorithm 2: Query Rewriting Algorithm under Open Decision

Input

Query form *s*: $Q(x_1,\ldots,x_n) \leftarrow c_i(x_i),\ldots,c_j(x_j),r_k(x_{k1}, x_{k2}),\ldots,r_m(x_{m1}, x_{m2}),aps$;
Policy set: *P*
Ontology: *O*

Output

Rewritten query $Q'(x_1,\ldots,x_{n'}) \leftarrow c_{i'}(x_{i'}),\ldots,c_{j'}(x_{j'}),r_{k'}(x_{k1'},x_{k2'}),\ldots,r_{m'}(x_{m1'},x_{m2'}),aps'$;

Process

1. **Identify applicable policies and create buckets to store the corresponding restrictions.** For each negative authorization policy (<*s'*, *v*, ->) in *P* that $s \leq s'$ and for each variable *x* in its view's head, check if it is semantically related to some variables in *Q's* head so as to identify all the applicable policies for the query *Q*. For each applicable policy, create a bucket to be used for storing restrictions related to its view *v*. Also, add the variables in *Q*'s head being "governed" by the policy to its "Related Variables" column.
2. **Match applicable policies' view bodies with the query body.** Establish a match Θ between the view *v* of each applicable policy and the query *Q* as those in Algorithm 1.

3. **Derive restriction expressions from the applicable policies and fill up the corresponding buckets.** Compare Θ(body(v)) with Q's body. If all concepts in Θ(body(v)) are found to subsume their matched counterparts in Q's body, the policy will for sure deny all the access to instances matched to the variables in Q, and thus add "Null" to v's bucket; or else, derive the following two kinds of restrictions from Θ(body(v)):
   a. **Subsumption Restriction:** For each c_i (or r_k) in Q with some sub-concept $c_{i'}$ (or sub-role $r_{k'}$) identified in Θ(body(v)), compute based on O a set of concepts {c'} which are subsumed by c_i and disjointed with $c_{i'}$ as its negation. For each element in {c'}, if Q's body contains c_i, add "$c_i \rightarrow c'$ " to the "Restricted Concepts" column of v's bucket; or else add or "+ $c'(x)$".
   b. **Additional Restriction:** After the subsumption restrictions are handled, locate the remaining expressions and compute their negations based on O. Then add them to the column "Restricted Expression" of v's bucket.
4. **Extract appropriate restrictions from buckets and rewrite the query accordingly.** If no "Null" exists in any bucket, rewrite Q as follows: For each row of the buckets, choose one restriction from its "Restricted Concepts" or "Restricted Expression" columns and add it to the column "Restricted Concepts" or "Restricted Expression" in the total bucket accordingly (see Table 2). Repeat that for all the rows. Then, rewrite query Q' according to annotations as "$c \rightarrow c'$" or "+$c'(x)$" in the column "Restricted Concepts" of the total bucket by replacing c with c' or adding "$c'(x)$" in Q's body. Then, add all expressions in the column "Restricted Expression" of the total bucket to Q's body.
   Repeat this step for all the possible choices of extracting the restrictions from the buckets to rewrite Q', and return $Q' = \cup Q'$ as the final rewritten query. Note that this step tries to compute an approximate of the maximally rewritten query.
5. **If Step 4 fails, check if Q can be rewritten with a reduced variable set so that some results can still be obtained.** If it fails to rewrite the query Q with all the variables in Q's head considered, find a rewritten version of Q with a reduced set of variables. In particular, remove all the variables with "Null" in their buckets, and then obtain the rewritten query Q' as Step 4 according to the buckets of the reduced variable set.
   Repeat this step to find all such Q', and return $Q' = \cup Q'$ as the output.
6. **If it fails to find a rewritten query Q' when all variables are removed from Q's head, return Φ.**

The buckets created for query Q_6 are shown in Table 2. As the restricted expressions resulted from applying e_{61} and e_{62} to Q_6's body are "Consume(x,z), z = Liquid fuel" and "HasRange(x,w), w>3000", we add their negated versions "Consume(x,z),

Table 2. The buckets created for rewriting Q_6 in Example 6

View's Buckets			
Views	**Related Variables**	**Restricted Concepts**	**Restricted Expression**
e_{61}:v_{61}	x, y		Consume(x,z), $z \neq$ Liquid Fuel
e_{62}:v_{62}	x		HasRange(x,w), $w \leq 3000$
e_{63}:v_{63}	y	SpecialBomb → BiologicalBomb	
		SpecialBomb → ChemicalBomb	
Total Bucket			
	Restricted Concepts		**Restricted Expression**
	SpecialBomb → BiologicalBomb or SpecialBomb → ChemicalBomb		Consume(x,z),$z \neq$ Liquid Fuel HasRange(x,w), $w \leq 3000$

$z \neq$ Liquid Fuel" and "HasRange(x,w), $w \leq 3000$" to v_{61} and v_{62}'s bucket respectively. As the concept "NuclearBomb" in v_{63}'s body conflicts with its super-concept "SpecialBomb" in Q_6's body, we reduce the concept "SpecialBomb" to the disjunction of "BiologicalBomb" and "ChemicalBomb" which is disjointed with "NuclearBomb" and add them to v_{63}'s bucket. The restricted expressions in v_{41} and are added to the total bucket as there exists no restriction annotation in their "Restricted Concepts" columns. Also, one of the restrictions "SpecialBomb→ BiologicalBomb" and "SpecialBomb→ ChemicalBomb" in v_{63}'s bucket can be added to the total bucket. The union of the two obtained rewritten queries Q'_{61} and Q'_{62} should be the final output.

Note that one crucial step for this algorithm is to compute the negation of the restrictive expressions described in the policy. To compute that using the domain ontology O, the domain experts together with the system administrator with semantic web knowledge have to work together to come up with the definition explicitly. In general, the problem of handling negation of ontology-based expression automatically in general is still open and is out of the scope of this paper.

4.3. Query Rewriting under Access Priority and Deny Priority Decisions

Access priority decision grants access if the access is allowed under either open or close decision. For deny priority decision, it grants access if the access is allowed under both open and close decisions. So, both positively authorized and negatively authorized policies should be taken into consideration, and involved in the corresponding querying rewriting algorithms.

Box 7. Example 7

Example 7. (Access Control: Open Decision / Deny Priority Decision)
Query from s:
$Q_7\,(x,y) \leftarrow$ Missile(x), Carry(x,y), SpecialBomb(y);
Policies:
e_{71}:<s,v,+>, $v_{71}(x,y) \leftarrow$ Missile(x), HasRange(x,w), Carry(x,y), SpecialBomb(y), $w<3000$;
e_{72}: <s,v,->, $v_{72}(x) \leftarrow$ Missile(x), Consume(x,z), z = Liquid Fuel;
e_{73}: <s,v,->, $v_{73}(y) \leftarrow$ NuclearBomb(y);

Referring to Example 7 (see Box 7), the rewritten query under close decision (only positive authorization policies involved) is given as:

$Q'_{71}\,(x,y) \leftarrow$ Missile(x),Carry(x,y),SpecialBomb(y), HasRange(x,w),$w<3000$,

and those under open decision (only negative authorization policies involved) are given as:

$Q'_{72}\,(x,y) \leftarrow$ Missile(x),Carry(x,y),BiologicalBomb(y), Consume(x,z), z = Solid Fuel;

$Q'_{73}\,(x,y) \leftarrow$ Missile(x),Carry(x,y),ChemicalBomb(y), Consume(x,z), z = Solid Fuel;

As all of their results will be granted access under access priority decision, the rewritten query is the disjunction of them: $Q' = Q'_{71} \cup (Q'_{72} \cup Q'_{73})$. However, under deny priority decision, only the results coming from Q'_{71} and $Q'_{72} \cup Q'_{73}$ are allowed for access. So the rewriting query should be a conjunction of them: $Q'_{71} \cap (Q'_{72} \cup Q'_{73})$. The restrictions due to Q'_{71} in fact can be added into the queries Q'_{72} and Q'_{73} so that they can be rewritten as:

$Q''_{72}(x,y) \leftarrow$ Missile(x),Carry(x,y), BiologicalBomb(y), Consume(x,z), z = Solid Fuel, HasRange(x,w),$w<3000$;

$Q''_{73}(x,y) \leftarrow$ Missile(x),Carry(x,y), ChemicalBomb(y), Consume(x,z), z = Solid Fuel, HasRange(x,w),$w<3000$;

The rewritten query of Q under deny priority decision can then be obtained as $Q' = Q''_{72} \cup Q''_{73}$.

The detailed query rewriting algorithms under access/deny priority decision are provided as follow:

Algorithm 3: Query Rewriting Algorithm under Access Priority Decision

Input

Query: $Q(x_1,\ldots,x_n) \leftarrow c_i(x_i),\ldots,c_j(x_j),r_k(x_{k1}, x_{k2}),\ldots,r_m(x_{m1}, x_{m2}),aps$;
Policy set: P
Ontology: O

Output

Rewritten Query Q' of Q on resources of O according to P:
$Q'(x_1,\ldots,x_{n'}) \leftarrow c_{i'}(x_{i'}),\ldots,c_{j'}(x_{j'}),r_{k'}(x_{k1'}, x_{k2'}),\ldots,r_{m'}(x_{m1'}, x_{m2'}),aps'$;

Process

1. Apply the query rewriting algorithm under open decision to Q according to policy set P and obtain the rewritten query Q'_1.
2. Apply the query rewriting algorithm under close decision to Q according to policy set P and obtain the rewriting query Q'_2.
3. Output $Q' = Q'_1 \cup Q'_2$ as the result.

Algorithm 4: Query Rewriting Algorithm under Deny Priority Decision

Input

Query: $Q(x_1,\ldots,x_n) \leftarrow c_i(x_i),\ldots,c_j(x_j),r_k(x_{k1}, x_{k2}),\ldots,r_m(x_{m1}, x_{m2}),aps$;
Policy set: P
Ontology: O

Output

Rewritten Query Q' of Q on resources of O according to P:
$Q'(x_1,\ldots,x_{n'}) \leftarrow c_{i'}(x_{i'}),\ldots,c_{j'}(x_{j'}),r_{k'}(x_{k1'}, x_{k2'}),\ldots,r_{m'}(x_{m1'}, x_{m2'}),aps'$;

Process

1. Apply the query rewriting algorithm under open decision to Q according to policy set P and obtain the rewritten query Q'_1.
2. For each Q'_{1i} in the rewritten query Q'_1 where $Q'_1 = \cup Q'_{1i}$, apply the query rewriting algorithm under close decision to the query Q'_{1i} according to policy set P and obtain the rewritten query Q'_{2i}.
3. Output $Q' = \cup Q'_{2i}$ as the result.

Figure 5. A conceptual system architecture for supporting the proposed access control model

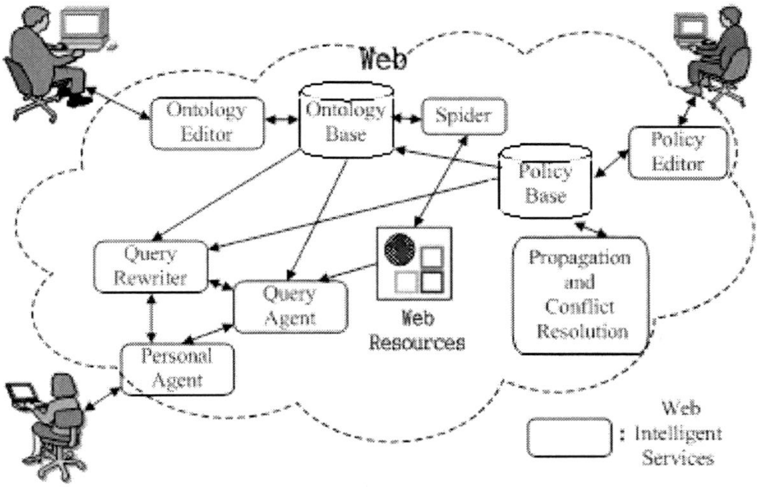

5. A CONCEPTUAL SYSTEM ARCHITECTURE FOR SUPPORTING POLICY-BASED ACCESS CONTROL IN THE SEMANTIC WEB

The policy-based query rewriting mechanisms described so far leverage on the Semantic Web technologies so that more flexible access control can be applied to on-line services. Figure 5 shows a conceptual system architecture illustrating how the proposed mechanisms can be deployed. Users first submit their retrieval requests to the Personal Agent service which translates the requests to queries taking the form as described in Definition 5. Before submitting the query to the Semantic Web data store, the queries should be rewritten by the Query Rewriter service which relies on the policies stored in a separate policy system which implements the query rewriting algorithms. The rewritten queries are then sent to the query agent to get the information of the resources to be retrieved, with the guarantee that all the access control polices once specified in the policy system will automatically be respected.

In order for the conceptual architecture to work, we make a few assumptions. First, we assume the ontologies which define the user concerned domain have been established, where domain experts are normally needed. Also, ontology learning methods also exist and can be integrated with Web spider to support semi-automatic ontology creation. Given the well-defined ontologies, the instance resources found in the Web can be annotated accordingly. Besides, we also assume that the access control requirements for the online resources are managed by some policy editors who have the expertise of specifying rule-based policies as what being described in this paper and should know clearly the implication of those policies. This is especially important in service-oriented environments as the deployment in principle can take effect in real time and the policies, if mis-specified, will affect all the systems which are consuming the controlled services. In general, intelligent software tools for helping the ontology and policy editors to validate their work before deployment should be of great help.

6. RELATED WORK

Policies are often used to define the authorities to access for security requirements in access control. There are roughly two types of policy languages, namely role-based and rule-based.

Role-base polices are intuitive as they endow or deprive subjects of the role with the rights to access objects. For example, the policies for access control in (Jajodia, et al., 2001) are in the form of $<o,s,\pm a>$ stating whether an authorization subject s can (for "$+a$") or cannot (for "$-a$") execute an action a on an authorization object o. As the subjects and objects are organized hierarchically according to the "is-a" relation between them, the policies can be propagated among them.

Rule-based policies use rules to define the authorization under certain conditions. Rei (Kagal, et al., 2003) is one of the representative ones where a policy language based on OWL-Lite was adopted for trust and security management in a pervasive computing environment. Based on the language, access control policies for allowable actions on particular resources can be expressed as rule-like constraints. In contrast with the rule-based policies as Rei (Kagal, et al., 2003), views on instance resources are newly introduced in this work to enhance the flexibility of the access control model. To support the introduction of views, a number of policy management issues have been carefully reconsidered in this paper.

For research work related to privacy in the Semantic Web, the use of policies languages for access control has been advocated in the literature. Bonatti, et al., (2006) discussed the requirements and research issues for semantic web policies. Also, Duma, et al., (2007) compared six prominent policy languages, namely Protune, Rei, Ponder, Trust-X, KeyNote and P3P-APPEL with respect to the needs to protect sensitive data in the context of the Semantic Web, and made some observations that aspects like trust and cooperation need further advancement. Damiani, et al., (2004) extended the XACML language with RDF statements for semantic web data, with an architecture called OntoPassport proposed.

Instead of studying merely access control policies languages, there also exists work studying ways to control access to ontologies for the Semantic Web. For instance, Li and Atluri (2003) proposed a policy-based concept-level access control model, in which the control is for access to concept-level entities, such as classes in ontologies. Jain et al. (2006) presented an access control model of secure RDF for protecting the RDF data. Policy propagation and conflict resolution are also addressed in their paper. Jeong et al. (2007) proposed the use of databases to store the OWL ontologies and users can be controlled to have access to only part of ontologies (also called ontology views). Kaushik et al. (2005) proposed a method, in which part of the ontology was suggested to be removed, hidden or modified to protect them from illegal access. Different from security control on ontologies themselves, our work addresses the security issue of resources which are specified using ontologies. Javanmardi et al. (2006) studied policy-based protection of concepts and instances in ontologies. Our work is different by the fact that we use the notion of views to specify the objects to be protected.

Query writing with views is an effective way for implementing access control in relational databases. Halevy (2001) presented a survey on techniques for answering queries using views, in which the bucket algorithm is described. Rizvi et al. (2004) proposed techniques to rewrite SQL queries according to authorized views. Lakshmanan et al. (2006) studied query answering using views for tree pattern queries. Cautis et al. (2007) presented an XML query rewriting approach for distributed access control, in which queries are modified when they are delivered between agents. Abel et al. (2007) proposed an algorithm for rewriting *SeRQL* queries with policies. It gets all restrictions for the triples in the from-clause of the queries and adds them to the where-clause of the original queries to obtain the rewritten queries. Compared with these methods, our queries are rule-based, and our algorithm considers views covering the required on-line resources.

7. CONCLUSION AND FUTURE WORK

In this paper, we explained the importance of providing the more flexible policy-based access control in a service-oriented environment to safe-guard sensitive information embedded in Semantic Web data not to be disclosed via ontology-based query services. In particular, we presented an access control model, in which authorizations for accessing the resources are defined using rule-based policies. The notion of views on instance resources is adopted in defining policies and the corresponding policy propagation and conflict resolution issues are both addressed in this paper. For controlling sensitive information from leaking via answers to users' queries, a query rewriting approach based on the access control policies is then proposed. Queries rewritten using the proposed algorithms can have their returned results free from policy violated resources information. For future work, we will implement a prototype based on the proposed query rewriting algorithms.

ACKNOWLEDGMENT

This work is partially supported by HKBU Faculty Research Grant (FRG/07-08/II-75).

REFERENCES

Abel, F., Coi, J., Henze, N., Koesling, A. W., Krause, D., & Olmedilla, D. (2007). Enabling advanced and context-dependent access control in RDF Stores. In *Proceedings of the Sixth International Semantic Web Conference* (pp. 1-14).

Beeri, C., Levy, Y. A., & Rousset, M.-C. (1997): Rewriting queries using views in description logics. Symposium on Principles of Database Systems. In A. Mendelzon & Z. M. Özsoyoglu (Eds.), In *Proceedings of the sixteenth ACM SIGACT-SIGMOD-SIGART symposium on Principles of database systems* (pp. 99-108). New York: ACM Press.

Bertino, E., Buccafurri, F., Ferrari, E., & Rullo, P. (1999): A Logical Framework for Reasoning on Data Access Control Policies. In B. Werner (Ed.), In *Proceedings of the 12th IEEE Computer Security Foundations Workshop (CSFW-12)* (pp. 175-189). Los Alamitos, CA: IEEE Computer Society Press.

Bonatti, P. A., Duma, C., Fuchs, N., Nejdl, W., Olmedilla, D., Peer, J., et al. (2006). Semantic Web policies - A discussion of requirements and research issues. In Y. Sure, & J. Domingue (Eds.), In *Proceedings of the European Semantic Web Conference* (pp. 712-724).

Brickley, D., & Guha, R. V. (2004). *RDF Vocabulary Description Language 1.0: RDF Schema.* Retrieved from http://www.w3.org/TR/rdf-schema/

Broekstra, J., Kampman, A., & van Harmelen, F. (2002). Sesame: A generic architecture for storing and querying RDF and RDF Schema. In I. Horrocks, & J. Hendler (Eds.), *Proceedings of the First International Semantic Web Conference* (pp. 54-68). Sardinia, Italy: Springer Verlag.

Cautis, B. (2007). Distributed access control: A privacy-conscious approach. In *Proceedings of the Twelfth ACM Symposium on Access Control Models and Technologies* (pp. 61-70). New York: ACM Press.

Damiani, E., De Capitani di Vimercati, S., Fugazza, C., & Samarati, P. (2004). Extending policy languages to the Semantic Web. In *Proceedings of the International Conference on Web Engineering* (pp. 330-343).

Duma, C., Herzog, A., & Shahmehri, N. (2007). Privacy in the semantic web: What policy languages have to offer. In *Proceedings of the Eighth IEEE International Workshop on Policies for Distributed Systems and Networks* (pp. 109-118).

Halevy, A. Y. (2001). Answering queries using views: A survey. *The VLDB Journal, 10*(4), 270–294. doi:10.1007/s007780100054

Heflin, J., Hendler, J., & Luke, S. (1999). *SHOE: A knowledge representation language for internet applications*. (Tech. Rep. No. 99-71). College Park, MD: University of Maryland, Dept. of Computer Science.

Jain, A., & Farkas, C. (2006). Secure resource description framework: An access control model. In *Proceedings of the Eleventh ACM Symposium on Access Control Models and Technologies* (pp. 121-129).

Jajodia, S., Samarati, P., Sapino, M. L., & Subrahmaninan, V. S. (2001). Flexible support for multiple access control policies. *ACM Transactions on Database Systems, 26*(2), 214–260. doi:10.1145/383891.383894

Javanmardi, S., Amini, M., & Jalili, R. (2006). An access control model for protecting Semantic Web resources. In *Proceedings of the Second International Semantic Web Policy Workshop*.

Jeong, D., Jing, Y., & Baik, D.-K. (2007). Access control model based on RDB security policy for OWL ontology. In Y. Shi, et al. (Eds.), In *Proceedings of the Seventh International Conference on Computational Science* (pp. 720-727).

Kagal, L., Finin, T., & Joshi, A. (2003). A policy based approach to security for the Semantic Web. In *Proceedings of the Second International Semantic Web Conference* (pp. 402-418). New York: ACM Press.

Kaushik, S., Wijesekera, D., & Ammann, P. (2005). Policy-based dissemination of partial web-ontologies. In *Proceedings of the 2005 Workshop on Secure Web Services* (pp. 43-52).

Lakshmanan, V. S. L., Wang, H., & Zhao, Z. (2006). Answering tree pattern queries using views. In *Proceedings of the Thirty Second International Conference on Very Large Databases* (pp. 571-582).

Li, Q., & Atluri, V. (2003). Concept-level access control for the Semantic Web. In *Proceedings of the 2003 ACM Workshop on XML Security* (pp. 94-103). New York: ACM Press.

McGuinness, D. L., & van Harmelen, F. (2004). *OWL Web Ontology Language Overview*. Retrieved from http://www.w3.org/TR/owl-features/

Prud'hommeaux, E., & Seaborne, A. (2008). *SPARQL Query Language for RDF*. Retrieved from http://www.w3.org/TR/rdf-sparql-query/

Rizvi, S., Mendelzon, A., Sudarshan, S., & Roy, P. (2004). Extending query rewriting techniques for fine-grained access control. In *Proceedings of 2004 ACM SIGMOD International Conference on Management of Data* (pp. 551-562). New York: ACM Press.

Sirin, E., & Parsia, B. (2007). SPARQL-DL: SPARQL Query for OWL-DL. In *Proceedings 3rd OWL Experiences and Directions Workshop (OWLED-2007)*.

Tim Berners-Lee, T., Hendler, J., & Lassila, O. (2001). The Semantic Web. *Scientific American, May*.

Wilkinson, K., Sayers, C., Kuno, H., & Reynolds, D. (2003). Efficient RDF storage and retrieval in Jena2. In *Proceeding of the First International Workshop on Semantic Web and Databases* (pp. 35-43).

ENDNOTES

1. See Table 1 for an illustration where each row corresponds to the bucket of a variable, and the concepts and the restriction expressions are stored in two separate main columns.
2. A set of views $\{v_1,\ldots,v_u\}$ cover the variable x if x appears in the head of any view v_i in this set. The minimal set of views for covering all variables is the view set that can't cover all variables any more if any view is removed from this view set. We can use a greedy algorithm to find the minimal set of views to cover all variables. It repeats the process that adding more view to current view set if the new view set covers more variables compared to the old one until the view set covers all variables.
3. The greatest lower bound of two concepts is considered as the most general sub-concept which is subsumed by both of them, e.g., "Special Bomb" is the greatest lower bound of the concepts "Bomb" and "Special Bomb" according to the ontology shown in Figure 1.

This work was previously published in International Journal of Organizational and Collective Intelligence, Volume 1, Issue 2, edited by Hideyasu Sasaki, pp. 46-66, copyright 2010 by IGI Publishing (an imprint of IGI Global).

Chapter 7
An Auction Mechanism Considering Seat Reservations in Movie Theater Services

Nariaki Nishino
The University of Tokyo, Japan

Koji Fukuya
The University of Tokyo, Japan

Kanji Ueda
National Institute of Advanced Industrial Science and Technology, Japan & The University of Tokyo, Japan

ABSTRACT

This paper proposes a new auction mechanism with seat reservations in movie theaters using an interdisciplinary approach. In movie theater services, the movie price is generally fixed, not depending on the quality of contents or the theater seat. It implies that such a service mechanism by fixed pricing might not reflect the value of movie contents. In this study, a new mechanism of theater services is proposed introducing the Vickrey–Clarke–Groves (VCG) mechanism and Gale–Shapley (GS) mechanism, which present effectiveness in the field of mechanism design. First derived is the theoretical predictions of equilibrium and how the mechanism works using experiments with human subjects. In addition, agent-based simulation is conducted using agents that make the decisions observed in the experiments. Consequently, the results present the validity of the proposed mechanism, showing an increase in the social surplus.

DOI: 10.4018/978-1-61350-135-1.ch007

INTRODUCTION[1]

Scientific studies of services have attracted attention over the years. According to one study of the relevant literature (Spohrer & Maglio, 2008), service innovations can impact service productivity and service quality. Especially in Japan, the government has initiated national projects for the promotion of service productivity and service innovation (Takenaka et al., 2009).

In addition, service engineering is proposed as a novel engineering method to evaluate and design services: Arai and Shimomura developed a service CAD system (Arai & Shimomura, 2004, 2005) and proposed method for evaluating services using service Quality Function Deployment (QFD) (Shimomura et al., 2009). Aurich et al. (2004) specifically examined the design of services from a product life-cycle perspective. Furthermore, the "Industrial Product–Service Systems (IPS2)" collaborative research project is established and several studies are conducted (Meier, 2010). The concept of "service-dominant logic" is proposed by Vargo and Akaka (2009).

This study addresses services in movie theaters as an actual example of service studies. Movies are a good example of a service and are now known worldwide as a popular leisure activity. In the movie theater service industry, both popular movies and uninteresting movies are usually provided at the same price. Moreover, especially in the case of Japan, that price is high. Therefore, it is doubtful whether the value of movies is reflected appropriately in the movie price. In general, according to market mechanisms, prices should be high if goods or services are in high demand, but prices should be low in the case of unpopular ones.

Another characteristic of movie theater services is that consumers receive services at seats in theaters. In addition to pricing, a problem is how seats in theaters are allocated according to consumer preferences. This study proposes a new movie service mechanism by considering seat allocation. In other words, we apply good findings in the field of mechanism design (Maskin, 2008) to the circumstances related to movie theater services. Then we examine the effectiveness of the proposed service mechanism using the methodology of experimental economics (Smith, 1976) and agent-based simulation.

This paper is organized as follows: the second section explains the approach for service design. The third section presents formulation of a basic framework of movie theaters. In the fourth section, the proposed mechanism is presented; the fifth section derives the Nash equilibrium of the proposed mechanism. Then, the sixth section presents a description of our economic experiment and its result. The seventh section presents agent-based simulation. Finally, the last section concludes the presentation of our analyses with a few remarks.

APPROACH FOR SERVICE DESIGN

An interdisciplinary approach is said to be necessary for service design (Takenaka et al., 2009). This study specifically examines experimental economics, mechanism design, and agent-based simulation. Each topic and its relation of service design are explained in the following subsections.

Experimental Economics

Economic experimentation has recently been used for social science study. Economic studies that adopt this experimental method are established as experimental economics (Smith, 1976, 1982; Friedman & Sunder, 1994; Kagel & Roth, 1995). Just as engineers and scientists do in other fields, an experimenter can design an economic experiment to examine a particular theory or an economic system. In an economic experiment, the experimenter constructs a laboratory environment under carefully controlled conditions. An important point is that subjects who are recruited for experiments are promised a monetary reward according to their performance in the experiments. According to the monetary reward, economic incentives are given to subjects. The experimenter observes their actions in the experiment to verify whether those actions reflect the theory as it was hypothesized.

Particularly in service studies, the methodology of experimental economics is useful. A salient issue in service design is the economic mechanism of services. Whether the proposed service is profitable or not is an absolutely critical problem. With respect to this problem, experiments based on experimental economics provide several new perspectives.

Mechanism Design

According to Maskin (2008), the theory of mechanism design can be regarded as the "engineering" side of economic theory. Mechanism design theory was initiated by Hurwicz (1972) and refined by Maskin (1999) and other researchers. The main goal in mechanism design is to design rules of a game or system to achieve a socially preferred outcome, even if each agent might be self-interested. Mechanism design theory generally uses the technique of game theory, and compares different rules or systems in terms of the equilibrium outcomes of these games. Mechanism design has produced numerous important insights in widely various applied contexts, influencing economic policy as well as market institutions.

When designing a new service, mechanism design theory offers deep insights in terms of service structure or the economic side of service. This approach can yield theoretical findings of incentive systems in service. Mechanism design is anticipated as a powerful tool for service design.

Agent-Based Simulation

Agent-based modeling is effective to clarify the process of service provision because it can readily include heterogeneity in individual preferences and its interactions (Takenaka & Ueda, 2008; Rahmandad, 2008). For example, agent-based simulations enable construction of a model in which economic agents act with bounded rationality or mutually interact in local behavior. Economic theory itself cannot address such factors easily. This approach yields precise insight into decision making in social systems including the process of service provision.

In this study, agent-based simulation is used for evaluating the proposed mechanism related to movie theater service. Using results of experiments with human subjects, agent models of several types are constructed. We simulate the mechanism and examine the effectiveness in the environment where those multiple agents are involved.

FORMULATION OF BASIC FRAMEWORK

The framework includes n consumers and a movie theater. The movie theater provides movies of one kind; the theater has M seats. Consumers obtain utility by enjoying the movie, whereas the theater earns a profit through consumers' payments for movie tickets. The details are explained as follows.

Movie Theater

The theater has l types of seats. Set L is defined as L=$\{1,2,\ldots,l\}$. The total number of seats is

$$M = \sum_{k \in L} m_k , \tag{1}$$

where m_k stands for the number of seats of type $k(\in L)$. The profit is represented as

$$\Pi=\beta\times n_b, \tag{2}$$

where β stands for price of a movie ticket and n_b stands for the number of consumers who bought a movie ticket. For simplicity, we assume that movies are provided at no cost.

Consumers

The set of consumers is defined as N={1,2,...,n}. Each consumer has a different preference for the type of seats; the preference is expressed as a sequence of the type of seats. Let $p_{ij} \in L$ represent the type of seats that consumer i likes the jth best; consequently, consumer i's preference can be described as $(p_{i1},p_{i2},\ldots,p_{il})$. For example, if L={1,2,3}, then a preference is expressed as (p_{i1},p_{i2},p_{i3})=(1,2,3), which means that the consumer likes the seats in order of type 1, type 3, and type 2.

In addition, each consumer has a reservation price for the movie and is willing to pay, at most, the reservation price. Consumer i's reservation price for the jth best type of seats is R_{ij}. That consumer's utility U_i ($i \in N$) is formulated as

$$U_i = \begin{cases} R_{ij} - \beta & (\text{If enjoying the movie}) \\ 0 & (\text{Otherwise}) \end{cases}. \quad (3)$$

PROPOSED AUCTION MECHANISM WITH SEAT RESERVATIONS

We propose a new mechanism in movie theater services. The mechanism consists of two parts: an auction to determine the movie price and seat-allocation to satisfy the consumers' request. The pricing and the seat-allocation are based on two famous mechanisms in the field of mechanism design: the Vickrey–Clarke–Groves (VCG) mechanism (Vickrey, 1961; Clarke, 1971; Groves, 1973) and the Gale–Shapley (GS) mechanism (Gale & Shapley, 1962). The VCG mechanism is applied to the pricing process; the GS mechanism is applied to a seat-allocation process. The mechanisms are explained in subsequent subsections.

Price Determination with VCG Mechanism

The price is determined using the VCG mechanism, which is a kind of auction that is famous for simultaneously satisfying incentive compatibility and Pareto efficiency. In the field of mechanism design, incentive-compatibility is defined as the strategy by which a player reporting private information is the dominant strategy for all players. In other words, revealing private information truthfully is the best strategy. An allocation is called Pareto efficient if no other feasible allocation makes both parties better off.

As described in the previous section, we assume that the movie theater provides movies of one kind. Accordingly, the price-determination auction, which uses the VCG mechanism, is described simply as follows.

1. Consumer i ($\in N$) bids price b_i for the movie
2. M consumers win in descending order of the bid prices
3. The M+1 th bid price in descending order is determined as the movie price β.

Here, a sealed bid auction is assumed: consumers cannot observe other bids. By this auction, M winners acquire movie tickets at the same price β, although they bid different prices. Additionally, we assume b_{max} as the upper limitation of bidding prices and assume that b_{max} is higher than any reservation price.

Seat Allocation Using GS Mechanism

After determining the movie price, the seat allocation process is conducted. We regard the seat-allocation as a matching problem between consumers and seats. To realize effective matching, a GS mechanism that can realize stable matching is introduced. The mechanism that is applied to a seat-allocation problem is explained in the following.

Step 0: First, each consumer and the movie theater declare their preferences. Concretely, consumers declare the order of favorite seat types and the movie theater declares the order of preferred consumers. In this case, we assume that the theater prefers consumers who bid high prices.

Step 1: Each consumer is temporarily allocated based on the first of the declared order. However, if the allocated consumers for the same type exceed the number of the seat types, consumers who bid higher prices are given priority. Consumers who bid a lower price are dropped from the temporal allocation. The outcome is determined randomly if consumers bid the same price.

Step *k*: Consumers who are dropped in step $k-1$ are reallocated to the next one in the declared order. Even if they are already allocated to other consumers, the seat types are reallocated in descending order of the bidding price.

Final Step: After these steps are repeated, if no consumer is dropped from the allocation, then the allocation is finished.

THEORETICAL EQUILIBRIUM

In this section, we derive the Nash equilibrium under complete information, which is defined in the field of game theory as a situation where each player knows all game-related information such as the game rules, possible actions, their payoffs, etc. Let us define some variables:

- Set of consumer *i*'s reservation price: $R_i=\{R_{ij} \mid j \in L$.
- Set of consumer *i*'s bidding action: $B_i=\{b_i | 0 \leq b_i \leq b_{max}\}$.
- Consumer *i*'s declaration of the order of favorite seat types: $c_i=(c_{i1},c_{i2},\ldots,c_{ij}) \in C_i$, where $0 \leq j \leq l$ and C_i is a set of c_i.
- Consumer *i*'s honest declaration of the order of favorite seat types: $c_i^j=(p_{i1},p_{i2},\ldots,p_{ij})$. c_i^j means that consumer *i* honestly declares the order of favorite seat types from the best to the *j*th best.
- Mapping from (R_i,β) to the number of elements in R_i which are greater than or equal to β: $\Gamma(R_i,\beta)$.
- Consumer *i*'s strategy: $s_i=(b_i,c_i) \in B_i \times C_i \equiv S_i$.
- Strategy profile: $s=s_1,s_2,\ldots,s_n) \in \prod_{i \in N} S_i \equiv S$.

Then, the Nash equilibrium is described as the following proposition.

*Proposition 1*$s^* \in S$ is the Nash equilibrium if s^* satisfies all the following conditions:

- **Condition 1:** The number of consumers who bid b_{max} equals *M*.
- **Condition 2:** The consumer who bids b_{max} declares the order of favorite seat types as $c_i = c_i^{\Gamma(R_i,\beta^*)}$, where β^* stands for the movie price derived by VCG mechanism under the strategy profile s^*.
- **Condition 3:** At least one of R_{ij} of the consumers who bids b_{max} is greater than or equal to β^*.
- **Condition 4:** The strategy of the consumer who bids other than b_{max} is that $0 \leq b_i^* \leq \min_i\{R_{i1} \mid b_i^* = b_{\max}\}$ and $c_i^* = c^{any}$. Herein, c^{any} means that the order of seat types does not matter and that every order of seat types is involved.

Proof[2]: We define $s_{-1}=(s_1,\ldots,s_{i-1},s_{i+1},\ldots,s_n)$ as the strategy profile without s_i, and $U_i(b_i,c_i,s_{-i})$ as the utility of consumer *i* in the strategy profile $s=(b_i,c_i,s_{-i})$.

First, we consider the set of the consumers who bid b_{max}: $N_1 \subset N$. The expected utility is decreasing if the consumer in N_1 lowers the bidding price from b_{max} because the number of other consumers who bid b_{max} is $M-1$ by condition (1) and accordingly the consumer who lowers the bidding price surely reduces the priority of seat allocation by the GS mechanism. Because the possibility that the good seat is allocated is decreasing, the expected utility is also lowered. Accordingly,

$$U_i(b_{max},c_i,s_{-i}) \geq U_i(b_i,c_i,s_{-i}) \text{ for } 0 \leq b_i \leq b_{max}. \tag{4}$$

This holds for all $i \in N_1$ under the conditions of Proposition 1. Therefore, b_{max} is the best response for the consumers in N_1. On the other hand, the honest declaration c_i^j weakly dominates the dishonest declarations by the characteristics of GS mechanism. Consequently, the dishonest ones can be eliminated. In addition, c_i^j maximizes the expected utility in case of $j=\Gamma(R_i,\beta^*)$ for the following reason. Because $\Gamma(R_i,\beta^*) \geq 1$ holds by condition (3), each consumer in N_1 has at least a reservation price by which the consumer can bring about a positive profit; the utility will decrease even if j becomes larger or smaller. In the case of larger j, the possibility of loss arises, whereas the opportunity of obtaining the positive profit is lost in case of smaller j. Accordingly, the following inequality can be derived as

$$U_i(b_i, c_i^{\Gamma(R_i,\beta(s))}, s_{-i}) \geq U_i(b_i, c_i^k, s_{-i}) \text{ for all } k\ (1 \leq k \leq I). \tag{5}$$

This equality holds for all $i \in N_1$ under the conditions of Proposition 1. Therefore, condition 2 means that $c_i^{\Gamma(R_i,\beta^*)}$ is the best response for all consumers in N_1.

Second, we consider a set of the consumers who do not bid b_{max}: $N_2 \subset N$. By Condition 1, the consumer in N_2 cannot obtain the seat allocation. The movie price is determined as $\beta = b_{max}$ and the consumer's utility becomes negative in case that the seat is allocated if the consumer in N_2 sets b_{max}. Therefore, the best response of the bidding price is $0 \leq b_i < b_{max}$. In addition, because the consumer in N_2 cannot obtain any seat, the seat declaration c^{any} is the best response and the utility is always zero.

However, if the consumer in N_2 set the bidding price b_i as

$$\min_{i \in N_1} R_{i1} < b_i < b_{\max}, \tag{6}$$

then the movie price β is increasing and not all consumers in N_1 have reservation price(s) that is greater than or equal to β. Accordingly, Condition 3 is not satisfied. Actually, b_{max} does not become the best response of the consumers in N_1 if such b_i is taken by the consumers in N_2. Therefore, between inequality (6), all strategies cannot be the best response. To obtain Nash equilibrium, the consumers in N_2 must set the bidding price as

$$0 \leq b_i \leq \min_{i \in N_1} R_{i1}. \quad (7)$$

Accordingly, the condition 4 must be satisfied.

From these discussions, results show that all strategies in s^* are the best response if Conditions 1–4 are satisfied. Therefore, s^* is the Nash equilibrium. Q. E. D

Numerical Example of Nash Equilibrium

We explain the Nash equilibrium using a numerical example. For simplicity, let us presume the following: N={1,2,3}, L={1,2}, M=2, R_1={1800,1440}, R_2={1500,1200}, and R_3={1200,960}; for all $i \in N$, B_i={2000,1500,1000}, $c_i^1 = (1, 0)$, and $c_i^2 = (1, 2)$ where zero in c_i^1 means that no declaration exists. From Proposition 1, the Nash equilibrium is described as follows. Two Nash equilibria exist: the first is $s_1^* = s_2^* = (2000, (1, 0))$, $s_3^* = (1500, c^{any})$; the second is $s_1^* = s_2^* = (2000, (1, 2))$, $s_3^* = (1000, c^{any})$.

In the case of the first equilibrium, the movie price is 1500. Consumers 1 and 2 bid the same prices and the first requested seat type is allocated randomly. Neither has a second request. Therefore one of them obtains the seat; the other obtains nothing. Next, in case of the second equilibrium, the movie price is 1000. Consumers 1 and 2 declare favorite seats until the second request. Consequently, because the bidding prices are the same, one of them is randomly allocated a seat of type 1; the other is allocated a seat of type 2. Consumer 3 cannot obtain the seat in either case.

Interpretation of Nash Equilibrium

The strategy profile of Nash equilibrium s^* is comprised of strategies of two kinds. Roughly speaking, one is the maximum bidding strategy. The other is the low bidding strategy. The strategies of two kinds are interpreted as follows.

- The consumer bids the maximum price if the movie price is less than the reservation price of the best-preferred seat type. The consumer honestly declares the seat types whose reservation price is greater than the movie price. The consumer can become a winner.
- The consumer bids the price that is less than the minimum one among winners' reservation prices of the best-preferred seat type if the movie price is greater than the reservation price of the best-preferred seat type. The declaration of the favorite seat types does not matter. The consumer cannot win a bid.

The Nash equilibrium was derived under the condition of complete information. It means that each consumer is able to know all the others' reservation prices and rationally calculate the utility. As a result of rationally pursuing the utility maximization, the Nash equilibrium is obtainable as a stable solution. Each consumer can then find which strategy is to be taken. However, a situation with complete information is rare in the real world. Consumers must make a decision under uncertainty such as situations in which consumers do not know other reservation prices. They must estimate whether to win a bid or not. Moreover, it is impossible to separate strategies into two parts appropriately under incomplete information.

Incomplete information would be necessary if one considered application to the real world. The experiments and simulation described in the subsequent section are presumed to be under incomplete information. The Nash equilibrium is used as a sort of standard to evaluate the behavior.

EXPERIMENTS WITH HUMAN SUBJECTS

To examine actual human behavior, experiments with human subjects were conducted based on the methodology of experimental economics.

Conducting Experiments

Photographs of the experimental room are presented in Figure 1. The experiments were conducted on January 8 and 24, 2008. Subjects were recruited from among graduate and undergraduate students of The University of Tokyo. Eight students in all participated in the experiments. For the experiments, z-Tree (Fischbacher, 2007) was used. It is general-purpose software package used for conducting economic experiments. Then, after finishing the experiments, participants were paid a show-up fee (1000 yen) and a monetary reward calculated at the rate of one yen per 10 points earned in experiments.

Parameters

Table 1 presents parameters used in experiments. Each subject is given a different reservation price R_{i1} that is predetermined randomly in the range of 300–3000. The set of seat types is assumed as $L=\{1,2,3\}$; its preference (p_{i1},p_{i2},p_{i3}) is selected randomly from (1, 2, 3), (1, 3, 2) and (2, 1, 3). In experiments, each subject makes a bidding decision during a period; the decision is repeated for a fixed number of periods. Both the reservation price and the preference are reset for each period.

Figure 1. Laboratory used for experiments

(a) Overview of the experimental room (b) A desk for a subject

Experimental Results

Experimental results are presented in Figure 2. The horizontal axis shows the reservation price. The vertical axis shows the bidding price. In the figure, all subjects' bidding prices are shown. The size of each circle represents the frequency of the occurrence of those same values. Therefore, a large circle means that many participants selected that value.

The figure shows that many subjects are apt to bid the reservation price honestly. In addition, for a reservation price of more than 1500, the maximum price is often bid. This is apparently an interesting feature. Subjects expect that the movie price determined by the auction is lower than their own reservation price. Then they bid the maximum bidding price to obtain good seats even at the risk of negative utility. This behavior is consistent with the feature of Nash equilibrium under complete information.

Figures 3 through 5 show the three typical patterns of subjects' behavior. Each figure presents all bids of a subject. The subject depicted in Figure 3 makes a decision to bid the reservation price honestly; the subject depicted in Figure 4 bids honestly in the case of a low reservation price, whereas the subject bids the maximum price in the case of a high reservation price. Figure 5 shows a subject with similar behavior to that of the subject depicted in Figure 4, but the subject often bids a lower price than his own reservation price.

Table 1. Parameters in experiments

Number of players	n=4
Number of seat types	l=3
Number of seats of each type	$m_1 = m_2 = m_3 = 1$
Percentage of reservation price for the best seat type of reservation price for the second-best seat type	$\frac{R_{i2}}{R_{i1}} = 0.8$
Percentage of reservation price for the best seat type of reservation price for the third-best seat type	$\frac{R_{i3}}{R_{i1}} = 0.6$
Maximum bidding price	b_{max}=3000
Minimum bidding price	b_{min}=0

Figure 2. Experimental results

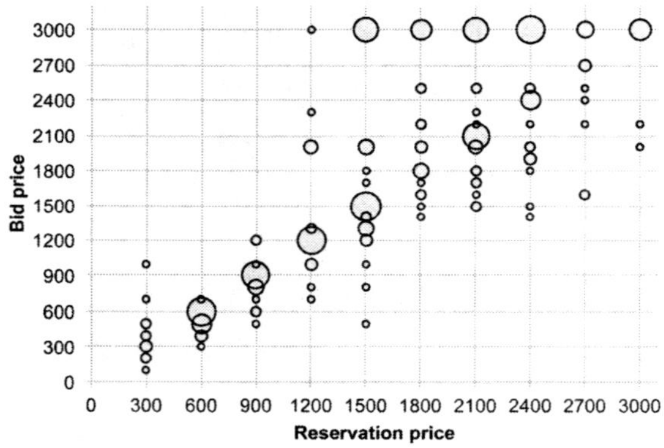

AGENT-BASED SIMULATION

We construct agents who make such decisions as outputs observed in experiments. Then, agent-based simulations including agents of several types are run to examine the effectiveness of the proposed mechanism.

Figure 3. Pattern 1: Honest bidding

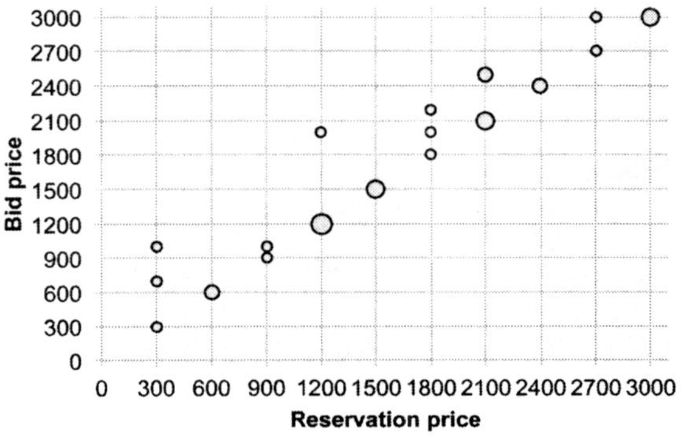

Figure 4. Pattern 2: Maximum bidding 1

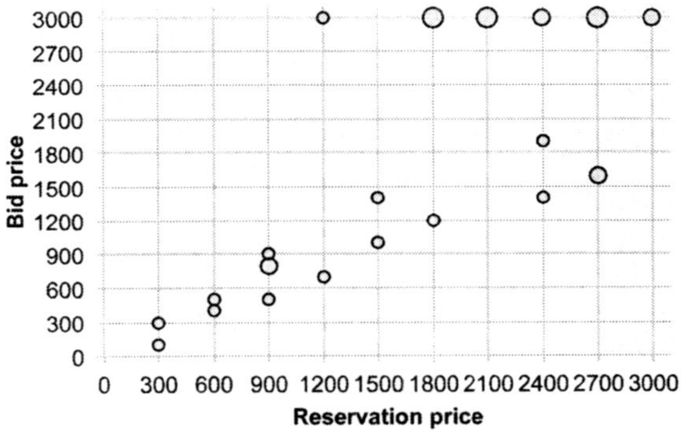

Figure 5. Pattern 3: Maximum bidding 2

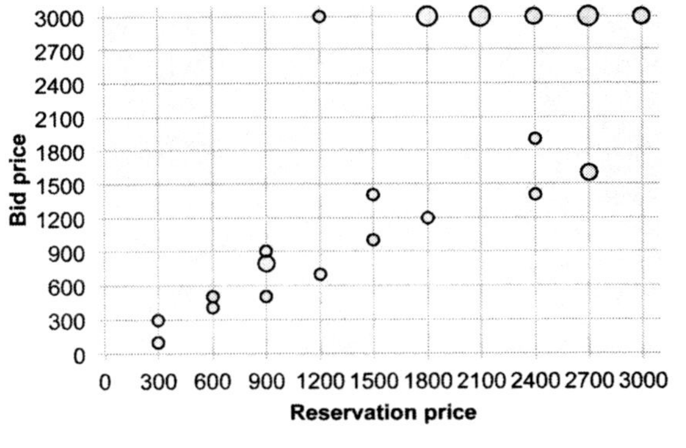

Consumer Agents

Based on results of experiments with human subjects, the following agents were constructed:

1. **Honest bidding:** Agents of this type bid the reservation price honestly. For the seat type preference, agents honestly declare the order of types in accordance with the given preference. This behavior corresponds to the experimental output presented in Figure 3.
2. **Maximum bidding 1:** Agents bid a maximum price if the given reservation price is equal to or higher than 1800. Otherwise, agents bid the reservation price. Regarding the preference of seat types, agents honestly declare the order of types in accordance with the given preference. The behavior of these agents is modeled based on the result shown in Figure 4.
3. **Maximum bidding 2:** Agents bid the maximum price if the given reservation price is equal to or higher than 2400. Agents bid honestly if the reservation price is between 900 and 2400. Otherwise, agents bid the reservation price minus 300. Regarding the preference of seat types, agents honestly declare the order of types in accordance with the given preference. This behavior is modeled considering the result shown in Figure 5.

In addition to agents of these types, agents with Q-learning are added. The Q-learning agents have no information about other agents, but they adaptively learn good behavior. The rule of behavior is the following: First, the agent perceives β and b_i in the previous period as the environments. Second, based on Boltzmann strategy, each agent selects a decision as a bidding action, either decreasing 100, same price, or increasing 100. Regarding the declaration of the order of seat types, each agent makes a decision, either declaring the best seat only, declaring the best and the second-best seat, or declaring all seats according to the order of seat preference. The obtained utility is used as a reward in Q-learning algorithm if an agent wins a bid for the seat and obtains utility U_i. The update equation of Q-value is shown below.

$$Q(s_{t+1}, a) \leftarrow (1-\alpha)Q(s_t, a) + \alpha(r + \gamma \max_a Q(s_{t+1}, a)) \qquad (8)$$

In that expressions s_t, a and r respectively stand for the environments in period t, the agent's action, and the reward. α is the learning rate, which is set as α=0.1; γ stands for the discount factor and γ =0.9.

Figure 6. Reservation price distribution

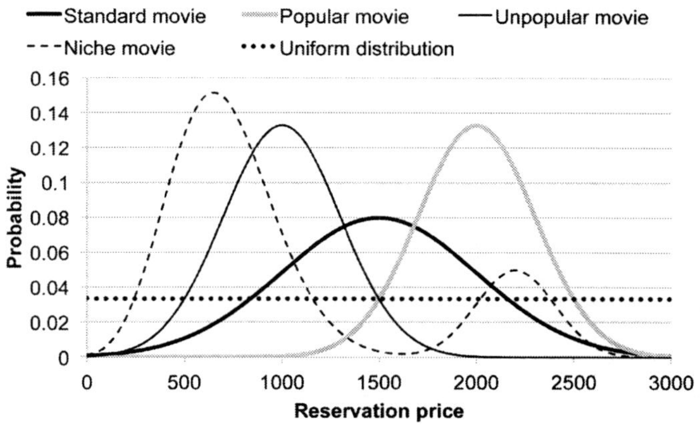

Table 2. Parameters used in simulation

Number of agents	n=50
Number of seat types	l=3
Number of seats of each type	$m_1 = m_2 = m_3 = 8$
Total number of seats	M=24

Reservation Price Distribution

In the simulation, the difference of movie quality is described as the difference of distribution of the reservation prices. For example, if many consumers have a high reservation price, then the movie can be regarded as being popular and of good quality. The following five distributions are used.

- **Standard movie:** Gaussian distribution of $N(1500, 500^2)$
- **Popular movie:** Gaussian distribution of $N(2000, 300^2)$
- **Unpopular movie:** Gaussian distribution of $N(1000, 300^2)$
- **Niche movie:** Poisson distribution with a small peak on the right
- **Unknown movie:** Uniform distribution of 0–3000

Figure 6 presents graphs of these distributions.

Table 3. Movie theater's profit

	Proposed mechanism	Fixed low price	Fixed high price
Standard	**35422**	14400	25492
Popular	**47446**	14400	32166
Unpopular	**23225**	14400	347
Niche	**17526**	14336	14638
Unknown	**36431**	14400	31224

Table 4. Consumers' surplus

	Proposed mechanism	Fixed low price	Fixed high price
Standard	5147	**19360**	3936
Popular	−1547	**27889**	4577
Unpopular	2187	**7996**	9.9
Niche	**12250**	11579	3380
Unknown	11768	**24743**	9420

Table 5. Social surplus

	Proposed mechanism	Fixed low price	Fixed high price
Standard	**40568**	33760	29428
Popular	**45899**	42289	36743
Unpopular	**25512**	22396	357
Niche	**29776**	25923	18018
Unknown	**48199**	39143	40644

Simulation Settings

The parameters in the simulation are presented in Table 2. The agents include 20 honestly bidding agents, 10 maximum bidding 1 agents, 10 maximum bidding 2 agents, and 10 Q-learning agents. Many subjects of the honest bidding type are observed in experiments. Therefore, we increase the number of honest bidding agents.

For comparison with other price mechanisms, two cases of fixed price are prepared: a fixed low price and a fixed high price. The movie prices are, respectively, 600 and 1800.

Simulation Results

Tables 3 through 5 present the simulation results. The tables respectively present the movie theater's profit, consumers' surplus, and the social surplus. Here, consumers' surplus is defined as the summation of all consumers' utility; the social surplus is defined as the summation of utility/profit of all agents. In the case of this simulation, it is a summation of consumers' utility and the movie theater's profit.

In the tables, the bold face numbers in the tables signify the highest surplus/profit of the three pricing mechanisms. From Table 3, results show that the proposed mechanism increases the theater's profit over that of other cases of fixed price. However, with respect to consumers' surplus, the low price case shows good performance (Table 4). Increasing the consumers' utility is natural: they can always watch movies at low prices. However, the proposed mechanism can increase consumers' surplus in cases of niche movies. Therefore, a niche demand is properly extracted. In Table 5, results show that, regarding the social surplus, the proposed mechanism outweighs other fixed price cases. Therefore, the result implies that the proposed mechanism might increase the efficiency of movie theater services.

CONCLUSION

Especially in Japan, most movie theaters provide services with rigid pricing systems. Both popular movies and unpopular movies are provided at the same price. That pricing format is only slightly efficient to create value in the industry of movie theater services. This study examines a proposed auction mechanism in movie theater services using the VCG mechanism and GS mechanism. First, we derive the Nash equilibrium under complete information. Then, experiments with human subjects are conducted to show that behavior patterns of three kinds are observed. In the experiments, three representative patterns of human behavior are observed: always honest bidding; maximum bidding with high reservation price and honest bidding with low reservation price; and maximum bidding with high reservation price and lower bidding with low reservation price. In addition, agents with those behavior patterns are constructed and agent-based simulations are run to examine the effectiveness of the proposed mechanism. Results reveal that the mechanism shows increases of the social surplus, which implies that the proposed mechanism works effectively to support movie theater services.

Although the current paper address on a mover theater service, our approach can be applicable to another cases in service design issues. In future work, we will apply the proposed approach to other services and will contribute toward the establishment of service design methodology.

REFERENCES

Arai, T., & Shimomura, Y. (2004). Proposal of service CAD system—a tool for service engineering. *CIRP Annals—Manufacturing Technology, 53*(1), 397-400.

Arai, T., & Shimomura, Y. (2005). Service CAD system—evaluation and quantification. *CIRP Annals—Manufacturing Technology, 54*(1), 463-466.

Aurich, J. C., Fuchs, C., & DeVries, M. F. (2004). An approach to life cycle oriented technical service design. *CIRP Annals—Manufacturing Technology, 53*(1), 151-154.

Clarke, E. H. (1971). Multipart pricing of public goods. *Public Choice, 11*(1), 17–33. doi:10.1007/BF01726210

Fischbacher, U. (2007). z-Tree: Zurich toolbox for ready-made economic experiments. *Experimental Economics, 10*(2), 171–178. doi:10.1007/s10683-006-9159-4

Friedman, D., & Sunder, S. (1994). *Experimental methods: A primer for economics*. London, UK: Cambridge University Press.

Gale, D., & Shapley, L. S. (1962). College admissions and the stability of marriage. *The American Mathematical Monthly, 69*(1), 9–15. doi:10.2307/2312726

Groves, T. (1793). Incentives in teams. *Econometrica, 41*(4), 617–631. doi:10.2307/1914085

Hurwicz, L. (1972). On informationally decentralized systems. In McGuire, C. B., & Radner, R. (Eds.), *Decision and Organization* (pp. 297–336). Amsterdam, The Netherlands: North-Holland.

Kagel, J., & Roth, A. (1995). *The handbook of experimental economics*. Princeton, NJ: Princeton University Press.

Maskin, E. (1999). Nash equilibrium and welfare optimality. *The Review of Economic Studies, 66*(1), 23–38. doi:10.1111/1467-937X.00076

Maskin, E. (2008). Mechanism design: How to implement social goals. *The American Economic Review, 98*(3), 567–576. doi:10.1257/aer.98.3.567

Meier, H., Roy, R., & Seliger, G. (2010). Industrial product-service systems—IPS. *CIRP Annals—Manufacturing Technology, 59*(2), 607-627.

Rahmandad, H., & Sterman, J. (2008). Heterogeneity and network structure in the dynamics of diffusion: Comparing agent-based and differential equation models. *Management Science, 54*(5), 998–1014. doi:10.1287/mnsc.1070.0787

Shimomura, Y., Hara, T., & Arai, T. (2009). A service evaluation method using mathematical methodologies. *CIRP Annals—Manufacturing Technology, 57*(1), 437-440.

Smith, V. L. (1976). Experimental economics – induced value theory. *The American Economic Review, 66*(2), 274–279.

Smith, V. L. (1982). Microeconomic systems as an experimental science. *The American Economic Review, 72*(5), 923–955.

Spohrer, J., & Maglio, P. P. (2008). The emergence of service science: Toward systematic service innovations to accelerate co-creation of value. *Production and Operations Management, 17*(3), 238–246. doi:10.3401/poms.1080.0027

Takenaka, T., Fujita, K., Nishino, N., Ishigaki, T., & Motomura, Y. (2009). Transdisciplinary approach to service design based on consumer value and decision making. *International Journal of Organizational and Collective Intelligence, 1*(1), 58–75. doi:10.4018/joci.2010100804

Takenaka, T., & Ueda, K. (2008). An analysis of service studies toward sustainable value creation. *International Journal of Sustainable Manufacturing, 1*(1-2), 168–179.

Vargo, S. L., & Akaka, M. A. (2009). Service-Dominant Logic as a Foundation for Service Science: Clarifications. *Service Science, 1*(1), 32–41.

Vickrey, W. (1961). Counterspeculation, auction, and competitive sealed tenders. *The Journal of Finance, 16*(1), 8–37. doi:10.2307/2977633

ENDNOTES

1. The topic of the current study was introduced briefly as one topic of brief examples in our preceding literature (Takenaka et al., 2009). Reports of the literature mainly address the methodology of transdisciplinary approach to service design and presented several examples related to its topic. The current paper presents a detailed description.
2. This is the proof for the necessary condition. Accordingly, the proof does not guarantee the nonexistence of any other Nash equilibrium.

This work was previously published in International Journal of Organizational and Collective Intelligence, Volume 2, Issue 1, edited by Hideyasu Sasaki, pp. 63-76, copyright 2010 by IGI Publishing (an imprint of IGI Global).

Section 2
Institutional Studies

Chapter 8
Legal Protection of the Web Page

Davide Mula
European University of Rome, Italy

Mirko Luca Lobina
University of Cagliari, Italy

ABSTRACT

Nowadays the Web Page is one of the most common media used by people, institutions, and companies to promote themselves, to share knowledge, and to get through to everybody in every part of the world. In spite of that, the web page isn't entitled to a specific legal protection, and because of this, every investment of time and money that stay off-stage aren't protected by an unlawfully used.

Seeing that no country in the world has specific legislation on this issue, in this chapter we develop a theory that wants to give legal protection to web pages using laws and treatment that are present in this moment. In particular we maintain that web pages can be considered as a database so to extend database's legal protection to the first one.

We start to analyze each component of database's definition and to find them in a web page so that we can compare those juridical goods. After that we analyze present legislation concern database and in particular World Intellectual Property Organization Copyright Treatments and European Directive 96/92/CE, which we consider as the best legislation in this field. In the end, we outline future trends that seem to appreciate and apply our theory.

DOI: 10.4018/978-1-61350-135-1.ch008

INTRODUCTION

Nowadays, thousands of web pages offer an heterogeneous variety of digital information (i.e., text, audio, video and images). Such contents can be available in a public way: an anonymous user could download, manipulate and use them maliciously, and, thus, establishing their ownership could be a serious problem in many circumstances.

The tendency is to face this problem at the same time, using technical and judicial approaches. On one hand, we can consider strategies oriented to the protection of the intellectual property, such as insertion of watermarks or, directly, limitations in the possibility of fruition of the contents published in the Web page (Braudaway, 2000). Secondly, we can refer to the judicial disciplines created expressly for the protection of the copyrights on digital information. In the specific, in this work, we explain our theory that try to give a legal protection to web page considering it as a database, judicial good that have a specific legislation.

The chapter is organized as follows. At first we look at a judicial generalization of the conception of database analyzing every its components and after we compare web page and database introducing the guardianship of the web page as a database. In the last part we refer about the future trends and propose our conclusions on this topic.

BACKGROUND

The first institution that had issue a database protection is the European Community by the directive 96/9/CE. The course to give a protection to database was started on April 15th, 1992, when the European Commission issued a formal proposal for a Directive on the legal protection of databases, which was later amended by the Commission on October 4th, 1993. After four years of discussions and proposals in the 1996 was approved the last version and issued the directive 96/9/CE.

The EU Database Directive was created to harmonize the intellectual property laws regarding databases of the 18 countries of the European Union by supplementing copyright to protect databases produced by *sweat of the brow* (Boyle, 2001). The Directive creates a new kind of intellectual property protection: a *sui generis* right. *Sui generis* is a Latin expression that means that something is linked to a specific requisite for admission, in other words this particular protection is given only to the database that meet all the requirements (Autelitano, 1999). Is important to observe that the term of protection is 15 years, but each time the database is updated significantly, the entire database and not just the updated parts receives another 15 years of protection. Consequently, active databases can be protected in perpetuity.

The Database Directive has created a two-tiered approach to the database's protection: on one hand database that by originality of selection and arrangement qualify for copyright protection under national laws will enjoy the same rights as other copyrighted works and, on the other hand, database that do not meet such requirements will, nonetheless, be protected against unfair extraction under the terms of the Directive.

The top tier provided copyright protection for original selection and arrangement of facts in the database. In other words the authorship is given when the web page has the requirement of originality of selection and arrangement and is important to observe that to have this legal protection the author doesn't need to demonstrate his investments in term of money or time.

A second tier provided *sui generis* protection, prohibiting the unfair extraction of a substantial part of a database reflecting significant investment. A database could simultaneously receive both types of protection: copyright protection for the expression, in other word the selection and arrangement of the data; and *sui generis* protection against the extraction of a qualitatively substantial part of the data itself. In other words the ownership, or *sui generis* protection, is given only when the author of the web page could prove his investments that must be considerable. About the concept of investment the European Court of Justice, in the case C-444 02, established that *The expression 'investment in ...the obtaining ...of the contents 'of a database in Article 7(1) of Directive 96/9 must be understood to refer to the resources used to seek out existing independent materials and collect them in the database. It does not cover the resources used for the creation of materials which make up the contents of a data-base.* Moreover we can observe that "The right provided for by the Directive allows the maker of a database to prevent the use of the data it contains under certain circumstances. It is intended to protect databases or their contents without protecting the information they contain as such. It thus indirectly protects the investment involved in the making of the database" (Court of Justice of the European Communites, 2004, p. 3).

The Directive provides that databases be protected by copyright under national legislation to the extent that their selection and arrangement are sufficiently original to constitute the author's own intellectual creation. Thus to prevent that in case a member nation did not provide similar protection under its laws it would be forced to amend them to comply with the term of the Directive (Marino, 2006; Bitton, 2008).

If the European Community has issued the first law that give a protection to database in USA even today there is not a specific law to protect database's owners and a soft form of protection is given only by WIPO Copyright Treatment (Braun, 2003). We think that is important to remember that the World Intellectual Property Organisation (WIPO) is a special organ of the UN that guarantees the interests and rights of inventors and those who hold the right of intellectual protection. Besides having eased the conclusion of multilateral accords for the protection of International patents, brands, design and copyrights, the WIPO is active in the field of technical cooperation and it backs member states in creating structures that allow the effective protection of immaterial goods. In spite of everything the course to issue database's law is begun in 1978, but nowadays is not concluded. In 1978 the National Commission on New Technological Uses of Copyrighted Works submitted a report, which states that computer databases fall within the protection of copyright as compilations. The House Report concluded that the term *literary work* includes computer databases but didn't gave to interpreters any clarification about the way to protect tangible database (Bitton, 2006).

In 1991, the Supreme Court addressed this question in *Feist Publications v. Rural Telephone Co.* Feist copied Rural's collection white page listing in order to compile its own (Gorman, 1992; Ghidini, 2001). The District Court granted summary judgment to Rural, relying on the *sweat of the brow* doctrine, which justified protection because of the work involved in selection and arrangement client's data. The Supreme Court rejected the District Court's sentence and the *sweat of the brow* doctrine because, with the Copyright Act of 1976, Congress made it clear that originality was a requirement for copyright protection, and in this particular case Rural's database does not have the originality requirement (Hayden, 1991; Askanazi, 2002). This sentence demonstrate that what the House Report said in 1978 was unclear and show how specific database's protection is necessary.

To explain the doctrine known as *sweat of the brow* we must consider that over the course of the nineteenth century, two rationales developed for protecting compilations under copyright. The earliest cases identified the constructor's effort, consider as his own expense, or skill, or labor, or money, as the critical contribution justifying protection. The *sweat of the brow* aims to protect the value of this effort extending copyright protection in a compilation beyond selection and arrangement to the facts themselves or, in other word, to the effort (Knight, 1999).

Before this Supreme Court sentence, several US District Courts had granted copyright protection to a collection of facts, such as a database, if the author of the database required a lot of effort to collect the facts or the data in general. Thus District Courts have applied the *sweat of the brow* theory that give protection to database as what we have said above. Under such protection, it was not even allowed to extract individual facts from the collection (Blanke, 2002).

Under US law, the eligibility for copyright protection of electronic databases depends on the interaction of two contrasting but well established principles: the non-copyrightability of facts and the copyrightbility of factual compilations (Eaddy, 2008).

At the end we can observe that in Europe database protection is effective and complete, but in USA there is not a specific protection for database and, for this reason, that the only way to protect database is to apply the Copyright Act and the WIPO Copyright Treatment (Derclaye, 2008). While under both the European

Union and the US approaches databases are eligible for copyright protection only if their selection and arrangement is sufficiently original, the *sui generis* protection offered by the directive 96/9/CE to non-copyrightable electronic databases has no counterpart under US law (McCurdy, 2003).

Up until here we have saw database's legislation in Europe and in USA but nothing about web page's protection. The reason is that any country in the word have issued a web page's law and for this reason we are trying to develop a theory that start from database legislation and arrive to give a specific protection to web page. We further our thesis because we think that is very important give a specific protection to web page, but at the same time we must consider which action are permitted by present legislation.

DEFINITION OF DATABASE AND WEB PAGE

The object of our research is to think about a legal protection to web page consider as a whole. Indeed before today we have a legal protection for music, movie, photographs and software, but there isn't any law or treatment that protect web page as a complete work in spite of the money that many company invest in this work.

We consider the web page as a judicial good which can be protected via an analogical interpretation of directive 96/9/CE and WIPO Copyright Treaty, adopted in Geneva on December 20, 1996, which is related to the judicial protection of database (Butler, 2000). Both of them consider databases as a collection of information, be they rough or elaborate, they are generally about determined topics or they contain material that has been organized in order to allow the user to research and get the information. Directive 96/9/CE define database as *a collection of independent works, data or other materials arranged in a systematic or methodical way and individually accessible by electronic or other means* and WIPO Copyright Treatment define database as *a compilations of data or other material, in any form, which by reason of the selection or arrangement of their contents constitute intellectual creations, are protected as such.*

We can observe that directive 96/9CE and WIPO Copyright Treatment give a similar definition of databases and, more or less, same rights to the owner of database (Brock, 1996). This point is very important because our research want to observe how we can compare web page and database to extend a judicial protection from the second to the first. Because the information can be about private subjects or companies, the risk that databases can affect the rights of various categories of subjects is real (Davidson, 2003). The latter are protected by many countries, we analyze how are protected in the European Union and in USA.

In foreseeing the specific forms of protection for that databanks, WIPO and UE tried to shield the tiring activity of data collection, selection and verification of questions. This type of protection intends to allow the creator of databanks to ban other subjects from putting their hands on full or partial information available in the databank (Wu, 2002).

With the birth of digital technology databases have acquired a major potential of stocking and collecting information without leaving out the crucial economic factor. The European Union and WIPO's Member State considers databases as an efficient and precious instrument for the growth of commerce and thus it each one have decided to extend a uniform and specific protection. The directive 96/9/CE has, on one hand, left protection via single orders untouched, adding, on another hand, a form of *sui generis* protection which allows the protection of investments made, by attributing to the constructor an exclusive right on the information container in the database (Hayes, 2000; Scanlan, 2005). Also the WIPO Copyright Treatment give a particular protection to database's constructor mentioning explicitly *without prejudice to any copyright subsisting in the data or material contained in the compilation*

Now that the reasons and interests in creating a specific protection of databases has been discussed, the judicial nature of this feat needs to be clarified, in order to then analyse the adaptability of this form of protection to the web pages.

The Database

The term "Data base" refers to all types of data collection, be they rough or elaborate, as long as they deal with specific topics and are organized in order to allow the user to research and obtain the said information.

It's too obvious that, explained in this manner, the definition of a database could include various entities, different because of content and the complexity (Hicks, 1987; Di Cocco, 2005). An encyclopaedia, dictionary, Jurisprudence material and even telephone directories could be included in these definitions; the common element between these entities is that they are instruments of collection and used for obtaining information, and thus, needing a specific protection against copy, especially in the digital format. It's obvious that digital technology offers greater possibilities than paper, be it in the proliferation of databases and even in their creation, allowing the insertion of texts, but even images, films and sounds (Grutzmacher, 1999; Gambino, 2009).

A legal definition of "database" is given by the community legislator via the directive 96/9/CE, which in art. 1 comma 2 declares that *for the purposes of this Directive, 'database` shall mean a collection of independent works, data or other materials arranged in a systematic or methodical way and individually accessible* *by electronic or other means*. In follow of what we say above we can assert that this definition could be consider good also from the WIPO Copyright Treatment point of view, indeed WIPO Treatment definition don't added anything and in general we can consider it less accurate than directive's definition (Greene, 1997).

Later on the legislator decided to add onto article 3 that *1. In accordance with this Directive, databases which, by reason of the selection or arrangement of their contents, constitute the author's own intellectual creation shall be protected as such by copyright. No other criteria shall be applied to determine their eligibility for that protection. 2. The copyright protection of databases provided for by this Directive shall not extend to their contents and shall be without prejudice to any rights subsisting in those contents themselves.*

The protection of databases in linkage with copyright had already been granted by art. 10 number 2 of the TRIPs on the 15th of April 1994. The following analysis is indispensable 'cause, if the community directive grants protection to the databases *which, by reason of the selection or arrangement of their contents, constitute the author's own intellectual creation*, art. 10 at number 2 of the TRIP accord grants similar protection to *all compiled data or material, that can be read from a machine or other form* without however providing a specific definition of databases (Douglas, 1996; Santamauro, 2007). As we have done above about WIPO we think that is important to remember that the TRIPS is an organ of the WTO which aims to enforce the intellectual property accords, monitoring the operations included in the accord and by promoting the transparency of the politics of the accord members. Moreover, it can be consulted by members in case of violation of the terms of the treaty.

About the European legal reality we can observe that the definition provided in the directive responds to the needs of the community legislator, in setting limits to the field of application of the directive and consequently, the obligations of harmonization imposed on the community members (Band, 1997). The limit imposed by the directive has the job of limiting the special *sui generis* protection which this grants to the databases. The precise definition is needed in order to define the reason for the protection, but also in order to establish the requisites needed for the protection. On the contrary no innovation has come about concerning the already present protection given by the copyright, not even in the sense of limiting its area of application.

From all the elements described above it can be seen that the dispositions included in the decree aren't in contrast with the details of the TRIPS accord and the WIPO treaty, 'cause databases that aren't included in the community law will be protected anyway by the copyright. In particular in this research we analyze European directive 'cause is more specific and 'cause a database protected by WIPO Treatment could not be included under directive's protection but not vice versa.

The elements that in particular characterize the legal notions of a database are (Auteri, 2003):

Collection of independent works, data or other materials: The collection must be viewed in the sense of a reunion and together with the latter a presentation of the selected elements, but always distinct in order to allow recognition individually or in reunion. In order to answer this need/requirement not only will the fixation be necessary but also the contextual reproduction of the elements, an easy task due to the information technology available today. Thus the nature of the elements inserted is apparently relevant, because it isn't just about words, but also numbers, images and sounds. It may be useful to state the definition of the International Standards Organization: *a representation of facts, concepts or instructions in a formalized manner suitable for communication, interpretation or processing by human beings or by automatic means* (Dommering, 1991).

The works are taken in consideration as the content of a database both when they are destined to provide facts on which they intend to give information and even as real and proper facts.

Is important to observe how, in last few years, new doctrine was developed concern copyright's protection of material content in database. In the case Oravec v. Sunny Isles Luxury Ventures, L.C., 527 F.3d 1218 (11th Cir. 2008), Oravec invoked the "effective registration doctrine", a doctrine which had not previously been adopted in the 11th Circuit but which has been embraced in a handful of other circuit court decisions. The Oravec court in effect affirmed the existence of the doctrine, but rejected Oravec's argument all the same. What must first be shown, however, is that the registration certificate for the derivative work, the certificate on which the theory relies, actually refers to the preexisting work as a work from which the registered work is derived. If such information is lacking, if the court has only the "current protestations" of the plaintiff that the certificate in fact is based on the underlying work in question, then the doctrine is unavailable to the plaintiff.

The effective registration doctrine holds, in substance, that if you own both a pre-existing work and a derivative work that incorporates elements of your original work, registration of the derivative work will, in certain circumstances, be deemed sufficient to permit an infringement suit "based on the underlying work, even if that work was not registered" (Milbrath, 2009).

Other materials: these being sounds, images, films, they can have an integrative role with respect to the information provided or more simply they can be primary sources of information.

Individually accessible by electronic or other means: This requisite is functional based on the accessibility of single units of information, possible as long as they remain distinct and do not mix with other elements which make up the work. The independence is request not only for other *elements* but also for pieces, work and data. The independence is thus seen as the faculty to find, learn and eventually extract information *by electronic or other means*. This requisite demands that the information must be presented according to some order or through a system that allows the recovery and individuation of specific information (Di Cocco, 2005).

Such a requisite isn't usually interpreted rigidly, unless there isn't the need for displaying single infos in a sequence, leaving to other elements, like indices and hypertext links, the job of giving the piece its sense of union (Musso, 1998; Spada, 1997).

The elasticity of interpretation of this element leads to the major or minor attribution of the specific *sui generis* protection.

Arranged in a systematic or methodical way: This is a requisite that arises with the same concept of filling in, which implies not only research, the choice or the unison of elements, but also a type of presentation of the information collected which allows the user to perceive the whole info and the independence of the data collected.

Both, the definition of the database in the directive and the one in the WIPO Copyright Treatment, recognise the author's creative support in the setting and placement of the material. The placing according to systematic criteria of the data collected is a basic notion of databases, but that doesn't mean that information has to be always displayed using the original method.

The term "Disposition" has in it the conception of coordination, intended as integration of data via a network of connections and the concept of organization, as the manifestation of a sequence, order of data placement.

On the one hand in the analogical databases, the disposition of the material is done using a topographical placement of information helping the user with indices and notes, the other side is the electronic database where disposition is via computer based on technical needs, which do not stick to the user's needs. On the other hand its important that the disposition of the material reveals only elements that can be perceived and used by the user.

The peculiarity of the electronic databases compared to the peculiarities of the analogical ones is that they do not reveal, with the aim of defining the database, as is the result by considering 21 of the EU Database Directive that states, it: *is not necessary for those materials to have been physically stored in an organized manner*.

Article 1 at comma 3 of the directive however excludes that protection given to the databases be extended to *computer programs used in the making or operation of databases accessible by electronic means*. However the same directive, when considering 20 adds that *protection under this Directive may also apply to the materials necessary for the operation or consultation of certain databases such as thesaurus and indexation systems*. By excluding software (used for constructing or the functioning of the database) from the protection, the directive excludes that the foreseen requisites for databases can be found in those same programmes.

The above is relevant for the attribution of the copyright protection, as the norm under examination seems to exclude from this protection the databanks whose creative character lies only in the disposition of the material thanks to the software used. The community legislator has distinguished between the necessary elements for the functioning and the elements necessary for the consultation of databases declaring that the protection should be extended even to such elements, even though he indicated as example the TESAURO and index systems. The question needs to be solved on a technical level, but in case this isn't possible an eventual extension of the protection shouldn't, according to the majority of the doctrine, create particular problems, after all the protection would be extended to these programmes only in the measure in which they are necessary for the functioning of a specific database (Linn, 2000; Saxby, 2005).

Accessible by electronic or other means: This requisite is intended in the sense of attributing to any user the faculty of accessing the single pieces of information available in the database, of learning about them and in the final case extracting them. The minority doctrine doesn't seem to follow this, according to it, it's enough if the technician has access to the information.

Related to the databases it's the same definition given by the norm which needs the availability of software specific for locating and for the picking-up of single pieces of information, but it however seems right to retain that for non digital databases the requisites should be more elastic.

The directive under examination recognises as the author of the database the physical or judicial person who creates the piece and gives him/her, in virtue of this classification, the original economic rights over it (Lipton, 2003). All member states haven't absorbed the directive in its totality, for example the Italian legislator has excluded the chance that a judicial person be considered as author of the database, admitting however that the subject can assume the position and have economic rights as a derived right (Beutler, 1996; Jarach, 1979). We must observe that WIPO Copyright Treatment move from contrary point of view 'cause don't distinguish between physical or judicial person. Thus 'cause WIPO treaty don't give any moral right to database's constitutor but only economic right.

The moral rights of the piece and the exclusive rights of making economical use are given to the author of the database. Concerning rights of every worker that collaborate to create a database, i.e. content creator, database designers or system developers we have to observe that the European Directive and the WIPO Treatment don't recognise moral and economic rights to each one of co-worker (Collie, 1994). Indeed we have to remember that database's legal protection is given only to the creation consider as whole at the same consideration have to be extended to the web page. Anyway co-worker have recognized moral and economic rights, but only for they specific job and as often as not these economic rights is automatically transferred from the co-worker to the owner by employment contract's regulations (Lai, 1999). In other words on one side we have specific right recognized to each collaborator and on the other side we have general right recognizes to the creation consider as whole.

The exclusive rights reserved for the database's author from article 5 of the directive 96/9/CE are:

1. *Temporary or permanent reproduction by any means and in any form, in whole or in part*, doesn't detect as per the norm the eventual private use of the copy made, which will be still equally subject to authorisation;
2. *Translation, adaptation, arrangement and any other alteration*, translations and individual pieces that are autonomously protected in their economic rights aren't subject to the database's author's authorization;
3. *Any form of distribution to the public of the database or of copies thereof. The first sale in the Community of a copy of the database by the right holder or with his consent shall exhaust the right to control resale of that copy within the Community;*
4. *Any communication, display or performance to the public;*
5. *Any reproduction, distribution, communication, display or performance to the public of the results of the acts referred to in* b.

Referring to point 3. it's important to underline that free delivery of examples for promotional reasons, teaching or scientific research, aren't to be considered as the exercising of the right of distribution. In the WIPO treaty there isn't any explicit limitation of the economical right, but the article 10 declares *Contracting Parties may, in their national legislation, provide for limitations of or exceptions to the rights granted to authors of literary and artistic works under this Treaty in certain special cases that do not conflict with a normal exploitation of the work and do not unreasonably prejudice the legitimate interests of the author* and later *Contracting Parties shall, when applying the Berne Convention, confine any limitations of or exceptions to rights provided for therein to certain special cases that do not conflict with a normal exploitation of the work and do not unreasonably prejudice the legitimate interests of the author*. From all the elements described above it can be seen that there isn't so much difference between European directive and WIPO Copyright Treatment.

Distribution is to be understood only as sale or transfer of property that can be done only with alienation or with the passing on of support material, that incorporates the original or its copy. With regard to the "passing on" it's important to distinguish between material and immaterial support, as exhaustion of the right of distribution exists only in the first case; it seems correct to believe that the simple placing of a database online for the public doesn't lead to any type of exhaustion of the right.

The right to distribute has two particular exceptions, clearly underlined at the second comma of article 5 of the present directive:

1. *In the case of reproduction for private purposes of a non-electronic database;*
2. *Where there is use for the sole purpose of illustration for teaching or scientific research, as long as the source is indicated and to the extent justified by the non-commercial purpose to be achieved;*
3. *Where there is use for the purposes of public security of for the purposes of an administrative or judicial procedure;*
4. *Where other exceptions to copyright which are traditionally authorized under national law are involved, without prejudice to points* 1., 2. *and* 3.

A part of the doctrine already held that given the importance of databases as sources of information, and their increasing relevance for some major social and economic activities, it was seen as necessary that the temperament of the exclusive rights via licences foresaw such restrictions in specific cases and with equal conditions for the author and the user (Giannantonio, 1997).

The maker of databases is completely another point, the community legislator has provided for the latter a specific point in art. 7, first comma, of the directive; this states: *Member States shall provide for a right for the maker of a database which shows that there has been qualitatively and/or quantitatively a substantial investment in either the obtaining, verification or presentation of the contents to prevent extraction and/or re-utilization of the whole or of a substantial part, evaluated qualitatively and/or quantitatively, of the contents of that database*. The community legislator has in the above wanted to protect the investment of the maker, not only from a quantitative view, in other words abased on the money invested, but also based on the qualitative point of view, considering for example the amount of time devoted (Winn, 2000). In this sense the qualification of constructor could be of a Judicial person participating in the entrepreneurial activity, equally of a physical person even if not an entrepreneur; essential requisite in both cases is that the constructor must come from one of the European countries.

The protection given to the investments is completely unlinked from that guaranteed by copyright, in fact if the copyright protects the structure of the database, the right of the maker aims at protecting the investments made by the parasite like competition. This difference of ends even in the most minimal duration of this *sui generis* protection which is reduced to fifteen years from the date of completing of the database.

In particular the maker can ban the extraction and the re-use of substantial parts. The article 7 comma 2 alphabet a of the directive defines the extraction as *the permanent or temporary transfer of all or a substantial part of the contents of a database to another medium by any means or in any form.* The same article continues to define the concept of re-us as *any form of making available to the public all or a substantial part of the contents of a database by the distribution of copies, by renting, by on-line or other forms of transmission. The first sale of a copy of a database within the Community by the rightholder or with his consent shall exhaust the right to control resale of that copy within the Community; Public lending is not an act of extraction or re-utilization.* In the definition shown above there are references to the concept of *substantial part*: the doctrine (Chimenti, 2001) shows that these words have to be interpreted with relation to single events and the problems caused to the legal owner. Besides banning extraction and the re-use of substantial parts of the compilation, the chance of ceding the activity is foreseen, even though a precise contractual form doesn't exist for it, the community legislator allows free space here for each member.

In the judgment C-203/02, BHB Case, November 9 2004, the Court of Justice of CE defined substantial part as *contents of [a] database' refers to the scale of the investment in the obtaining, verification or presentation of the contents of the subject of the act of extraction and/or re-utilisation, regardless of whether that subject represents a quantitatively substantial part of the general contents of the protected database. Any part which does not fulfil the definition of a substantial part, evaluated both quantitatively and qualitatively, falls within the definition of an insubstantial part of the contents of a database* (Gledhill, 2001).

The Court made clear that the Copyright Clause does not protect a group of facts merely based on the amount of resources one invests in creating the database or compilation (Chalton, 1997). This is consistent with the notion that factual information is something that should be left in the public domain (Smith, 2009). Proponents of database legislation argue that business models emerging in the information age need *sweat of the brow* protection. Collections of information, especially those readily accessible via the Internet, related to news, stock market activity, travel, health, Internet usage patterns, and customer lists have become valuable commodities. While companies invest substantial resources in gathering and maintaining such databases, Internet allows the cost of copying and disseminating such information to decrease rapidly. As the amount of free riders increases, incentive to invest resources in such databases will decrease if creators do not reap enough market return, through increased competitors and less licenses or subscriber fees (Blanke, 2002).

If what the Court said about database is important to database's constructor, we think that is more important to web page's creator, not only for the investment, but also for the moral right that creation of web page should give to the constructor.

The Protection of Web Pages as a Databases

After having focused on the basic characteristics of databases, its now easier to discover the differences between typical elements of a web page and those of a database.

It can be stated without much difficulty that a general similarity between the elements of a single website and those delineated in the definition of databases. The first requisite predicted for database in the directive is the *collection of independent works, data or other materials.* The meaning of this expression used by the legislator has been clarified above, and thus it isn't too ring to say that all elements which are generally found in a web page are included fully in the definition given to the content of a database.

An analysis of a similar result can be done also for the second requisite of databases: *individually accessible by electronic or other means*. The independence of single data in a web page is highlighted by various elements; in particular the division of information in single files and their connection using hypertext links denotes the independence and, at the same time, the interconnection of the elements. It must added that when all elements are in a single file its always possible to distinguish the single elements by making them independent, not only from a technical point of view, but also in content. Indeed elaborator and software, every browser in particular, are able to distinguish the data in every single element, even though they are presented in the same way and the user can, using simple operations, manage to separate the single parts and eventually get the files that the user is interested in (Johnston, 2009).

The third requisite for databases imposes that *data be arranged in a systematic or methodical way*. When comparing a web page with a database we cannot forget what has already been mentioned about this requisite for this type of databases. In fact for this characteristic it must be said that system and method must be felt when the user uses the site, not in the physical disposition of the information which must answer the creator and the software's needs. It might be useful based on what has been said till now to confirm and remind again what the article 21 of the directive 96/9/CE states *whereas it is not necessary for those materials to have been physically stored in an organized manner* (Sims, 2009).

The last requisite states that it be *accessible by electronic or other means* it's a characteristic that can be checked by the simple presence of research instruments by the pieces of information available on the site or furnished by browsers used for surfing the web. Thus it seems right to state that all the requisites needed for the definition of databases can be used directly for the web page (Hollander, 2009).

About requisites contained in WIPO Copyright Treatment we can observe that only one of them is not explicitly included in directive 96/9/CE and is the requisite for database *to by reason of the selection or arrangement of their contents constitute intellectual creations*. Any way we think that this requisite we can find in every web page, also if is created on a software's model, because each page must be different about the content and the elements used. If we find two similar page we can sustain that is a copy or a plagiarized work and in this case the first creator could use this theory to protect what have he done (Unsworth, 1997).

At this point we think could be useful to summarize similarities and differences between web page and database. A web page is composed by different kind of components as text, image, music, film clip, software (i.e. games on line) and each element has a specific legal protection of itself. Those elements are the same components that we can find in a database, in fact databank can contains text, image, music, film clip and software. Going over we can observe that everyone can research each web page's elements and access to them individually, as the European Directive requires for database. Withal we can observe that database's requisites of *data arranged in a systematic or methodical way* and of *accessible by electronic or other means* are attended in web page's nature, indeed web page's prologue requires to respect a specific grammar or, in other words, to use a systematic or methodical way. At the end we can sustain that database and web page have the same structure and compositions, in fact web page could be consider as a database and database could be consider as a web page. The only difference that we can point out is that paper database doesn't lose its inner nature, i.e. telephone book, on the contrary paper web page lose web page's inner nature. At the end of this short summarize we can sustain that in general we can extend database's legal protection to web page (Gambino, 2009).

The directive and the modality with which single member states have accepted the situation, offers a kind of in-elastic protection and it isn't very adaptable to new events.

In fact the derogations which create a restricted space for free utilisation are not applied to extraction, not even for private use of data from an electronic database. From what has been said, it can be deduced that even where a database is diffused free of charge, no private user could, based on the literal interpretation of the norm, consult it, or even less download files on their hard disks or auxiliary memory units. About the faculty of consulting we have to observe that the ban arises as even for simple consultation of a data on the network its necessary that this be stored in the user's RAM and cache memory, in fact all this process is part of the idea of extraction. We shouldn't forget that for the connections, it's wrong to talk about hypertext connections as the link only provides the server's address where the file can be found, it doesn't connect the two datas. In the World Wide Web, as in other hyper textual systems, link is a sign of interconnection from a source to a destination. A link on a text, on a photo or on other multimedia object permit to open another file or page (Smith, 2009).

Interpreted in the way as explained above it will be extremely difficult for the *sui generis* protection to be applied to search engines, the access here is generally free and only in rare cases there is a work behind the scenes, work related to the gaining of data, based on connections and other sites (Tyson, 1997; Derclaye, 2008).

This type of discipline could be applicable for information groupings which are accessed via passwords, but we must consider that in these sites a password is indispensable in order to access the various services. While the ban of re-use can be included in the contract for adhesion, while a rigid application on the network could result as an excessive restriction, potentially it could mine the intrinsic nature of internet (Tai, 2003; Stazi, 2004). In fact if it were attributed to selected information that is diffused with the protection, impeding the reproduction as the info is part of a database, the whole physiognomy of the internet would be radically changed from a virtual area where information is diffused so that it be freely available and usable. What needs to be protected isn't the generality of information present on internet, but the particular realities that need the investment of time and money and which for their economic relevancy require particular attention (Westermeier, 2009).

More over we must observe that in the recent past many legal theory have been developed to give a legal protection to software when there were not any treatment (Derclaye, 2000) and the same thing have been done about games and other judicial goods that in the past didn't have specific protection. Indeed technology's develop go over faster than every legislator's work or law's evolution. In other words frequently has happened that when something new appear on the world scene, in particular in the digital environment, and these things have a considerable economic value lawyer begin to think about a legal protection that have to guarantee investments that stay off-stage and, in this way, also the develop of new technology (Cohen, 1991; Colston, 2002).

In particular we want underline that this theory try to protect not only the economic investment made by big company but also and above all the time investment of single person or small associations (Crews, 1998; Hollander, 2009). To demonstrate better what we have just said we can remember what is write in WIPO site's home page: *The World Intellectual Property Organization (WIPO) is a specialized agency of the United Nations. It is dedicated to developing a balanced and accessible international intellectual property (IP) system, which rewards creativity, stimulates innovation and contributes to economic development while safeguarding the public interest.*

For all that has been mentioned up to this point, it seems legitimate to believe that directive 96/9/CE for databases and WIPO Copyright Treatment can be extended to web pages. However it seems right that inside this theory there be a distinction between web page with restricted access, for which a protection seems necessary and rightful, from web pages to free access, for which a protection seems necessary and rightful (Mansani, 1996; Bonelli, 2002) for the one that has to do with copyright and for the web page considered a whole. In fact if the web page with restricted access needs protection not only from the point of view of copyright but also about the investment that has done, web page to free access needs only a copyright protection.

FUTURE TRENDS

The explained theory is followed by few authors as, i.e., by the University of Leicester which on his web site tell about protection of itself: *The University of Leicester World Wide Web site, as a database, is eligible for protection under copyright and Database Right. These rights are owned by the University of Leicester.* In simple language the University of Leicester agrees with our thesis and for the first time pay attention to the copyright of a web page.

Analyzing over what the University of Leicester's web site tell about protection of itself we found that University attributes to himself every moral and economic rights not only related to the content of each page but also related to *all original content (including text, code, page design, graphics and sound)*[…].

University of Leicester link the protection of his web site to the Copyright and Rights in Database Regulations 1997, the UK law that has acknowledged the European directive 96/9/CE. This link permit to the writer to sustain all the more so what said above.

European University of Rome, as University of Leicester, in his law review's web site, Diritto Mercato Tecnologia, concerning copyright protection writes that the web site is protect as a database under Copyright Italian law (Figure 1).

As well, also Milan Court in 2007 define web page as database giving legal protection to a homemade web site concerning pet, that was stolen by a publisher that used web site's information and photo to create his own site (Resta, 2007).

Above mentioned case represents the first sentence on web page's legal protection and shows his relevance 'cause Italian court analyzed few different form of legal protection. In particular, judges take into their analysis not only copyright law, but also criminal and civil law but round off sentence underlined that the best way to protect web page is referred to database copyright law.

The state of thing we didn't find any theory against the our thesis, moreover we think that in future the doctrine and the jurisprudence, as done, still follow this road considering in particular that a lot of web site are starting to adopting the same policy of European University of Rome's web site.

Figure 1. Italian copyright

DIRITTO
MERCATO TECNOLOGIA

| Home | Presentazione | Redazione | Studi in corso | Eventi e Convegni | Call for paper |

| Segnalazioni editoriali | Siti d'interesse | Normativa | Osservatorio di Diritto Comparato |

Cerca

DIRITTO E MERCATO

Cultura, industria e proprietà intellettuale

Mercato, concorrenza e regolazione

Pratiche commerciali e tutela dei consumatori

DIRITTO E TECNOLOGIA

Biotecnologie, ogm e vita

Comunicazioni elettroniche, audiovisivo e garanzie

Responsabilità e privacy on line

Copyright

La navigazione sul sito è completamente GRATUITA ed ogni informazione e relazione scambiata tra il titolare del sito ed i navigatori avviene senza scopo di lucro ed al di fuori di ogni attività commerciale o professionale.

Il presente sito web è oggetto di tutela ai sensi della legge n.633 del 1941, come banca di dati ai sensi degli artt. 64-quinquies e seguenti.

Il contenuto del sito è tutelato da copyright e può essere liberamente stampato ed utilizzato solo per uso personale e non commerciale.

Non si garantisce l'accuratezza e l'integrità delle informazioni riportate e pertanto si declina ogni responsabilità per eventuali problemi o danni causati da errori o omissioni, anche nel caso tali errori o omissioni risultino da negligenza, caso fortuito o altra causa.

Il titolare del sito declina ogni responsabilità in merito al contenuto dei siti collegati tramite link, o in altra forma, al loro mancato aggiornamento o ad altri danni che possono verificarsi all'utente dalla navigazione sugli stessi. I titolari dei siti linkati che non gradissero il rinvio possono segnalarlo e saranno immediatamente rimossi.

Questo sito non rappresenta una testata giornalistica e viene aggiornato senza alcuna periodicità, esclusivamente sulla base della disponibilità del materiale. Pertanto, non è un prodotto editoriale sottoposto alla disciplina di cui all'art. 1, comma III della L. n. 62 del 7.03.2001.

Il sito è curato e coordinato dal Prof. Avv. Andrea Stazi e dal Dott. Davide Mula a solo scopo divulgativo ed informativo.

L'utente prende atto che la navigazione nel sito avviene a suo esclusivo rischio. Né il titolare del sito, né altri soggetti che hanno collaborato nella creazione, produzione o immissione in rete dello stesso saranno responsabili per qualunque danno derivante dalla navigazione, comprese le operazioni di downloading, l'utilizzo di materiali scaricati, i problemi di trasmissione, errori, omissioni, inesattezze di qualsiasi tipo, interruzioni o ritardi, virus o altro.

Per ogni eventuale lite che insorgesse in merito all'accesso o all'uso del sito, o in relazione al download o all'uso del materiale inviato, o a qualsiasi altro titolo, tra il navigatore ed il titolare del sito o altri soggetti che hanno collaborato, collaborano o collaboreranno alla realizzazione e alla gestione dello stesso, l'utente accetta la giurisdizione dello stato italiano ed, in ogni caso, l'applicazione della legge italiana in vigore al momento della lite, indipendentemente dal proprio domicilio o dalla propria sede.

Essendo esclusa ogni attività commerciale, di vendita o di consegna all'interno del sito dimt.it, tutte le attività tramite esso poste in essere hanno carattere privato e si intendono verificatesi in Italia.

Privacy policy | Contattaci | ©2008 Diritto Mercato e Tecnologia

CONCLUSION

From what has been said, it can be deduced that even where a database is diffused free of charge, no private user could, based on the literal interpretation of the norm, consult it, or even less download files on their hard disks or auxiliary memory units (Mulholland, 2005). We shouldn't forget that for the connections, it's wrong to talk about hypertext connections as the link only provides the server's address where the file can be found, it doesn't connect the two data.

Interpreted in the way, as explained above, it will be extremely difficult for the *sui generis* protection to be applied to search engines, the access here is generally free and only in rare cases there is a work behind the scenes, work related to the gaining of data, based on connections and other sites (Patel, 2007). This type of discipline could be applicable for information groupings which are accessed via passwords, while a rigid application on the network could result as an excessive restriction, potentially it could mine the intrinsic nature of internet (Slay, 2008). In fact if it were attributed to selected information that is diffused with the protection, impeding the reproduction as the info is part of a database, the whole physiognomy of the internet would be radically changed from a virtual area where information is diffused so that it be freely available and usable. What needs to be protected isn't the generality of information present on internet, but the particular realities that need the investment of time and money and which for their economic relevancy require particular attention (Falce, 2009).

Waiting for an ad-hoc protection that will contemplate all specifics that could arise regarding the web sites this interpretative solution could be taken up and used not only by big company to protect their web site but also by each private constitutor that spend a lot of time to create their private web site.

We think that this thesis don't damage internet's philosophy of free information and free circulation of them (Correa, 2002) but that permit to every web page's creator to have a recognition of his work and moral and economic rights related to it.

REFERENCES

Askanazi, J., Caplan, G., Descoteaux, D., Donohue, K., Glasser, D., Johnson, A., & Mena, E. (2002). *The future of database protection in U.S. Copyright Law*. Retrieved November 27, 2006, from http://www.law.duke.edu/journals/dltr/articles/2001dltr0017.html

Autelitano, F. (1999). Banche dati. La rilevanza delle banche dati nel sistema del "cyberlaw". *I Contratti*, *10*, 925–935.

Auteri, P. (2003). Attuazione della direttiva 96/9/CE relativa alla tutela giuridica delle banche dati. *Le Nuove Leggi Civili Commentate*, *4-5*, 1175–1230.

Band, J., & Gowdy, J. S. (1997). Sui generis database protection - Has its time come? *D-Lib Magazine.* Retrieved September 25, 2006, from http://www.dlib.org/dlib/june97/06band.html

Beutler, S. (1996). The protection of multimedia products through the EC's directive. *Entertainment Law Review*, *7*, 317.

Bitton, M. (2006). Trends in protection for informational works under copyright law during the 19th and 20th centuries. *Michigan Telecommunications and Technology Law Review*, *1*, 126.

Bitton, M. (2008). Exploring European Union copyright policy through the lens of the database directive. *Berkeley Technology Law Journal*, *4*, 1417.

Blanke, J. M. (2002). Vincent van Gogh, sweat of the brow, and database protection. *American Business Law Journal*, *4*, 662.

Bonelli, G. (2002). Il sito web quale opera dell'ingegno. *Diritto dell'informazione e dell'informatica, 1*, 201.

Boyle, J. (2001). Comment & analysis: Whigs and hackers in cyberspace: Copyright regulations before the European Parliament should be treated as skeptically as they were by the Victorians. *Financial Times*, pp. 21.

Braudaway, G., & Mintzer, F. (2000). Automatic recovery of invisible image watermarks from geometrically distorted images. *Journal of Electronic Imaging*, *9*(4), 477. doi:10.1117/1.1287836

Braun, N. (2003). The interface between the protection of technological measures and the exercise of exceptions to copyright and related rights: comparing the situation in the United States and in the European community. *EIPR*, *25*(11), 496.

Brock, F. (1996). Diritti d'autore. Opera collettiva. Autorizzazione alla riproduzione di articolo di rivista. Potere del direttore della rivista di rappresentare l'editore. *Rivista di diritto industriale, 3,* 227.

Butler, K. (2000). *Databases are latest battleground in the intellectual property debate* (p. 28). Investor's Business Daily.

Chalton, S. (1997). The effect of the E.C. database directive on United Kingdom copyright law in relation to databases: A comparison of features. *EIPR*, *6*, 278.

Chimenti, L. (2001). I data bases nella direttiva 9/96 e nel d.lgs. 6 maggio 1999, n. 169. *Il diritto dell'informazione e dell'informatica, 1,* (pp. 199-211).

Cohen, J. H. (1991). Hybrids on the borderline between copyright and industrial property law. *Intellectual Property Journal*, *2*(4), 190.

Collie, I. (1994). Multimedia and moral rights. *Arts and Entertainment Law Review*, *6*, 194.

Colston, C. (2002). Challenges to information retrieval – A global solution? *International Journal of Law and Information Technology*, *10*(3), 294. doi:10.1093/ijlit/10.3.294

Correa, C. M. (2002). Fair use in the digital era. *IIC*, *4*, 535.

Court of Justice of the European Communites. (2004). *Press release n° 46/04/EN, 2004*, (p. 3).

Crews, K. D. (1998). Harmonization and the goals of copyright: Property rights or cultural progress? *Indiana Journal of Global Legal Studies*, *6*, 117.

Davidson, M. J. (2003). *The legal protection of database*. UK: Cambridge.

Derclaye, E. (2000). Software copyright protection: Can Europe learn from American case law. *EIPR*, *22*(1), 7.

Derclaye, E. (2008). *The legal protection of databases: A comparative analysis*. UK: Edward Elgar.

Di Cocco, C. (2005). *L'opera multimediale*. Italy: Giappichelli.

Dommering, J., & Hugenholtz, A. (1991). *An introduction to information law. Work of fact at the crossroads of freedom and protection, in copyright, freedom of expression and information law*. Boston, MA: The Hague.

Douglas, J. (1996). The challenge of multimedia: reform the Copyright Act? *Computers and Law*, *31*, 47.

Eaddy, J. H. (2008). Database copyright analysis for dummies: Protecting your intellectual investment is about the design, not the data. *New England Law Review*, *2*, 319.

Falce, V. (2009). The (over)protection of information in the knowledge economy. Is the Directive 96/9/EC a *faux pas? Rivista di Diritto d'Autore*, *4*, 180.

Gambino, A. M., & Stazi, A. with Mula, D. (2009). *Diritto dell'informatica e della comunicazione*. Italy: Giappichelli.

Ghidini, G., & Falce, V. (2001). Intellectual property on communications standards: Balancing innovation and competition through the essential facilities doctrine. *Diritto d'Autore*, *3*, 315.

Giannantonio, E. (1997). *Manuale di diritto dell'informatica*. Italy: Giuffré.

Gledhill, D. (2001). *William Hill takes racing database fight to OFT* (p. 10). The Independent.

Gorman, R. A. (1992). The Feist case: Reflection on a path breaking copyright decision. *Rutgers Computer & Technology Law Journal*, *18*, 731.

Greene, L. H. (2007). Database protection legislation: views from the United States and WIPO. *Copyright World*, *66*, 38.

Grutzmacher, M. (1999). *Urheber, leistungs-und sui-generis-shutz von datenbanken*. Germany: Baden-Baden.

Hayden, J. F. (1991). Copyright protection of computer databases after Feist. *Harvard Journal of Law & Technology*, *5*, 215.

Hayes, B. S. (2000). Integrating moral rights into U.S. law and the problem of the works for hire doctrine. *Ohio State Law Journal*, *61*, 1013.

Hicks, W. B. (1987). Copyright and computer database: Is traditional compilation law adequate? *Texas Law Review*, *65*, 993.

Hollander, W. H. (2009). New intellectual property database is a powerful tool. *Federal Lawyer*, *56*, 19.

Jarach, G. (1979). Considerazioni sui rapporti tra autori e utilizzatori delle opere dell'ingegno. *Il diritto di autore, 2*(3), 587-598.

Johnston, R. (2009). Recent developments in intellectual property law that will impact the Internet. *Computer & Internet Lawyer*, *26*, 12.

Knight, G. A. (1999). The fall and rise of sweat of the brow. *Intellectual Property Journal*, *3*, 342.

Lai, S. (1999). Digital copyright and watermarking. *EIPR*, *21*(4), 171.

Linn, A. (2000). History of database protection: Legal issues of concern to the scientific community. Retrieved September 25, 2006, from http://www.codata.org/data_access/linn.html

Lipton, J. (2003). Databases as intellectual property: New legal approaches. *EIPR*, *25*(3), 139.

Mansani, L. (1996). *La protezione dei database in Internet* (p. 149). AIDA.

Marino, F. (2006). Database protection in the European Union. Retrieved September 15, 2006, from www.jus.unitn.it/cardozo/Review/Students/Marino1.html

McCurdy, G. V. S. (2003). Intellectual property and competition: Does the essential facilities doctrine shed any new light? *EIPR*, *20*(10), 473.

Milbrath, S. D. (2009). The 11th Circuit's new copyright standard for architectural works. *The Florida Bar Journal*, *83*, 50.

Mulholland, H. (2005). *U-turn on child protection database*. Retrieved September 6, 2006, from www.societyguardian.co.uk

Musso, A. (1998). *Ipertesti e thesauri nella disciplina del diritto d'autore* (p. 10). AIDA.

Patel, K. (2007). Authors v internet archives: The copyright infringement battle over web pages. *Journal of the Patent and Trademark Office Society*, *89*, 418.

Resta, F. (2007). Banche di dati on-line. I limiti della tutela penale. *Giurisprudenza di Merito*, *7-8*, 2053.

Santamauro, J. (2007). Reducing the rhetoric: Reconsidering the relationship of the TRIPs agreement, CBD and proposed new patent disclosure requirements relating to genetic resources and traditional knowledge. *European Intellectual Property Review*, *3*, 92.

Saxby, S. (2005). European Court of Justice interprets key aspect of database directive. *Computer Law & Security Report*, *21*, 2. doi:10.1016/j.clsr.2005.01.022

Scanlan, G. (2005). The database directive — Sui Generis and copyright — A practicable distinction? *The Journal of Business Law*, pp. 432.

Sims, B. M. (2009). Collaborative sites. *GPsolo*, *26*, 27.

Slay, C. L. (2008). Myspace or whose space? Digital Millenium Copyright Act's impact on web sites. *The Maryland Bar Journal*, *41*, 20.

Smith, H. (2009). Interpretation of the terms "extraction" and "substantial part" in relation to infringement. *European Intellectual Property Review*, *31*, 58.

Spada, P. (1997). *Banche dati e diritto d'autore* (p. 5). AIDA.

Stazi, A. (2004). *La pubblicità commerciale on line*. Italy: Giuffrè.

Tai, E. T. T. (2003). Exhaustion and online delivery of digital works. *EIPR*, *25*(5), 207.

Tyson, L., & Sherry, E. (1997). Statutory protection for databases: Economic and public policy issues. Retrieved August 25, 2006, from www.infoindustry.org/ppgrc/doclib/grdoc016.htm

Unsworth, J. (1997). *New copyright and database regulations: USPTO, WIPO, and you*. London, UK: University of London & Oxford University.

Westermeier, J. T. (2009). Protecting content on the Internet. *Computer & Internet Lawyer*, *26*, 8.

Winn, E. (2000). Who owns the customer? The emerging law of commercial transactions in electronic customer data. *Business Law*, *56*, 213.

Wu, X. (2002). E.C. database directive. *Berkeley Technology Law Journal*, *1*, 974.

Chapter 9
Collaborative Production, the Knowledge Commons and the Application of Open Content Licenses

Natalie Pang
Nanyang Technological University, Singapore

ABSTRACT

In recent years impacts of information and communication technologies, market enclosures, and the opposing struggle to retain community and public goods have had significant impacts on the social interactions of communities. This chapter examines communities in the context of the knowledge commons – a space by which "a particular type of freedom" (Benkler, 2004) can be practised. It also provides an appropriate lexicon to the examination and discourse of communities and the ways they work. As Castells (2003) notes, self-knowledge "is always a construction no matter how much it feels like a discovery" –this construction is enabled when people work or associate themselves with each other. In particular, the chapter is concerned about the structure of open content licenses operating within such domains. The chapter first explores the concept of the knowledge commons to understand the types of intellectual property that are distinctive to communities (public, communal, and private). Thereafter, licenses as a structure are examined as they may apply within such contexts. A significant influence on the discussion is the contemporary media environment that communities operate in today, resulting in the breaking down of boundaries, the blurring of distinctions between an original and a copy, and shifting the nature of production in communities. These debates lead to a case for open content licenses as an appropriate structural mechanism for communities.

DOI: 10.4018/978-1-61350-135-1.ch009

INTRODUCTION

A struggle is emerging in the world, as highlighted by Slater (2005). It is a struggle to produce and protect what is referred to as the knowledge commons, a space and vicinity of 'common' goods produced by communities of people. The idea of a commons is not new – it has been around since the first human cooperation and collective action. Men hunting together for food, sharing and complementing their skills and produce for their villages – the commons is rooted in communities of social trust and cooperation (Bollier, 2004). Originating from the historical commons, the commons as defined by Benkler (2003) generally are 'institutional spaces, in which we can practice a particular type of freedom – freedom from the constraints we normally accept as necessary preconditions to functional markets'. Moritz (2004) defines the knowledge commons as 'zones of free and equitable use for data, information and knowledge', consisting of physical, logical and content layers of resources (Bollier, 2004).

Almost at the same time, the knowledge commons can be thought of a form of defiance against contemporary organisations of enclosures around knowledge and informational goods. It is certainly so – and before the issues of copyrights and open content licenses can be discussed it is necessary to first understand the motivations by the communities who create, defend, and are sustained by it.

The Romans in the ancient ages identified three types of property (Diegeser, 2003): *res privatae*, *res publicæ* and *res communes.* Res privatae identified property that is possessed by an individual, family or a company. The second type of property is associated with things that are used by the state, and these are commonly seen today as public parks, roads, and buildings. The last type of property, *res communes*, recognized resources that are common to all, such as resources in the natural world (e.g. water and air).

The knowledge commons as it exists and referred to in this paper associates itself with the last type of property. Commonly referred to as the public domain today, property that exists in this space are distinct from things in the private sphere, though this chapter asserts a further distinction between the public and the commons domains. Copyright as it was first conceptualized was intended to benefit creators, while at the same time ensuring a healthy level of works to be available publicly. Copyright as a system of checks and balances maintains such protection and circulation. This chapter argues that technological changes and fundamental shifts in the media environment of today call for an alternative mechanism to copyright. Though the boundaries between the private, the public, and the commons (especially the last two domains) have disintegrated over the years but it is important for this discussion to shed light on these distinctions. They are also essential in order to

Figure 1. A visual imagination of the commons and enclosures

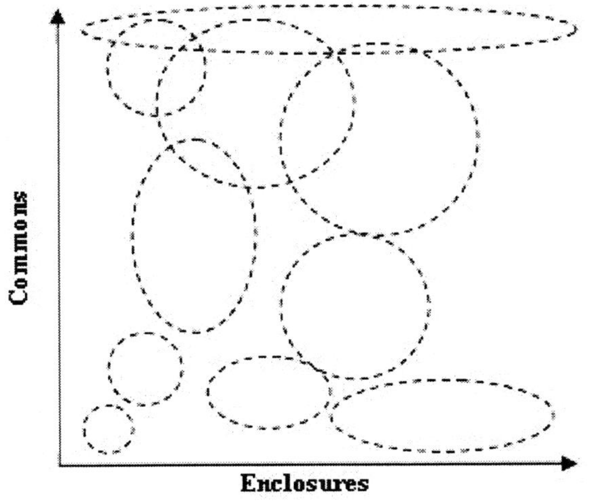

understand the contemporary scenarios of today and their impacts, which will be discussed later in this chapter.

One of the most significant ideas to explore in attempting to understand the original concept of the commons are enclosures. Simply, it refers to privatization and in the contemporary context - usually fronted by corporations in the namesakes of efficiency and quality. Yet privatization in terms of resources (e.g. financial and knowledge gained) is not the only thing that is happening. The enclosure movement, which originated in the 18th century amongst farmers in England, caused boundaries around intellectual property contained in resources to be formed. What once belonged to many now only belonged to a few. It resembles somewhat like the exclusive club where if one becomes a member (insider), there is plenty to be gained and an array of privileges to be capitalized on – and the distance with the non-member (outsider) widens intentionally. Therefore if we were to visualize the original concept of the commons, where all common resources is represented on one axis, and compare that with the effect that enclosures have on them, it might resemble something like Figure 1.

In this figure, the commons is conceptualized on the vertical axis as a space where all common resources reside. Enclosures on the other hand, are conceptualized on the horizontal axis. The circles representing collective communities that appear within this interaction are constantly evolving, expanding and contracting, as shown by the dotted lines around them. These groups form enclosures within themselves around the commons' space, and these enclosures grow larger as they traverse on the horizontal axis. This can be thought of as the exclusive club mentioned earlier, where a large yet private group of members enjoy equal and exclusive privileges. As a non-member, access to those knowledge, resources, or privileges is almost impossible. Such groups are low in terms of their openness in the commons space – yet within those boundaries there is still a pool of resources brought together by a collective or through collective action. But because of this, there are very little overlaps between these communities: they remain in silos because of these enclosures.

On the other hand, as communities increase in their openness (see vertical axis) in the commons and members of one community frequently find themselves belonging to other communities on the same basis of interactions, overlaps often happen at this level as communities collaborate and share knowledge with one another. There are mechanisms in place for these communities to facilitate such collaboration, such as a free-to-all membership so long as there is sufficient interest aligned between the individual and the community, partnerships and collaboration programs, and communication tools within and between these communities. And then there are communities that share their resources to all; yet one must be a member in order to contribute. The Cooperation Commons (http://www.cooperationcommons.com/) founded by Howard Rheingold (Rheingold, 2002) is based on this principle. As the site states: *'You do not need a login to view the documents, the blog, or any section of this site. You do need a login to add an entry to the summary documents or to blog. If you are interested in summarizing or blogging, or in being a member of our Google Group discussion, contact... '* Many research groups take on this form as well, where there is a limited membership but unlimited access to the resources created within the community. On the highest level there is very little or no enclosures, and plenty of collaboration to create resources in the commons. Such communities often have almost invisible boundaries surrounding its memberships and ownerships; and knowledge and other resources produced are co-owned, shared, and freely available for all to access. These communities do this on the principle that the more there is collaboration around knowledge and the creation of resources, the higher would be the value and credibility on such knowledge and resources. On the other hand, one could also visualize these communities as differentiated by the extent by which they share benefits and privatize costs. A contemporary example is Wikipedia, where a relatively small number of authors contribute encyclopedia entries (privatized costs) for all to use (shared benefits).

Understanding the enclosures or the lack of them (in the commons) is critical to the discussion in this chapter – the relevance (or irrelevance) of copyright in the groups and resources created described, and the case for open content licenses in especially in the contemporary media environment. Still, Figure 2 is a somewhat simplistic presentation of the commons and the enclosures that have been formed

Figure 2. A park in the commons, China

and it is only thus visualized for the purpose of this discussion. It must also be highlighted that even in these two paradigms there are different forms and levels continuously evolving.

What are open content licenses and how different are they from the role of copyright and licenses? How do they provide protection for intellectual property? Some initial background here aims to provide contextual understandings on scenarios in the contemporary media environment which open content licenses are the most relevant. This is not to say that copyright is not useful or irrelevant. Copyright has been around for nearly three hundred years; and have been used by all creators of literary works, artists, musicians, and so on. There are still scenarios where copyright is useful – but it is not within the scope of this chapter to discuss them at length.

Before proceeding with the discussion, it should be clarified that copyright usually consists of a bundle of rights (Liang, 2004, pp 25):

- **Reproduction rights:** The right to reproduce copies or the work (for example making copies of a book from a manuscript)
- **Adaptation rights:** The right to produce derivative works based on the copyrighted work (for example creating a film based on a book)
- **Distribution rights:** The right to distribute copies of the work (for example circulating the book in bookshops)
- **Performance rights:** The right to perform the copyrighted work publicly, (for example having a reading of the book or a dramatic performance of a play)

- **Display rights:** The right to display the copyrighted work publicly (for example showing a film or work of art)

These rights are available to original works of authorship but in the context of copyright law, originality 'only refers to the fact that the work was not copied from another or to the point of origin' (Liang, 2004, pp 25). So long as a certain piece of work can demonstrate that it has not been copied from somewhere else or some effort was needed in creating a final outcome of a work then the condition of originality would have been satisfied. As the discussion unfolds later there are extreme difficulties in trying to maintain such distinctions especially in the contemporary media environment.

The chapter now turns to the next discussion – significant in providing background knowledge to realizing the relevance and value of open content licenses, and applying them to appropriate scenarios. Thereafter, the commons based model of production is discussed, along with several examples to illustrate its relevance in the contemporary media environment. This is then examined through the lens of open content licenses.

RES PRIVATAE, RES PUBLICÆ AND RES COMMUNES IN MODERN SOCIETY

As discussed earlier in the chapter, three main domains of production exist: res privatae, res publicæ, and res communes. This section will talk about them but concentrate on the last two, and their common misunderstandings.

Res Privatae: Referring to the private domain, all works that are produced and not freely shared belong to the private domain. Profit-making organisations often work within this domain. Personal works such as literature, paintings, music scores and compositions exist in this domain when they are first created but can be later articulated to the different domains of private, public or the community using licenses.

Res Publicæ: Quite simply, this refers to all resources that exist in the public domain. Examples of institutions in the public domain are public libraries, museums, parks, and public broadcasting agencies. Works produced in the public domain are free and equal for all to use and provide a space of respite from the market forces. The ancient understanding of the Romans project that that things that are owned or defined by the state government is also the equivalent of the commons domain (in the next discussion) – but it should be maintained that this is not necessarily the case – even though they do contribute to the commons domain in many ways.

Res Communes: This refers to the domain, where resources that are common to all are found. It is necessary to discuss the enclosures within this domain; where people form enclosures around the commons and access is fragmented not by the market, but by the memberships, interests or clubs of people. Although within many of such memberships and clubs the resources are similar to those of the commons – they are collectively owned, collaborative, there is equal access, and is often free but such features are contingent upon the maintenance of membership or interests. Property produced by such enclosed communities is not necessarily transferred to the commons domain; but it must be highlighted that many of such groups do contribute to the commons by contributing free resources that are of quality (as they have been collectively produced) and to do this they use certain structural mechanisms such as open content licenses. This domain must also not be confused with the earlier domain, referred to as the public domain. Quite often the commons domain is larger that what is state owned and there are occasions where what is state owned may not be in public interest or access. But undeniably, both domains frequently visit and invigorate one another.

Having said that, it should also be mentioned that within this domain many levels of *res communes* exist – some are more exclusive than others, and some are active in the commons by their contributions and members frequently move from one group to another because of this. It is however, not within the scope of this chapter to talk about these levels of differentiations. But it is must be recognized that this domain of resources has grown significantly especially in recent times – and because of certain groups this domain has become one of the main ways by which the commons and the public domain is nurtured and maintained.

By now it should be clear that the three domains of res privatae, res publicæ, and res communes as originally conceptualized by the Romans are now significantly different in the modern society. While it remains that res privatae still refer to individual and market forces, the other two domains are frequently misunderstood. At the same time, these domains of property become less dichotomous in nature, with actions of the market, the state, and the larger human and civil community moving across the various domains.

When copyright began, there were clear distinctions between the three domains of resources: the private, the public and the community domain; and copyright was effectively used to regulate resources in these three domains. More so in recent times, the use of copyright licenses has moved towards a heightened regulation of resources in the private sphere instead; and the alternative, the open content licenses, is seen as the way and counteract against that; in their goal to nurture and ensure a healthy level of contributions to the public and commons domains (Lessig, 2004).

COPY: RIGHT AND LEFT LICENSES

The concept of copyright is multifaceted according to its use and application to various contexts such as the types of collections, organisation, and creators. Liang (2004, pp 13) stated quite simply and importantly that copyright 'in a broad historical and cultural view…is a recent and by no means universal concept'.

The Renaissance period which saw Europe emerge out of darkness towards a revival of learning also saw the appearance of great scientists, inventors, artists and other geniuses such as Leonardo Da Vinci, Donatello, and Michelangelo. It is important to note that it was also marked with institutional revelations, such as the establishment of the Vatican Library in Italy in the 1400s, the formation of the Laurentian Library by the famous Florentine family (Pang, 2009). Universities began and also grew, and accompanying this growth were the developments of university libraries (Johnson, 1970; Pang, 2009). Bookmaking was revolutionalised by Gutenberg, replacing handwritten books with printed ones. Large volumes of printed books were then placed on open shelves in bookshops and libraries – making the written word accessible to the masses (Krasner-Khait, 2001). This period marked a golden age of literacy, where the absorption and the creation of knowledge in various disciplines such as the arts, literature, science, architecture, and technology were equally matched by their dissemination. Also marking this period was the rise of commerce and exploration, and the knowledge amassed by people and institutions of this period translated into rich and diverse collections found in personal, private institutional, public libraries and also in commercial institutions in the market such as bookshops.

Such was the world that needed copyright. At the beginning of the period, printers were freely reprinting popular books without getting permissions or paying royalties – and copyright was an effective way by which this industry could be regulated. It was a system that wanted to function as a system of checks, benefiting original authors and allow non-commercial institutions (such as the public library) or groups to 'exist as an alternative, non-commercial' distribution channels for the storage and use of knowledge works – and more importantly, to facilitate learning and further inspirations based on such learning and exchanges over these works.

In many ways, copyright is still doing what it has set out to do – but with the rapid establishments of market forces, copyright as a system to benefit original creators has been displaced – and fallen into the hands of media corporations such as recording labels and publishing houses instead. Many examples of how copyright is used today demonstrate a common deviation from its original purpose of regulating the publishing industry – to regulating consumers, content creators, and audiences of these works. Consider the following:

- Many works that are created are rewritten interpretations or adaptations of an original work, such as the many adaptations of *Faustus*, by Christopher Marlowe, Fernando Peddoa, Alfred Jarry, Thomas Mann and Michel Butor (Liang, 2004).
- Numerous works are inspired by real stories, events, narratives contained in personal journals, diaries, and letters. Confucius stated once 'I have finished my greatest work and I am proud to say that not a single idea in it is mine' (Liang, 2004, pp 13).
- Many works exist publicly and are common to all, such as folktales, and spread by storytellers across generations. These works exist through a concerted and collective effort, and no one could claim authority over any version as the 'original'. The *Tales of the 1001 Nights* is one such example.
- Again, for the same works, copyright cannot stop commercial corporations from appropriating these works and turn them into proprietary and copyrighted products of the corporation. Walt Disney Corporation established its wealth on fairytales such as Snow White and Sinbad (Liang, 2004).
- Copyright has originally little or no application to music composition. Most musical themes 'were freely adapted and copied from one composer to another. Bach's *Concerto in D Major BWV 972* for example is simply a re-orchestration of the ninth movement of Vivaldi's *L'Estro Armonica'* (Liang, 2004, pp 15). Copyright only began for music and its use, distribution, and composition with the growth of the recording industry in 20th century.

It must be realized that copyright accounts for much of the enclosures that exist against the global knowledge commons. Take this example of a public park in China that has been built collectively by generations of people in a village, and has existed for many decades. Trees, grass, benches, and stories are freely available in the park and are in the commons – there is no claim of ownership over them because these resources are jointly held by people in the village. It is a powerful collective endeavour, demonstrated by the size, facilities, infrastructure, stories, and recreation found in the park (see Figure 2). Yet it is also highly possible that because there are no claims, a corporation intending to turn this park into a theme park can come along to appropriate the things that are of value, and start charging for entries, or the use of facilities in them. Copyright cannot stop such actions. Such practices are already rampant on the internet and in digital media; and even though the distinction between the original and the copy is blurred, copyright tries to artificially maintain them (Liang, 2004). The fact that distinctions are blurring is significant to the discussion of intellectual property protection; and this will be discussed in greater detail later. Such examples of copyright use only demonstrate how copyright is in the hands of large corporations and not in the best interests of the community or creators. The sometimes ignored and neglected outcome is the shrinking and fragmentation of the commons, and the public domain.

It is essential at this point to recognize a recent movement that is quickly becoming very popular and commonly augmented as alternatives to copyright. Broadly referred to as the 'copyleft' movement, it serves as a discourse to restrictions imposed by copyright. The copyleft movement is rooted in the principles of open source, free, or shared software – incorporating the ideologies of 'free distribution, usage and collaborative development' (Liang, 2004, pp 18). Yet it is far from being a model that abandons what copyright was intended to do. Within the existing legal framework, this model allows one to stipulate a certain degree of freedom to the way resources that are created are used, and distributed. It is a model that seeks to intervene with what has become an inherent 'tyranny' in copyright (Boynton, 2004). In 1790, copyright protection lasted for 14 years and was renewable only once before a certain work or resource entered the public domain. From 1831-1909, the term was increased from 28 to 56 years. The tenure seems to grow worse: and as of today, copyright protection for individual lasts for 70 years after the death of the creator, and for corporations, 95 years after publication. Because of such shifts in favour of the private domain, the amount and flow of resources in the public and commons domains have been sluggish (Boynton, 2004). This provides a strong motivation for an alternative to copyright. In general, it is copyleft, as most people know it. More specifically, we refer to a category of open content licenses which is based on the same principles and have seen significant developments in recent years.

THE CONTEMPORARY MEDIA ENVIRONMENT

The use and impact of technology on everyday lives have often been heard and researched on. There are profound shifts in the way communities interact because of the changing nature of mediating technologies. But the contemporary media environment we now reside in is not limited to simply changing the way people interact – they have changed the nature of organisations, groups, production, and soon to be revealed in later discussions, the continuum of the private and public boundaries that are so important to the knowledge commons. Most of these are nothing new to us – but it is our intention to examine the ways the contemporary media environment has changed the relevance (irrelevance) of copyright, and the three domains of resources: private, public, and the commons. Highlighting these changes is also crucial to towards driving the case for open content licenses. Through a number of examples, this section aims to demonstrate pragmatic scenarios challenging the assumptions of traditional copyright and licenses.

Boundaries in the Contemporary Media Environment

Before the realization of the Internet and distributed networks, there were boundaries. These were boundaries that existed to distinct the private from the public, and all forms of common property. These boundaries were necessary for a number of reasons. Property and information inherent in them was distributed. Such distribution separates action from the private and the community and the public – and it is in such order that collective action can be seen (Olson, 1965). The second reason differentiates an action from participating in the commons or the public domain; and this reason is found in the traditional collective action theory as originally conceptualized by Olson (1965) and others (Olson & Zeckhauser, 1966; Oliver & Marwell, 1988): that in order to participate or contribute, there must be a conscious, coordinated, and known intentions amongst people in a community and no one member or individual may be able to contribute to the public or communal good for the benefit of others – only widespread contributions can.

Perhaps in some cases these boundaries still exist – but with contemporary information and communication technologies such boundaries are breaking down both on micro and structural levels. Participation can now happen without knowledge of others in a community, or the conscious intention of contributing to property with communal or public good properties. Bimber, Flanagin, and Stohl (2005) refer to this as the second-order communality; and there are many examples of such actions in our everyday lives: as unconscious as the sharing of a bookmark with others, and as conscious as adding value through the posting of a review on a web page or community blog. Value is derived from the communal or public good through such sharing and retrieval of useful information that has also been value-added by the contributions of others. Contemporary technologies and the media environment, along with its communities of people, provide such functionalities and make it possible for knowledge to increase in value the more it is used and shared.

Another implication that comes with the breaking down of boundaries is that information and property continually move back and forth between the private, the public and the commons realms. While copyright that has been an effective framework to regulate property with distinctive boundaries, it may no longer be effective to maintain them just so that copyright can be applied. It must be realized that we are operating in a world that has significantly changed its nature of production, and there must be at least parallel efforts in aligning changes to the policies that regulate such modes of production.

The Nature of Production in Communities

Isolation is deadly (Pang, Denison, Johanson, Schauder, & Williamson, 2006). And the use and growth of the number of linked pages on the Internet has certainly proved how this revelation is already inherent in people. When copyright began, it was a time when the expressions of ideas, and the sharing of them, were limited to people with political, social, or economic causes. With the Internet and usable communication technologies, and simply because it is now so easy to share, the world is seeing an exponential growth of what Lessig (2004) refer to as noncommercial publishing. It is more than a mere platform of expression, but one that reflects a paradigm shift in the way people create knowledge, communicate, collaborate, interact, and distribute their works. Benkler (c.f. Boynton, 2004) once said, 'No one writes from nothing…we all take the world as it is and use it, remix it.' And very much so, as we see even in times of old, that one story inspires another, and one's knowledge is the amassed wisdom of a few others. The well known impressionist movement in painting was largely influenced by earlier artistic movements, such as the Classicism and Realism. Pioneers of the movement: Auguste Renoir, Claude Monet, Alfred Sisley and Frederic Bazille knew each other from common and conventional painting classes and shared the common goal to defy the conventional definitions of art in that era. Thereafter this group grew, and through working together and influencing one another, knowledge of similar approaches and techniques were shared and the movement was born lasting from 1867 to 1886 (Pioch, 2006)

Amassed and collective wisdom works pretty much the same way. Useful contributions emerge from an interactive process where one sees participation in groups, forums, discussion lists, and the integrated reflection of one's thoughts such as writing (in today's context, blogging – but even though blogging can be a solitary pursuit, it is often mediated and networked by track backs and thoughts from interested people). Rather than the explicit pursuit of a goal or purpose, knowledge is produced collectively with other people, and interactively through participation.

The networked environment is a platform permitting individuals and communities to come together for collective action using 'decentralized cooperation strategies' (Benkler, 2006, pp 63). Before this environment came about collective action was thought to be extremely difficult unless there was a centralized coordinating body ensuring the congruent pursuit of explicit goals and minimizing the problem of free-riding by individuals (Olson, 1965).

The commons, and in this context, the collaborative model of knowledge production has been around since the first human cooperation – and the Internet and other information and communication technologies have made the social networks integrated in this model faster, and much more transparent. Social networks, once amplified by information and communication technologies, enable broader, faster, and lower cost of coordination of activities (Schauder & Pang, 2006).

Take for example, projects in the open source movement. The successful case of the Linux operating system and efforts such as the 'open source unionism' (Freeman and Rogers, 2002) demonstrate new types of 'cooperative endeavours and organizing structures' (Bimber, Flanagin, & Stohl, 2005, pp 375). Far exceeding these structural changes is a model that accepts that intelligence in communities cannot help but be distributed; and creates unique advantages out of such distributed intelligence.

But the open source story is also about the social network enabled via the collaborative production. It is a social network that has been enabled with distributed networks made efficiently possible by information and communication technologies. Such is the nature of production increasingly witnessed in the contemporary media environment. This model is efficient for a number of reasons. Knowledge and the production of property appreciates in its worth because of the additional value and dialogues contributed by other participants in a community, and increases in significance through higher global usage. At the same time, inefficiencies imposed by copyright and the intellectual property regime can be addressed through this model (Kogut & Metiu, 2001) with the decentralization of innovation – from mega content owners to creators.

What's in a Copy?

Satirically speaking, there is a new disorder on the Internet. A disorder that is altogether welcoming and hostile, depending on whose side you are on. Fondly known as the copy, it refers to duplicates of a file (property) that could be distributed on the Internet. The difference that the Internet makes should be realized. In the past when the world is without it, copies were made by teachers for use in the classroom, by singers creating samples of their works, and by art galleries creating portfolios of artists for showcasing purposes, just to name a few examples. It was an act that was somewhat acceptable simply because copies were simply inferior to the original, and replicates were akin to clones – like the original but not quite authentic, and not quite the same. Let us first say that the Internet was not originally conceptualized to encourage the disorder we speak of – the original versus the copy. When the World Wide Web was conceptualized, and the Internet was born, it was assumed that links (to an original) were favoured over having a copy that was probably inferior to the original. On top of this, digital storage was expensive and cumbersome. The Internet was born to facilitate networks, and through links and references one's knowledge and property could be referred to another and the sharing of resources could be encouraged.

Yet an almost parallel transformation of technologies was taking place alongside developments of the Internet – with media storage, file types and formats – which were also adapted for use on the Internet. Media storage has now become relatively inexpensive, playing back copies of a file is easy, and file formats and types are becoming interoperable as vendors understand benefits in collaboration. There is little (or rather, almost none) loss of quality in a copy to speak of, and it has become much easier to include a copy of a property instead of a link to an original.

As a result a copy is inconsistently referenced to an original, or returned to an original server; rendering the distinction between an original and a copy of intellectual property almost non-existent on the Internet. The copyright framework tries to artificially maintain these distinctions (Liang, 2004) but it must be realized that there is a need to reexamine ways by which the goals of copyright can be better achieved with alternatives. In addition, the costs of making copies in the contemporary media environment has also become relatively insignificant compared to the time when copyright was effective for physical copies of books, cassettes, videos, and photographs. In the media environment of today, the marginal costs of reproduction or distribution has lost its meaning (Schlachter, 1997).

As earlier presented, while there is nothing in the copyright framework to stop corporations from appropriating resources in the public and commons domain for commercial purposes, copyright as it functions on the Internet is perhaps even worse – with the ability to remain anonymous. The copying and pirating of works is now easily achievable without the disclosure of identity or bearing any risks or losses (Schlachter, 1997).

THE CASE FOR OPEN CONTENT LICENSES

The chapter has so far presented a number of arguments towards the need for open content licenses, and they are quickly recaptured as below:

- The nature of knowledge production is one that require dialogues and sharing of knowledge, which in turn encourages innovation and sustain communities
- Friendly structures are needed to ensure a healthy level of resources and knowledge in the commons and public domains
- Changes in the media environment result in paradigm shifts in the way people interact; create, retrieve, share and use knowledge
- The changed media environment result in empowering communities to optimize shared knowledge in a powerful and dynamic manner, thus enabling greater levels of creation of intellectual property

- Breaking down of boundaries defining private, public and community resources reflect the need for a new structure regulating the creation, use, and dissemination of resources in these domains

Beyond these reasons there lies a social perspective to the need for open content licenses. In order to avoid the balkanization of content and communities, license structures that are friendly to open content are desirable to promote creation, innovation, and encourage communities to grow by leveraging on a healthy knowledge commons. Contrary to popular belief, the knowledge commons is not necessarily unsympathetic to market forces (Bollier, 2004) as both are needed to encourage and inspire each other. Most open content licenses allow people to add proprietary works to the knowledge commons so long as they are used in ways as specified by the creators. This permits businesses and professionals to contribute to the public and community domains without necessarily giving away all of their work.

At the same time, most successful projects based on the open content license and collaborative production model reflect a hybrid of networks: between the large, disconnected and distributed groups, and the smaller, cohesive, and occasionally hierarchically organized groups. Whatever their structures – they are based on a peer to peer sharing model and the more cohesive they are, they likelier they are to generate their own norms and ways of production. These are seen as strong and weak ties in social network theory and are both necessary (Granovetter, 1983) in order to provide individuals and communities with, respectively, bonding and bridging links to knowledge, resources, and one another for assistance and support (Schauder & Pang, 2006, keynote). Healthy social networks are essential to a healthy public sphere (Boeder, 2005).

This also explains how, in the context of online participations, some individuals can participate as a passive looker sometimes and an active contributor at times even with only partial knowledge of the network. In the case of communities, open content licenses act as structures by which collective action is possible within a media environment that is highly decentralized and emergent (Bimber, Flanagin & Stohl, 2005; Benkler, 2006). The growth and adoption of open content licenses by businesses, cultural communities, and governments worldwide plainly illustrate their case, and the adaptability of them in various settings. Though not intended to be an exhaustive list, some examples are discussed here.

In July 2006, the Croatian government 'adopted an open software policy and issued guidelines for developing and using open source software in government institutions' (Vervloesem, 2006). Said Domagoj Juricic, Deputy State Secretary of the Central State Administrative Office for e-Croatia, '...the Croatian government has recognized the importance of market alternatives considering the platforms, tools, and other solutions that could help us build a qualitative e-society...the policy is not about replacing something, it is about treating things equally' (Vervloesem, 2006). Croatia is not the only country that has adopted the open source movement and as part of that movement, embraced the use of open content licenses in its public policies. Indonesia has also adopted an open source policy towards the use of software and content creation; and considers it as a strategic move to counter piracy problems (Antara, 2006). Similar benefits have also been found for using open content licenses in publishing, especially in developing countries (Papin-Ramcharan & Dawe, 2006).

Many collaborative software productions such as those found at the Fresh Meat Community (www.freshmeat.net), and even commercial content management systems such as Plone and Drupal have also widely adopted open content licenses. One of the most popular forms of open content license is the GNU General Public License, widely used in open source software developments. Significantly different from the usual copyright model, this license relies on the user community to also be co-producers of software. Derivative works that are produced must also be licensed with the GNU General Public License; preventing proprietary works from being produced based on the collective contributions of others. Unlike copyright, this license would also ensure that software codes once contributed, would always stay in the knowledge commons for others to use.

The charm of open content licenses is spreading to individual home computer users. Other than avoiding exorbitant fees that come with proprietary software (Yaqoob, 2006), many users have also found motivation in using software that are not only legal and affordable, but also allow them to take ownership of the growth, and development of the very same software they were using (Ali, 2006).

But the model is not limited to software and policies. The open content licensing model is also used widely in the creation of content, such as the very popular Wikipedia. The license being used by Wikipedia is the GNU Free Documentation License, to fulfill Wikipedia's goal of '... Wikipedia content can be copied, modified, and redistributed so long as the new version grants the same freedoms to others and acknowledges the authors of the Wikipedia article used (a direct link back to the article satisfies our author credit requirement). Wikipedia articles therefore will remain free forever and can be used by anybody subject to certain restrictions, most of which serve to ensure that freedom...' (Wikipedia, 2006). As one would observe, this license is used to grant the same type of freedom one would find in the earlier software example. In a similar form Flickr, a web application allowing users to upload and share photos with others, also makes use of the open content licenses to facilitate such sharing.

A BRIEF GUIDE TO OPEN CONTENT LICENSES

Recalling in earlier discussion the rights that are contained in the copyright framework, the open content license model differ fundamentally in that it seeks to grant to the user a certain number of freedoms. Some uses of open content licenses have already mentioned in earlier text – and it must be warranted that there are several other examples, applicable to various content and media domains. One of the most well-known initiatives is the Creative Commons licenses, which are also localized for different jurisdictions such as India, China, Japan, Korea, Australia, Italy, Taiwan, Brazil, Netherlands, France, Austria, Spain, United Kingdom, Croatia, and so on. It is not within the scope of this chapter to speak about the different types of open content licenses; there are already several excellent works written such as Liang (2004) and Laurent (2004) and this chapter refers to those works for that purpose.

The following lists the common characteristics of open content licenses (Liang, 2004, pp 43). Most of them are already explained in detail by Liang (2004); however it is the intention of this section to discuss them as they relate to the knowledge commons and the nature of production in communities:

Basis / validity of the license: Although open content licenses allow certain freedom to be granted to users, they also assert the copyright of the author ensuring that derivative works that are produced are not restrictive or proprietary.

This allows trust to be developed and sustained in a network; therefore avoiding problems of selfish appropriations of collectively produced work. Hardin (1968)'s infamous article symbolized this idea, where he puts forward that when a scarce resource is used as a common by individuals, the environment and resources would be degraded over time. In a nutshell, Hardin (1968) concluded that having the commons also implied setting oneself up for a tragedy: 'Therein is the tragedy. Each man is locked into a system that compels him to increase his herd without limit – in a world that is limited. Ruin is the destination toward which all men rush, each pursuing his own best interest in a society that believes in the freedom of the commons' (Hardin, 1968). Already with the media environment there is already a degree of fragmentation of resources and open content licenses as a structure could help to better address such potential problems of appropriations.

Rights granted: Unlike most copyright licenses, in open content licenses users are granted freedom by granted certain rights; such as the right to copy and distribute the work, and in some cases, the right to modify, create and distribute derivative works.

Recalling the discussion around enclosures, these rights granted through the open content licenses effectively breaks down the enclosures and boundaries surrounding resources, communities, and the production of knowledge. This also explains why we often find that members of one community grounded in the principles of the knowledge commons are often members of multiple communities. Rights granted under the open content licenses allow them to actively bring their knowledge to a vast diversity of communities – and in turn enable them to apply what they learn from others in these communities to their own areas.

Derivative works: Refer to any work that is produced based on an original work. In open content licenses, any derivative work that are allowed to produce must also carry with it the same open content license that the original work was tagged with. The right to create derivate work usually includes the right to create it in all media.

The way open content licenses deal with derivative work is significantly different from copyright licenses. Quite plainly, the structure ensures that works that have been produced for the public and commons domain cannot be easily taken out of for commercial purposes. In doing so a healthy level of resources in the public and commons domain is nurtured; this in turn cultivates the communities which thrive on using such knowledge.

Commercial / non-commercial usage: The common assumption is that by using open content licenses, all works are granted for free. Not necessarily so – the creator do have the option to indicate whether or not a certain work is to be used for both commercial and non-commercial purposes, or only for non-commercial purposes.

As mentioned in earlier discussion, although the commons is distinct from the market, there must be a healthy level of both the market and the commons in order to invigorate one another (Bollier, 2004). This aspect of open content licenses allows the nurturing of both market and social communities in one single structure.

Procedural requirements imposed: Most open content licenses also impose procedural requirements when a user wants to distribute an original or derivate work. This requires that the distribution is accompanied by a copy of the license, or the inclusion of any other sign, symbol, or information about the nature of the license, and indication of where this license may be obtained.

Appropriate credits: Open content licenses are very strict in making sure that appropriate credits are given to the creator of a work, when the work is distributed to a third party, and when modifications are made or derivative works are created.

By these characteristics all rights and obligations imposed under the license, and the appropriate credits would also be passed onto third parties acquiring a certain piece of work. In social network theory, this further strengthens strong or bonding ties that are already formed in a community. At the same time, weak ties between a closely-knitted community and those outside the community (third parties) can be effectively bridged (Granovetter, 1983; Schauder & Pang, 2006). Like before, these aspects of open content licenses will not only allow trust to be nurtured and a community to be cultivated; they will also ensure that proper acknowledgements be accorded to creators.

They do not effect fair use rights: Unlike copyright licenses, open content licenses ensures a certain degree of fair use of a work even if there is disagreement with the terms and conditions imposed by the license.

This ensures that members in a community are empowered to still remain in participation even if they do not agree, or only have partial knowledge of the community network. This is especially effective in the contemporary media environment, where a certain level of participation exist in the form of usage.

Absence of warranty: Most open content licenses state that there is no warranty for the work, and it is provided on an 'as is' basis; though there are options for warranties to be arranged between the licensee and the third party.

While many might regard this as a possible drawback of open content licenses, it reflects an important character of the knowledge commons in the way the user is conceptualized. The term 'user' is in fact inadequate: within the knowledge commons most users are also seen as co-producers of a work – even if they do not direct modify or create derivative works, their feedback in using the work is used to further improve the work itself. Works are seen as continuously evolving, with time and the collective knowledge of others.

Other standard legal clauses, such as severability, limitation on liability, and termination are commonly applied in open content licenses (Liang, 2004). The section has discussed characteristics of open content licenses in a way that demonstrates their implications for communities, and in the context of this paper, the knowledge commons. While demonstrating that there are more than enough reasons to examine open content licenses as they apply to communities, the discussion has also attempted to show how they are essential to function as a type of structure for communities to operate under.

FUTURE TRENDS

As modern information and communication technologies become more pervasive and ubiquitous, communities – whether it is communities of practice or those that make up civil society (Pang and Schauder, 2006) – work increasingly within such environments. Open content licenses will increase in their usage and popularity because of their applications in the contemporary media environment. Since the first conceptualization of open content licenses there has been a significant increase in its use, and growth in the community that supports them. Open content licenses are also increasing in their desirability for governments seeking to cultivate growth and healthy public and community domains within cultural institutions, businesses, and social communities.

Yet the well-known tension remains, between the commons and the market, and in this case between advocates of open content models and proprietary market forces. This tension is already well manifested in the conflicts between creators of software (Antara, 2006); and as more and more cultural institutions, governments, and community organisations adopt open content licenses, one can also expect opposing market forces to rise against such movements. Nevertheless, with more communities realizing that only with an appropriate structure can constructive collective action be possible, the growth of open content licenses is inevitable as they provide such a structure for communities.

It is therefore not surprising that large corporations are already turning around and attempting to adopt certain aspects of open content licenses, though the reasons for doing so are many: recognition of its benefits, and sometimes it has been a change directed by the demands of customers (Ricciuti, 2002; Mears, 2006). There is also a rise of smaller market entities that begin their businesses using the open content licensing model (Mears, 2006). Being small entities, such companies depend on the collective knowledge they can gain outside of their corporative network to grow – and they realize that such benefits can be gained through the open content licensing model. But this is changing, as many larger companies are also jumping on this wagon in recognition of the benefits that open content models and its licenses can give (Ricciuti, 2002). Amazon.com and Air New Zealand are some of such examples (Ricciuti, 2002).

However, there are still organizations and institutions that are struggling to catch up in terms of efficiently adapting the open content licensing model to its operational contexts. Cultural institutions such as museums for example, are deeply rooted in their traditional models of curation and even though there are engagements with local communities to co-create meanings around artifacts in collections, how open content licenses may be used to effectively facilitate such participation and sharing is still under-researched.

The creation and dissemination of knowledge resources in community networks is increasingly a reflexive state of affairs: comprising of reflections and actions, the thinking and the doing between people in a community network. The protection of intellectual property in such contexts is no longer a prescriptive process and has to be carefully considered. As more community networks realize their benefits, it is expected that there will be proliferation of open content models and its licensing structures in community networks; and the larger civil society.

With the intensification of these trends over time and the creation and distribution of intellectual property by communities become increasingly robust in the contemporary media environment, the reality of copyright to function in such contexts may decrease in its application and importance (Schlachter, 1997).

CONCLUSION

Changes in the media environment have made it difficult for copyright to be enforced in communities. Other than the threats imposed by the media environment for the copyright framework, the dynamics of collective action and production in communities have also presented the need for alternative licensing mechanisms. These make up the scenarios presented in the chapter arguing for the case of using open content licenses as structural mechanisms for communities. Because they function to ensure rights to be granted to users, they become powerful and effective empowerment for communities that needed dialogues, collaboration, and innovation.

Beyond the knowledge commons lies the unforgettable community: it is a concept of collaboration, co-production, and one that allow communities to thrive on the using and sharing of collective wisdom – and open content licenses function as a paradigm by which intellectual property in such constructs can be governed. Theorists often wonder why open source projects have become so popular in recent years. The chapter has also demonstrated that users of open content licenses do not deprive themselves of their rights to creation, or disregard intellectual property in any way. Whether or not open content licenses are to be used remains a choice that one must make; but as this chapter has discussed, although the popularity and growth of open content licenses may not have been well anticipated ahead of its time, it is perhaps clear in hindsight.

REFERENCES

Ali, N. D. (2006). The open and closed case. *SPIDER, September 2006*, 7-9.

Antara. (2006). *IBM, Microsoft protest Indonesia's open source policy.* Retrieved October 1, 2006, from http://www.antara.co.id/en/seenws/?id=16383

Benkler, Y. (2003). The political economy of commons. *UPGRADE: European Journal for the Informatics Professional*, *4*(3), 6–9.

Benkler, Y. (2006). *The wealth of networks: How social production transforms markets and freedom*. London, UK: Yale University Press.

Bimber, B., Flanagin, A. J., & Stohl, C. (2005). Reconceptualizing collective action in the contemporary media environment. *Communication Theory*, *15*(4), 365–388. doi:10.1111/j.1468-2885.2005.tb00340.x

Boeder, P. (2005). Habermas' heritage: The future of the public sphere in the network society. *First Monday, 10*(9). Retrieved October 13, 2006, from http://firstmonday.org/issues/issue10_9/boeder/index.html

Bollier, D. (2004). Why we must talk about the information commons. *Law Library Journal, 96*(2), 267–282.

Boynton, R. S. (2004, January 24). The tyranny of copyright? *The New York Times.* Retrieved October 8, 2006, from http://www.nytimes.com/2004/01/25/magazine/25COPYRIGHT.html?ei=5007&en=9eb265b1f26e8b14&ex=1390366800&partner=USERLAND&pagewanted=all&position=

Castells, M. (2003). *The power of identity.* Malden, MA: Blackwell Publishing.

Digeser, E. D. (2003). Citizenship and the roman res publica: Cicero and a Christian corollary. *Critical Review of International Social and Political Philosophy, 6*(1), 5–21. doi:10.1080/13698230510001702643

Freeman, R. B., & Rogers, J. (2002). Open source unionism: Beyond exclusive collective bargaining. *Working USA: Journal of Labor and Society, 5*, 3–4.

Granovetter, M. (1983). The strength of weak ties: a network theory revisited. *Sociological Theory, 1*, 201–233. doi:10.2307/202051

Hardin, G. (1968). The tragedy of the commons. *Science, 62*, 1243–1248.

Johnson, E. D. (1970). *History of libraries in the western world.* Metuchen, NJ: Scarecrow Press Inc.

Kogut, B., & Metiu, A. (2001). Open-source software development and distributed innovation. *Oxford Review of Economic Policy, 17*, 248–264. doi:10.1093/oxrep/17.2.248

Krasner-Khait, B. (2001). Survivor: The history of the library. *History Magazine, (October/November)*. Retrieved July 11, 2006, from http://www.history-magazine.com/libraries.html

Laurent, A. M. S. (2004). *Understanding open source and free software licensing.* Cambridge, UK: O'Reilly.

Lessig, L. (2004). *Free culture: The nature and future of creativity.* New York, NY: Penguin Books.

Liang, L. (2004). *A guide to open content licenses.* Netherlands: Piet Zwart Institute.

Mears, J. (2006). Open source unlocks options for many small-to-medium sized businesses. *Network World.* Retrieved October 11, 2006, from http://www.linux-world.com/cgi-bin/mailto/x_linux.cgi

Moritz, T. D. (2004). Conservation partnerships in the commons? Sharing data and information, experience and knowledge, as the essence of partnerships. *Museum International*, *56*(4), 24–31. doi:10.1111/j.1468-0033.2004.00046.x

Oliver, P., & Marwell, G. (1988). The paradox of group size in collective action: A theory of the critical mass, II. *American Sociological Review*, *53*, 1–8. doi:10.2307/2095728

Olson, M. (1965). *The logic of collective action*. Cambridge, MA: Harvard University Press.

Olson, M., & Zeckhauser, R. (1966). An economic theory of alliances. *The Review of Economics and Statistics*, *48*, 266–279. doi:10.2307/1927082

Pang, N. (2009). Digital libraries as centres of knowledge. In Theng, Y. L., & Foo, S. (Eds.), *Handbook of digital libraries* (pp. 506–515). Hershey, PA: IGI Global. doi:10.4018/978-1-59904-879-6.ch052

Pang, N., Denison, T., Johanson, G., Schauder, D., & Williamson, K. (2006, October). *Empowering communities through memories: The role of public libraries*. Paper presented at the 3rd Prato International Community Informatics Conference, Prato, Italy.

Pang, N., & Schauder, D. (2006). User-centred design and the culture of knowledge creating communities: A theoretical reassessment. In Burstein, F. V., & Linger, H. (Eds.), *The local and global in knowledge management - Why culture matters* (pp. 151–166). Kew, Australia: Australian Scholarly Publishing.

Papin-Ramcharan, J. I., & Dawe, R. A. (2006). Open access publishing: A developing country view. *First Monday, 11* (6). Retrieved October 1, 2006, from http://firstmonday.org/issues/issue11_6/papin/index.html

Pioch, N. (2006). *Impressionism.* Retrieved October 1, 2006, from http://www.ibiblio.org/wm/paint/glo/impressionism/

Rheingold, H. (2002). *Smart mobs: The next social revolution*. Cambridge, UK: Perseus Books Group.

Ricciuti, M. (2002). Open source: Rebels at the gate. *Business Tech: CNet News.* Retrieved October 12, 2006, from http://news.com.com/2009-1001-961354.html

Schauder, D., & Pang, N. (2006). *Keynote presentation: Digital storytelling.* Paper presented at the Museums Australia 2006 Seminar: Storytelling Through Emerging Technologies. Victoria, Australia.

Schlachter, E. (1997). The intellectual property renaissance in cyberspace: Why copyright law could be unimportant on the Internet. *Berkeley Technology Law Journal, 12*(1). Retrieved October 12, 2006, from http://btlj.boalt.org/data/articles/12-1_spring_1997_symp_2-schlachter.pdf

Slater, J. B. (2005). When America sneezes. *Mute*, *2*(1), 5.

Vervloesem, K. (2006). Croatian government adopts open source software policy. *News Forge.* Retrieved October 16, 2006, from http://www.newsforge.com/article.pl?sid=06/08/11/1855229

Wikipedia. (2006). *Wikipedia: Copyrights*. Retrieved October 13, 2006, from http://en.wikipedia.org/wiki/Wikipedia:Copyrights

Yaqoob, N. (2006). My Ubuntu experience. *SPIDER, September 2006*, 10-12.

Chapter 10
Managing Collective Intelligence in Semantic Communities of Interest

Stefano Montanelli
Università degli Studi di Milano, Italy

Silvana Castano
Università degli Studi di Milano, Italy

Alfio Ferrara
Università degli Studi di Milano, Italy

Gaia Varese
Università degli Studi di Milano, Italy

ABSTRACT

In this paper, the authors present a reference P2P architecture based on autonomous, self-emerging semantic communities of interest (CoIs) for collective intelligence creation and management. An approach for enabling knowledge organization and management at the level of a single peer is presented in the paper, as well as techniques for supporting a peer to participate to the construction of a shared community vocabulary, according to the terminological preferences automatically extracted from its personal knowledge. Furthermore, an application example in the e-health domain is presented in the framework of the iCoord system for P2P semantic coordination to show the use of a manifesto-based collective intelligence for enforcing effective collaboration in a real case study.

DOI: 10.4018/978-1-61350-135-1.ch010

INTRODUCTION

In a modern vision, P2P systems are seen as effective collaboration platforms where data and knowledge belonging to a possibly large set of peers can be shared in an effective way (Androutsellis-Theotokis & Spinellis, 2004). In this context, the traditional approaches based on peer-to-peer knowledge discovery and data exchange are being replaced by more articulated architectures where the notion of *semantic community of interest* (*CoI*) is introduced to explicitly give shape to the *collective intelligence* of a group of peers with similar expertise/resources (Avrithis, Kompatsiaris, Staab, & Vakali, 2008). Semantic CoIs allow to shift from a network of units to a network of coalitions where the community itself (and not the peers on their own) has the role to support queries and specific collaboration needs that can rise in a given moment. Creation and maintenance of a community-level collective intelligence push a novel attention to the critical aspects of distributed knowledge management in the P2P environment, where the goal of establishing a shared agreement among a set of peers conflicts with the intrinsic P2P nature that pursues peer autonomy, communication scalability, and rapid change propagation. In this direction, recent approaches based on P2P communities show interesting solutions to improve the efficiency of query distribution and to increase data availability, apart from the accessibility of the single peers (Aiello & Alessi, 2007; Das, Nandi, & Ganguly, 2009). However, methods and techniques for collaboratively building and negotiating any form of P2P community intelligence are still at a basic level of development and only preliminary results are currently available (Aleman-Meza, Halaschek-Wiener, & Arpinar, 2005; Ren, Anumba, & Ugwu, 2002).

In this paper, we propose a reference P2P architecture for collective intelligence creation and management based on autonomous, self-emerging semantic CoIs. In our architecture, a semantic CoI emerges from the P2P network by aggregating those peers that autonomously agree to contribute with their own data and knowledge to the construction of a collective intelligence about a certain topic of interest. The collective intelligence of a semantic CoI is made explicit in the form of a *community manifesto*, containing both an ontological description of the community interests and a shared community vocabulary. An approach for enabling knowledge organization and management at the level of a single peer is presented in the paper, as well as techniques for supporting a peer to participate to the construction of a shared community vocabulary, according to the terminological preferences automatically extracted from its personal knowledge. As far as we know, the capability of enabling a group of independent peers to autonomously define a shared community vocabulary without relying on any centralized authority is an original contribution per sé. Furthermore, an application example in the e-health domain is presented in the framework of the iCoord system for P2P semantic coordination, to show the

Figure 1. A reference P2P architecture for collective intelligence creation and management

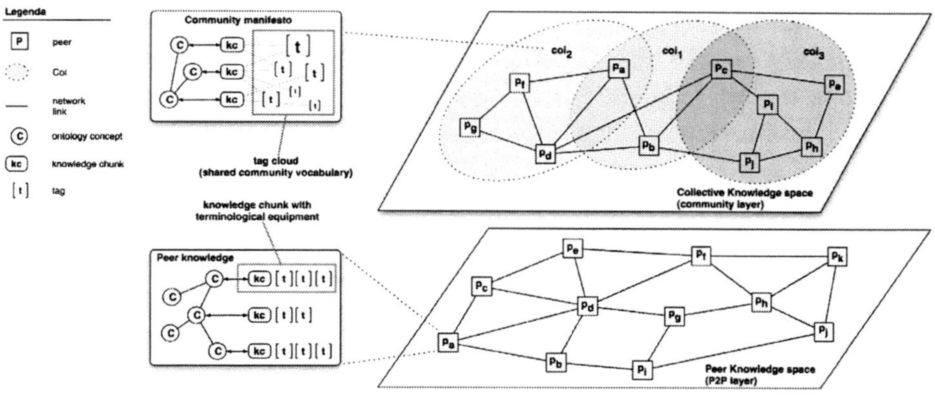

use of a manifesto-based collective intelligence for enforcing effective collaboration in a real case study. For the sake of clarity, an appendix is finally provided to summarize the notations adopted in the overall paper.

REFERENCE P2P ARCHITECTURE AND KNOWLEDGE MODEL

In the field of P2P systems, the notion of community refers to the capability of the network to autonomously recognize and aggregate groups of peers with common interests and similar resources to share (Castano & Montanelli, 2005; Gu & Wei, 2006). We borrow this notion of P2P community and we define a *semantic community of interest*, from now on simply called *CoI*, as a community of peers where the term "semantic" denotes that the peers participating to the community agree on the "meaning" of the resources to share, and such a meaning is formalized through an ontology-based manifesto. The manifesto gives shape to the *collective intelligence* of a CoI, which is gradually set up in a collaborative way through progressive enrichments performed by all the community members.

For creation and management of a collective intelligence in a CoI, we propose the reference P2P architecture shown in Figure 1, where the upper layer, namely the *Collective Knowledge space*, is in charge of managing CoI formation and management, and the lower layer, namely the *Peer Knowledge space*, is in charge of ensuring connectivity and standard communication among the overall network peers.

Formation of a CoI. The formation of a community in a P2P network is typically characterized by the adoption of a *supervised approach* where the peer promoting the community (i.e., the *community founder*) controls the formation process by leading the phases of member identification and community commitment. In other words, the supervised approach is characterized by an explicit phase of negotiation where the approval/rejection of a new peer is determined by the choice of the community founder and the list of community members is "network-aware" (Bloehdorn, Haase, Hefke, Sure, & Tempich, 2005). In our reference P2P architecture, for CoI formation and management, we define a Collective Knowledge space characterized by the use of an *unsupervised approach*, thus exhibiting the following key features.

- **Implicit negotiation:** The choice of joining the community is autonomously taken by each peer according to its level of interest in the topic(s) addressed in the community. No coordination authority (e.g., community founder, superpeer) is expected to manage approval/rejection of the potential members.
- **Soft membership:** The complete list of community members is not made explicit within the community. This means that, at a given moment, the community members are not aware of the other peers currently joining the community.

A CoI is created by a founding peer by defining an initial community manifesto. The community manifesto is the repository of collective intelligence within a CoI and it is continuously circulating throughout the network for advertising the community existence and for enabling all the members to progressively contribute to its enrichment. A peer receiving a community manifesto can autonomously decide to join the community and to become a community member according to its level of interest in the CoI interests.

Network connectivity: A number of solutions can be adopted to enforce effective communications within a P2P network, spanning from classical approaches based on message flooding, like Gnutella (The Gnutella Protocol, 2001), up to modern strategies based on gossiping and periodic exchange of peer neighborhood, like Shuffling (Voulgaris, Gavidia, & Van Steen, 2005). Most of the available solutions in this field are different in terms of generated network traffic and accuracy of the discovery procedures, and a comparative analysis can be found in Androutsellis-Theotokis and Spinellis (2004) and in Hose, Roth, Zeitz, Sattler, and Naumann (2008). In our reference P2P architecture, to enforce network connectivity and to support CoI formation, we define a Peer Knowledge space characterized by the use of a gossiping approach. In particular, through gossiping, all the messages exchanged by peers, like for example query/answer messages and community advertisements, can be effectively propagated throughout the network, thus enforcing the phase of implicit negotiation of the unsupervised approach described above. This is due to the fact that, in a gossiping-based P2P network, a peer is connected to a small set of randomly-chosen nodes that are continuously updated through periodic exchange of neighborhood with other nodes. This way, a message (e.g., a query, an answer, a community advertisement) that needs to be propagated is piggybacked on ordinary gossiping operations and it epidemically reaches all the peers without causing traffic overhead.

Modeling Knowledge at the Peer Level

Each peer is considered as a single agent having view only of its personal knowledge, namely the *peer ontology*, describing its own contents/resources. Given a peer P_i, the peer ontology $PO(P_i)$ is a semantic-web resource like a RDF(S) repository or an OWL ontology, where N is the set of element names, P is the set of property/relation names, and L is the set of datatypes and literal values in the signature of $PO(P_i)$, respectively. The elements of the peer ontology $PO(P_i)$, either concepts and instances, are formalized as a set of knowledge chunks $KC(P_i)$.

Given an element $e \in PO(P_i)$ (concept or instance), a *knowledge chunk kc(e)* $\in KC(P_i)$ provides a synthetic representation of the constituent axioms/assertions of *e*, both explicitly and implicitly defined in $PO(P_i)$. A knowledge chunk *kc(e)* is defined as a set of axioms $kc(e) = \{a_1, a_2, ..., a_n\}$ constituting the specification of the corresponding element *e*. An axiom $a_i(kc(e))$ with $i \in [1,n]$ has the form $a_i(kc(e)) = <n(kc), r(a_i), v(a_i)>$, where:

- $n(kc) \in N$ is the name of the knowledge chunk *kc(e)*, that is the name of *e*;
- $r(a_i) \in P \cup \{\equiv, \subseteq\}$ is a semantic relation contained in the definition of *e*;
- $v(a_i) \in N \cup L$ is the value of the corresponding relation $r(a_i)$.

Moreover, a knowledge chunk *kc(e)* is associated with a terminological equipment *E(kc(e))* and a change-log timestamp *TS(kc(e))*.

The *terminological equipment E(kc(e))* denotes the set of tags (i.e., terms) featuring *e* in $PO(P_i)$. For a given knowledge chunk *kc(e)*, the corresponding terminological equipment *E(kc(e))* is computed by considering the tags describing the element *e*, that is, the terms appearing in the set of all axioms in $PO(P_i)$ containing a reference to *e* (i.e., concept names, property names, annotation labels, and comments). Before insertion in *E(kc(e))*, a tag is submitted to a normalization/tokenization procedure. In this phase, various terminology-related procedures are executed, like for example a procedure to split compound tags and a procedure to derive lemmas/synonyms from a terminological thesaurus (e.g., WordNet). A detailed description of how to derive knowledge chunks and associated terminological equipments from OWL ontology specifications is provided in Castano, Ferrara, and Montanelli (2009).

Table 1. Knowledge Chunks of the Peer a

$KC(P_a)$ – Set of knowledge chunks of the peer P_a		
Knowledge chunk (*n(kc)*)	**Semantic relation (*$r(a_i)$*)**	**Relation value (*$v(a_i)$*)**
Drug	rdf:subClassOf	Pharmaceutical_Preparation
Drug	hasIngredient	Chemical
Drug	hasIngredient	Active_Ingredient
Therapeutic_Procedure	uses	Drug
Therapeutic_Procedure	treats	Disease

The *change-log timestamp TS(kc(e))* denotes the timestamp of the last update involving the specification of *kc(e)*. Each time the peer P_i performs an update to an element $e \in PO(P_i)$, the corresponding knowledge chunk *kc(e)*, the terminological equipment *E(kc(e))* and the change-log timestamp *TS(kc(e))* are updated accordingly.

Example 1. As an example of peer knowledge, we consider a peer P_a with a portion of a peer ontology $PO(P_a)$ in the e-health domain. Given the following OWL-DL axioms:

- Drug $\subseteq$ Pharmaceutical_Preparation
- Drug $\subseteq$ ∃hasIngredient.Active_Ingredient
- Therapeutic_Procedure $\subseteq$ ∃uses.Drug
- Therapeutic_Procedure $\subseteq$ ∃treats.Disease

The knowledge chunks kc(Drug) and kc(Therapeutic_Procedure) are inserted in the set $KC(P_a)$ (Table 1).

According to the specification in $PO(P_a)$, the terminological equipments associated with the knowledge chunks of $KC(P_a)$ are:

E(kc(Drug)) = {active, chemical, drug, ingredient, pharmaceutical, preparation}

E(kc(Therapeutic_Procedure)) = {disease, drug, procedure, use, therapeutic, treat}

We note that verbs are inserted in the terminological equipments in their basic form (e.g., treats → treat), compound tags are tokenized (e.g., Therapeutic_Procedure → therapeutic, procedure), and auxiliary verbs are not considered (e.g., hasIngredient → ingredient). Finally, the change-log timestamp t_0 is set for both the knowledge chunks kc(Drug) and kc(Therapeutic_Procedure), that is TS(kc(Drug)) = TS(kc(Therapeutic_Procedure)) = t_0.

Modeling Knowledge at the CoI Level

The consensus reached in a CoI around a topic/concept of interest is called collective intelligence and it is expressed in the form of a *community manifesto*. For a community *coi*, a community manifesto *m(coi)* is defined as a 4-tuple of the form: *m(coi) = <KC(coi), E(KC(coi)), TC(coi), CP(coi)>*, where:

- *KC(coi)* denotes the set of knowledge chunks describing the concepts of the focused ontology featuring the interests of *coi*;
- $E(KC(coi)) = \{E(kc) \mid kc \in KC(coi)\}$ denotes the set of terminological equipments associated with the knowledge chunks in *KC(coi)*;
- $TC(coi) = \{<t_i, k>\}$ denotes a tag cloud representing the shared vocabulary of *coi*, where $t_i \in E(kc)$ $(E(kc) \in E(KC(coi)))$ is a tag, and $k \in N$ denotes the frequency counter of t_i, namely the number of peers using the tag t_i;
- $CP(coi) = \{<ID(P_i), TS(P_i)>\}$ is the list of contributing peers, namely the peers that have worked on *m(coi)*, where $ID(P_i)$ is the identifier of the peer P_i, and $TS(P_i)$ is the timestamp of the last update applied by P_i to the manifesto.

The founder of the community *coi* has the role to define the initial focused ontology *KC(coi)*. This set remains unchanged during the overall community life-cycle and it is used by the peers receiving the manifesto *m(coi)* to assess their level of interest in *coi*. On the opposite, the set *E(KC(coi))* initially coincides with the terminological equipments associated with the knowledge chunks in *KC(coi)* of the founder, and it is progressively enriched by the community members according to the terminology used for describing their own resources. The tags in *E(KC(coi))* are used to feed the tag cloud *TC(coi)* where they are stored together with the associated frequency counters expressing their popularity in the community. The cloud *TC(coi)* enables each community member to become aware of the terminology used by other peers with similar interests and to enforce consolidation and standardization of a shared community vocabulary.

Due to the progressive enrichment of the manifesto *m(coi)* performed by the community members, a number of different versions of *m(coi)* are generated during the overall life-cycle of the community *coi*. We denote as $v_1(m(coi))$ the initial version of the community manifesto *m(coi)* created by the founder of the community, while the jth version of the manifesto *m(coi)* is denoted as $v_j(m(coi))$.

Example 2. As an example of community manifesto, we consider a community coi_1 about medical drugs founded by the peer P_a with an initial manifesto $v_1(m(coi_1))$ defined in Table 2.

Table 2. Knowledge chunks of community manifesto

$KC(coi_1)$ – Set of knowledge chunks of the community manifesto of coi_1		
Knowledge chunk (*n(kc)*)	**Semantic relation (*$r(a_i)$*)**	**Relation value (*$v(a_i)$*)**
Drug	rdf:subClassOf	Pharmaceutical_Preparation
Drug	hasIngredient	Chemical
Drug	hasIngredient	Active_Ingredient

- $E(KC(coi_1)) = E(kc(Drug)) = \{active, chemical, drug, ingredient, pharmaceutical, preparation\}$
- $TC(coi_1) = \{(active,1), (chemical,1), (drug,1), (ingredient,1), (pharmaceutical,1), (preparation,1)\}$
- $CP(coi_1) = \{<P_a, t_1>\}$

The community manifesto $v_1(m(coi_1))$ is defined by the peer P_a by specifying $KC(coi_1) = \{kc(Drug)\}$ with $kc(Drug) \in KC(P_a)$. The tag cloud $TC(coi_1)$ initially coincides with the terminological equipment E(kc(Drug)) and the popularity of each tag is set by default to 1. Finally, the set $CP(coi_1)$ initially contains only the community founder P_a and the timestamp t_1.

CONSTRUCTION OF THE COLLECTIVE INTELLIGENCE

In the Peer Knowledge space, the gossiping mechanism enforces the advertisement of the existing CoIs by disseminating the associated community manifestos. When a peer P_i receives from the network the manifesto $v_j(m(coi))$, the following tasks are executed.

1. The peer P_i evaluates its level of interest in the community *coi* (*matching task*).
2. If the community is joined, the peer P_i contributes to the collective intelligence of the community *coi* by enriching the manifesto $v_j(m(coi))$ with its terminological preferences (*contribution task*). The updated version $v_{j+1}(m(coi))$ of the community manifesto is generated by the peer P_i.
3. This updated version of the community manifesto is propagated throughout the P2P network to advertise the other community members of the changes (*propagation task*).

Matching task. The goal of the matching task is to determine whether the peer P_i is interested in the incoming manifesto $v_j(m(coi))$, and thus in the community *coi*. The criterion adopted in our approach is featured by an affinity-based interest, which means that a peer is interested in a CoI if its knowledge "has to do" with the topics described by the manifesto. Thus, the knowledge in the peer ontology of P_i is matched against the focused ontology of the CoI. To this end, we employ our ontology matching engine HMatch 2.0 which has been specifically conceived to match semantic web ontologies in open distributed systems, like P2P systems. HMatch 2.0 has been successfully tested and evaluated over the 2006, 2007, and 2009 benchmarks of the Ontology Alignment Evaluation Initiative (OAEI)[1], and over real datasets in the framework of the BOEMIE research project[2].

HMatch 2.0 takes as input two ontologies and returns as output the mappings between pairs of concepts with the same or the closest intended meaning in the two ontologies. HMatch 2.0 measures the semantic affinity of two concepts by exploiting the information of their corresponding knowledge chunk representations. Given two knowledge chunks kc' and kc'', the function $SA(kc',kc'') \rightarrow [0,1]$ calculates their semantic affinity value as the linear combination of a linguistic affinity value $LA(kc',kc'')$ and a contextual affinity value $CA(kc',kc'')$. In particular, $LA(kc',kc'')$ is calculated by comparing the name of kc' and kc''. For evaluating $LA()$, HMatch 2.0 relies on a thesaurus of terms and terminological relationships automatically extracted from the WordNet lexical system. The contextual affinity function of HMatch 2.0 provides a measure of similarity between two knowledge chunks by taking into account the number of their matching axioms as follows:

$$CA(kc',kc'') = \frac{2 \cdot |\{matching\ axioms\ of\ kc'\ and\ kc''\}|}{|kc'| + |kc''|}$$

where $|kc'|$, $|kc''|$, and $|\{matching\ axioms\ of\ kc'\ and\ kc''\}|$ denote the number of axioms of kc', the number of axioms of kc'', and the number of matching axioms between kc' and kc'', respectively.

Conditions for considering a pair of axioms (a_i,a_j) as matching axioms depend on the kind of involved semantic relations $r(a_i)$ and $r(a_j)$ and on their corresponding values $v(a_i)$ and $v(a_j)$, respectively (see Table 3).

In particular, three different cases can occur.

- $r(a_i)$ and $r(a_j)$ are both object properties. In this case, the corresponding values $v(a_i)$ and $v(a_j)$ are concept names. Thus, a_i and a_j are considered as matching axioms iff the linguistic affinity of $r(a_i)$ and $r(a_j)$ is greater than or equal to a given threshold th_1 and the linguistic affinity of $v(a_i)$ and $v(a_j)$ is greater than or equal to a given threshold th_2.

Table 3. Conditions for matching axioms

Kind of semantic relations	Conditions for matching axioms
$r(a_i)$ and $r(a_j)$ are object properties	$LA(r(a_i),r(a_j)) \geq th_1$ AND $LA(v(a_i),v(a_j)) \geq th_2$
$r(a_i)$ and $r(a_j)$ are datatype properties	$LA(r(a_i),r(a_j)) \geq th_1$ AND $v(a_i)$, $v(a_j)$ *are compatible ranges*
$r(a_i)$ is a datatype property and $r(a_j)$ is an object property	$LA(r(a_i),r(a_j)) \geq th_1$

- $r(a_i)$ and $r(a_j)$ are both datatype properties. In this case, the values $v(a_i)$ and $v(a_j)$ are the corresponding datatype ranges. Two datatype ranges are considered as matching ranges when they are compatible. For example, a range xsd:numeric is compatible with other numeric datatypes like xsd:float or xsd:integer. A set of compatibility rules has been defined in HMatch 2.0 to code the main range-type compatibilities featuring OWL ontologies.
- $r(a_i)$ is a datatype property and $r(a_j)$ is an object property (or vice versa). In this case, the corresponding values $v(a_i)$ and $v(a_j)$ are incomparable. Thus, we assume that the axioms a_i and a_j match when the linguistic affinity of $r(a_i)$ and $r(a_j)$ is greater than or equal to a given threshold th_1.

A comprehensive Semantic Affinity value of *kc'* and *kc"* is calculated as follows:

$$SA(kc',kc'') = W_{LA} \cdot LA(kc',kc'') + (1 - W_{LA}) \cdot CA(kc',kc'')$$

where $W_{LA} \in [0,1]$, is a weight expressing the relevance assigned to the Linguistic Affinity in the overall computation of $SA(kc',kc'')$. The use of the weight W_{LA} in $SA(kc',kc'')$ is motivated by the need of enabling a peer P_i to support a flexible matching process. In some circumstances, the Semantic Affinity value can be calculated on the basis of the Linguistic Affinity only, thus excluding the computation of the Contextual Affinity (i.e., $W_{LA} = 1$). This is suggested, for example, when poor computational resources are available on a peer P_i, and a fast matching execution is required. Instead, a balanced use of the weight W_{LA} is suggested when a more accurate semantic affinity evaluation is requested by the peer P_i and both Linguistic and Contextual Affinity need to be calculated (i.e., $W_{LA} = 0.5$). In the examples of this paper, we work with a default value $W_{LA} = 0.5$. For the selection of such a default value of W_{LA}, we chose the value that provided more satisfactorily results in the ontology matching experiments performed over the OAEI benchmarks and the BOEMIE datasets. A more detailed description of HMatch 2.0 and related ontology matching models and techniques is provided in Castano, Ferrara, and Montanelli (2006).

The result of the matching task is a mapping set $MAP(P_i,coi) = \{<kc',kc''>\}$ composed by the pairs of matching knowledge chunks $kc' \in KC(P_i)$ and $kc'' \in KC(coi)$, respectively. Each peer defines its own set of *join constraints* which are used to configure HMatch 2.0 and to specify the minimal matching conditions that are required in order to join a community. For example, the join constraints used by a peer P_i can be based on the set cardinality $k = |MAP(P_i,coi)|$, namely on the number of matching knowledge chunks discovered by HMatch 2.0 between the peer knowledge and the community knowledge. The peer P_i tunes its "willingness" to join a CoI by setting appropriate constraints on the value of the cardinality k. If a peer P_i aims at participating to a high number of CoIs a low value of k is set (e.g., $k = 1$), while a more selective community participation is determined by a high value of k (e.g., $k > 1$). When the join constraints are satisfied, the peer enters the community and the manifesto $v_j(m(coi))$ is locally stored, otherwise the manifesto $v_j(m(coi))$ is discarded.

We note that, for a given semantic community *coi*, the peer P_i executes the matching task only at the arrival of the first manifesto *m(coi)*, disregarding the number of the received version. Subsequent arrivals of any version of *m(coi)* are not submitted to matching since the knowledge chunks *KC(coi)* are unchanged and the mapping set $MAP(P_i,coi)$ is already calculated.

Contribution task. The goal of the contribution task is to enable the peer P_i to enrich the manifesto $v_j(m(coi))$ with its own terminological preferences. The key point of this task is that, due to the gossiping mechanism, multiple and different versions of a manifesto *m(coi)* can coexist in the network at a certain moment and can be received by a peer P_i. Thus, P_i has the need to detect whether an incoming manifesto $v_j(m(coi))$ has been already received in the past and which are the tags in its peer ontology that have to be considered for insertion in the tag cloud $TC(coi) \in v_j(m(coi))$. For this reason, the contribution task is implemented through timestamp-based techniques, similarly to what is done for transaction management in distributed database systems (Ozsu & Valduriez, 1999). When a manifesto $v_j(m(coi))$ is received, the list of contributing peers $CP(coi) \in v_j(m(coi))$ is exploited by the peer P_i. The following scenarios can occur.

1. $\boldsymbol{ID(P_i) \notin CP(coi)}$. This means that $v_j(m(coi))$ is the manifesto of a new CoI at its first arrival. In this case, given the mapping set $MAP(P_i,coi) = \{<kc',kc''>\}$ calculated in the matching task, the terminological equipment $E(kc')$ of a matching knowledge chunk $kc' \in KC(P_i)$ is added to the terminological equipment $E(kc'')$ of the corresponding matching knowledge chunk $kc'' \in KC(coi)$, namely $E(kc'') = E(kc'') \cup E(kc')$.

Table 4. Knowledge Chunks of the Peer b

$KC(P_b)$ – Set of knowledge chunks of the peer P_b		
Knowledge chunk (*n(kc)*)	**Semantic relation (*r(a_j)*)**	**Relation value (*v(a_j)*)**
Malaria	rdf:subClassOf	Parasitic_Disease
Malaria	hasSymptom	Intermittent_Fever
Malaria	hasSymptom	Anemia
Antimalarial_Drug	rdf:subClassOf	Medicine
Antimalarial_Drug	Treats	Malaria

Moreover, the tags of the terminological equipment $E_{kc'}$ are added to the community tag cloud $TC(coi)$. Given a tag $t_i \in E(kc')$, the pair $<t_i, 1>$ is inserted in $TC(coi)$ if the tag t_i is missing in the tag cloud, otherwise the pair $<t_i, k> \in TC(coi)$ is updated to $<t_i, k+1>$. Finally, the identifier $ID(P_i)$ is added to $CP(coi)$ with an updated timestamp $TS(P_i)$.

2. ***$ID(P_i) \in CP(coi)$***. This means that another version of $v_j(m(coi))$ was already received in the past and processed by the peer P_i. In this case, P_i has to update the manifesto by considering only the changes that occurred to its own knowledge (chunks) after the execution of the last contribution task. To this end, given the mapping set $MAP(P_i,coi)$, the peer P_i calculates the set of tags $T_{new}(coi)$ as $T_{new}(coi) = \{t_j \mid t_j \in E(kc'), TS(kc') > TS(P_i)\}$, where $kc' \in KC(P_i)$, $<kc', kc''> \in MAP(P_i,coi)$, $TS(kc')$ is the timestamp of the last change-log on kc', and $TS(P_i) \in CP(coi)$ is the timestamp of the last contribution task performed by P_i on $v_j(m(coi))$. For each $t_j \in T_{new}(coi)$, both $E(kc'')$ and $TC(coi)$ are updated by including t_j in $E(kc'')$ and by increasing the frequency counter of t_j in $TC(coi)$. Finally, the timestamp $TS(P_i)$ is updated in $CP(coi)$. A updated version $v_{j+1}(m(coi))$ of the community manifesto is then generated

Propagation task. The goal of the propagation task is to propagate the version v_{j+1} of the manifesto $m(coi)$ over the Peer Knowledge layer. After the execution of the contribution task, $v_{j+1}(m(coi))$ is passed to the gossiping mechanism and it is forwarded to the neighboring peers of P_i for advertisement.

Example 3. We consider three peers, namely P_a, P_b, and P_c where the peer P_a is the founder of the community coi_1 introduced in Example 2, whose knowledge chunks $KC(P_a)$ are shown in Example 1. Assume that the following knowledge chunks are stored by P_b and P_c in their respective peer knowledge (Table 4, Table 5).

Table 5. Knowledge Chunks of the Peer c

KC(P_c) – Set of knowledge chunks of the peer P_c		
Knowledge chunk (*n(kc)*)	**Semantic relation (*r(a_i)*)**	**Relation value (*v(a_i)*)**
Drug	hasIngredient	Chemical
Drug	treats	Malaria
Halfan	rdf:subClassOf	Drug
Quinine	rdf:subClassOf	Drug
Vibravenos	rdf:subClassOf	Drug

- E(kc(Malaria)) = {anemia, disease, fever, intermittent, malaria, parasitic, symptom}
- E(kc(Antimalarial_Drug)) = {antimalarial, drug, malaria, medicine, treat}
- TS(kc(Malaria)) = TS(kc(Antimalarial_Drug)) = t_0
- E(kc(Drug)) = {drug, chemical, ingredient, malaria, treat}
- E(kc(Halfan)) = {drug, halfan}
- E(kc(Quinine)) = {drug, quinine}
- E(kc(Vibravenos)) = {drug, vibravenos}
- TS(kc(Drug)) = TS(kc(Halfan)) = TS(kc(Quinine)) = TS(kc(Vibravenos)) = t_0

Through gossiping, the initial version of the community manifesto v_1(m(coi_1)) produced by the peer P_a is propagated to P_b and P_c. In Figure 2, we show the process of convergence of the community manifesto of coi_1. To highlight the results of the contribution task, for each version of the community manifesto produced by the various peers during convergence, in Figure 2, we only report the content of the tag cloud TC(coi_1).

Receiving v_1(m(coi_1)), the peer P_b matches its knowledge chunks KC(P_b) against the knowledge chunks KC(coi_1), discovering that SA(Antimalarial_Drug,Drug) = 0.6; thus the mapping set MAP(P_b,coi_1) = {<kc(Antimalarial_Drug), kc(Drug)>} is produced by HMatch 2.0. Assuming that at least one matching knowledge chunk is required to join a CoI ($|MAP(P_b,coi_1)| \geq 1$), P_b joins the community coi_1 and it stores the manifesto v_1(m(coi_1)). Moreover, in the contribution task, the peer P_b enriches E(kc(Drug)) ∈ E(KC(coi_1)) and TC(coi_1) by inserting the terminological equipment E(kc(Antimalarial_Drug)). This originates the following version v_2(m(coi_1)) of the community manifesto (Table 6).

- E(KC(coi_1)) = E(kc(Drug)) = {active, antimalarial, chemical, drug, ingredient, malaria, medicine, pharmaceutical, preparation, treat}

Figure 2. Example of manifesto convergence from v_1 to v_5

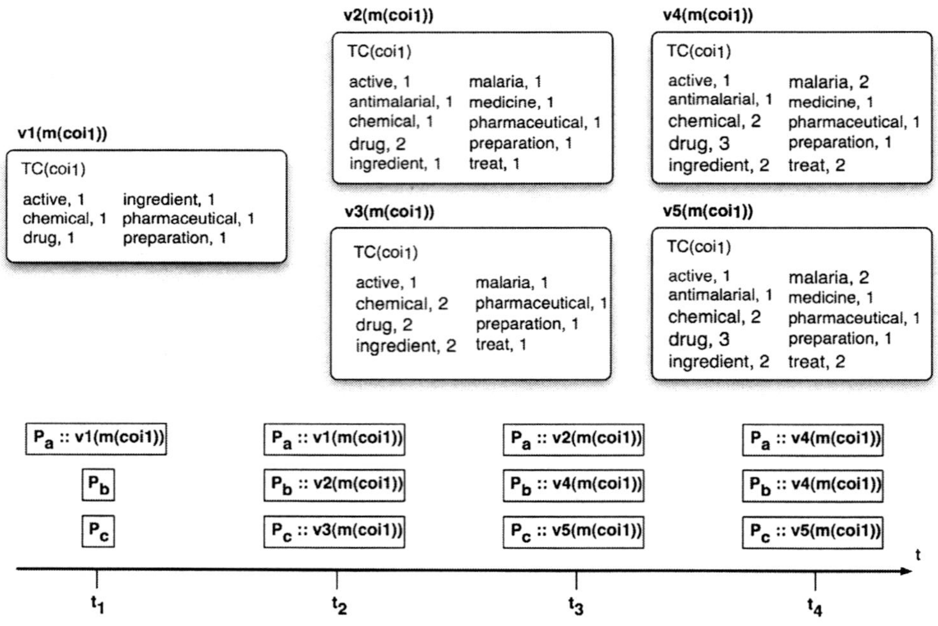

Table 6. Knowledge Chunks of the Community Manifesto

KC(coi_1) – Set of knowledge chunks of the community manifesto of coi_1		
Knowledge chunk (*n(kc)*)	**Semantic relation (*r(a_j)*)**	**Relation value (*v(a_j)*)**
Drug	rdf:subClassOf	Pharmaceutical_Preparation
Drug	hasIngredient	Chemical
Drug	hasIngredient	Active_Ingredient

- TC(coi_1) = {(active,1), (antimalarial,1), (chemical,1), (drug,2), (ingredient,1), (malaria,1), (medicine,1), (pharmaceutical,1), (preparation,1), (treat,1)}
- CP(coi_1) = {<P_a, t_1>, <P_b, t_2>}

At the same time, receiving v_1(m(coi_1)), the peer P_c joins the community coi_1 due to the mapping set MAP(P_c,coi_1) = {<kc(Drug), kc(Drug)>} produced by HMatch 2.0, since SA(Drug,Drug) = 0.7. A version v_3(m(coi_1)) of the community manifesto is produced by P_c and it is propagated over the Peer Knowledge layer through gossiping. When P_b receives the version v_3(m(coi_1)), the contribution task is executed to include the terminological equipment E(kc(Antimalarial_Drug)) also in v_3(m(coi_1)). A version v_4(m(coi_1)) is then produced and propagated. Similarly, a

Table 7. Knowledge Chunks of the Community Manifesto

KC(coi_1) – Set of knowledge chunks of the community manifesto of coi_1		
Knowledge chunk ($n(kc)$)	**Semantic relation ($r(a_i)$)**	**Relation value ($v(a_i)$)**
Drug	rdf:subClassOf	Pharmaceutical_Preparation
Drug	hasIngredient	Chemical
Drug	hasIngredient	Active_Ingredient

version $v_5(m(coi_1))$ is produced by P_c when it receives $v_2(m(coi_1))$. In Figure 2, it is simple to note that the versions v_4 and v_5 are identical and each of them represents the final community manifesto of coi_1 as follows (Table 7).

- $E(KC(coi_1)) = E(kc(Drug))$ = {active, antimalarial, chemical, drug, ingredient, malaria, medicine, pharmaceutical, preparation, treat}
- $TC(coi_1)$ = {(active,1), (antimalarial,1), (chemical,2), (drug,3), (ingredient,2), (malaria,2), (medicine,1), (pharmaceutical,1), (preparation,1), (treat,2)}
- $CP(coi_1) = \{<P_a, t_1>, <P_b, t_2>, <P_c, t_3>\}$

This version of the manifesto is progressively received and stored by all the community members. Further updates to the community manifesto are not required until changes to the peer ontology of the community members will occur.

Considerations and Contributions

To better remark the contribution of our work, we give some considerations on the P2P convergence of a community manifesto and on the relationships between our work about CoIs and the state-of-the-art solutions about ontology-based Communities of Practice (CoPs).

Propagation and convergence of a community manifesto. The path followed by a community manifesto during propagation throughout the network cannot be predicted in advance due to the random exchange of peer neighborhoods adopted by the gossiping mechanism. This means that a certain manifesto $v_j(m(coi))$ can be received multiple times by a peer P_i, and two versions $v_j(m(coi))$ and $v_l(m(coi))$ of a manifesto can be received in a different order by two community members P_i and P_k. Thus, at a given moment for the same community *coi*, two members P_i and P_k can store two different versions of the *coi* manifesto $v_j(m(coi))$ and $v_l(m(coi))$, respectively. The manifestos v_j and v_l have the same set of knowledge chunks *KC(coi)* (i.e., those defined by the founder), but they can differ in the terminological equipments *E(KC(coi))*, or in the tag cloud *TC(coi)*, or in the list of contributing peers *CP(coi)*.

For this reason, a member of *coi* storing a certain version v_j of the manifesto *m(coi)* can not be sure that this version is fully representative of the actual terminological preferences of all the community members. However, the various manifesto versions tend to converge towards a unique and comprehensive community manifesto under the (reasonable) assumption that the changes to the peer ontology of the community members are non-frequent events. In this case, the time required for reaching the manifesto convergence depends on the size of the network, on the number of community members, and on the configuration of the gossiping mechanism for what concerns the frequency of the neighbor-exchange operations.

CoIs vs. CoPs. The considered problem of collective intelligence creation within a CoI has a number of analogies with the problem of knowledge management within a Community of Practice (CoP). A CoP is a group of people within (or sometimes across) organizations who share a common set of information, needs or problems (Seely-Brown & Duguid, 1991). Knowledge management issues for CoPs are widely discussed in the literature due to the need to explicitly and formally capture the common conventions, languages, tool usage, and standards that characterize the community. Usually, ontologies are employed to specify the CoP knowledge, both at the level of a single member, where an ontology provides a semantic representation of the knowledge shared by a given community member; and at the level of an overall community, where an ontology formalizes the shared practices of the entire set of community member s (Alani, Dasmahapatra, O'Hara, & Shadbolt, 2003; Davies, Duke, & Sure, 2004). Moreover, ontology mediation techniques are sometimes proposed to discover possible points of convergence between different community members (Spaniol & Klamma, 2004). As far as we know, the existing approaches to CoP knowledge management consider web-based infrastructures where a centralized repository is used to store the shared community knowledge and a coordinating authority has the role to resolve possible conflicts between members. The focus of the approach we propose in this paper places the accent more on the problem of how to coordinate a collective intelligence that is autonomously emerging in an open distributed system, like a P2P network, rather than on the problem of how to model the different kinds of knowledge (e.g., an interest, a practice) that can be shared by a group of members. In a P2P network, a central knowledge repository as well as a coordination authority is almost missing or difficult to maintain during time. For this reason, we propose to describe the collective intelligence of a CoI through a community manifesto that is continuously circulating throughout the P2P network for enabling the community members to contribute to the progressive enrichment of the collective intelligence.

Adaptation of our approach to CoPs. In our P2P approach, the correct evolution of the collective intelligence of a CoI is guaranteed by the contribution task that is periodically executed by the community member and by the subsequent propagation task that enables to advertise the updates applied to the manifesto. We stress that the P2P approach we propose can be suitably adopted also in the case of a web-based CoP by storing the community manifesto in a centralized repository. The formalism of knowledge chunks enables a community member to model its practices and the matching task is exploited to discover similarities between the knowledge of a specific community member and the centrally-stored manifesto. The contribution task is executed by a community member when a change occurs in its local knowledge and the propagation task is no more required since any community member can acquire the up-to-date manifesto by accessing the centralized repository.

APPLICATION TO THE E-HEALTH DOMAIN

The proposed architecture based on the notion of CoI and collective intelligence has been implemented within the iCoord system for P2P semantic coordination (The iCoord System, 2008). In iCoord, coordination means the capability of each single peer to automatically retrieve and effectively share the data of interest by also dealing with the need of evolving its own knowledge over time to correctly assimilate the new external knowledge acquired from outside partners during collaboration/interaction (Castano, Ferrara, Lorusso, & Montanelli, 2008). Key features of iCoord are i) the adoption of a shuffling-based approach to enforce peer-to-peer communications in the Peer Knowledge space (Voulgaris et al., 2005), and ii) the development of advanced techniques to enable semantic query answering and tool-assisted knowledge design capable of exploiting the collective intelligence of specialized CoIs available in the network, as will be described in the following.

As application example, we consider a case study in the e-health domain, based on a P2P network of medical structures (i.e., hospitals and specialized research labs) that need to cooperate for knowledge and data sharing. Each peer of the network represents a medical structure and it is equipped with a software toolkit for accessing the functionalities of the iCoord system. In the example, we consider the community coi_1 about medical drugs, and the community members P_a, P_b, and P_c presented in Example 3.

Exploiting CoIs for Query Answering

The joined CoIs are exploited by a peer to retrieve from the network the available matching knowledge chunks about a certain concept of its own interest. Data/resource search is performed by a requesting peer P_i by formulating a *probe query pq* with an ontological specification of a target concept of interest expressed in the form of one or more knowledge chunks. For a given query *pq*, a matching-based

Table 8. Knowledge Chunks Featuring Probe Query

pq_1 – Set of knowledge chunks featuring the probe query		
Knowledge chunk (*n(kc)*)	**Semantic relation (*r(a$_j$)*)**	**Relation value (*v(a$_j$)*)**
Malaria	rdf:subClassOf	Disease
Medicine	Treats	Malaria

routing mechanism, called *routing-by-community*, is provided in iCoord to choose the most appropriate recipients of *pq*, namely those CoIs whose members are most likely capable of providing relevant results for the query target. In this respect, for a community *coi*, the set *KC(coi)* in the manifesto *m(coi)* is exploited to evaluate the relevance of *coi* for the query *pq*. In particular, the HMatch 2.0 system is invoked by the requesting peer P_i to match *pq* against the manifestos of the joined communities. A community *coi* is considered as a candidate recipient for the query *pq* when at least one matching knowledge chunk $kc \in KC(coi)$ is found for *pq* by HMatch 2.0. The communities with the most relevant matching results are finally selected as query recipients by the routing-by-community mechanism. Queries are propagated throughout the network with shuffling and, given the community *coi* as query recipient, the peer members of *coi* can filter all the incoming queries by considering for processing only the requests sent to *coi*. A detailed description of the routing-by-community mechanism and related query propagation techniques are provided in Montanelli & Castano (2008).

Receiving *pq*, a peer P_k invokes HMatch 2.0 to compare the incoming probe query against its knowledge chunks $KC(P_k)$ and to identify possible semantic affinities. In particular, *SA(pq, kc)* is calculated by the peer P_k for each knowledge chunk $kc \in KC(P_k)$. A (possibly empty) list of matching knowledge chunks is returned by HMatch 2.0. If a non-empty result is produced, these matching knowledge chunks are used to compose an answer to *pq* that is returned to the requesting peer P_i. Collecting all the query answers, the peer P_i evaluates all the returned matching concepts and decides whether to further peer-to-peer interact with one or more answering peers for effective data acquisition.

Example 4. The peer P_a is interested in discovering network nodes that are capable of providing relevant knowledge about malaria and possible drugs for treating this disease. A probe query pq_1 is formulated by P_a containing the following knowledge chunks (Table 8).

By matching pq_1 against $KC(coi_1)$ with HMatch 2.0, the peer P_a obtains SA(Medicine,Drug) = 0.5.The community coi_1 is then selected as query recipient by the routing-by-community mechanism and pq_1 is submitted to the network for propagation to the coi_1 members P_b and P_c. In the peer P_b, HMatch 2.0 is invoked

Table 9. Semantic affinities

SA(Medicine, Drug) = 0.83
SA(Medicine, Halfan) = 0.4
SA(Medicine, Quinine) = 0.4
SA(Medicine, Vibravenos) = 0.4

to compare pq_1 against the knowledge chunks $KC(P_b)$ and the semantic affinities SA(Medicine,Antimalarial_Drug) = 0.73 and SA(Malaria,Malaria) = 0.75 are returned as a result. Thus, a query answer containing the knowledge chunk kc(Antimalarial_Drug) and kc(Malaria) are sent by the peer P_b to the requesting peer P_a as a reply. At the same time, in the peer P_c, the following semantic affinities are returned by HMatch 2.0 as matching results between the query pq_1 and the knowledge chunks $KC(P_c)$ (see Table 9).

A query answer containing the knowledge chunks kc(Drug), kc(Halfan), kc(Quinine), and kc(Vibravenos) are sent by the peer P_c to the requesting peer P_a as a reply. By exploiting the received replies, P_a recognizes that the peer P_b provides a symptomatical description of malaria and antimalarial drugs, while the peer P_c stores knowledge about drugs to treat malaria. Since the peer P_a is interested in retrieving data about drugs for malaria, the peer P_c is selected as a partner for the subsequent data acquisition phase. State-of-the-art techniques can be exploited to acquire data from matching peers (see for instance Halevy et al. (2004) for further details).

Exploiting Collective Intelligence for Knowledge Design and Evolution

The collective intelligence of the joined CoIs is exploited by a peer when it needs to update its own knowledge for specifying new ontology concepts as well as for changing/enriching the specification of existing ones. To this end, a tool-assisted environment for knowledge design, called NLE, is provided in iCoord, based on grammar-controlled syntax and natural-language descriptions of the edited concepts (Ferrara, Montanelli, Varese, & Castano, 2009). In the NLE tool environment, editing is performed on a *concept draft* which can be manually specified "from scratch" by the expert user in case of insertion of a new concept, or can be derived from a concept currently stored in the peer ontology in case of enrichment of an existing concept. In both cases, the specification of a concept axiom is performed by providing a natural-language sentence, whose structure is controlled by a formal grammar capable of supporting the *intuitive* definition of a correct OWL axiom, by hiding most of the technical details generally required to use an ontology language.

During editing of a concept draft with the NLE tool, the role of the collective intelligence is twofold. On one side, the knowledge chunks $KC(coi_i)$ of a joined community coi_i are exploited to provide possible suggestions for reuse. The idea is that a knowledge chunk specified in the manifesto of a CoI can be used as a template during the manual specification of a concept using the NLE tool. This approach to knowledge design allows to enforce the reuse of existing knowledge within a CoI and to promote the diffusion of common design patterns among the members of a given community. The HMatch 2.0 system is invoked to match the concept draft under definition against the set $KC(coi_i)$ of each joined CoI, with the aim to discover the best matching knowledge chunks that can be provided as relevant suggestions. An initial set of matching knowledge chunks is provided in the editor at the beginning of the editing session, but new chunks are continuously retrieved on the fly as long as new assertions are specified in the editor and the matching operation becomes more precise. On the other side, the tag cloud $TC(coi_i)$ of a joined community coi_i is exploited to provide terminological hints during typing of name/structural definitions of the concept axiom under definition. The idea is that the popularity of a tag within a community of peers having similar interests/expertise can provide relevant suggestions in order to choose the most suitable terms in the specification of a given concept axiom. The linguistic affinity techniques of HMatch 2.0 are employed to evaluate the level of match between a given term t in the concept draft under definition and the tags in the tag cloud $TC(coi_i)$ of each joined community. A set of tag suggestions $T_{hint} = \{t' \mid t' \in TC(coi_i) \wedge LA(t,t') > th\}$ is produced by HMatch 2.0 as a result, where coi_i is a joined community and th is a threshold setting the minimum level of semantic affinity required for considering a tag $t' \in TC(coi_i)$ as a relevant suggestion for the considered concept draft. The tags in the set T_{hint} are ranked according to their frequency (i.e., popularity) and they are provided as suggestions of alternative tags for t in the axiom specification. Tag reuse and terminology sharing allow peers to consolidate a shared vocabulary within a community, thus eliciting the effectiveness of the knowledge sharing functionalities.

Once that the editing phase is completed, the concept draft is assimilated in the peer ontology. The NLE tool automatically translates the natural-language specification of the draft into a corresponding OWL specification. During translation, validation is performed with the Pellet DL reasoner[3] to detect possible inconsistencies. Furthermore, after assimilation of the concept draft c, the corresponding knowledge chunk $kc(c)$ is updated in the peer knowledge as well as the terminological equipment $E(kc(c))$ and the timestamp $TS(kc(c))$.

Example 5. The peer P_b has the need to enrich the specification of its concept Antimalarial Drug, whose knowledge chunk kc(Antimalarial_Drug) is shown in Example 3.

In iCoord, the expert user of the peer P_b can visualize the list of concepts stored in its peer ontology (left panel of Figure 3) and it can start the editing phase by dragging the concept Antimalarial Drug, namely the concept draft, into the editing area (central panel of Figure 3). A matching knowledge chunk kc(Drug) $\in$ KC(coi_1) is discovered by HMatch 2.0 and it is shown in the suggestion area (right panel of Figure 3). In iCoord, the specifications of both concepts and suggestions are shown through the natural language descriptions produced by the NLE tool. The expert user can decide to reuse the suggestion of kc(Drug) by dragging this knowledge chunk into the editing area. In this case, the axioms of kc(drug) are appended to the axioms of the concept draft Antimalarial Drug and the expert user can choose to partially reuse the suggestion by removing those axioms that are considered as inappropriate and by modifying those terms that are considered as non-satisfactory. In particular, the axioms Drug is something that hasIngredient a Chemical and Drug is something that hasIngredient a Active Ingredient are reused, while the axiom Drug is a Pharmaceutical Preparation is dropped. Moreover, the term Drug is manually replace by the tag Antimalarial Drug. Thus, the concept draft is finally composed by the following axioms:

- Antimalarial Drug is a Medicine
- Antimalarial Drug is something that treats a Malaria
- Antimalarial Drug is something that hasIngredient a Chemical
- Antimalarial Drug is something that hasIngredient a Active Ingredient

At the same time, the linguistic matching techniques of HMatch 2.0 are invoked to compare the terms in the concept draft against the tags of the tag cloud TC(coi_1). Since the term Medicine matches the tag Drug $\in$ TC(coi_1) and since Drug has a high popularity in coi_1 (i.e., frequency = 3), the replacement of the term Medicine with the tag Drug in proposed in the editing area (see the terminological suggestions in Figure 3). Such a suggestion can be accepted or rejected by the expert user according to its terminological preferences and to the frequency of the proposed tags.

RELATED WORK

In the field of open distributed systems, like P2P and Grid, work related to CoI formation and management is mainly concerned with semantics-based P2P systems, with particular focus on those systems where the notion of peer community is ex-

Figure 3. The knowledge design environment of iCoord

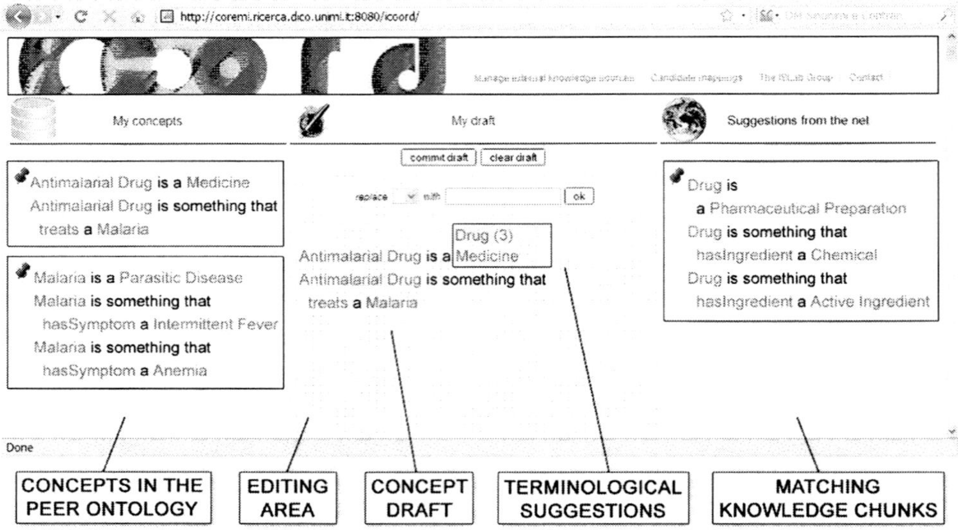

plicitly supported. In this context, some interesting approaches have been emerging in the recent years. For example, in Khambatti, Ryu, and Dasgupta (2002), *escalation techniques* are employed to advertise within the network the peer interests expressed through attributes (i.e., keywords) and to allow the receiving nodes to detect the existence of common interest and thus communities. A similar approach is proposed in Das et al. (2009) where the advertisement phase of peer interests is used by the network nodes to build routing indexes that are subsequently exploited in the search phase to improve the efficiency of query propagation.

In Liu, Bhaduri, Das, Nguyen, and Kargupta (2006), a statistical mechanism based on the *quantile* measure is used to evaluate the similarity among the advertised peer interests. In the proposed approach, a peer can decide to promote the formation of a new community according to the level of similarity between its own interests and the received advertisements. An invitation procedure is then enforced by the community creator to initiate and supervise the concrete formation of the group. Peer interests can be inferred through mining techniques as proposed in Gu and Wei (2006). In that work, each community is defined as a vector of topics and it is assigned to a community manager which has the role of periodically advertising the community topics. The main limit of this kind of approaches is the traffic overhead due to community advertisement.

To overcome such a restriction, the use of a shared and centralized taxonomy of community topics is usually enforced. The list of communities is thus prefixed and a peer can choose one or more preferred communities to join by simply matching its interests with the centralized topics taxonomy. In Crespo and Garcia-Molina (2004), communities are clusters of similar peers whose contents are classified according to a predefined classification hierarchy (i.e., a tree of concepts). Keyword-based matching techniques are used by peers to determine the clusters to join. In most of these examples, both peer interests and community topics are expressed as keywords and basic string matching techniques are exploited in the community formation process to enable peers to choose the most interesting communities to join.

The use of Semantic Web technologies (i.e., ontologies and ontology-based matching techniques) has being recently exploited to provide a semantically rich representation of peer interests and/or community descriptions and to support similarity-based query/answer mechanisms. In Bloehdorn et al. (2005), ontologies are used for representing both the shared conceptualization of the allowed community topics and the expertise of each system node. The use of a shared ontology is enforced also in Wang and Vassileva (2004) where the notions of team, coalition, and congregation are proposed to distinguish among three different levels of cohesion when creating a peer community. However, methods and techniques for enabling peers to perform a coordinated exploitation of the collective knowledge/intelligence of a community are only marginally considered in the current literature.

In Aiello and Alessi (2007), the notion of collective knowledge is introduced to denote the knowledge fragments about a certain concept of interest that are interlinked across different nodes. In other approaches like Sigurbjörnsson and van Zwol (2008), collective knowledge is defined to support recommendation systems for multimedia resource annotation. The idea is that the system suggests the tags to use for annotation by analyzing statistics on tag co-occurrence derived from the experience of other users. As a general remark, we observe that all the considered systems deal (at different levels) with the notion of collective semantics, and they propose their own idea of "Social Network Analysis" aimed at enforcing effective knowledge retrieval (Avrithis et al., 2008).

Original contribution. The goal of our approach is to go beyond the existing state-of-the-art solutions for P2P community formation and management by adopting an unsupervised approach where the choice of joining/leaving a community is autonomously taken by each interested peer according to its own preferences. Moreover, the use of Semantic Web technologies like ontologies and ontology-based matching techniques allows to enforce a semantically rich approach to community and peer content description thus overcoming the need of a centralized/shared taxonomy. Furthermore, the collective construction of a community manifesto with a shared, preference-based vocabulary within a CoI represents a concrete attempt to combine the benefits of recently emerging social-based approaches with more consolidated P2P and Semantic Web technologies (Gruber, 2008).

CONCLUSION

In this paper, we presented a reference P2P architecture based on autonomous, self-emerging semantic communities of interest (CoIs) for collective intelligence creation and management. Techniques for enabling a group of independent peers to autonomously define their shared community vocabulary have been also discussed. We believe that the collective intelligence of a CoI expressed in the form of an ontology-based community manifesto can play an important role for the development of more effective P2P collaboration platforms. The iCoord system and the e-health example presented in the paper provide a significant result in this direction.

Currently, a prototype version of iCoord has been developed and it is available online as a web application (The iCoord System, 2008). Furthermore, experiments to evaluate the size of a community manifesto and associated vocabulary in real collaboration scenarios are being implemented. In particular, tests on the convergence issues of the community manifestos are being considered. In future work, we plan to investigate semantic clustering techniques based on the linguistic matching techniques of HMatch 2.0 for improving the organization of the vocabulary of a CoI by grouping tags that are semantically related.

REFERENCES

Aiello, G., & Alessi, M. (2007). DNK-WSD: a Distributed Approach for Knowledge Discovery in Peer to Peer Networks. In *Proceedings of the 15th EUROMICRO International Conference on Parallel, Distributed and Network-Based Processing (PDP'07)*, Naples, Italy (pp. 325-332).

Alani, H., Dasmahapatra, S., O'Hara, K., & Shadbolt, N. (2003). Identifying Communities of Practice through Ontology Network Analysis. *IEEE Intelligent Systems*, *18*(2), 18–25. doi:10.1109/MIS.2003.1193653

Aleman-Meza, B., Halaschek-Wiener, C., & Arpinar, I. B. (2005). Collective Knowledge Composition in a P2P Network. In L. C. Rivero, J. H. Doorn, & V. E. Ferraggine (Eds.), *Encyclopedia of Database Technologies and Applications* (pp. 74-77). Hershey, PA: IGI Global.

Androutsellis-Theotokis, S., & Spinellis, D. (2004). A Survey of Peer-to-Peer Content Distribution Technologies. *ACM Computing Surveys*, *36*(4), 335–371. doi:10.1145/1041680.1041681

Avrithis, Y., Kompatsiaris, Y., Staab, S., & Vakali, A. (Eds.). (2008). *Proceedings of the CISWeb (Collective Semantics: Collective Intelligence and the Semantic Web) Workshop, located at the 5th European Semantic Web Conference (ESWC 2008)*, Tenerife, Spain.

Bloehdorn, S., Haase, P., Hefke, M., Sure, Y., & Tempich, C. (2005). Intelligent Community Lifecycle Support. In *Proceedings of the 5th International Conference on Knowledge Management (I-KNOW 05)*, Graz, Austria.

Castano, S., Ferrara, A., Lorusso, D., & Montanelli, S. (2008). Ontology Coordination: The iCoord Project Demonstration. In *Proceedings of the 27th International Conference on Conceptual Modeling (ER 2008)*, Barcelona, Spain (pp. 512-513).

Castano, S., Ferrara, A., & Montanelli, S. (2006). Matching Ontologies in Open Networked Systems: Techniques and Applications. *Journal on Data Semantics, 5*, 25–63. doi:10.1007/11617808_2

Castano, S., Ferrara, A., & Montanelli, S. (2009). The iCoord Knowledge Model for P2P Semantic Coordination. In *Proceedings of the 6th Conference of the Italian Chapter of AIS*, Costa Smeralda (Nu), Italy.

Castano, S., & Montanelli, S. (2005). Semantic Self-Formation of Communities of Peers. In *Proceedings of the ESWC Workshop on Ontologies in Peer-to-Peer Communities*, Heraklion, Greece.

Crespo, A., & Garcia-Molina, H. (2004). Semantic Overlay Networks for P2P Systems. In *Proceedings of the 3rd International Workshop on Agents and Peer-to-Peer Computing (P2PC 2004)*, New York (pp. 1-13).

Das, T., Nandi, S., & Ganguly, N. (2009). Community Formation and Search in P2P: A Robust and Self-Adjusting Algorithm. In *Proceedings of the 3rd Workshop on Intelligent Networks: Adaptation, Communication & Reconfiguration (IAMCOM 2009)*, Bangalore, India.

Davies, J., Duke, A., & Sure, Y. (2004). OntoShare - An Ontology-based Knowledge Sharing System for virtual Communities of Practice. *The Journal of Universal Computer Science, 10*(3), 262–283.

Ferrara, A., Montanelli, S., Varese, G., & Castano, S. (2009). *Natural Language Ontology Authoring in iCoord. International Journal of Information Technology and Database Systems*. IJITDAS.

Gruber, T. (2008). Collective Knowledge Systems: where the Social Web meets the Semantic Web. *Journal of Web Semantics*, *6*(1), 4–13. doi:10.1016/j.websem.2007.11.011

Gu, W., & Wei, W. (2006). Automatic Community Discovery in Peer-to-Peer Systems. In *Proceedings of the 5th International Conference on Grid and Cooperative Computing Workshops (GCC 2006)*, Changsha, Hunan, China (pp. 110-116).

Halevy, A., Ives, Z., Madhavan, J., Mork, P., Suciu, D., & Tatarinov, I. (2004). The Piazza Peer Data Management System. *IEEE Transactions on Knowledge and Data Engineering*, *16*(7), 787–798. doi:10.1109/TKDE.2004.1318562

Hose, K., Roth, A., Zeitz, A., Sattler, K.-U., & Naumann, F. (2008). A Research Agenda for Query Processing in Large-Scale Peer Data Management Systems. *Information Systems*, *33*(7-8), 597–610. doi:10.1016/j.is.2008.01.012

Khambatti, M., Ryu, K. D., & Dasgupta, P. (2002). Efficient Discovery of Implicitly Formed Peer-to-Peer Communities. *International Journal of Parallel and Distributed Systems and Networks*, *5*(4), 155–164.

Liu, K., Bhaduri, K., Das, K., Nguyen, P., & Kargupta, H. (2006). Client-side Web Mining for Community Formation in Peer-to-Peer Environments. *SIGKDD Explorations*, *8*(2), 11–20. doi:10.1145/1233321.1233323

Montanelli, S., & Castano, S. (2008). Semantically Routing Queries in Peer-based Systems: the H-Link Approach. *The Knowledge Engineering Review*, *23*(1), 51–72. doi:10.1017/S0269888907001257

Ozsu, M. T., & Valduriez, P. (1999). *Principles of Distributed Database Systems* (2nd ed.). Upper Saddle River, NJ: Prentice Hall.

Ren, Z., Anumba, C. J., & Ugwu, O. O. (2002). Negotiation in a Multi-Agent System for Construction Claims Negotiation. *Applied Artificial Intelligence*, *16*(5), 359–394. doi:10.1080/08839510290030273

Seely-Brown, J., & Duguid, P. (1991). Organisational Learning and Communities of Practice. *Organization Science*, *2*(1).

Sigurbjörnsson, B., & Van Zwol, R. (2008). Flickr Tag Recommendation based on Collective Knowledge. In *Proceedings of the 17th International Conference on World Wide Web (WWW 2008)*, Beijing, China (pp. 327-336).

Spaniol, M., & Klamma, R. (2004). Mediating Ontologies for Communities of Practice. In *Proceedings of the 5th International Conference on Practical Aspects of Knowledge Management (PAKM 2004)*, Vienna, Austria (pp. 330-342).

The Gnutella Protocol. (2001). *The Gnutella Protocol Specification v0.4*. Retrieved from http://www9.limewire.com/developer/gnutella_protocol_0.4.pdf

The iCoord System. (2008). *The ISLab Knowledge Coordination Platform*. Retrieved from http://islab.dico.unimi.it/icoord/

Voulgaris, S., Gavidia, D., & Van Steen, M. (2005). CYCLON: Inexpensive Membership Management for Unstructured P2P Overlays. *Journal of Network and Systems Management*, *13*(2), 197–217. doi:10.1007/s10922-005-4441-x

Wang, Y., & Vassileva, J. (2004). Trust-Based Community Formation in Peer-to-Peer File Sharing Networks. In *Proceedings of the IEEE/WIC/ACM International Conference on Web Intelligence (WI'04)*, Beijing, China (pp. 341-348).

ENDNOTES

1 http://islab.dico.unimi.it/content/oaei2009/

2 http://www.boemie.org

3 http://pellet.owldl.com

APPENDIX

A summary table of the notations adopted in the paper is provided in Table 10.

Table 10. Notations

Notation	Description
coi	Semantic Community of Interest
P_i	i[th] peer of the network
$PO(P_i)$	Peer ontology of the peer P_i
N	Set of element names in $PO(P_i)$
P	Set of property/relation names in $PO(P_i)$
L	Set of datatypes and literal values in $PO(P_i)$
$KC(P_i)$	Set of knowledge chunks of the peer P_i
e	Element (concept or instance) of $PO(P_i)$
$kc(e)$	Knowledge chunk of the element e
a_i	i[th] axiom of a knowledge chunk
$n(kc)$	Name of the knowledge chunk kc
$r(a_i)$	Semantic relation of the axiom a_i
$v(a_i)$	Relation value of the axiom a_i
$E(kc(e))$	Terminological equipment of $kc(e)$
$TS(kc(e))$	Timestamp of the last change-log on $kc(e)$
$m(coi)$	Manifesto of the community coi
$KC(coi)$	Set of knowledge chunks of the community coi
$E(KC(coi))$	Set of terminological equipments of the community coi
$TC(coi)$	Tag cloud of the community coi
$CP(coi)$	Peers contributing to the manifesto of the community coi
t_i	i[th] tag in a tag cloud
$ID(P_i)$	Identifier of the peer P_i
$TS(P_i)$	Timestamp of the last update on a community manifesto performed by the peer P_i
$v_i(m(coi))$	i[th] version of the community manifesto for the community coi
$LA(kc',kc'')$	Linguistic Affinity value between kc' *and kc''*
$CA(kc',kc'')$	Contextual Affinity value between kc' *and kc''*
$SA(kc',kc'')$	Semantic Affinity value between kc' *and kc''*
W_{LA}	Weight of the linguistic affinity in the computation of $SA(kc',kc'')$
$MAP(P_i,coi)$	Set of similarity mappings between the knowledge chunks in $KC(P_i)$ and the knowledge chunks in $KC(coi)$
$T_{new}(coi)$	Set of new tags to insert in the tag cloud of the community coi
pq	Probe query
$T_{hint}(coi)$	Set of tags belonging to the tag cloud of the community coi that are exploited as suggestions during editing of a concept draft

This work was previously published in International Journal of Organizational and Collective Intelligence, Volume 1, Issue 4, edited by Hideyasu Sasaki, pp. 40-60, copyright 2010 by IGI Publishing (an imprint of IGI Global).

Chapter 11
A Social Bookmarking-Based People Search Service:
Building Communities of Practice with Collective Intelligence

Jeff J.S. Huang
National Central University, Taiwan

Stephen J.H. Yang
National Central University, Taiwan

Jeng C.C Chen
National Central University, Taiwan

Irene Y.S. Li
National Central University, Taiwan

Indy Y.T. Hsiao
National Central University, Taiwan

ABSTRACT

The emergence of Web 2.0 has brought along the trend of community. It is also the trend that contributes to socialization of the Internet. The essence of Web 2.0 is creation and sharing which give rise to social networking communities such as Blog, Wikipedia and Facebook. Through Wikipedia, Blogs, Facebook and other kinds of social networking websites, interactive relationship and bridge of knowledge sharing have been built up successfully. This paper attempts to propose an effective way

DOI: 10.4018/978-1-61350-135-1.ch011

to locate people with shared interests. By using Internet resources bookmarked by the users, the similarity of interests between them can be analyzed. Based on this relationship, people could build communities. Also, through community activities, the innovation and exchange of collective intelligence are accomplished.

INTRODUCTION

The emergence of Web 2.0 not only accelerates the development of diverse communities but also promotes socialization of the Internet. Lots of social software is created along with Web 2.0. The socialization of the Internet has become powerful and trendy. It inspires social networking websites such as Blog, Facebook, etc. The mechanism of socialized internet improves close interpersonal relationship and provides nonverbal communication media such as multimedia audio-visual objects, images, pictures, and other diverse media. By communicating and sharing with others through the resourceful media, the interpersonal interaction becomes closer.

Furthermore, through the services of Social Software such as Blog, Wiki, Facebook, Del.icio.us, Flickr, etc., Social Networking between users is established. This social networking helps users locate people with shared interests and form CoP(Communities of Practice). Through these social platforms, collective intelligence is realized. Afterwards, people can bring different CoPs together to form CoIs (Communities of interest) which can provide unique opportunities to bring social creativity alive by transcending individual perspectives (Fischer, 2001). Accordingly, some researchers assert that Social Network mainly emphasizes building various CoP so that users can share and exchange information with each other based on their similar interests (Rachel, 2008).

Indeed, products of knowledge sharing and creating by users are mostly on a certain social platform. For example, Flicker allows users to share pictures or images and Del.icio.us allows users to share bookmarks. These products are the aggregate of collective intelligence. However, real collective intelligence should not be limited to the sharing and creating products. The most significant resources are producers of these products. As Diederich & Iofciu (2006) pointed out, "using tag-based profile can give more recommendations than standard object-based user profiles." It means that producers play an important part in forming collective intelligence. If users can find those who share the same interests with them and interact with each other, innovation of knowledge and new world would be inspired by collective intelligence. Therefore, this paper mainly focuses on finding out people of shared interests by analyzing collaborative tags. By doing so, new knowledge communities are established. On the other hand, the use of similarity algorithm and Tag Cloud inspires the power of Web 2.0 collective intelligence, leads to communities of collective intelligence, and promotes innovative thinking and creativity.

WEB SEARCH SERVICE IN PEOPLE SEARCH AND RESOURCE SEARCH

The various social networking websites can be roughly categorized into two types (Guo & Zhao, 2008). One is human-centered which refers to the websites such as MySpace, FaceBook, etc. These websites emphasize online connection between people. The so-called "connection" here refers to the interaction such as "Electronic Mail", "Chat", "Blog", etc. These kinds of interaction will leave some records. By analyzing these records, researchers will have the information that shows the interrelationship between people. Early in 1993, Schwartz et al. had made use of the interactive records of interpersonal electronic mails along with Heuristic Graph Algorithms to explore people with shared interests or other relevant resources(Schwartz & Wood. 1993). Furthermore, Adamic & Adar (2005) pointed that interpersonal relationships can be analyzed by investigating the interactive process of electronic mail. Besides, Ali-Hasan and Adamic (2007) also indicated that the interests and specialties shared among people could be identified by analyzing the interactive records between bloggers and readers.

The other type is object-centered. The representative websites are Del.icio.us, YouTube, Flickr, etc. These websites put emphasis on sharing object. Several articles have been devoted to the studies of object-centered websites. For example, Heymann et al (2008) conducted research on Del.icio.us to discuss whether social bookmarking improves web search (Heymann et al., 2008, Yanbe et al., 2007). Kato et al. (2008) also conducted research on Del.icio.us to discuss whether social tagging improves web image (Kato et al., 2008, Bustos et al., 2005). However, the studies mentioned above do not focus on the interaction between people. Thus, we attempt to analyze objects shared by people in the object-centered websites and find out the interrelationship between people. We take Del.icio.us as our experimental object. The data extracted from Del.icio.us are analyzed to locate people with shared interests. Through this mechanism, communities of collective intelligence are established. In 2007, some relevant research conducting by well-known researchers such as Vu et al. analyzed and search people who have similar specialties by calculating similarity between documents they use on the Internet(Vu et al., 2007). Guo et al. (2005) and Sripanidkulchai (2003) investigated people's interests from peer-to-peer web resources sharing and saving. They found the interests shared by people by analyzing documents uploaded and downloaded by the users.

PEOPLE SEARCH SERVICE WITH COLLECTIVE INTELLIGENCE

"Human" is a set of knowledge or content producer. However, current search techniques are all fixed on "objects" such as the files, resources, and the specific information and knowledge documents located by Google Search. However, this search technique ignores the producers behind these resources - "human." Therefore, in this paper, "human" is considered as "intelligence resources" and the "objects" shared by these people on Del.icio.us, namely bookmarking resources, are considered as "knowledge resources." However, how can "intelligence resources" and "knowledge resources" be identified through the platforms of networking websites? Undoubtedly, this is what this paper discusses and centers on, especially the "intelligence resources." Therefore, the Internet resources tagged by collaborative tags are used as the medium to analyze the similarities between each other's interests. From this relationship, "intelligence resources" that include similar interests are located. Furthermore, through further interaction, communities of practice are established. Through community activities in these communities, innovation and sharing of collective intelligence are realized. On the other hand, people can find relevant "knowledge resources" they need through collaborative tags.

Moreover, there is research that centers on "human." Artiles et al. (2005) used "people name" to locate people. In this way, they solved problems of naming ambiguity and same name. They designed WePS(Web People Search)as a test platform. Users input "people names" and search relevant people rank as results on the list. Although searching by people names is helpful to find people, it is possible to lose people similar to the users. Accordingly, research of locating people of similar field by analyzing documents is conducted. Wan et al. proposed a method to search relevant "people" from relevant people-document and conducted resolution of people names to find out people of relevant field (Wan, Gao, Li, & Ding, 2005). Diederich and Iofciu (2006) proposed another method to locate people in the website. They used tag-based profiles to find people with similar interests. In terms of this, if people of similar fields can be located in social network and gather them to form CoP, through community activities, collective intelligence is realized. It will highlight the efforts of people search service. Other researchers such as Mori et al. (2008) proposed an important finding. They discovered that finding relevant people in certain fields is important to Collaborative System. Thus, they recommend a people search interface and tool which requires users to input information about those who are searched for before people search. In this way, search results of the target people can be more accurate. According to the forth mentioned relevant research, the research of using "human" as a resource in the era of Web 2.0 becomes significant. In this paper, the research emphasizes searching "human" and forming CoP.

BUILDING COP FROM COLLABORATIVE SOCIAL TAGGING

Social Interesting Sharing in Collaborative Social Tagging

Social Tagging is also known as Free tagging or Collaborative Tagging. It allows users to place tags which has the function of classification on web resources. Therefore, Harry, Valentin, & Hana (2007) claimed that "Tagging systems allow much greater malleability and adaptability in organizing information than do formal classification systems." In addition, with the rise of Web 2.0, the Threshold of classification transforms from specialist classification into direct classification by general users. This method of direct classification has been more approachable, socialized, and popularized for common users. Therefore, the Vander (2005) first coined the new term "Folksonomy" which is the combination of "Folks"and "Taxonomy." Folksonomy, a bottom-up classification, means that members in the society all participate in the classification, which could also be interpreted as "popularized classification" (Stefan, 2007).

Besides, due to the trend of Web 2.0 which drives the Internet ecology of virtual communities, the focus on the knowledge within the corporation itself was gradually shifted to emphasis on exterior resources and human resources in a way of global thinking. Thus, the interior professionals in corporations have been transferred into exterior global human resources. This global thinking contributes to the space for collective cooperation. For instance, Wikipedia is one of the successful models in collective cooperation; it not only gathers people who share the same interests or professionals from various fields to create collectively but also brings the intelligence and power of the Internet crowd into full play through social networking platforms. Therefore, the trend of interdisciplinary cooperation with collective intelligence is inspired. Moreover, the tagging techniques of Web 2.0 have brought distinct effect on the application of collective collaboration. The techniques help people classify the sharing. For example, the social bookmarking, a kind of tagging techniques, has a distinct effect on improving searching quality. (Heymann et al., 2007) The social bookmarking provided by Del.icio.us is a good model of collective collaboration. Del.icio.us used tagging techniques to classify social bookmarkings shared by users. This mechanism provides an important foundation in connecting "learning new things" with "new members".

We especially take Del.icio.us as our study material. Del.icio.us not only provides the function for users to collect their favorite resource pages but also provides the mechanism for users to share their resource pages. For example, it provides resource pages which are more popular and are posted recently for users to refer to and collect. Besides, it provides the mechanism for users to build up personal People Network manually. Users can add people with shared interests to their People Network.

However, Del.icio.us does not provide the function for users to find people with shared interests. Furthermore, Del.icio.us provides lists which are the most popular and recent resource pages. Although the lists are preferred by most people, it does not mean that everyone prefers the most popular and recent resources. There are differences in users' preference. Therefore, it is too arbitrary to conclude that the most popular resources are preferred by every user.

Building CoP Based on People Search Service

The term "Community of Practice" was first proposed by Etienne C. Wenger in 1998. He thought that community of practice was an informal group in the corporation. He also claimed that it was not an organization aiming at completing specific tasks and missions. Thus, it was different from the organized units of formal task-oriented missions. Instead, it belonged to spontaneous informal groups formed by sharing specialized knowledge and emotions. Through the social interaction and exchanges in this group, members could learn social skills, share knowledge and the process of problem-solving, and even develop innovative thinking. In this way, collective intelligence was realized.

Furthermore, Wenger made a simple definition to CoP (Communities of Practice). He said, "Communities of Practice are groups of people who share a passion for something they do and who interact regularly to learn how to do it better." (Wenger,2000). Wenger further said, "A CoP is a group of professionals who share a common interest for a domain or a specific topic." (Wenger,1998; Wenger, McDermott, & Snyder, 2002). That is, the passion of sharing and the interests of people are the driving force of CoP. Based on the passion of sharing and the interests of people, this paper used the global website of social sharing, Del.icio.us, as the experimental data set. By analyzing the resources users were interested in and the tags people placed on the resources, we could get the similarity degree between users and then formed CoP. CoP bridged their relationship through the same interest, provided motivation to one another, and developed the interactive model of new innovative collaborations.

In terms of Wenger's viewpoints, this paper tries to analyze the degree of similarity between users from the sharing mechanism of social tagging. Thus, Del.icio.us is used as the data set of this experiment. After calculating by the revised algorithm, people with similar interests are analyzed and located. The experimental platform is presented in Figure 1. Users input key words or phrases in section A for analysis of tags, resources and people. The results of analysis are displayed by names in section D. After searching and comparison, the relevant resources are listed in section B. When users click on the names listed in section D, the system will display all the information about the target group in section C.

Figure 1. Building CoP based on People Search Service

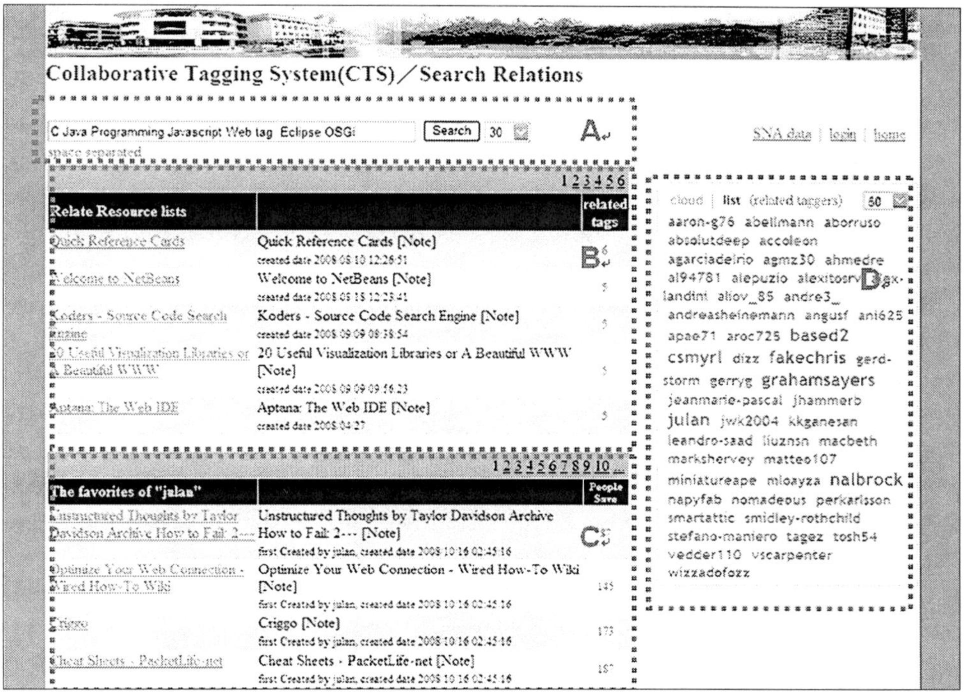

Through this mechanism, the original static sharing is replaced by interactive sharing of dynamic communication. It realizes community ecology of collective intelligence. Owing to the communities, passive users are inspired to share actively.

SOCIAL BOOKMARKING-BASED PEOPLE SEARCH SERVICE

Applying VSM to Find Similar Interest People

Vector Space Model (VSM), first proposed by Salton in 1984(Salton et al., 1984), was originally used to categorize documents. Firstly, the related characteristic of the content of the documents was asserted, and then the representative characteristic items were extracted from each document. After that, Vector Space was transformed by these characteristic items, and used to calculate similarity. Finally, these documents were categorized by the degree of similarity. However, similarity-based method was used not only in verbal texts but also in nonverbal fields (You & Chen, 2006). As long as characteristic points related to objects were identified, and transformed into digital vector space model, similarity measurement could be conducted, such as measuring similarity between graphs (Xifeng, Philip, Jiawei, 2005), Web Page (Hou & Zhang, 2003) and so on.

The research and application of similarity have been generally adopted in many fields as a mean of computing similarity between objects. Cosine similarity-based method was first used in this field to measure similarities between contents (Salton, 1989). Through the measurement, documents could be categorized. On the other hand, some researchers used similarity-based method in searching documents. They computed the similarity between key words and the content of the documents, ordered it based on the degree of similarity, and displayed the results to the users (Yencken et al., 2008).

Cosine similarity utilizes the distance between two identical sets of base and dimension vectors to measure the angle between two context vectors (You & Chen, 2006). The value is among 0 to 1. When the angle between two vectors is smaller, the cosine value is smaller and close to 1 which means that the similarity between the two vectors is considerable. On the contrary, the similarity between the two vectors is low when the value is close to 0. For example, the assumptions in the two n-dimensional vector space, namely a and b, respectively, the vector [a1, a2, ..., an] and [b1, b2, ..., bn], then a and b cosine similarity degree in mathematics as follows:

$$Sim(a,b) = \cos ine\theta = \frac{a \bullet b}{|a||b|} = \frac{\sum_{i=1}^{n} a_i * b_i}{\sqrt{\sum_{i=1}^{n} a_i^2} * \sqrt{\sum_{j=1}^{n} b_j^2}}$$

Basically, users are interested in the topic of tag made by the users. If a user use a tag to note the number of network resources several times that means the users are interested in the topic. On the other hand, they note few times that means the users are less interested in the topic. For example, an user, Jeff, places thirty tags of e-learning on Del.icio.us website and three tags of Java. Therefore, there is a possibility that Jeff is interested in e-learning. We try to apply vector space model on social networking of delicious. Exploring common interests between people according to the historical data of the tags are used and the information of network resources by users. Finally, users who share the same interest become a community of practice.

The sample of this paper was based on the data from Del.icio.us. Thus, from the website, we collected three items of data including "people", "tag", and "resource". According to the relation of these three essential factors, the three-dimension space vector was constituted, and this relation meant some person could do the action that he could tag on the resources randomly. Therefore, everyone possessed the Tag Set that had been noted. That is, everyone possessed his own tag, namely the Resource Set. Accordingly, this paper defined two space vector set, Users Tags Vector Set and Tags Vector Set with common interesting resources were included.

Definition 1. *A user U places n tags labeled as t1, t2, ..., tn to the resources R1, R2,..., Rm. This process is called Users Tags Vector Set with Resource. The formula of Tags vector set can be presented as T=(Rt1, Rt2,..., Rtn). Rti is the amount of tags ti user U places to the resources. N is the dimension of the vector space.*

For example, User 1, User 2 and User 3 use 3 tags, 2 tags and 1 tag respectively (see Figure 2). The Vector Spaces here are 3 dimensions. User 1 uses T1 to mark two different resources R1 and R2 (the [$User_1$,T_1] position in the left table). User 2 uses T2 to mark three different resources R4, R5 and R2 (the [$User_2$,T_2] position in the left table). Finally, the data which is recorded by system will be transformed into digital tags vector set. The output is presented in the right table.

Definition 2. *A reference user U_B places n tags labeled as t1,t2, ..., tn to resources R1, R2,..., Rm. The amount of tags placed by U_B are the tags vector dimensions. R_1, R_2,..., R_m are the resources that interest the reference user U_B and compared user u_i. Under the condition that the reference user and the compared user place same tags to the same resources, Tags Vector Set with Common Interesting Resources is formed. The formula of Tags Vector Set with Common Interesting Resources can be presented as $T=(T_{1Ri}, T_{2Ri}, ..., T_{nRi})$. T_{iRi} represents the amount of same tags that are used by the reference user and compared user.*

User 1 and User 2, the compared users, use eight tags and two tags to mark resources respectively. No matter how many tags the compared users use, we take the tags used by the reference user as the base. For example, the reference user $User_{Base}$ uses three tags in Figure 3. The tags vectors here are three dimensions. User 1 and $User_{Base}$ use the same tag T1 to mark resource R1(the [$User_1$,T_1] position in the left

Figure 2. Tags vector set

	T1	T2	T3
$User_{Base}$	R1,R2	R1,R3,R5,R7,R9	R2,R4,R6,R8
User1	R1	R1,R3,R9	R2,R6
User2	0	R5,R7	0

	T1	T2	T3
$User_{Base}$	2	5	4
User1	1	3	2
User2	0	2	0

table). They use tag T2 to mark resource R1, R3 and R9. (the [$User_1$,T_2] position in the left table). Finally, the data which is recorded by system will be transformed into digital tags vector set. The output is presented in the right table.

People Search Service Process Based on Social Bookmarking

To put Social Community into practice, this paper was based on the social platform, Del.icio.us, to collect the experimental data. In figure 4, we designed Web Crawler to collect data, and then obtain users' behavior data through analyzing and extracting mechanism. These behavior data including the three related essential factors, "people", "tags" and "resources", formed the Data Set of User Tagging Behavior Profile. Finally, the people similar to the users would be found by the formula for calculating similarity we amended, and the partners could be accommodated to the loginers. That is, once the users login into the system, the system will automatically show the people having the similar interests to the users by people clouds.

Furthermore, the system provides a community multiple dimensions of practice, and the community multiple dimensions of practice is composed of multi-interest or professional searching inputted by users. For example, when users input three key words, C++, Java, and ASP, the system will find partners concurrently satisfy these three interests, and show them to users by People Clouds.

After we collected data from Del.icio.us, we used the following algorithm to find people with similar interests. The algorithm was as follows:

Algorithm for Similar People Search
Require: User tagging behavior profile
Data set:from Del.icio.us

1. Read the User tagging behavior profile
2. behavior profile Convert to Users Tags vector set with resource
3. behavior profile Convert to Tags Vector Set with Common interesting resources
4. **for** all Users Tags vector with resource **do**
5. Calculate *sima(Ub, Ui)*
6. **end for**
7. **for** all Tags Vector Set with Common interesting resources **do**
8. Calculate *simb(Ub, Ui)*
9. **end for**
10. **return** Sort *sima+simb*

Figure 3. Tags vector set with common interesting resources

	T1	T2	T3
User1	R1,R2	R3,R5	R2,R4,R6,R8
User2	R1	R4,R5,R6	0
User3	0	R2	0

→

	T1	T2	T3
User1	2	2	4
User2	1	3	0
User2	0	1	0

Figure 4. People search service process

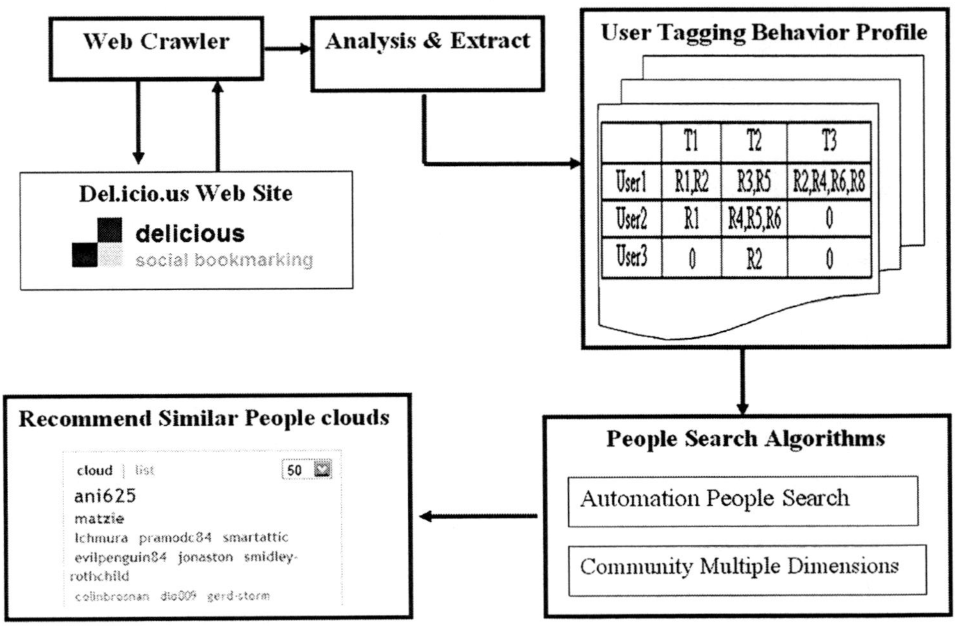

EXPERIMENTS AND EVALUATION

The experiment's data were retrieved from the Del.icio.us for the experiment data set. This data set contained three related elements including people, tags and resources. To find users sharing similar interests and to recommend to the loginers of the system from importing Cosine similarity algorithm. Furthermore, to find who share similar interests from verifying the algorithms that is having high accuracy. Therefore, the control group in this experiment using the FCA (formal concept analysis) algorithm to compare and verification.

The data were collected from April, 2008 to October, 2008. It took approximately half a year. In this period, the system continuously collected experimental data every two hours from Del.icio.us. The aggregated data were as follows:

˙Tagger:435,940 users ˙Resource:73,445 items ˙Tag:212,076 items

The limitation of this experiment was that the amount of tags marked by some taggers was too small to be taken into consideration. To make this experiment representative, we selected a tagger who marked enough tags as the "reference user" of the experiment. Then, we analyzed the data by the following steps:

1. The control group adopted the FCA algorithm to recommend people with similar interests.
2. The experimental group adopts the revised Cosine similarity algorithm to recommend people with similar interests.
3. Compare the results of step 3 and step 4, and find out the differences between the rankings listed by FCA and revised Cosine similarity algorithm.
4. Conduct the correlation analysis to the differences found in step 3, and search the database by SQL-like.
5. Use the result of step 4 as evidence. Observe and compare the results of step 1 and 2.

Quantitative Evaluation and Discuss

The experimental results are showed in figure 5. We chose Julan as the reference user. Besides, we also chose ten users whose interests were similar to Julan's as the recommended users. The users in the left table were found by the revised Cosine similarity algorithm and recommended according to the ranking. The users in the right table were found by FCA (Formal Concept Analysis) algorithm and recommended according to the ranking. When we examined the first three recommended users in these two tables, we can see that the rankings were different. We might infer that the accuracy of these two algorithms was different. In the remaining section, we will discuss the accuracy of these algorithms. We will further prove that the revised Cosine similarity algorithm is more accurate.

The FCA algorithm only uses the amount of same tags to analyze the similarity value between the reference user and the recommended users. From figure 5, we can see that smartattic and Julan have 577 identical tags while ani625 and Julan have 506 identical tags. By using FCA algorithm, smartattic is the first recommended users in the ranking and ani625 the second. The ranking of the rest recommended users are showed in the right table.

The revised Cosine similarity algorithm not only considers the amount of same tags between the reference user and the recommended user, but also considers whether the reference user and the recommended user marked the same tags to the same resources. By using the revised Cosine similarity algorithm, we can see that the

Figure 5. Our approach and FCA algorithm for people search ranking

Our Ranking	Top 10 Taggers	Similar with Julan Score
1.	ani625	131.078
2.	smartattic	103.954
3.	matzie	90.073
4.	lchmura	68.854
5.	pramodc84	63.400
6.	smidley-rothchild	53.605
7.	evilpenguin84	46.508
8.	JonAston	42.225
9.	agiletimes	40.612
10.	colinbrosnan	37.954

FCA Ranking	Top 10 Taggers	Similar with Julan tags number
1.	smartattic	577
2.	matzie	543
3.	ani625	506
4.	agiletimes	479
5.	pramodc84	447
6.	netsuke	430
7.	tewfiq	428
8.	smidley-rothchild	425
9.	colinbrosnan	418
10.	JonAston	400

similarity value of ani625 and Julan is 131.078. Therefore, the first recommended user in the ranking is ani625. The second recommended user is smartattic. The rest recommended users are showed in the left table.

In the following section, we will compare smartattic, the first recommended user by FCA algorithm, with ani625, the first recommended user by revised Cosine similarity algorithm. For smartattic, we adopt FCA to conduct statistical analysis. As for ani625, we use revised Cosine similarity algorithm to conduct statistical analysis. The experimental result is showed in figure 6. The x-axis represents the intervals of re-used tag numbers. The y-axis shows the degree of similarity between smartattic & Julan and ani625 & Julan (in percentage). The observations and analysis are as follows:

- FCA only uses the amount of same tags to analyze the similarity value between the reference user and the recommended user. It neglects the amount of tags that are marked repeatedly. For example, ani625 places the tag *e-learning* 21 times. However, it will be counted only once by using FCA algorithm. Thus, if some tags are used repeatedly, the similarity value calculated by FCA algorithm will not be so accurate.
- Based on the above phenomena, we use the factor “the amount of tags that are used repeatedly” to evaluate the accuracy of FCA and revised Cosine similarity algorithm. We divide “the amount of tags that are used repeatedly” into four intervals. The intervals are 1-10, 11-20, 21-30 and above 30.
- In figure 6, we can see clearly that by using FCA algorithm, smartattic will be the first recommended user in interval 1-10. In other words, if all of the tags

Figure 6. smartattic and ani625 for Julan similar

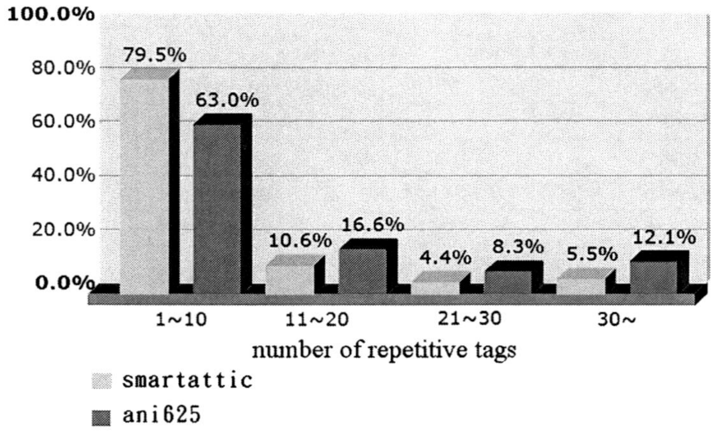

are marked once and will not be used repeatedly, FCA algorithm can recommend users accurately. However, users' actual behaviors are not so limited.

- If a tag is used more than 11 times by a user, the revised Cosine similarity shows its influence on the result. The revised Cosine similarity shows higher degree of similarity than FCA. We can see from figure 6 that ani625 is the first person to be recommended in interval 11-20.
- The revised Cosine similarity has higher accuracy than FCA in interval 21-30 and interval above 30.
- We can infer from the experiment that the threshold of "tags that used repeatedly" is 11. In other words, if a user repeatedly places a tag more than 11 times, the revised Cosine similarity will have higher accuracy in recommending users.

CONCLUSION AND FUTURE WORK

This paper proposes people search algorithm to recommend people with similar interests and form a community. We analyze tags marked by users and the resources that users are interested in to find people with similar interests. People with similar interests will be the driving force to form CoP which realizes the innovation and communication of collective intelligence. Because data set of the system are extracted from Del.icio.us, there may be privacy problems. Therefore, it is hard for us to trace the subsequent interaction between users. Fortunately, we have had obvious contribution to the social networking, especially in recommending people with similar interests on the global tag-sharing data set. The platform we develop can not only find people with similar interests, but also input some interest items to find multi- profession people and form multi-dimension community. In the future, we will conduct Social knowledge mining to the community. Then, we will use Social Network Analysis to analyze the roles everyone acts, and further form the Knowledge Network.

ACKNOWLEDGMENT

This work is supported by National Science Council, Taiwan under grants NSC96-2628-S-008-008-MY3, NSC98-2511-S-008-006-MY3 and NSC98-2511-S-008-007-MY3.

REFERENCES

Adamic, L. A., & Adar, E. (2005). How to search a social network. *Social Networks*, *27*(3), 187–203. doi:10.1016/j.socnet.2005.01.007

Ali-Hasan, N., & Adamic, L. (2007). Expressing social relationships on the blog through links and comments. *In Proc. of International Conference on Weblogs and Social Media, Mar*.

Artiles, J., Gonzalo, J., & Verdejo, F. (2005). A testbed for people searching strategies in the WWW. In Proceedings of the 28th annual International ACM SIGIR conference on Research and Development in Information Retrieval (SIGIR'05), 569-570.

Bustos, B., Keim, D. A., Saupe, D., Schreck, T., & Vranic, D. V. (2005). Feature-based similarity search in 3D object databases. *ACM Computing Surveys*, 345–387. doi:10.1145/1118890.1118893

Diederich, J., & Iofciu, T. (2006). Finding communities of practice from user profiles based on folksonomies. *In Proceedings of the 1st International Workshop on Building Technology Enhanced Learning Solutions for Communities of Practic*e.

Ehrlich, K., Lin, C. Y., & Griffiths-Fisher, V. (2007). Searching for experts in the enterprise: Combining text and social network analysis. [ACM Press.]. *Group*, *07*, 117–126.

Fischer, G. (2001). Communities of interest: Learning through the interaction of multiple knowledge systems, *The 24th IRIS Conference*, Bergen, Norway, 1-14.

Guo, L., Jiang, S., Xiao, L., & Zhang, X. (2005). Fast and low-cost search schemes by exploiting localities in p2p networks. *Journal of Parallel and Distributed Computing, 65*(6), 729–742. doi:10.1016/j.jpdc.2005.01.007

Halpin, H., Robu, V., & Shepherd, H. (2007). The complex dynamics of collaborative tagging, *in Proceedings of the 16th International Conference on World Wide Web*, 211–220, New York, USA. ACM Press.

Hasan, A. N., & Adamic, L. (2007). Expressing social relationships on the blog through links and comments. *In Proc. of International Conference on Weblogs and Social Media*, Mar.

Heymann, P., Koutrika, G., & Garcia-Molina, H. (2008). Can social bookmarking improve web search? *In Proceedings of WSDM'2008*. ACM, 195-206.

Hou, J., & Zhang, Y. (2003). Utilizing Hyperlink Transitivity to Improve Web Page Clustering, in Klaus Dieter-Schewe (ed.), Database Technologies 2003: Proceedings of the Fourteenth Australasian Database Conference. *Conferences in Research and Practice in Information Technology*, 49-57, Australian Computer Society Inc., Australia.

Mori, J., Basselin, N., Kroner, A., & Jameson, A. (2008). Find me if you can: designing interfaces for people search. *In Proceedings of IUI*. 2008, 377-380.

Rachel, P. (2008). Communities of practice: using the open web as a collaborative learning platform, *iLearning Forum 2008 Proceedings*, Paris.

Salton, G. (1989). *Automatic text processing: the transformation, analysis, and retrieval of information by computer*. Boston, MA: Addison-Wesley Longman Publishing Co., Inc.

Salton, G., & McGill, M. J. (1984). *Introduction to Modern Information Retrieval*. McGraw-Hill.

Schwartz, M. F., & Wood, D. C. M. (1993). Discovering shared interests among people using graph analysis of global electronic mail traffic. *Communications of the ACM, 36*(8), 78–89. doi:10.1145/163381.163402

Schwartz, M. F., & Wood, D. C. M. (1993). Discovering shared interests using graph analysis. *Communications of the ACM, 36*(8), 78–89. doi:10.1145/163381.163402

Sripanidkulchai, K., Maggs, B., & Zhang, H. (2003). Efficient content location using interest-based locality in peer-to-peer systems. *In Proc. of INFOCOMM*, Mar.

Vander, W. T. (2005). Explaining and showing broad and narrow folksonomies. http://www.personalinfocloud.com/2005/02/explaining_and_.html.

Vu, Q. M., Masada, T., Takasu, A., & Adachi, J. (2007). Disambiguation of people in web search using a knowledge base. *In Proceedings of International Conference on Research, Innovation & Vision for the Future Information & Communication Technologies (IEEE RIVF'07)*, 185-191.

Wan, X., Gao, J., Li, M., & Ding, B. (2005). Person resolution in person search results: Webhawk. *In CIKM '05: Proceedings of the 14th ACM international conference on Information and knowledge management*, 163-170, New York, USA, ACM Press.

Wenger, E. (1998). *Communities of practice: Learning, meaning, and identity.* Cambridge University Press.

Wenger, E. and Snyder, Williams. (2000). Communities of practice: the organizational frontier. *Harvard Business Review*, (January-February): 139–145.

Wenger, E., McDermott, R., & Snyder, W. M. (2002). *Cultivating communities of practice*. Harvard Business School Press.

Yan, X., Yu, P. S., & Han, J. (2005). Substructure similarity search in graph databases. *SIGMOD Conference 2005*, 766-777.

Yanbe, Y., Jatowt, A., Nakamura, S., & Tanaka, K. (2007) Can social bookmarking enhance search in the web? *In Proceedings of JCDL'2007*. 107-116

Yencken, L., & Baldwin, T. (2008). Orthographic similarity search for dictionary lookup of Japanese words, *In Proc. of the 22nd International Conference on Computational Linguistics* (COLING 2008), Manchester, UK.

You, J. M., & Chen, K. J. (2006). Improving context vector models by feature clustering for automatic thesaurus construction. *Proceedings of the Fifth SIGHAN Workshop on Chinese Language Processing.*

Yu, B., & Singh, M. P. (2003). Searching social networks. *AAMAS, 2003*, 65–72.

This work was previously published in International Journal of Organizational and Collective Intelligence, Volume 1, Issue 2, edited by Hideyasu Sasaki, pp. 83-95, copyright 2010 by IGI Publishing (an imprint of IGI Global).

Compilation of References

Abel, F., Coi, J., Henze, N., Koesling, A. W., Krause, D., & Olmedilla, D. (2007). Enabling advanced and context-dependent access control in RDF Stores. In *Proceedings of the Sixth International Semantic Web Conference* (pp. 1-14).

Adamic, L. A., & Adar, E. (2005). How to search a social network. *Social Networks, 27*(3), 187–203. doi:10.1016/j.socnet.2005.01.007

Agi, I., & Gong, L. (1996). An empirical study of MPEG video transmissions. In *Proceedings of the Internet Society Symposium on Network and Distributed System Security*, San Diego, CA, (pp. 137-144).

Ahn, J., Shim, H., Jeon, B., & Choi, I. (2004). Digital video scrambling method using intra prediction mode. *PCM2004. Springer LNCS, 3333*, 386–393.

Aiello, G., & Alessi, M. (2007). DNK-WSD: a Distributed Approach for Knowledge Discovery in Peer to Peer Networks. In *Proceedings of the 15th EUROMICRO International Conference on Parallel, Distributed and Network-Based Processing (PDP'07)*, Naples, Italy (pp. 325-332).

Aihara, K. (1990). Chaotic neural networks. In Kawakami, H. (Ed.), *Bifurcation phenomena in nonlinear system and theory of dynamical systems* (*Vol. 8*, pp. 143–161). Advanced Series on Dynamical Systems.

Alani, H., Dasmahapatra, S., O'Hara, K., & Shadbolt, N. (2003). Identifying Communities of Practice through Ontology Network Analysis. *IEEE Intelligent Systems, 18*(2), 18–25. doi:10.1109/MIS.2003.1193653

Aleman-Meza, B., Halaschek-Wiener, C., & Arpinar, I. B. (2005). Collective Knowledge Composition in a P2P Network. In L. C. Rivero, J. H. Doorn, & V. E. Ferraggine (Eds.), *Encyclopedia of Database Technologies and Applications* (pp. 74-77). Hershey, PA: IGI Global.

Ali, N. D. (2006). The open and closed case. *SPIDER, September 2006*, 7-9.

Ali-Hasan, N., & Adamic, L. (2007). Expressing social relationships on the blog through links and comments. *In Proc. of International Conference on Weblogs and Social Media, Mar.*

Anderson, R., & Manifavas, C. (1997). Chamleon – A new kind of stream cipher. In *Lecture Notes in Computer Science, Fast Software Encryption*, (pp. 107-113P. Springer-Verlag. Blakley, G. R. (1979). Safeguarding cryptographic keys. In. *Proceedings of the National Computer Conference, 48*, 313–317.

Androutsellis-Theotokis, S., & Spinellis, D. (2004). A Survey of Peer-to-Peer Content Distribution Technologies. *ACM Computing Surveys, 36*(4), 335–371. doi:10.1145/1041680.1041681

Antara. (2006). *IBM, Microsoft protest Indonesia's open source policy.* Retrieved October 1, 2006, from http://www.antara.co.id/en/seenws/?id=16383

Arai, T., & Shimomura, Y. (2004). Proposal of service CAD system—a tool for service engineering. *CIRP Annals—Manufacturing Technology, 53*(1), 397-400.

Arai, T., & Shimomura, Y. (2005). Service CAD system—evaluation and quantification. *CIRP Annals—Manufacturing Technology, 54*(1), 463-466.

Arnold, M., Schmucker, M., & Wolthusen, S. D. (2003). *Techniques and applications of digital watermarking and content protection.* Norwood, MA: Artech House.

Arnold, M., & Schiltz, K. (2002). Quality evaluation of watermarked audio tracks. *SPIE Electronic Imaging, 4675*, 91–101.

Arnold, M. (2000). Audio watermarking: features, applications and algorithms. *IEEE International Conf. Multimedia and Expo, 2*, 1013-1016.

Artiles, J., Gonzalo, J., & Verdejo, F. (2005). A testbed for people searching strategies in the WWW. In Proceedings of the 28th annual International ACM SIGIR conference on Research and Development in Information Retrieval (SIGIR'05), 569-570.

Askanazi, J., Caplan, G., Descoteaux, D., Donohue, K., Glasser, D., Johnson, A., & Mena, E. (2002). *The future of database protection in U.S. Copyright Law*. Retrieved November 27, 2006, from http://www.law.duke.edu/journals/dltr/articles/2001dltr0017.html

Atal, B. S. (1976). Automatic recognition of speakers from their voices. *Proceedings of the IEEE, 64*, 460–475. doi:10.1109/PROC.1976.10155

Aurich, J. C., Fuchs, C., & DeVries, M. F. (2004). An approach to life cycle oriented technical service design. *CIRP Annals—Manufacturing Technology, 53*(1), 151-154.

Autelitano, F. (1999). Banche dati. La rilevanza delle banche dati nel sistema del "cyberlaw". *I Contratti, 10*, 925–935.

Auteri, P. (2003). Attuazione della direttiva 96/9/CE relativa alla tutela giuridica delle banche dati. *Le Nuove Leggi Civili Commentate, 4-5*, 1175–1230.

Avrithis, Y., Kompatsiaris, Y., Staab, S., & Vakali, A. (Eds.). (2008). *Proceedings of the CISWeb (Collective Semantics: Collective Intelligence and the Semantic Web) Workshop, located at the 5th European Semantic Web Conference (ESWC 2008)*, Tenerife, Spain.

Band, J., & Gowdy, J. S. (1997). Sui generis database protection - Has its time come? *D-Lib Magazine.* Retrieved September 25, 2006, from http://www.dlib.org/dlib/june97/06band.html

Baptista, M. S. (1998). Cryptography with chaos. *Physics Letters. [Part A], 240*(1-2), 50–54. doi:10.1016/S0375-9601(98)00086-3

Barni, M., Bartiloni, F., Cappellini, V., & Piva, A. (1998). A DCT domain system for robust image watermarking. *Signal Processing, 66*(3), 357–372. doi:10.1016/S0165-1684(98)00015-2

Barni, M., Bartiloni, F., & Piva, A. (2001). Improved wavelet based watermarking through pixel wise masking. *IEEE Transactions on Image Processing, 10*, 783–791. doi:10.1109/83.918570

Bassia, P., Pitas, I., & Nicholaidis, N. (2001). Robust audio watermarking in the time domain. *IEEE Transactions on Multimedia, 3*, 232–241. doi:10.1109/6046.923822

Baumgarte, F., Ferekidis, C., & Fuchs, H. (1995). *A nonlinear psychoacoustic model applied to the ISO MPEG layer 3 coder*. Preprint 4087, 99th AES Convention.

BCC Research. (2007). *The global biometrics market*.

Beeri, C., Levy, Y. A., & Rousset, M.-C. (1997): Rewriting queries using views in description logics. Symposium on Principles of Database Systems. In A. Mendelzon & Z. M. Özsoyoglu (Eds.), In *Proceedings of the sixteenth ACM SIGACT-SIGMOD-SIGART symposium on Principles of database systems* (pp. 99-108). New York: ACM Press.

Bellare, M., & Rogaway, P. (1995). Optimal asymmetric encryption - How to encrypt with RSA. *Extended abstract in Advances in Cryptology - Eurocrypt 94 Proceedings* [Springer-Verlag.]. *Lecture Notes in Computer Science*, 950.

Bender, W., Gruhl, D., Morimoto, N., & Lu, A. (1996). Techniques for data hiding. *IBM Systems Journal, 35*(3-4).

Bender, W., Gruhl, D., & Morimoto, H. (1995). Techniques for data hiding. *Proceedings of the Society for Photo-Instrumentation Engineers, 2020*, 2420–2440.

Benkler, Y. (2003). The political economy of commons. *UPGRADE: European Journal for the Informatics Professional, 4*(3), 6–9.

Benkler, Y. (2006). *The wealth of networks: How social production transforms markets and freedom*. London, UK: Yale University Press.

Bertino, E., Buccafurri, F., Ferrari, E., & Rullo, P. (1999): A Logical Framework for Reasoning on Data Access Control Policies. In B. Werner (Ed.), In *Proceedings of the 12th IEEE Computer Security Foundations Workshop (CSFW-12)* (pp. 175-189). Los Alamitos, CA: IEEE Computer Society Press.

Beutler, S. (1996). The protection of multimedia products through the EC's directive. *Entertainment Law Review, 7*, 317.

Bhatnagar, G., & Raman, B. (2009a). A new robust reference watermarking scheme based on DWT-SVD. *Computer Standards & Interfaces, 31*(5), 1002–1013. doi:10.1016/j.csi.2008.09.031

Bhatnagar, G., & Raman, B. (2009b). Robust reference watermarking scheme using wavelet packet transform and bidiagonal-singular value decomposition. *International Journal of Image and Graphics, 9*(3), 449–477. doi:10.1142/S0219467809003538

Bhatnagar, G., & Raman, B. (2010). Distributed multiresolution discrete Fourier transform and its application to watermarking. *International Journal of Wavelets, Multresolution, and Information Processing*, *8*(2), 225–241. doi:10.1142/S021969131000347X

Bhatnagar, G., & Raman, B. (2009c). Robust watermarking using distributed MR-DCT and SVD. In *Proc. Int. Conf. on Advances in Pattern Recognition* (pp. 21-24). Kolkatta, India: IEEE Press.

Bimber, B., Flanagin, A. J., & Stohl, C. (2005). Reconceptualizing collective action in the contemporary media environment. *Communication Theory*, *15*(4), 365–388. doi:10.1111/j.1468-2885.2005.tb00340.x

Bitton, M. (2006). Trends in protection for informational works under copyright law during the 19th and 20th centuries. *Michigan Telecommunications and Technology Law Review*, *1*, 126.

Bitton, M. (2008). Exploring European Union copyright policy through the lens of the database directive. *Berkeley Technology Law Journal*, *4*, 1417.

Blanke, J. M. (2002). Vincent van Gogh, sweat of the brow, and database protection. *American Business Law Journal*, *4*, 662.

Bloehdorn, S., Haase, P., Hefke, M., Sure, Y., & Tempich, C. (2005). Intelligent Community Lifecycle Support. In *Proceedings of the 5th International Conference on Knowledge Management (I-KNOW 05)*, Graz, Austria.

Blonder, G. E. (2005). *Graphical password.* US Patent 5559961, Lucent Technologies Inc., Murray Hill, NJ.

Bochner, S., & Chandrasekharan, K. (1949). *Fourier transforms*. New York, NY: Princeton University Press.

Boeder, P. (2005). Habermas' heritage: The future of the public sphere in the network society. *First Monday, 10*(9). Retrieved October 13, 2006, from http://firstmonday.org/issues/issue10_9/boeder/index.html

Bollier, D. (2004). Why we must talk about the information commons. *Law Library Journal*, *96*(2), 267–282.

Bonatti, P. A., Duma, C., Fuchs, N., Nejdl, W., Olmedilla, D., Peer, J., et al. (2006). Semantic Web policies - A discussion of requirements and research issues. In Y. Sure, & J. Domingue (Eds.), In *Proceedings of the European Semantic Web Conference* (pp. 712-724).

Bonelli, G. (2002). Il sito web quale opera dell'ingegno. *Diritto dell'informazione e dell'informatica, 1*, 201.

Boney, L., Tewfik, A. H., & Hamdy, K. N. (1996). Digital watermarks for audio signals. *IEEE Proceedings of the International Conference on Multimedia Computing and Systems*, (pp. 473-480).

Boyle, J. (2001). Comment & analysis: Whigs and hackers in cyberspace: Copyright regulations before the European Parliament should be treated as skeptically as they were by the Victorians. *Financial Times*, pp. 21.

Boynton, R. S. (2004, January 24). The tyranny of copyright? *The New York Times.* Retrieved October 8, 2006, from http://www.nytimes.com/2004/01/25/magazine/25COPYRIGHT.html?ei=5007&en=9eb265b1f26e8b14&ex=1390366800&partner=USERLAND&pagewanted=all&position=

Bracewell, R. (1965). *The Fourier transform and its applications*. New York, NY: McGraw-Hill.

Brandenburg, K., & Stoll, G. (1992). *The ISO/MPEG-audio codec: A generic standard for coding of high quality digital audio*. 92nd AES-Convention, preprint 3336.

Brassil, J., & O'Gorman, L. (1996). Watermarking document images with bounding box expansion. *Proceedings of the First International Information Hiding Workshop*, vol. 1174 (pp. 227-235).

Brassil, J., Low, S., Maxemchuk, N. F., & O'Gorman, L. (1994). Electric marking and identification techniques to discourage document copying. *Proceedings of IEEE INFOCOM'94*, vol. 3 (pp. 1278-1287).

Braudaway, G., & Mintzer, F. (2000). Automatic recovery of invisible image watermarks from geometrically distorted images. *Journal of Electronic Imaging*, *9*(4), 477. doi:10.1117/1.1287836

Braun, N. (2003). The interface between the protection of technological measures and the exercise of exceptions to copyright and related rights: comparing the situation in the United States and in the European community. *EIPR*, *25*(11), 496.

Brickley, D., & Guha, R. V. (2004). *RDF Vocabulary Description Language 1.0: RDF Schema.* Retrieved from http://www.w3.org/TR/rdf-schema/

Brigham, E. O. (2002). *The fast Fourier transform*. New York, NY: Prentice-Hall.

Brock, F. (1996). Diritti d'autore. Opera collettiva. Autorizzazione alla riproduzione di articolo di rivista. Potere del direttore della rivista di rappresentare l'editore. *Rivista di diritto industriale, 3,* 227.

Broekstra, J., Kampman, A., & van Harmelen, F. (2002). Sesame: A generic architecture for storing and querying RDF and RDF Schema. In I. Horrocks, & J. Hendler (Eds.), *Proceedings of the First International Semantic Web Conference* (pp. 54-68). Sardinia, Italy: Springer Verlag.

Broomhead, D., & Lowe, D. (1988). Multivariable functional interpolation and adaptive networks. *Complex Systems*, *2*, 321–355.

Burr, W. E. (2000). Data encryption standard. In NIST (Ed.), *A century of excellence in measurements, standards, and technology: A chronicle of selected NBS/NIST publications, 1901-2000*. Retrieved from http://nvl.nist.gov/pub/nistpubs/sp958-lide/250-253.pdf

Bustos, B., Keim, D. A., Saupe, D., Schreck, T., & Vranic, D. V. (2005). Feature-based similarity search in 3D object databases. *ACM Computing Surveys*, 345–387. doi:10.1145/1118890.1118893

Butler, K. (2000). *Databases are latest battleground in the intellectual property debate* (p. 28). Investor's Business Daily.

Campbell, F. W., & Kulikowski, J. J. (1966). Orientation selectivity of the human visual system. *The Journal of Physiology*, *187*, 437–445.

Campbell, J. P. (1997). Speaker recognition: A tutorial. *Proceedings of the IEEE*, *85*(9), 1437–1462. doi:10.1109/5.628714

Carroll, J. M., Verhagen, J., & Wong, P. T. (1992). Chaos in cryptography: The escape from the strange attractor. *Cryptologia*, *16*(1), 52–72. doi:10.1080/0161-119291866766

Castano, S., Ferrara, A., & Montanelli, S. (2006). Matching Ontologies in Open Networked Systems: Techniques and Applications. *Journal on Data Semantics, 5*, 25–63. doi:10.1007/11617808_2

Castano, S., & Montanelli, S. (2005). Semantic Self-Formation of Communities of Peers. In *Proceedings of the ESWC Workshop on Ontologies in Peer-to-Peer Communities*, Heraklion, Greece.

Castano, S., Ferrara, A., Lorusso, D., & Montanelli, S. (2008). Ontology Coordination: The iCoord Project Demonstration. In *Proceedings of the 27th International Conference on Conceptual Modeling (ER 2008)*, Barcelona, Spain (pp. 512-513).

Castano, S., Ferrara, A., & Montanelli, S. (2009). The iCoord Knowledge Model for P2P Semantic Coordination. In *Proceedings of the 6th Conference of the Italian Chapter of AIS*, Costa Smeralda (Nu), Italy.

Castells, M. (2003). *The power of identity*. Malden, MA: Blackwell Publishing.

Cautis, B. (2007). Distributed access control: A privacy-conscious approach. In *Proceedings of the Twelfth ACM Symposium on Access Control Models and Technologies* (pp. 61-70). New York: ACM Press.

Chalton, S. (1997). The effect of the E.C. database directive on United Kingdom copyright law in relation to databases: A comparison of features. *EIPR, 6*, 278.

Chandra, D. V. S. (2002). Digital image watermarking using singular value decomposition. In *Proc. Midwest Sym. on Circuits and Systems* (pp. 264–267). Tulsa, OK: IEEE Press.

Chang, C. C., Tsai, P., & Lin, C. C. (2005). SVD-based digital image watermarking scheme. *Pattern Recognition Letters, 26*, 577–1586. doi:10.1016/j.patrec.2005.01.004

Chang, Y.-F., & Chang, C.-C. (2004). A secure and efficient strong-password authentication protocol. *ACM SIGOPS Operating Systems Review, 38*(3), 79–90. doi:10.1145/1035834.1035844

Chang, C. Y., & Su, S. J. (2005). Apply the counterpropagation neural network to digital image copyright authentication. *2005 9th International Workshop on Cellular Neural Networks and Their Applications IEEE* (pp. 110-113).

Chellappa, R., Wilson, C. L., & Sirohey, S. (1995). Human and machine recognition of faces: A survey. *Proceedings of the IEEE, 83*, 705–740. doi:10.1109/5.381842

Chen, B., & Wornell, G. W. (1999). Dither modulation: A new approach to digital *watermarking* and information embedding. *Proceedings of the SPIE – Security and Watermarking of Multimedia Contents, 3657*, (pp. 342-353).

Cheng, H., & Li, X. (2000). Partial encryption of compressed images and videos. *IEEE Transactions on Signal Processing, 48*(8), 2439–2451. doi:10.1109/78.852023

Chimenti, L. (2001). I data bases nella direttiva 9/96 e nel d.lgs. 6 maggio 1999, n. 169. *Il diritto dell'informazione e dell'informatica, 1,* (pp. 199-211).

Clarke, E. H. (1971). Multipart pricing of public goods. *Public Choice, 11*(1), 17–33. doi:10.1007/BF01726210

Cohen, J. H. (1991). Hybrids on the borderline between copyright and industrial property law. *Intellectual Property Journal, 2*(4), 190.

Collie, I. (1994). Multimedia and moral rights. *Arts and Entertainment Law Review*, *6*, 194.

Colston, C. (2002). Challenges to information retrieval – A global solution? *International Journal of Law and Information Technology*, *10*(3), 294. doi:10.1093/ijlit/10.3.294

Correa, C. M. (2002). Fair use in the digital era. *IIC*, *4*, 535.

Court of Justice of the European Communites. (2004). *Press release n° 46/04/EN, 2004*, (p. 3).

Cox, I. J., Killian, J., Leighton, F. T., & Shamoon, T. (1997). Secure spread spectrum watermarking for multimedia. *IEEE Transactions on Image Processing*, *6*(12), 1673–1687. doi:10.1109/83.650120

Cox, I. J., Miller, M. L., & Bloom, J. A. (2001). *Digital watermarking*. San Francisco, CA: Morgan Kaufmann.

Cox, I. J., Miller, M. L., & Muttoo, S. K. (2002). *Digital watermarking*. Morgan Kaufmann Pub.

Cox, I. J., Miller, M. L., & Bloom, J. A. (2000). Watermarking applications and their properties. In *Proc. Int. Conf. on Information Technology* (pp. 1-5). Las Vegas, NV: IEEE Press.

Craver, S., & Memon, N., & Yeo, B.-L., & Yeung, M. (1996). Can invisible watermarks resolve rightful ownerships? *IBM Research Technical Report RC 20509 IBM CyberJournal*.

Craver, S., Memon, N., Yeo, B.-L., & Yeung, M. (1997). Resolving rightful ownerships with invisible watermarking techniques: Limitations, attacks and implications. *IBM Research Technical Report RC 20755 IBM CyberJournal*.

Crespo, A., & Garcia-Molina, H. (2004). Semantic Overlay Networks for P2P Systems. In *Proceedings of the 3rd International Workshop on Agents and Peer-to-Peer Computing (P2PC 2004)*, New York (pp. 1-13).

Crews, K. D. (1998). Harmonization and the goals of copyright: Property rights or cultural progress? *Indiana Journal of Global Legal Studies*, *6*, 117.

Cvejic, N., Keskinarkaus, A., & Seppanen, T. (2001). *Audio watermarking using m-sequences and temporal masking* (pp. 227–230). IEEE Workshops on Applications of Signal Processing to Audio and Acoustics.

Dachselt, F., & Wolfgang, S. (2001). Chaos and cryptography. *IEEE Trans. Circuits Syst. I*, *48*(12), 1498–1509. doi:10.1109/TCSI.2001.972857

Damiani, E., De Capitani di Vimercati, S., Fugazza, C., & Samarati, P. (2004). Extending policy languages to the Semantic Web. In *Proceedings of the International Conference on Web Engineering* (pp. 330-343).

Das, T., Nandi, S., & Ganguly, N. (2009). Community Formation and Search in P2P: A Robust and Self-Adjusting Algorithm. In *Proceedings of the 3rd Workshop on Intelligent Networks: Adaptation, Communication & Reconfiguration (IAMCOM 2009)*, Bangalore, India.

Datta, R., Li, J., & Wang, J. Z. (2009). Exploiting the human-machine gap in image recognition for designing Captchas. *IEEE Transactions on Information Forensics and Security*, *4*(3), 504–518. doi:10.1109/TIFS.2009.2022709

Daubechies, I. (1992). *Ten lectures notes on wavelet*. Philadelphia, PA: SIAM.

Daugman, J. G. (1994). *United States Patent No. 5,291,560: Biometric personal identification system based on iris analysis.* Washington DC: U.S. Government Printing Office.

Davidson, M. J. (2003). *The legal protection of database*. UK: Cambridge.

Davies, J., Duke, A., & Sure, Y. (2004). OntoShare - An Ontology-based Knowledge Sharing System for virtual Communities of Practice. *The Journal of Universal Computer Science*, *10*(3), 262–283.

Davis, K. J., & Najarian, K. (2001). Maximizing strength of digital watermarks using neural networks. *IEEE Proceedings of International Joint Conference on Neural Neworks*, vol. 4 (pp. 2893-2898).

Delaigle, J. F., Devleeschouwer, C., Macq, B., & Langendijk, L. (2002). Human visual system features enabling watermarking. *Proceedings of Multimedia and Expo, ICME02*, 489–492.

Delaigle, J. F., De Vleeschouwer, C., & Macq, B. (1998). Watermarking algorithm based on a human visual model. *Signal Processing*, *66*, 319–335. doi:10.1016/S0165-1684(98)00013-9

Derclaye, E. (2000). Software copyright protection: Can Europe learn from American case law. *EIPR*, *22*(1), 7.

Derclaye, E. (2008). *The legal protection of databases: A comparative analysis*. UK: Edward Elgar.

Devaney, R. L. (2003). *An introduction to chaotic dynamical systems*. Colorado, US: Westview Press.

Dhamija, R. (2000). *Hash visualization in user authentication*. Computer Human Interaction Conference.

Dhamija, R., & Perrig, A. (2000). *Déjà vu: A user study using images for authentication.* 9th Usenix Security Symposium.

Di Cocco, C. (2005). *L'opera multimediale*. Italy: Giappichelli.

Diederich, J., & Iofciu, T. (2006). Finding communities of practice from user profiles based on folksonomies. *In Proceedings of the 1st International Workshop on Building Technology Enhanced Learning Solutions for Communities of Practic*e.

Digeser, E. D. (2003). Citizenship and the roman res publica: Cicero and a Christian corollary. *Critical Review of International Social and Political Philosophy*, *6*(1), 5–21. doi:10.1080/13698230510001702643

Djurovic, I., Stankovic, S., & Pitas, I. (2001). Digital watermarking in the fractional fourier transformation domain. *Journal of Network and Computer Applications*, *24*(4), 167–173. doi:10.1006/jnca.2000.0128

Do van. T., Jorstad, I., Jonvik, T., & Do van, T. (2009). Strong authentication with mobile phone as security token. *International Conference on Mobile Adhoc and Sensor Systems*, (pp. 777-782).

Dommering, J., & Hugenholtz, A. (1991). *An introduction to information law. Work of fact at the crossroads of freedom and protection, in copyright, freedom of expression and information law*. Boston, MA: The Hague.

Douglas, J. (1996). The challenge of multimedia: reform the Copyright Act? *Computers and Law*, *31*, 47.

Driscoll, D. (1994). Fingerprint ID systems. *Advanced Imaging (Woodbury, N.Y.)*, *9*(20).

Duma, C., Herzog, A., & Shahmehri, N. (2007). Privacy in the semantic web: What policy languages have to offer. In *Proceedings of the Eighth IEEE International Workshop on Policies for Distributed Systems and Networks* (pp. 109-118).

Duncan, M. V., Akhtari, M. S., & Bradford, P. G. (2004). Visual security for wireless handheld devices. *The Journal of Science & Health at the University of Alabama, 2*. Retrieved from http://www.bama.ua.edu/~joshua/archive/may04/Duncan%20et%20al.pdf

Eaddy, J. H. (2008). Database copyright analysis for dummies: Protecting your intellectual investment is about the design, not the data. *New England Law Review*, *2*, 319.

Echizen, I., Yoshiura, H., Arai, T., Himura, H., & Takeuchi, T. (1999). General quality maintenance module for motion picture watermarking. *IEEE Transactions on Consumer Electronics*, *45*, 1150–1158. doi:10.1109/30.809196

Eckhorn, R., Reitboeck, H. J., Arndt, M., & Dicke, P. (1990). Feature linking via synchronization among distributed assemblies: Simulations of results from cat visual cortex. *Neural Computation*, *2*, 293–307. doi:10.1162/neco.1990.2.3.293

Eggers, J. J., Su, J. K., & Girod, B. (2000). A blind *watermarking* scheme based on structured codebooks. *Secure Images and Image Authentication-IEE Colloquium*, 4/1-4/6.

Ehrlich, K., Lin, C. Y., & Griffiths-Fisher, V. (2007). Searching for experts in the enterprise: Combining text and social network analysis. [ACM Press.]. *Group*, *07*, 117–126.

Elman, J. (1994). Finding structure in time. *Cognitive Science*, *14*, 179–211. doi:10.1207/s15516709cog1402_1

Elnashaie, S. S. E. H., & Abasha, M. E. (1995). On the chaotic behaviour of forced fluidized bed catalytic reactors. *Chaos, Solitons, and Fractals*, *5*(5), 797–831. doi:10.1016/0960-0779(95)93891-F

Epshtein, D., & Krawczyk, H. (2002). *Image-based authentication of public keys and applications to SSH. Project report*. Technion – Dept. of Electrical Engineering, Technion.

Falce, V. (2009). The (over)protection of information in the knowledge economy. Is the Directive 96/9/EC a *faux pas? Rivista di Diritto d'Autore*, *4*, 180.

Faundez-Zanuy, M. (2005). Biometric verification of humans by means of hand geometry. *39th Int. Carnahan Conf. on Security Technology CCST 2005*, (pp. 61-67).

Feng, Z., Xiaomin, M., & Shouyi, Y. (2005). Multiple-chirp typed blind watermarking algorithm based on fractional Fourier transform. In *Proc. Int. Sym. on Intelligent Signal Processing and Communication Systems* (pp. 141–144). Philadelphia, PA: IEEE Press. doi:10.1109/ISPACS.2005.1595366

Ferrara, A., Montanelli, S., Varese, G., & Castano, S. (2009). *Natural Language Ontology Authoring in iCoord. International Journal of Information Technology and Database Systems*. IJITDAS.

Ferwerda, J. A., Pattanaik, S. N., Shirley, P., & Greenberg, D. P. (1997)... *Computer Graphics*, *31*, 143–152.

Fischbacher, U. (2007). z-Tree: Zurich toolbox for ready-made economic experiments. *Experimental Economics*, *10*(2), 171–178. doi:10.1007/s10683-006-9159-4

Fischer, G. (2001). Communities of interest: Learning through the interaction of multiple knowledge systems, *The 24th IRIS Conference*, Bergen, Norway, 1-14.

Freeman, R. B., & Rogers, J. (2002). Open source unionism: Beyond exclusive collective bargaining. *Working USA: Journal of Labor and Society*, *5*, 3–4.

Fridrich, J. (1997). *Secure image ciphering based on chaos*. Final Technical Report RL-TR-97-155, Rome Laboratory, New York.

Friedman, D., & Sunder, S. (1994). *Experimental methods: A primer for economics*. London, UK: Cambridge University Press.

Fu, M. S., & Au, A. C. (2004). Joint visual cryptography and watermarking. *Proceedings of the International Conference on Multimedia and Expro (ICME2004)*, (pp. 975-978).

Fukuhara, T., Ando, K., Watanabe, O., & Kiya, H. (2002). *Partial-scrambling of JPEG2000 images for security applications*. ISO/IEC JTC 1/SC29/WG1, N2430.

Furht, B. (1999). *Handbook of internet and multimedia systems and applications*. CRC Press.

Furht, B., & Kirovski, F. (2004). *Multimedia security handbook*. CRC Press.

Gale, D., & Shapley, L. S. (1962). College admissions and the stability of marriage. *The American Mathematical Monthly*, *69*(1), 9–15. doi:10.2307/2312726

Gambino, A. M., & Stazi, A. with Mula, D. (2009). *Diritto dell'informatica e della comunicazione*. Italy: Giappichelli.

Gang, L., Akansu, A. N., Ramkumar, M., & Xie, X. (2001). Online music protection and mp3 compression. In *Proc. of Int. Symposium on Intelligent Multimedia, Video and Speech Processing*, Hong Kong, China, May, 13-16.

Ganic, E., & Eskicioglu, A. M. (2005). Robust embedding of visual watermarks using DWT-SVD. *Journal of Electronic Imaging*, *14*, 043004. doi:10.1117/1.2137650

Ganic, E., Zubair, N., & Eskicioglu, A. M. (2003). An optimal watermarking scheme based on singular value decomposition. In *Proc. Int. Conf. on Communication, Network, and Information Security* (pp. 85-90). Uniondale, NY: Acta Press.

Ghidini, G., & Falce, V. (2001). Intellectual property on communications standards: Balancing innovation and competition through the essential facilities doctrine. *Diritto d'Autore*, *3*, 315.

Giannantonio, E. (1997). *Manuale di diritto dell'informatica*. Italy: Giuffré.

Ginesu, G., Giusto, D. D., & Onali, T. (2005). *Application-scalable image-based authentication framework with JPEG2000*. IEEE International Workshop on Multimedia Signal Processing MMSP05.

Ginesu, G., Giusto, D. D., & Onali, T. (2006). Mutual image-based authentication framework with JPEG2000 in wireless environment. *EURASIP Journal on Wireless Communications and Networking*.

Gish, H., & Schmidt, M. (1994). Text-independent speaker identification. *IEEE Signal Processing Magazine*, *11*(4), 18–32. doi:10.1109/79.317924

Gledhill, D. (2001). *William Hill takes racing database fight to OFT* (p. 10). The Independent.

Gordy, J. D., & Bruton, L. T. (2000). Performance evaluation of digital audio watermarking algorithms. *Proceedings of the 43rd Midwest Symposium on Circuits and Systems*.

Gorman, R. A. (1992). The Feist case: Reflection on a path breaking copyright decision. *Rutgers Computer & Technology Law Journal*, *18*, 731.

Gorodetski, V. I., Popyack, L. J., Samoilov, V., & Skormin, V. A. (2001). SVD-based approach to transparent embedding data into digital images. In *Proc. Int. Workshop on Mathematical Methods, Models and Architectures for Computer Network Security* (pp. 263-274). St. Petersburg, Russia: Springer.

Goyal, V., Kumar, V., Singh, M., Abraham, A., & Sanyal, S. (2005). CompChall: Addressing password guessing attacks. *ITCC05, 1*, (pp. 739-744).

Granovetter, M. (1983). The strength of weak ties: a network theory revisited. *Sociological Theory*, *1*, 201–233. doi:10.2307/202051

Greene, L. H. (2007). Database protection legislation: views from the United States and WIPO. *Copyright World*, *66*, 38.

Grosbois, R., Gerbelot, P., & Ebrahimi, T. (2001). Authentication and access control in the JPEG 2000 compressed domain. *Proc. of SPIE 46th Annual Meeting, Applications of Digital Image Processing XXIV, vol. 4472*, (pp. 95-104). San Diego, July 29th-August 3rd, 2001.

Groves, T. (1793). Incentives in teams. *Econometrica*, *41*(4), 617–631. doi:10.2307/1914085

Gruber, T. (2008). Collective Knowledge Systems: where the Social Web meets the Semantic Web. *Journal of Web Semantics*, *6*(1), 4–13. doi:10.1016/j.websem.2007.11.011

Gruhl, D., Lu, A., & Bender, W. (1996). Echo hiding. *Proceedings of the First International Information Hiding Workshop*, vol. 1174 (pp.295-316).

Grutzmacher, M. (1999). *Urheber, leistungs- und sui-generis-shutz von datenbanken*. Germany: Baden-Baden.

Gu, W., & Wei, W. (2006). Automatic Community Discovery in Peer-to-Peer Systems. In *Proceedings of the 5th International Conference on Grid and Cooperative Computing Workshops (GCC 2006)*, Changsha, Hunan, China (pp. 110-116).

Guo, L., Jiang, S., Xiao, L., & Zhang, X. (2005). Fast and low-cost search schemes by exploiting localities in p2p networks. *Journal of Parallel and Distributed Computing*, *65*(6), 729–742. doi:10.1016/j.jpdc.2005.01.007

Halevy, A. Y. (2001). Answering queries using views: A survey. *The VLDB Journal*, *10*(4), 270–294. doi:10.1007/s007780100054

Halevy, A., Ives, Z., Madhavan, J., Mork, P., Suciu, D., & Tatarinov, I. (2004). The Piazza Peer Data Management System. *IEEE Transactions on Knowledge and Data Engineering*, *16*(7), 787–798. doi:10.1109/TKDE.2004.1318562

Haller, N. M. (1994). The S/KEY (TM) one-time password system. *Proceedings of Internet Society Symposium on Network and Distributed System Security*, (pp. 151-158).

Halpin, H., Robu, V., & Shepherd, H. (2007). The complex dynamics of collaborative tagging, *in Proceedings of the 16th International Conference on World Wide Web*, 211–220, New York, USA. ACM Press.

Hardin, G. (1968). The tragedy of the commons. *Science*, *62*, 1243–1248.

Hasan, A. N., & Adamic, L. (2007). Expressing social relationships on the blog through links and comments. *In Proc. of International Conference on Weblogs and Social Media*, Mar.

Hashemi, J., & Fatemizadeh, E. (2005). Biometric identification through hand geometry. *International Conference on Computer as a Tool EUROCON 2005, 2*, (pp. 1011-1014).

Hayden, J. F. (1991). Copyright protection of computer databases after Feist. *Harvard Journal of Law & Technology, 5*, 215.

Hayes, B. S. (2000). Integrating moral rights into U.S. law and the problem of the works for hire doctrine. *Ohio State Law Journal, 61*, 1013.

Heflin, J., Hendler, J., & Luke, S. (1999). *SHOE: A knowledge representation language for internet applications*. (Tech. Rep. No. 99-71). College Park, MD: University of Maryland, Dept. of Computer Science.

Herkiloglu, K., Sener, S., & Gunsel, B. (2004). Robust audio watermarking by adaptive psychoacoustic masking. *Proceedings of 12th IEEE Conference on Signal Processing and Communications Applications*, (pp. 29-32).

Heymann, P., Koutrika, G., & Garcia-Molina, H. (2008). Can social bookmarking improve web search? *In Proceedings of WSDM'2008*. ACM, 195-206.

Hicks, W. B. (1987). Copyright and computer database: Is traditional compilation law adequate? *Texas Law Review, 65*, 993.

Ho, C., & Hsu, W. (2005). *Image protection system and method*. US Patent: US2005114669.

Hollander, W. H. (2009). New intellectual property database is a powerful tool. *Federal Lawyer, 56*, 19.

Holt, L., Maufe, B. G., & Wiener, A. (1988). *Encoded marking of a recording signal*. UK Patent, GB 2196167A.

Hong, F., Shi, L., & Luo, T. (2004). A semi-fragile watermarking scheme based on neural network. *IEEE Proceedings of the Third International Conference on Machine Learning and Cybernetics*, vol. 6 (pp. 3536-3541).

Hopfield, J. J., & Tank, D. W. (1985). Neural computation of decisions in optimization problems. *Biological Cybernetics, 52*, 141–152.

Hose, K., Roth, A., Zeitz, A., Sattler, K.-U., & Naumann, F. (2008). A Research Agenda for Query Processing in Large-Scale Peer Data Management Systems. *Information Systems, 33*(7-8), 597–610. doi:10.1016/j.is.2008.01.012

Hou, J., & Zhang, Y. (2003). Utilizing Hyperlink Transitivity to Improve Web Page Clustering, in Klaus Dieter-Schewe (ed.), Database Technologies 2003: Proceedings of the Fourteenth Australasian Database Conference. *Conferences in Research and Practice in Information Technology*, 49-57, Australian Computer Society Inc., Australia.

Huang, J., & Shi, Y. Q. (2002). Adaptive image watermarking scheme based on visual masking. *Electronics Letters, 34*(8), 748–750. doi:10.1049/el:19980545

Hurwicz, L. (1972). On informationally decentralized systems. In McGuire, C. B., & Radner, R. (Eds.), *Decision and Organization* (pp. 297–336). Amsterdam, The Netherlands: North-Holland.

Hwang, M. S., Chang, C. C., & Hwang, K. F. (1999). A watermarking technique based on one-way hash functions. *IEEE Transactions on Consumer Electronics*, *45*(2), 286–294. doi:10.1109/30.793411

International Biometric Group. (2006). *Biometrics market and industry report 2006-2010*. Retrieved from http://www.biometricgroup.com/reports/public/market_report.html

Introna, L. D., & Nissenbaum, H. (2009). *Facial recognition technology: A survey of policy and implementation issues*. Center for Catastrophe Preparedness and Response. New York University, July, 22, 2009.

Jain, A. K., Bolle, R., & Pankanti, S. (1999). *Biometrics: Personal identification in networked society*. Kluwer Academic Publishers.

Jain, A., & Farkas, C. (2006). Secure resource description framework: An access control model. In *Proceedings of the Eleventh ACM Symposium on Access Control Models and Technologies* (pp. 121-129).

Jajodia, S., Samarati, P., Sapino, M. L., & Subrahmaninan, V. S. (2001). Flexible support for multiple access control policies. *ACM Transactions on Database Systems*, *26*(2), 214–260. doi:10.1145/383891.383894

Jansen, W., Gavrila, S., Korolev, V., Ayers, R., & Swanstrom, R. (2003). *Picture password: A visual login technique for mobile devices*. NIST IR 7030.

Jarach, G. (1979). Considerazioni sui rapporti tra autori e utilizzatori delle opere dell'ingegno. *Il diritto di autore, 2*(3), 587-598.

Javanmardi, S., Amini, M., & Jalili, R. (2006). An access control model for protecting Semantic Web resources. In *Proceedings of the Second International Semantic Web Policy Workshop*.

Jeong, D., Jing, Y., & Baik, D.-K. (2007). Access control model based on RDB security policy for OWL ontology. In Y. Shi, et al. (Eds.), In *Proceedings of the Seventh International Conference on Computational Science* (pp. 720-727).

Jermyn, I., May, A., Monrose, F., Riter, M., & Rubin, A. (1999). *The design and analysis of graphical passwords*. 8th USENIX Security Symposium.

Johnson, J. L. (1994). Pulse-coupled neural nets: Translation, rotation, scale, distortion and intensity signal invariances for images. *Applied Optics*, *33*(26), 6239–6253. doi:10.1364/AO.33.006239

Johnson, E. D. (1970). *History of libraries in the western world*. Metuchen, NJ: Scarecrow Press Inc.

Johnston, R. (2009). Recent developments in intellectual property law that will impact the Internet. *Computer & Internet Lawyer*, *26*, 12.

Kagal, L., Finin, T., & Joshi, A. (2003). A policy based approach to security for the Semantic Web. In *Proceedings of the Second International Semantic Web Conference* (pp. 402-418). New York: ACM Press.

Kagel, J., & Roth, A. (1995). *The handbook of experimental economics*. Princeton, NJ: Princeton University Press.

Kahn, D. (1996). The history of steganography. [Information Hiding, Springer-Verlag.]. *Lecture Notes in Computer Science*, *1174*, 1–5.

Katzenseisser, S., & Petitcolas, F. A. P. (2000). *Information hiding techniques for steganography and digital watermarking*. London, UK: Artech House.

Kaushik, S., Wijesekera, D., & Ammann, P. (2005). Policy-based dissemination of partial web-ontologies. In *Proceedings of the 2005 Workshop on Secure Web Services* (pp. 43-52).

Kazakeviciute, G., Januskevicius, E., Rosenbaum, R., & Schumann, H. (2005). Tamper-proof image *watermarking*, based on existing public key infrastructure. *Informatica, 16*(1).

Khambatti, M., Ryu, K. D., & Dasgupta, P. (2002). Efficient Discovery of Implicitly Formed Peer-to-Peer Communities. *International Journal of Parallel and Distributed Systems and Networks, 5*(4), 155–164.

Kharrazi, M., Sencar, H. T., & Memon, N. (2004). *Image steganography: Concepts and practice*. Lecture Note Series, Institute for Mathematical Sciences, National University of Singapore, April 2004.

Kim, H. J., & Yeo, I. (2003). Modified patchwork algorithm: A novel audio watermarking scheme. *Transactions on Speech and Audio Processing, 11*(4), 381–386. doi:10.1109/TSA.2003.812145

Kim, H. (2000). Stochastic model based audio watermark and whitening filter for improved detection. *IEEE International Conference on Acoustics, Speech, and Signal Processing, 4*, (pp. 1971-1974).

Kim, H. J. (2003). *Audio watermarking techniques*. Pacific Rim Workshop on Digital Steganography. ISO/IEC Joint Technical Committee 1. (1993). *Subcommittee 29 working group 11, information technology-coding of moving pictures and associated audio for digital storage media at up to about 1.5 Mbit/s, Part 3: Audio*. ISO/IEC 11172-3.

Kim, H. O., Lee, B. K., & Lee, N. Y. (2001). *Wavelet-based audio watermarking techniques: Robustness and fast synchronization*. Research Report 01-11, Division of Applied Mathematics-Kaist.

Kim, Y. C., Byeong, C., & Choi, C. (2002). Two-step detection algorithm in a HVS-based blind watermarking on still images. *Revised Papers of Digital Watermarking First International Workshop IWDW 2002*, vol. 2613 (pp. 235-248).

Knight, G. A. (1999). The fall and rise of sweat of the brow. *Intellectual Property Journal, 3*, 342.

Kogut, B., & Metiu, A. (2001). Open-source software development and distributed innovation. *Oxford Review of Economic Policy, 17*, 248–264. doi:10.1093/oxrep/17.2.248

Kohonen, T. (1982). Self-organized formation of topologically correct feature maps. *Biological Cybernetics, 43*, 59–63. doi:10.1007/BF00337288

Kohonen, T. (1995). *Self-organizing maps*. Springer-Verlag.

Krasner-Khait, B. (2001). Survivor: The history of the library. *History Magazine, (October/November)*. Retrieved July 11, 2006, from http://www.history-magazine.com/libraries.html

Kundur, D., & Hatzinakos, D. (2004). Towards robust logo watermarking using multiresolution image fusion. *IEEE Transactions on Multimedia, 6*, 185–197. doi:10.1109/TMM.2003.819747

Kundur, D., & Karthik, K. (2004). Video fingerprinting and encryption principles for digital rights management. *Proceedings of the IEEE, 92*(6), 918–932. doi:10.1109/JPROC.2004.827356

Kung, S. Y., Mak, M. W., & Lin, S. H. (2004). *Biometric authentication: A machine learning approach.* Prentice Hall.

Kunkelmann, T., & Reineman, R. (1997). A scalable security architecture for multimedia communication standards. *Proceedings of the 4th IEEE International Conference on Multimedia Computing and Systems.* Darinstadt Univ. of Technology, IT0. D-64283 Darmstadt, Germany, (pp. 660-663).

Lai, S. (1999). Digital copyright and watermarking. *EIPR, 21*(4), 171.

Lakshmanan, V. S. L., Wang, H., & Zhao, Z. (2006). Answering tree pattern queries using views. In *Proceedings of the Thirty Second International Conference on Very Large Databases* (pp. 571-582).

Lambrecht, C., & Verscheure, O. (1996). Perceptual quality measure using a spatio-temporal model of the human visual system. *Proceedings of the Society for Photo-Instrumentation Engineers, 2668*, 450–461.

Lasota, A., & Mackey, M. C. (1997). *Chaos, fractals, and noise-stochastic aspects of dynamics.* New York, NY: Springer.

Laurent, A. M. S. (2004). *Understanding open source and free software licensing.* Cambridge, UK: O'Reilly.

Leclerc, F., & Plamondon, R. (1994). Automatic signature verification: The state of the art - 1989-1993. *International Journal of Pattern Recognition and Artificial Intelligence, 8*(3), 643–660. doi:10.1142/S0218001494000346

Lee, J., & Jung, S. (2001). A survey of watermarking techniques applied to multimedia. *Proceedings 2001 IEEE International Symposium on Industrial Electronics (ISIE2001), 1,* (pp. 272-277).

Legge, G. E., & Foley, J. M. (1980). Contrast masking in human vision. *Journal Optical Society, 70*, 1458–1470. doi:10.1364/JOSA.70.001458

Lessig, L. (2004). *Free culture: The nature and future of creativity.* New York, NY: Penguin Books.

Li, S. Z., & Jain, A. K. (2005). *Handbook of face recognition.* Springer.

Li, Q., & Atluri, V. (2003). Concept-level access control for the Semantic Web. In *Proceedings of the 2003 ACM Workshop on XML Security* (pp. 94-103). New York: ACM Press.

Li, Q., Yuan, C., & Zong, Y. Z. (2007). Adaptive DWT-SVD domain image watermarking using human visual model. In *Proc. Int. Conf. Advanced Communication Technology* (pp. 1947-1951). Gangwon-Do, Korea: IEEE Press.

Li, S., Li, C., Chen, G., & Bourbakis, N. G. (2004). *A general cryptanalysis of permutation-only multimedia encryption algorithms.* IACR's Cryptology ePrint Archive: Report 2004/374.

Lian, S. (2008e). Digital rights management for the home TV based on scalable video coding. *IEEE Transactions on Consumer Electronics*, *54*(3), 1287–1293. doi:10.1109/TCE.2008.4637619

Lian, S. (2009b). Secure video distribution scheme based on partial encryption. [Wiley-Blackwell Publisher]. *International Journal of Imaging Systems and Technology*, *19*(3), 227–235. doi:10.1002/ima.20199

Lian, S. (2009c). Quasi-commutative watermarking and encryption for secure media content distribution. [Springer.]. *Multimedia Tools and Applications*, *43*(1), 91–107. doi:10.1007/s11042-008-0258-4

Lian, S., Kanellopoulos, D., & Ruffo, G. (2009a). Recent advances in multimedia information system security. *Informatica. Slovenian Society Informatika*, *33*(1), 3–24.

Lian, S., Liu, Z., Ren, Z., & Wang, H. (2006a). Secure advanced video coding based on selective encryption algorithms. *IEEE Transactions on Consumer Electronics*, *52*(2), 621–629. doi:10.1109/TCE.2006.1649688

Lian, S., Liu, Z., Ren, Z., & Wang, H. (2006c). Commutative watermarking and encryption for media data. *International Journal of Optical Engineering*, *45*(8), 0805101–0805103.

Lian, S., Liu, Z., Ren, Z., & Wang, H. (2007). Commutative encryption and watermarking in compressed video data. *IEEE Transactions on Circuits and Systems for Video Technology*, *17*(6), 774–778. doi:10.1109/TCSVT.2007.896635

Lian, S., & Wang, Z. (2008). Collusion-traceable secure multimedia distribution based on controllable modulation. *IEEE Transactions on Circuits and Systems for Video Technology*, *18*(1), 1462–1467. doi:10.1109/TCSVT.2008.2002829

Lian, S., & Zhang, Y. (2009a). *Handbook of research on secure multimedia distribution*. Hershey, PA: IGI Global. doi:10.4018/978-1-60566-262-6

Lian, S., & Zhang, Y. (2009b). Protecting mobile TV multimedia content in DVB/GPRS heterogeneous wireless networks. *Journal of Universal Computer Science*, *15*(5), 1023–1041.

Lian, S. (2009d). Secure multimedia transcoding for scalable video streams. In Ahmad, A. M. A., & Khalil Ibrahim, I. (Eds.), *Multimedia transcoding in mobile and wireless networks*. Hershey, PA: IGI Global.

Lian, S. (2008d). Traitor tracing in mobile multimedia communication. In Khalil Ibrahim, I. (Ed.), *Handbook of research on mobile multimedia* (2nd ed.). Hershey, PA: IGI Global. doi:10.4018/978-1-60566-046-2.ch030

Lian, S. (2008c). Secure multimedia content distribution scheme based on watermarking technology. In Li, C.-T. (Ed.), *Multimedia forensics and security*. Hershey, PA: IGI Global. doi:10.4018/978-1-59904-869-7.ch002

Lian, S. (2008b). Multimedia encryption and watermarking in wireless environment. In Zhang, Y., Zheng, J., & Ma, M. (Eds.), *Handbook of research on wireless security*. Hershey, PA: IGI Global. doi:10.4018/978-1-59904-899-4.ch016

Lian, S. (2008a). *Multimedia content encryption: techniques and applications*. Auerbach Publication, Taylor & Francis Group, September 2008.

Lian, S. (2009a). *Multimedia communication security: Recent advances*. Nova Publishers, April 2009.

Lian, S. (2010a). *Content and service protection for the ubiquitous TV based on convergent networks*. Wireless Personal Communication. Springer. DOI 10.1007/s11277-009-9783-3

Lian, S. (2010b). *Secure service convergence based on scalable content and service protection*. Telecommunications System. Springer. DOI 10.1007/s11235-009-9233-2

Lian, S., Chen, X., Dong, Y., & Wang, H. (2010). *On the secure multimedia distribution scheme based on partial encryption*. IEEE ICC 2010.

Lian, S., Dong, Y., & Wang, H. (2009b). *A secure solution for ubiquitous multimedia broadcasting*. 2009 IEEE International Conference on Communications (ICC 2009), Dresden, Germany, 13-18 June, 2009.

Lian, S., Liu, Z., Dong, Y., & Wang, H. (2008a). On the security of the delay-based fingerprint embedding scheme. *Proceedings of 2008 International Conference on Communication in China* (ChinaCom2008), IEEE Publisher, Aug. 25-27, 2008, Hangzhou, China, (pp. 699–703).

Lian, S., Liu, Z., Dong, Y., & Wang, H. (2008b). On the joint audio fingerprinting and decryption scheme. *Proceedings of 2008 IEEE International Conference on Multimedia and Expo* (ICME2008), IEEE Publisher, June 23-26, 2008, Hannover, Germany, (pp. 261-264).

Lian, S., Liu, Z., Ren, Z., & Wang, H. (2006b). *Secure distribution scheme for compressed data streams*. Accepted by 2006 IEEE Conference on Image Processing (ICIP 2006).

Lian, S., Liu, Z., Ren, Z., & Wang, Z. (2005). Selective video encryption based on advanced video coding. In *Proceedings of 2005 Pacific-Rim Conference on Multimedia (PCM2005), Part II, Springer LNCS, 3768*, (pp. 281-290).

Lian, S., Sun, J., & Wang, Z. (2004b). Perceptual cryptography on SPIHT compressed images or videos. *Proceedings of IEEE International Conference on Multimedia and Expro (I)* (ICME 2004), Taiwan, China, June 2004, 3, (pp. 2195-2198).

Lian, S., Sun, J., & Wang, Z. (2004d). A novel image encryption scheme based-on JPEG encoding. In *Proceedings of the Eighth International Conference on Information Visualization* (IV04), London, UK, July, (pp. 217-220).

Lian, S., Sun, J., & Wang, Z. (2004e). Perceptual cryptography on JPEG2000 encoded images or videos. *Proceedings of International Conference on Computer and Information Technology*, (pp. 78-83).

Lian, S., Sun, J., Zhang, D., & Wang, Z. (2004a). A selective image encryption scheme based on JPEG2000 codec. *2004 Pacific-Rim Conference on Multimedia (PCM2004), Springer LNCS, 3332*, (pp. 65-72).

Lian, S., Wang, Z., & Sun, J. (2004c). A fast video encryption scheme suitable for network applications. *Proceedings of International Conference on Communications, Circuits and Systems*, Chengdu, China, 1, (pp. 566-570).

Liang, L. (2004). *A guide to open content licenses*. Netherlands: Piet Zwart Institute.

Lin, C. L., Sun, H. M., & Hwang, T. (2001). Attacks and solutions on strong-password authentication. *IEICE Transactions on Communications. E (Norwalk, Conn.), 84-B*(9), 2622–2627.

Lin, C.-W., Shen, J.-J., & Hwang, M.-S. (2003). Security enhancement for optimal strong-password authentication protocol. *ACM Operating System Review, 37*(3), 12–16. doi:10.1145/881783.881785

Lin, C. H., Jen, J. S., & Kuo, L. C. (2006). Distributed discrete wavelet transformation for copyright protection. In *Proc. Int. Workshop on Image Analysis for Multimedia Interactive Services* (pp. 53-56). Incheon, Korea: Springer.

Linn, A. (2000). History of database protection: Legal issues of concern to the scientific community. Retrieved September 25, 2006, from http://www.codata.org/data_access/linn.html

Lipton, J. (2003). Databases as intellectual property: New legal approaches. *EIPR, 25*(3), 139.

Liu, R., & Tan, T. (2002). An SVD-based watermarking scheme for protecting rightful ownership. *IEEE Transactions on Multimedia, 4*(1), 121–128. doi:10.1109/6046.985560

Liu, K., Bhaduri, K., Das, K., Nguyen, P., & Kargupta, H. (2006). Client-side Web Mining for Community Formation in Peer-to-Peer Environments. *SIGKDD Explorations, 8*(2), 11–20. doi:10.1145/1233321.1233323

Liu, Q., & Jiang, X. (2005). Design and realization of a meaningful digital watermarking algorithm based on RBF neural network. *IEEE International Conference on Neural Networks and Brain*, vol. 1 (pp. 214-218).

Lou, D. C., Liu, J. L., & Hu, M. C. (2003). Adaptive digital watermarking using neural network technique. *Proceedings of IEEE 37th Annual 2003 International Carnahan Conference on Security Technology*, (pp.325-332).

Lubin, J. (1993). *The use of psychophysical data and models in the analysis of display system performance. Digital images and human vision* (pp. 163–178). A. B. Watson.

Ma, X., McCrindle, R., & Cheng, X. (2006). *Verifying and fixing password authentication protocol*. SNPD'06.

Macq, B., & Quisquater, J. (1995). Cryptology for digital TV broadcasting. *Proceedings of the IEEE, 83*, 944–957. doi:10.1109/5.387094

Mallat, S. G. (1989). A theory for multiresolution signal decomposition: The wavelet representation. *IEEE Transactions on Pattern Analysis and Machine Intelligence, 11*, 674–693. doi:10.1109/34.192463

Maltoni, D., Maio, D., Jain, A. K., & Prabhakar, S. (2009). *Handbook of fingerprint recognition* (2nd ed.). Springer. doi:10.1007/978-1-84882-254-2

Mansani, L. (1996). *La protezione dei database in Internet* (p. 149). AIDA.

Mansour, M. F., & Tewfik, A. H. (2001). Audio watermarking by time-scale modification. *International Conference on Acoustics, Speech, and Signal Processing, 3,* (pp. 1353-1356).

Mao, Y. B., Chen, G. R., & Lian, S. G. (2004). A novel fast image encryption scheme based on the 3D chaotic baker map. *International Journal of Bifurcation and Chaos in Applied Sciences and Engineering, 14*(10), 3613–3624. doi:10.1142/S021812740401151X

Marino, F. (2006). Database protection in the European Union. Retrieved September 15, 2006, from www.jus.unitn.it/cardozo/Review/Students/Marino1.html

Marr, D. (1982). *Vision: A computational investigation into the human representation and processing of visual information*. San Francisco, CA: W. H. Freeman.

Maskin, E. (1999). Nash equilibrium and welfare optimality. *The Review of Economic Studies*, *66*(1), 23–38. doi:10.1111/1467-937X.00076

Maskin, E. (2008). Mechanism design: How to implement social goals. *The American Economic Review*, *98*(3), 567–576. doi:10.1257/aer.98.3.567

Matias, Y., & Shamir, A. (1987). A video scrambling technique based on space filling curves. *Proceedings of Advances in Cryptology-CRYPTO'87* [Springer.]. *LNCS*, *293*, 398–417.

Maxwell, T., Giles, C., Lee, T. C., & Chen, H. H. (1986). Nonlinear dynamics of artificial neural systems. *AIP Conference Proceedings*, *151*, 299–304. doi:10.1063/1.36227

McCulloch, W. S., & Pitts, W. H. (1943). A logical calculus of the ideas immanent in nervous activity. *The Bulletin of Mathematical Biophysics*, *5*, 115–133. doi:10.1007/BF02478259

McCurdy, G. V. S. (2003). Intellectual property and competition: Does the essential facilities doctrine shed any new light? *EIPR*, *20*(10), 473.

McGuinness, D. L., & van Harmelen, F. (2004). *OWL Web Ontology Language Overview*. Retrieved from http://www.w3.org/TR/owl-features/

Me, G., Pirro, D., & Sarrecchia, R. (2006). *A mobile based approach to strong authentication on Web* (p. 67). International Multi-Conference on Computing in the Global Information Technology.

Mears, J. (2006). Open source unlocks options for many small-to-medium sized businesses. *Network World*. Retrieved October 11, 2006, from http://www.linuxworld.com/cgi-bin/mailto/x_linux.cgi

Meerwald, P., & Uhl, A. (2001). A survey of wavelet-domain watermarking algorithms. In *Proc. SPIE, Electronic Imaging, Security and Watermarking of Multimedia Contents III, 4314*. San Jose, CA: SPIE.

Meier, H., Roy, R., & Seliger, G. (2010). Industrial product-service systems—IPS. *CIRP Annals—Manufacturing Technology*, *59*(2), 607-627.

Meyer, Y. (1989). Orthonormal wavelets. In Combes, J. M. (Ed.), *Wavelets: Time-frequency methods and phase spaces (Lecture Notes on IPTI)* (pp. 21–37). New York, NY: Springer Verlag.

Milbrath, S. D. (2009). The 11th Circuit's new copyright standard for architectural works. *The Florida Bar Journal*, *83*, 50.

Mitchell, D. S., Bin, Z., Tewfik, A. H., & Boney, L. (1998). Robust audio watermarking using perceptual masking. *IEEE Signal Processing*, *66*(3), 337–355. doi:10.1016/S0165-1684(98)00014-0

Mitchell, C. (1989). Limitations of challenge-response entity authentication. *IEEE Electronic Letters*, *25*(17), 1195–1196. doi:10.1049/el:19890801

Mohanty, S. P. (1999). Digital watermarking: A tutorial review. In *Report on Dept. of Electrical Engineering*. Bangalore, India: Indian Institute of Science.

Mollin, R. A. (2006). *An introduction to cryptography*. CRC Press.

Monrose, F., & Rubin, A. D. (2000). Keystroke dynamics as a biometric for authentication. *Future Generation Computer Systems*, *16*(4), 351–359. doi:10.1016/S0167-739X(99)00059-X

Montanelli, S., & Castano, S. (2008). Semantically Routing Queries in Peer-based Systems: the H-Link Approach. *The Knowledge Engineering Review*, *23*(1), 51–72. doi:10.1017/S0269888907001257

Moody, J. E., & Darken, C. (1989). Fast learning in networks of locally-tuned processing units. *Neural Computation*, *1*, 281–294. doi:10.1162/neco.1989.1.2.281

Mori, J., Basselin, N., Kroner, A., & Jameson, A. (2008). Find me if you can: designing interfaces for people search. *In Proceedings of IUI*. 2008, 377-380.

Moritz, T. D. (2004). Conservation partnerships in the commons? Sharing data and information, experience and knowledge, as the essence of partnerships. *Museum International*, *56*(4), 24–31. doi:10.1111/j.1468-0033.2004.00046.x

Muharemagic, E., & Furht, B. (2004). *Multimedia security: Watermarking techniques*. Chicago, IL: Comprehensive Report on Information Security, International Engineering Consortium.

Mulholland, H. (2005). *U-turn on child protection database*. Retrieved September 6, 2006, from www.societyguardian.co.uk

Muntean, T., Grivel, E., Nafornita, I., & Najim, M. (2002). *Audio digital watermarking for copyright protection*. International Workshop on "Trends and Achievements in Information Technology.

Musso, A. (1998). *Ipertesti e thesauri nella disciplina del diritto d'autore* (p. 10). AIDA.

Nakajima, N., & Yamaguchi, Y. (2004). Enhancing registration tolerance of extended visual cryptography for natural images. *Journal of Electronic Imaging*, *13*(3), 654–662. doi:10.1117/1.1758729

Nallusamy, R., & Paul, S. (2009). Strong authentication for secure content access in converged networks. *International Symposium on Advanced Networks and Telecommunication Systems*, 2009, (pp. 1-3).

Naor, M., & Shamir, A. (1994). Visual cryptography. In De Santis, A. (Ed.), *Advances in Cryptology-Eurocrypt '94, Lecture Notes in Computer Science, Springer-Verlag, 950* (pp. 1–12). Berlin.

Naor, M., & Pinkas, B. (1997). Visual authentication and identification. In Kaliski, B. (Ed.), *Advances in Cryptology – Crypto '97, 1294* (pp. 322–336).

Nitin Sehgal, V. K., Chauhan, D. S., Sood, M., & Hastir, V. (2008). Image based authentication system with sign-in seal. *Proc. of the World Congress on Engineering and Computer Science 2008, WCECS 2008*, October 22 - 24, 2008, San Francisco, USA.

Norcen, R., & Uhl, A. (2003). Selective encryption of the JPEG2000 bitstream. *IFIP International Federation for Information Processing. Springer LNCS, 2828*, 194–204.

Oliver, P., & Marwell, G. (1988). The paradox of group size in collective action: A theory of the critical mass, II. *American Sociological Review*, *53*, 1–8. doi:10.2307/2095728

Olson, M. (1965). *The logic of collective action*. Cambridge, MA: Harvard University Press.

Olson, M., & Zeckhauser, R. (1966). An economic theory of alliances. *The Review of Economics and Statistics*, *48*, 266–279. doi:10.2307/1927082

Omura, J. K. (1990). Novel applications of cryptography in digital communications. *IEEE Communications Magazine*, *28*(5), 21–29. doi:10.1109/35.54344

Onali, T., & Ginesu, G. (2006). Transmission-efficient image-based authentication for mobile devices. *Lecture Notes in Computer Science*, 3893.

ORuanaidh, J. J. K., & Pun, T. (1998). Rotation, scale and translation invariant spread spectrum digital image watermarking. *Signal Processing*, *66*, 303–317. doi:10.1016/S0165-1684(98)00012-7

Ozsu, M. T., & Valduriez, P. (1999). *Principles of Distributed Database Systems* (2nd ed.). Upper Saddle River, NJ: Prentice Hall.

Pan, D. (1995). A tutorial on MPEG/audio compression. *IEEE MultiMedia*, *2*(2), 60–74. doi:10.1109/93.388209

Pang, N., & Schauder, D. (2006). User-centred design and the culture of knowledge creating communities: A theoretical reassessment. In Burstein, F. V., & Linger, H. (Eds.), *The local and global in knowledge management - Why culture matters* (pp. 151–166). Kew, Australia: Australian Scholarly Publishing.

Pang, N. (2009). Digital libraries as centres of knowledge. In Theng, Y. L., & Foo, S. (Eds.), *Handbook of digital libraries* (pp. 506–515). Hershey, PA: IGI Global. doi:10.4018/978-1-59904-879-6.ch052

Pang, N., Denison, T., Johanson, G., Schauder, D., & Williamson, K. (2006, October). *Empowering communities through memories: The role of public libraries*. Paper presented at the 3rd Prato International Community Informatics Conference, Prato, Italy.

Pantle, A., & Sekuler, R. W. (1969). Contrast response of human visual mechanisms sensitive to orientation and direction of motion. *Vision Research*, *9*, 397–406. doi:10.1016/0042-6989(69)90087-X

Papin-Ramcharan, J. I., & Dawe, R. A. (2006). Open access publishing: A developing country view. *First Monday*, *11* (6). Retrieved October 1, 2006, from http://firstmonday.org/issues/issue11_6/papin/index.html

Parnes, R., & Parviainen, R. (2001). Large scale distributed watermarking of multicast media through encryption. In *Proc. IFIP Int. Conf. Communications and Multimedia Security, Issues of the New Century,* Darmstadt, Germany, (pp. 21-22).

Passfaces, T. M. (n.d.). *Website*. Retrieved from http://www.realuser.com

PassPicc. (n.d.). *Website*. Retrieved from http://www.authord.com/PassPic/

Patel, K. (2007). Authors v internet archives: The copyright infringement battle over web pages. *Journal of the Patent and Trademark Office Society*, *89*, 418.

Pennebaker, W. B., & Mitchell, J. L. (1993). *JPEG: Still image data compression standard.* Van Nostrand Reinhold.

Perrig, A., & Song, D. (1999). *Hash visualization: A new technique to improve real-world security.* International Workshop on Cryptographic Techniques and E-Commerce CrypTEC '99.

Petitcolas, F. A. P., Anderson, R. J., & Kuhn, M. G. (1999). Information hiding – A survey. *Proceedings of the IEEE - Special Issue on Protection of Multimedia Content, 87*(7), 1062-1078.

Pfarrhofer, R., & Uhl, A. (2005). Selective image encryption using JBIG. *Communications and Multimedia Security, 2005*, 98–107. doi:10.1007/11552055_10

Phillips, P. J., Moon, H., Rauss, P., & Rizvi, S. (1997). The FERET evaluation methodology for face-recognition algorithms. *Proceedings IEEE Conference Computer Vision and Pattern Recognition CVPR, 97*, 137–143. doi:10.1109/CVPR.1997.609311

Phillips, P. J., Flynn, P. J., Scruggs, T., Bowyer, K. W., Chang, J., & Hoffman, K. … Worek, W. (2005). Overview of the face recognition grand challenge. *Proceedings of the 2005 IEEE Computer Society Conference on Computer Vision and Pattern Recognition* (CVPR'05), volume 1.

Phillips, P. J., Scruggs, T., O'Toole, A. J., Flynn, P. J., Bowyer, K. W., Schott, C. L., & Sharpe, M. (2007). *FRVT 2006 and ICE 2006 large-scale results*. National Institute of Standards and Technology, March 2007.

Pichler, F., & Scharinger, J. (1996). Finite dimensional generalized Baker dynamical systems for cryptographic applications. *Lecture Notes in Computer Science, 1030*, 465–476. doi:10.1007/BFb0034782

Pierce, J. D., Warren, M. J., Mackay, D. R., & Wells, J. G. (2004). Graphical authentication: Justifications and objectives, *Proceedings of the 2nd Australian Information Security Management Conference, Securing the Future* (AISM 2004), (pp. 49-63).

Pioch, N. (2006). *Impressionism.* Retrieved October 1, 2006, from http://www.ibiblio.org/wm/paint/glo/impressionism/

Podesser, M., Schmidt, H. P., & Uhl, A. (2002). Selective bitplane encryption for secure transmission of image data in mobile environments. In CD-ROM *Proceedings of the 5th IEEE Nordic Signal Processing Symposium (NORSIG 2002)*, Tromso-Trondheim, Norway, October.

Poggio, T., & Girosi, F. (1990). Regularization algorithms for learning that are equivalent to multilayer networks. *Science, 247*(4945), 978–982. doi:10.1126/science.247.4945.978

Pointsec Mobile Technologies. (n.d.). *Home*. Retrieved from http://www.pointsec.com

Poirson, A., & Wandell, B. (1993). Appearance of colored patterns. *Journal of the Optical Society of America, 10*(12), 2458–2470. doi:10.1364/JOSAA.10.002458

Probst, R., Lonsbury-Martin, B. L., & Martin, G. K. (1991). A review of otoacoustic emissions. *Journal of Acoustic Society, 89*, 2027–2067. doi:10.1121/1.400897

Prokoski, F. J. (1997). *Security and non-diagnostic medical uses for thermal imaging.* American Academy of Thermology 1997 Annual Meeting, Pittsburgh.

Prud'hommeaux, E., & Seaborne, A. (2008). *SPARQL Query Language for RDF.* Retrieved from http://www.w3.org/TR/rdf-sparql-query/

Pu, Y., Liao, K., Zhou, J., & Zhang, N. (2004). A public adaptive watermark algorithm for color images based on principal component analysis of generalized Hebb. *IEEE Proceedings of International Conference on Information Acquisition*, (pp. 484-488).

Qi, D., Zou, J., & Han, X. (2000). A new class of scrambling transformation and its application in the image information covering. [English Edition]. *Science in China - Series E*, *43*(3), 304–312. doi:10.1007/BF02916835

Qiao, L., & Nahrstedt, K. (2000). Comparison of MPEG encryption algorithm. *International Journal on Computers and Graphics*, *22*(4), 437–448. doi:10.1016/S0097-8493(98)00033-8

Qiao, L., & Nahrstedt, K. (1997). A new algorithm for MPEG video encryption. In *Proceeding of the First International Conference on Imaging Science, Systems and Technology (CISST'97)*, Las Vegas, Nevada, July, (pp. 21-29).

Quan, X., & Zhang, H. (2004). Audio watermarking for copyright protection based on psychoacoustic model and adaptive wavelet packet decomposition. *Proceedings of 2004 International Symposium on Intelligent Multimedia, Video and Speech Processing*, (pp. 282–285).

Rachel, P. (2008). Communities of practice: using the open web as a collaborative learning platform, *iLearning Forum 2008 Proceedings*, Paris.

Rahmandad, H., & Sterman, J. (2008). Heterogeneity and network structure in the dynamics of diffusion: Comparing agent-based and differential equation models. *Management Science*, *54*(5), 998–1014. doi:10.1287/mnsc.1070.0787

Reither, M. K., & Rubin, A. D. (1998). Crowds anonymity for Web transactions. *ACM Transactions on Information and System Security*, *1*(1), 66–92. doi:10.1145/290163.290168

Ren, Z., Anumba, C. J., & Ugwu, O. O. (2002). Negotiation in a Multi-Agent System for Construction Claims Negotiation. *Applied Artificial Intelligence*, *16*(5), 359–394. doi:10.1080/08839510290030273

Resta, F. (2007). Banche di dati on-line. I limiti della tutela penale. *Giurisprudenza di Merito*, *7-8*, 2053.

Rey, C., & Dugelay, J. (2002). A survey of watermarking algorithms for image authentication. *EURASIP Journal on Applied Signal Processing*, *6*, 613–621. doi:10.1155/S1110865702204047

Rheingold, H. (2002). *Smart mobs: The next social revolution*. Cambridge, UK: Perseus Books Group.

Ricciuti, M. (2002). Open source: Rebels at the gate. *Business Tech: CNet News*. Retrieved October 12, 2006, from http://news.com.com/2009-1001-961354.html

Rivest, R., Shamir, A., & Adleman, L. (1998). A method for obtaining digital signatures and public-key cryptosystems. *Communications of the ACM*, *21*(2), 120–126. doi:10.1145/359340.359342

Rizvi, S., Mendelzon, A., Sudarshan, S., & Roy, P. (2004). Extending query rewriting techniques for fine-grained access control. In *Proceedings of 2004 ACM SIGMOD International Conference on Management of Data* (pp. 551-562). New York: ACM Press.

Robert, A., & Picard, J. (2005). On the use of *masking models* for image and audio *watermarking. IEEE Transactions on Multimedia, 7*(4), 727–739. doi:10.1109/TMM.2005.846781

Robinson, D. J. M., & Hawksford, M. J. (1999). Time-domain auditory model for the assessment of high-quality coded audio. *107th Convention of the Audio Engineering Society* - preprint 5071.

Romeo, A., Romdotti, G., Mattavelli, M., & Mlynek, D. (1999). Cryptosystem architectures for very high throughput multimedia encryption: The RPK solution. *Proceedings of the 6th IEEE International Conference on Electronics, Circuits and Systems*, 1, 5-8 Sept., (pp. 261-264).

Rosenblatt, F. (1985). The Perceptron: Probabilistic model for information storage and organization in the brain. *Psychological Review*, *65*, 386–408. doi:10.1037/h0042519

Rudin, N., & Inman, K. (2001). *An introduction to forensic DNA analysis* (2nd ed.). CRC Press. doi:10.1201/9781420058505

Rummelhart, D. E., & McClelland, J. L.PDP Research Group. (1986). *Parallel Distributed Processing* (*Vol. 1*). The MIT Press.

Said, A. (1996). A new fast and efficient image codec based on set partitioning in hierarchical trees. *IEEE Transactions on Circuits and Systems for Video Technology*, *6*(3), 243–250. doi:10.1109/76.499834

Salton, G. (1989). *Automatic text processing: the transformation, analysis, and retrieval of information by computer*. Boston, MA: Addison-Wesley Longman Publishing Co., Inc.

Salton, G., & McGill, M. J. (1984). *Introduction to Modern Information Retrieval*. McGraw-Hill.

Samal, A., & Lyengar, P. A. (1992). Automatic recognition and analysis of human faces and facial expressions: A survey. *Pattern Recognition*, *25*, 65–77. doi:10.1016/0031-3203(92)90007-6

Sanchez-Reillo, R., Sanchez-Avila, C., & Gonzalez-Marcos, A. (2000). Biometric identification through hand geometry measurements. *IEEE Transactions on Pattern Analysis and Machine Intelligence*, *22*(10), 1168–1171. doi:10.1109/34.879796

Sandirigama, M., Shimizu, A., & Noda, M. T. (2000). Simple and secure password authentication protocol (SAS). *IEICE Transactions on Communications. E (Norwalk, Conn.)*, *83-B*(6), 1363–1365.

Santamauro, J. (2007). Reducing the rhetoric: Reconsidering the relationship of the TRIPs agreement, CBD and proposed new patent disclosure requirements relating to genetic resources and traditional knowledge. *European Intellectual Property Review*, *3*, 92.

Saxby, S. (2005). European Court of Justice interprets key aspect of database directive. *Computer Law & Security Report*, *21*, 2. doi:10.1016/j.clsr.2005.01.022

Scanlan, G. (2005). The database directive — Sui Generis and copyright — A practicable distinction? *The Journal of Business Law*, pp. 432.

Scharinger, J. (1998). Kolmogorov systems: Internal time, irreversibity and cryptographic applications. In D. Dubois, (Ed.), *Proceedings of the AIP Conference on Computing Anticipatory Systems, 437*. Woodbury, NY: Amer. Inst. of Phys.

Schauder, D., & Pang, N. (2006). *Keynote presentation: Digital storytelling.* Paper presented at the Museums Australia 2006 Seminar: Storytelling Through Emerging Technologies. Victoria, Australia.

Schlachter, E. (1997). The intellectual property renaissance in cyberspace: Why copyright law could be unimportant on the Internet. *Berkeley Technology Law Journal, 12*(1). Retrieved October 12, 2006, from http://btlj.boalt.org/data/articles/12-1_spring_1997_symp_2-schlachter.pdf

Schneier, B. (1995). *Applied cryptography* (2nd ed.). Wiley.

Schwartz, M. F., & Wood, D. C. M. (1993). Discovering shared interests among people using graph analysis of global electronic mail traffic. *Communications of the ACM, 36*(8), 78–89. doi:10.1145/163381.163402

Schyndle, R. G. V., Tirkel, A. Z., & Osbrone, C. F. (1994). A digital watermark. In *Proc. of Int. Conf. on Image Processing,* vol. 2 (pp. 86-90). Austin, TX: IEEE Press.

Seely-Brown, J., & Duguid, P. (1991). Organisational Learning and Communities of Practice. *Organization Science, 2*(1).

Servetti, A., Testa, C., Carlos, J., & Martin, D. (2003). Frequency-selective partial encryption of compressed audio. Paper presented at the *International Conference on Audio, Speech and Signal Processing*, Hong Kong, April 5, (pp. 668-671).

Shamir, A. (1979). How to share a secret. *Communications of the ACM, 22*(1), 612–613. doi:10.1145/359168.359176

Shapiro, J. M. (1993). Embedded image coding using zerotrees of wavelet coding. *IEEE Transactions on Signal Processing, 41*(12), 3445–3462. doi:10.1109/78.258085

Shi, C., & Bhargava, B. (1998). A fast MPEG video encryption algorithm. In *Proceedings of the 6th ACM International Multimedia Conference*, Bristol, UK, September, (pp. 81-88).

Shi, C., Wang, S., & Bhargava, B. (1999). MPEG video encryption in real-time using secret key cryptography. In *Proc. of PDPTA'99*, Las Vegas, Nevada, Computer Science Research, Education and Application Press, (pp. 2822-2828).

Shimomura, Y., Hara, T., & Arai, T. (2009). A service evaluation method using mathematical methodologies. *CIRP Annals—Manufacturing Technology, 57*(1), 437-440.

Sigurbjörnsson, B., & Van Zwol, R. (2008). Flickr Tag Recommendation based on Collective Knowledge. In *Proceedings of the 17th International Conference on World Wide Web (WWW 2008)*, Beijing, China (pp. 327-336).

Simon, C., & Goldstein, I. (1935). A new scientific method of identification. *New York State Journal of Medicine, 35*(18), 901–906.

Sims, B. M. (2009). Collaborative sites. *GPsolo, 26*, 27.

Sirin, E., & Parsia, B. (2007). SPARQL-DL: SPARQL Query for OWL-DL. In *Proceedings 3rd OWL Experiences and Directions Workshop (OWLED-2007)*.

Slater, J. B. (2005). When America sneezes. *Mute, 2*(1), 5.

Slay, C. L. (2008). Myspace or whose space? Digital Millenium Copyright Act's impact on web sites. *The Maryland Bar Journal, 41*, 20.

Smith, V. L. (1976). Experimental economics – induced value theory. *The American Economic Review, 66*(2), 274–279.

Smith, V. L. (1982). Microeconomic systems as an experimental science. *The American Economic Review*, *72*(5), 923–955.

Smith, H. (2009). Interpretation of the terms "extraction" and "substantial part" in relation to infringement. *European Intellectual Property Review*, *31*, 58.

Smith, J. O., & Abel, J. A. (1999). *Bark and ERB bilinear transforms*.

Sobrado, L., & Birget, J. C. (2002). Graphical passwords. *The Rutgers Scholar, 4*.

Spada, P. (1997). *Banche dati e diritto d'autore* (p. 5). AIDA.

Spaniol, M., & Klamma, R. (2004). Mediating Ontologies for Communities of Practice. In *Proceedings of the 5th International Conference on Practical Aspects of Knowledge Management (PAKM 2004)*, Vienna, Austria (pp. 330-342).

Spohrer, J., & Maglio, P. P. (2008). The emergence of service science: Toward systematic service innovations to accelerate co-creation of value. *Production and Operations Management*, *17*(3), 238–246. doi:10.3401/poms.1080.0027

Sridharan, S., Dawson, E., & Goldburg, B. (1991). Fast Fourier transform based speech encryption system. *IEE Proceedings of Communications. Speech and Vision*, *138*(3), 215–223. doi:10.1049/ip-i-2.1991.0029

Sripanidkulchai, K., Maggs, B., & Zhang, H. (2003). Efficient content location using interest-based locality in peer-to-peer systems. *In Proc. of INFOCOMM*, Mar.

Stazi, A. (2004). *La pubblicità commerciale on line*. Italy: Giuffrè.

Suo, X., Zhu, Y., & Owen, G. S. (2005). *Graphical passwords: A survey*. 21st Annual Computer Security Applications Conference (ACSAC 2005), Tucson AZ.

Sverldov, A., Dexter, S., & Eskicioglu, A. M. (2005). Robust DCT-SVD domain image watermarking for copyright protection: Embedding data in all frequencies. In *Proc. European Signal Processing Conference*. Antalya, Turkey: Curran Associates, Inc.

Swanson, M. D., Bin, Z., & Tewfik, A. H. (1998). Multiresolution scene-based video watermarking using perceptual models. *IEEE Journal on Selected Areas*, *16*(4), 540–550. doi:10.1109/49.668976

Swanson, M. D., Zhu, B., & Tewfil, A. H. (1996). Transparent robust image watermarking. *Proceedings of International Conference on Image Processing*, *3*, 211–214.

Szepanski, W. (1979) A signal theoretic method for creating forgery-proof documents for automatic verification. In *Proc. Carnahan Conf. on Crime Countermeasures* (pp. 101-109). Lexington, KY.

Tai, E. T. T. (2003). Exhaustion and online delivery of digital works. *EIPR*, *25*(5), 207.

Takada, T., & Koike, H. (2003). Awase-E: Image-based authentication for mobile phones using user's favorite images. *Proceedings of 5th International Symposium, Mobile HCI 2003*, (pp. 347-351). Springer.

Takefuji, Y., Lee, K., & Aiso, H. (1992). An artificial maximum neural network: A winner-take-all neuron model forcing the state of the system in a solution domain. *Biological Cybernetics*, *67*, 243–251. doi:10.1007/BF00204397

Takenaka, T., Fujita, K., Nishino, N., Ishigaki, T., & Motomura, Y. (2009). Transdisciplinary approach to service design based on consumer value and decision making. *International Journal of Organizational and Collective Intelligence*, *1*(1), 58–75. doi:10.4018/joci.2010100804

Takenaka, T., & Ueda, K. (2008). An analysis of service studies toward sustainable value creation. *International Journal of Sustainable Manufacturing*, *1*(1-2), 168–179.

Tanaka, T., & Kubo, N. (2004). Biometric authentication by hand vein patterns. *SICE 2004 Annual Conference, 1,* (pp. 249-253).

Tang, L. (1996). Methods for encrypting and decrypting MPEG video data efficiently. In *Proceedings of the Fourth ACM International Multimedia Conference (ACM Multimedia'96)*. Boston, MA, November 1996, (pp. 219-230).

The Gnutella Protocol. (2001). *The Gnutella Protocol Specification v0.4*. Retrieved from http://www9.limewire.com/developer/gnutella_protocol_0.4.pdf

The iCoord System. (2008). *The ISLab Knowledge Coordination Platform*. Retrieved from http://islab.dico.unimi.it/icoord/

Tilki, J. F., & Beex, A. A. (1996). Encoding a hidden digital signature onto an audio signal using psychoacoustic masking. *Proceedings 1996 7th International Conference on Signal Processing* (pp. 476-480).

Tim Berners-Lee, T., Hendler, J., & Lassila, O. (2001). The Semantic Web. *Scientific American, May.*

Torrubia, A., & Mora, F. (2002). Perceptual cryptography on MPEG Layer III bit-streams. *IEEE Transactions on Consumer Electronics*, *48*(4), 1046–1050. doi:10.1109/TCE.2003.1196437

Torrubia, A., & Mora, F. (2003). Perceptual cryptography of JPEG compressed images on the JFIF bit-stream domain. *Proceedings of the IEEE International Symposium on Consumer Electronics*, ISCE, 17-19 June 2003, (pp. 58-59).

Tosun, A. S., & Feng, W. C. (2000). Efficient multi-layer coding and encryption of MPEG video streams. *Proceedings of IEEE International Conference on Multimedia and Expo.*, *1*, 119–122.

Tosun, A. S., & Feng, W. C. (2001). Lightweight security mechanisms for wireless video transmission. *Proceedings International Conference on Information Technology: Coding and Computing*, *2-4*(April), 157–161. doi:10.1109/ITCC.2001.918783

Tosun, A. S., & Feng, W. C. (2001). On error preserving encryption algorithms for wireless video transmission. *Proceedings of the ACM International Multimedia Conference and Exhibition*, IV, Ottawa, Ont, (pp. 302-308).

Tovée, M. J. (1996). *An introduction to the visual system* (pp. 180–202). Cambridge University Press.

Trichili, H., Bouhlel, M.-S., Solaiman, B., & Kamoun, L. (2003). Exploitation of the HVS features for the enhancement of image watermarking techniques. *ISPA03, 2,* (pp. 1076–1081).

Trikel, A. Z., Rankin, G. A., Schyndel, R. M. V., Ho, W. H., Mee, N. R. A., & Osborne, C. F. (1993). Electronic water-mark. In *Proc. Digital Image Computing: Techniques and Applications* (pp. 666-672). Macquarie University, Sydney.

Tyson, L., & Sherry, E. (1997). Statutory protection for databases: Economic and public policy issues. Retrieved August 25, 2006, from www.infoindustry.org/ppgrc/doclib/grdoc016.htm

Uchida, K. (2005). Fingerprint identification. *NEC Journal of Advanced Technology, 2*(1).

Uehara, T. (2001). *Combined encryption and source coding*. Retrieved from http://www.uow.edu.au/~tu01/CESC.html.

Unsworth, J. (1997). *New copyright and database regulations: USPTO, WIPO, and you*. London, UK: University of London & Oxford University.

Vander, W. T. (2005). Explaining and showing broad and narrow folksonomies. http://www.personalinfocloud.com/2005/02/explaining_and_.html.

Vargo, S. L., & Akaka, M. A. (2009). Service-Dominant Logic as a Foundation for Service Science: Clarifications. *Service Science*, *1*(1), 32–41.

Vervloesem, K. (2006). Croatian government adopts open source software policy. *News Forge*. Retrieved October 16, 2006, from http://www.newsforge.com/article.pl?sid=06/08/11/1855229

Vickrey, W. (1961). Counterspeculation, auction, and competitive sealed tenders. *The Journal of Finance*, *16*(1), 8–37. doi:10.2307/2977633

Viskey. (n.d.). *Home*. Retrieved from http://www.viskey.com

VisualPass. (n.d.). *Home*. Retrieved from http://penguin.poly.edu/seminars/visualpass/visualpasswords.ppt

Voulgaris, S., Gavidia, D., & Van Steen, M. (2005). CYCLON: Inexpensive Membership Management for Unstructured P2P Overlays. *Journal of Network and Systems Management*, *13*(2), 197–217. doi:10.1007/s10922-005-4441-x

Vu, Q. M., Masada, T., Takasu, A., & Adachi, J. (2007). Disambiguation of people in web search using a knowledge base. *In Proceedings of International Conference on Research, Innovation & Vision for the Future Information & Communication Technologies (IEEE RIVF'07)*, 185-191.

Wan, X., Gao, J., Li, M., & Ding, B. (2005). Person resolution in person search results: Webhawk. *In CIKM '05: Proceedings of the 14th ACM international conference on Information and knowledge management*, 163-170, New York, USA, ACM Press.

Wang, S. H., & Lin, Y. P. (2004). Wavelet tree quantization for copyright protection watermarking. *IEEE Transactions on Image Processing*, *13*(2), 154–165. doi:10.1109/TIP.2004.823822

Wang, R. D., Xu, D. W., & Qian, L. (2005). Audio watermarking algorithm based on wavelet packet and psychoacoustic model. *PDCAT*, *2005*, 812–814.

Wang, Y., & Vassileva, J. (2004). Trust-Based Community Formation in Peer-to-Peer File Sharing Networks. In *Proceedings of the IEEE/WIC/ACM International Conference on Web Intelligence (WI'04)*, Beijing, China (pp. 341-348).

Wee, S. J., & Apostolopoulos, J. G. (2001). Secure scalable video streaming for wireless networks. In *Proceedings of the IEEE International Conference on Acoustics, Speech, and Signal Processing*. Salt Lake City UT, May 4, (pp. 2049-2052).

Wee, S. J., & Apostolopoulos, J. G. (2003). Secure scalable streaming and secure transcoding with JPEG-2000. *Proceedings of IEEE International Conference on Image Processing, 1,* (pp. 205-208). Sept. 14-17.

Wei, L. (2002). *Password.* Retrieved from http://wlu-share.tripod.com/ImgPasswd.htm

Weinshall, D. (2004). *Secure authentication schemes suitable for an associative memory.* Leibniz Center for Research in Computer Science, Technical Report 2004-00.

Wen, J., Sevra, M., Luttrell, M., & Jin, W. (2001). A format-compliant configurable encryption framework for access control of multimedia. In *Pro. IEEE Workshop on Multimedia Signal Proc*. Cannes, France, Oct., (pp. 435-440).

Wenger, E. (1998). *Communities of practice: Learning, meaning, and identity*. Cambridge University Press.

Wenger, E. and Snyder, Williams. (2000). Communities of practice: the organizational frontier. *Harvard Business Review*, (January-February): 139–145.

Wenger, E., McDermott, R., & Snyder, W. M. (2002). *Cultivating communities of practice*. Harvard Business School Press.

Weragama, N. S., & Sandirigama, M. (2007). SAS-3: A polynomial based strong password authentication protocol. *International Conference on Industrial and Information Systems, 2007,* (pp. 41-46).

Westen, S. J. P., Lagendijk, R. L., & Biemond, J. (1996). Optimization of JPEG color image coding using a human visual system model. *Proceedings of the Society for Photo-Instrumentation Engineers, 2657*, 370–381.

Westermeier, J. T. (2009). Protecting content on the Internet. *Computer & Internet Lawyer, 26*, 8.

Wikipedia. (2006). *Wikipedia: Copyrights*. Retrieved October 13, 2006, from http://en.wikipedia.org/wiki/Wikipedia:Copyrights

Wilkinson, K., Sayers, C., Kuno, H., & Reynolds, D. (2003). Efficient RDF storage and retrieval in Jena2. In *Proceeding of the First International Workshop on Semantic Web and Databases* (pp. 35-43).

Winn, E. (2000). Who owns the customer? The emerging law of commercial transactions in electronic customer data. *Business Law, 56*, 213.

Wolfe, P. J., & Godsill, S. J. (2000). Towards a perceptually optimal spectral amplitude estimator for audio signal enhancement. *Proceedings of the IEEE International Conference on Acoustics, Speech, and Signal Processing, 2*, 821–824.

Wu, C. P., Su, P. C., & Kuo, C. C. J. (2000). Robust and efficient digital audio watermarking using audio content analysis. [SPIE]. *Security and Watermarking of Multimedia Contents, 3971*, 382–392.

Wu, X. (2002). E.C. database directive. *Berkeley Technology Law Journal, 1*, 974.

Wu, C., & Kuo, C. C. (2000). Fast encryption methods for audiovisual data confidentiality. In *SPIE International Symposia on Information Technologies 2000, Proceedings of SPIE, 4209*, Boston, MA, USA, Nov. 2000, (pp. 284-295).

Wu, C., & Kuo, C. C. (2001). Efficient multimedia encryption via entropy codec design. In *SPIE International Symposium on Electronic Imaging 200, Proceedings of SPIE, 4314,* San Jose, CA, USA, Jan. 2001, (pp. 128-138).

Wu, M., & Liu, B. (1998). Watermarking for image authentication. *Proceedings of 1998 IEEE International Conference on Image Processing*, 2, (pp. 437-441).

Xia, X., Boncelet, C. G., & Arce, G. R. (1997). A multiresolution watermark for digital images. In *Proc. Int. Conf. on Image Processing*, vol. 3 (pp. 548-551). Santa Barbara, CA: IEEE Press.

Xie, G., & Shen, H. (2005). Toward improved wavelet-based watermarking using the pixel-wise Masking Model. *ICICP2005, 1*, (pp. 689-692).

Xing, H., & Scordilis, M. S. (2005). Improved spread spectrum digital audio watermarking based on a modified perceptual entropy psychoacoustic model. *Proceedings of IEEE Southeast Conference*, (pp. 283-286).

Yan, X., Yu, P. S., & Han, J. (2005). Substructure similarity search in graph databases. *SIGMOD Conference 2005*, 766-777.

Yanbe, Y., Jatowt, A., Nakamura, S., & Tanaka, K. (2007) Can social bookmarking enhance search in the web? *In Proceedings of JCDL'2007*. 107-116

Yaqoob, N. (2006). My Ubuntu experience. *SPIDER, September 2006*, 10-12.

Ye, Y., Yang, Q., & Wang, Y. (2003). Magic cube encryption for digital image using chaotic sequence. *Journal of Zhejiang University of Technology*, *31*(2), 173–176.

Yen, J. C., & Guo, J. I. (1999). A new MPEG encryption system and its VLSI architecture. *IEEE Workshop on Signal Processing Systems*, Taipei, (pp. 430-437).

Yencken, L., & Baldwin, T. (2008). Orthographic similarity search for dictionary lookup of Japanese words, *In Proc. of the 22nd International Conference on Computational Linguistics* (COLING 2008), Manchester, UK.

Yeo, I. K., & Kim, H. J. (2003). Modified patchwork algorithm: A novel audio watermarking scheme. *IEEE Transactions on Speech and Audio Processing, 11*(4).

You, J. M., & Chen, K. J. (2006). Improving context vector models by feature clustering for automatic thesaurus construction. *Proceedings of the Fifth SIGHAN Workshop on Chinese Language Processing.*

Yu, B., & Singh, M. P. (2003). Searching social networks. *AAMAS, 2003*, 65–72.

Yu, F. Q., Zhangi, Z. K., & Xu, M. H. (2006). A digital watermarking algorithm for image based on fractional Fourier transform. In *Proc. IEEE Conf. on Industrial Electronics and Applications* (pp. 1-5). Singapore: IEEE Press.

Yu, H., & Yu, X. (2003). Progressive and scalable encryption for multimedia content access control. *Proceeding of IEEE International Conference on Communications*, (pp. 547-550).

Yuan, C., Zhu, B., Wang, Y., Li, S., & Zhong, Y. (2003). Efficient and fully scalable encryption for MPEG-4 FGS. *IEEE Int. Symp. Circuits and Systems*, May, (pp. 620-623).

Yuhang, D., Dayan, Z., & Kejun, W. (2005). A study of hand vein recognition method. *IEEE International Conference Mechatronics and Automation, 4*, (pp. 2106-2110).

Yun, Y. W. (2002). The "123" of biometric technology. *Synthesis Journal, 2002.*

Zeng, W., & Lei, S. (2003). Efficient frequency domain selective scrambling of digital video. *IEEE Transactions on Multimedia, 5*(1), 118–129. doi:10.1109/TMM.2003.808817

Zhang, X. D., Feng, J., & Lo, K. T. (2003). Image watermarking using tree-based spatial-frequency feature of wavelet transform. *Journal of Visual Communication and Image Representation, 14*, 474–491. doi:10.1016/S1047-3203(03)00047-6

Zhang, F., & Zhang, H. (2004). Applications of neural network to watermarking capacity. *IEEE International Symposium on Communications and Information Technology 2004*, vol. 1 (pp. 340-343).

Zhang, J., Wang, N. C., & Xiong, F. (2002). Hiding a logo watermark into the multiwavelet domain using neural networks. *Proceedings of 14th IEEE International Conference on Tools with Artificial Intelligence*, (pp. 477-482).

Zhang, X., & Zhang, F. (2005). A blind watermarking algorithm based on neural network. *ICNN&B '05 International Conference on Neural Networks and Brain IEEE,* vol. 2 (pp. 1073-1076).

Zhang, Z. M., Li, R. Y., & Wang, L. (2003). Adaptive watermark scheme with RBF neural networks. *Proceedings of the 2003 International Conference on Neural Networks and Signal Processing IEEE,* vol. 2 (pp. 1517-1520).

Zhao, W., Chellappa, R., Rosenfeld, A., & Phillips, P. J. (2003). Face recognition: A literature survey. *ACM Computing Surveys*, 399–458. doi:10.1145/954339.954342

Zwicker, E., & Zwicker, U. T. (1991). Audio engineering and psychoacoustics: Matching signals to the final receiver: The human auditory system. *Journal of the Audio Engineering Society. Audio Engineering Society, 39*(3), 115–126.

About the Contributors

Hideyasu Sasaki, a graduate of the University of Tokyo in 1994, received an LLM from the University of Chicago Law School in 1999, and an MS and a PhD in Cybernetic Knowledge Engineering (Media and Governance) with honors from Keio University in 2001 and 2003, respectively. He has been tenured as an Associate Professor at Department of Information Science and Engineering, Ritsumeikan University since 2005. He was an Assistant Professor at Keio University from 2003 to 2005. His research interests include decision science, computational intelligence, soft computing, and service computing. He has been admitted to practice as an attorney-and-counselor at law in the New York State Bar since 2000. He was awarded IARIA Fellow in 2010. He is the founding and current Editor-in-Chief of *International Journal of Organizational and Collective Intelligence*. He serves as a reviewer for *ACM Transactions on TAAS and KDD*. His recent co-authored journal article from IJSSOE is selected as a best paper of the year in 2010. He is active at international program committees of numerous computational intelligence and service computing: ACM MEDES, CICN, SoCPaR, IARIA ICIW, WISS, et cetera.

* * *

Gaurav Bhatnagar has been a member of the Computer Vision and Sensing Systems Laboratory in the Department of Electrical and Computer Engineering at University of Windsor since 2009. He received his BSc from C.C.S. University in 2003 and MSc in Applied Mathematics from Indian Institute of Technology Roorkee in 2005. He has submitted his Ph.D. from Indian Institute of Technology Roorkee, India in 2009. So far he has published 1 book chapter, 8 international journals and 14 conference proceedings. His areas of research include digital watermarking, multimedia encryption, cryptography, image analysis, image fusion, biometrics, and wavelet analysis.

Silvana Castano is full professor of Computer Science at the Università degli Studi di Milano, where she chairs the Information systems & knowledge management (ISLab) group. She received the Ph.D. degree in Computer and Automation Engineering from Politecnico di Milano. Her main research interests are in the area of databases and information systems and ontologies and Semantic Web, with focus on ontology matching and evolution, emergent semantics, knowledge discovery in open networked systems, semantic integration and interoperability. On these topics, she has been working in several national and international research projects, such as EU FP6 BOEMIE, EU FP6 INTEROP-NoE, PRIN ESTEEM, COFIN D2I, FIRB WEB-MINDS. She has been serving as PC member for several important database, information systems, and Semantic Web conferences. In 2009, she is PC co-chair of the ER 2009 conference. Since November 2008, she is the President-Elect of GRIN, the Italian association of University Professors in Informatics.

Chrong-Cheng Chen received his master degree in the Department of Computer Science and Information Engineering from National Central University in 2008. He is now a senior programmer in Industrial Technology Research Institute of Taiwan. His research interests include Web 2.0, OSGi, Cloud Computing, and people search.

William K. Cheung is currently an Associate Professor in the Department of Computer Science, Hong Kong Baptist University. He received the BSc and MPhil degrees in electronic engineering from the Chinese University of Hong Kong and the PhD degree in computer science in 1999 from the Hong Kong University of Science and Technology. He has served as co-chairs and program committee members of a number of international workshops/conferences, as well as guest editors of journals in areas including artificial intelligence, Web intelligence, data mining, Web services, and e-commerce technologies. He is the Managing Editor of the IEEE Intelligent Informatics Bulletin since 2007. His research interests include artificial intelligence and machine learning, as well as their applications to collaborative filtering, Web mining, distributed data mining, planning under uncertainty, and Web services management.

Alfio Ferrara is assistant professor of Computer Science at the University of Milano, where he received his Ph.D. in Computer Science in 2005. His research interests include database and semi-structured data integration, Web-based information systems, ontology engineering, and knowledge representation and evolution. On these topics, he works in national and international research projects, including the recent EU FP6 BOEMIE project, the EU FP6 INTEROP NoE, and the ESTEEM PRIN project funded by the Italian Ministry of Education, University, and Research. He is also author of several articles and papers in international journals and conferences about ontology management and matching.

Koji Fukuya received B.E. from the University of Tokyo in 2008. He studies auction mechanism at Research into Artifacts, Center for Engineering in the University of Tokyo. His research interests include a service modelling using multi-agent system and elucidation of service mechanism by experiments with human subjects.

Giaime Ginesu graduated (MS) in Electronic Engineering (2001), discussing a thesis on thermal image processing and pattern recognition and received PhD degree in Electronic Engineering (2005) from the University of Cagliari, Italy. During 2001, he was at the Institute for Telecommunications of the Technical University of Braunschweig (Germany), to work on thermographic image processing. In 2003 he stayed as visiting scholar at the Rensselaer Polytechnic Institute (Troy, NY), to work on volumetric data coding. Since 2007 he has been working in the ICT project development sector at Regione Autonoma della Sardegna. He teaches Image and video processing for the course of Telecommunications at the Faculty of Engineering, University of Cagliari. His interests are mainly related to signal processing and transmission (image and video processing, coding and transmission and JPEG2000/MPEG standards). He is member of IEEE and of the CNIT research unit in Cagliari.

Daniele Giusto is Director of CNIT@UniCA Lab of Multimedia Communications and Professor of Telecommunications at the Faculty of Engineering, University of Cagliari, Italy, where he teaches Communication Systems and Image Processing and Transmission. He is also a Visiting Professor of Image Processing at the International Advanced School of Optical Technologies, Nuoro, Italy. His research interests are in the area of video/image processing and communication. He is the recipient of the 1993 AEI Ottavio Bonazzi best paper award, and co-recipient of a 1998 IEEE Chester Sall best paper award. Dr. Giusto is a senior member of IEEE, and a member of AEI, EURASIP, and SPIE; he is also a member of the board of CNIT, the Italian University Consortium for Telecommunications, an Evaluator/Auditor for the European Commission, and the Italian National Delegate in the ISO JTC_1/SC_29/WG_1 (JPEG) standardization committee. He has been General Chair for the PACKET VIDEO 2000 International Workshop.

Indy Y.T. Hsiao studied Electric Engineering in DYIT college and graduated in 1996. He then studied Information Management in Tamkang University (TKU) after retiring from the army. His research subject was about how to filter table information to match small device users' needs. He then worked in TKU Information Processing Center right after receiving his master degree. He had worked there for almost 7 years. His major work was maintaining the Teaching Support Platform of TKU, which is the most important teaching related platform of TKU and he had learned a lot from the job. He is now a PhD student at the Department of Computer

Science and Information Engineering in National Central University, Taiwan. His research interests include Web 2.0, e-Portfolio, and Second Life.

Jeff J.S. Huang received his B.S. degree in the Department of information management from Tatung University in 1997 and M.S. degree in the Department of Computer Science and Information Engineering from Tamking University in 2000. He taught at Hsing Kuo University of Management in 2001. He is now a PhD student in the Department of Computer Science and Information Engineering in National Central University. He severed as a Program Committee member of ICCE 2008 (International Conference on Computers in Education). His research interests include Web 2.0, social networking, social computing, context aware ubiquitous computing, Computer-Supported Collaborative Learning, Computer Supported Cooperative Work, e-learning, and knowledge management.

Irene Y.S. Li received her M.A. degree in Graduate Institute of Foreign Languages and Literatures from National Chiao Tung University in 2009. Her research interest was neurolinguistics. She had her teaching practice in Linkou senior high school. Now, she is a research assistant. She works at Department of Computer Science and Information Engineering, National Central University, Taiwan. She assists Ph.D students in making teaching experiment. Her currently research interests include TESL, e-learning, Web 2.0.

Jian Li received the BS and MA degrees in computer science from Wuhan University in 1998 and 2001, respectively, and the PhD degree in computer science from the Institute of Software, Chinese Academy of Sciences, in 2007. He is currently a postdoctoral fellow in the Department of Computer Science at Hong Kong Baptist University. His research interests include semantic web, information integration, and artificial intelligence with applications to data mining.

Shiguo Lian received his PhD from Nanjing University of Science & Technology. He was a Research Assistant in EE Department of City University of Hong Kong in 2004. He has been with France Telecom R&D (Orange Labs) Beijing since 2005. He is the member of IEEE, SPIE, EURASIP, and Chinese Association of Graphics and Images. His research interests include multimedia communication and security, intelligent multimedia analysis, and ubiquitous communication and services.

Mirko Luca Lobina (M'00) is a researcher in telecommunications at the University of Cagliari, Italy. He received PhD in EE and CS from the University of Cagliari in 2004. His main research topics include: privacy and watermarking.

Stefano Montanelli has a Post Doc position in Computer Science at the University of Milano, where he received his Ph.D. in Computer Science in 2006. His main research interests include Semantic Web, ontology matching and evolution, semantic knowledge coordination, and emergent semantics in open distributed systems. On these topics, he is involved in national and international research projects, including the recent EU FP6 BOEMIE project (Bootstrapping Ontology Evolution with Multimedia Information Extraction), the EU FP6 INTEROP NoE (Interoperability Research for Networked Enterprises Applications and Software), and the ESTEEM PRIN project (Emergent Semantics and cooperaTion in multi-knowledgE EnvironMents) funded by the Italian Ministry of Education, University, and Research. He is also author of articles and papers in international journals and conferences about ontology and instance matching, P2P semantic routing and ontology-based P2P community management.

Davide Mula graduated in Business Law at the University LUISS Guido Carli - Roma in 2007, discussing a thesis on legal protection of the web page. He has a Master's degree in "Globalization of Markets and Consumer Protection", Roma Tre University. Today, he is a Lecturer in Informatics and Communication Law at the Europea University of Rome, School of Law and School of Economics and PhD student in Public and Private in Business Law at the European University of studies in Rome. He has been a speaker at Congresses and Seminars and member of several research projects and groups on competition, intellectual property, advertising, communications and new technology law. His main research topics include: IP, consumer, and telecommunications.

Kensuke Naoe graduated the faculty of Environment and Information Studies at Keio University in 2002. He received the Master degree in 2004 and PhD in 2009 from Graduate School of Media and Governance at Keio University. His major is artificial neural network and information security. He is interested in the area of research in digital watermarking and image hashing using neural network, machine learning, network intrusion detection, and cryptography.

Nariaki Nishino is an associate professor at Department of Technology Management for Innovation, School of Engineering, the University of Tokyo. He received his B.E. and M.E. from Kobe University and Ph.D. from the University of Tokyo in 2004. He was an assistant professor of Co-creation Engineering Research Division, Research into Artifacts, Center for Engineering (RACE) in the University of Tokyo from 2007 to 2009. He is engaged in the studies of social systems introducing the method of experimental economics and agent-based simulation. His research interests include game theories, network externalities, auction theories, and service system design. He is also active in collaborative researches on decision-making problems with manufacturing and service industries in Japan.

Natalie Pang received her PhD from Monash University, Australia. Her interdisciplinary research examined community participation in digital or transmedia contexts, and the role of institutions/technology sanctioning or facilitating cooperation in such shared spaces. Her research has been awarded the Vice Chancellor's Commendation for Doctoral thesis excellence, and the Faculty of IT Doctoral Medal at Monash University for 2009. Other research interests include: the study of common pool resources, records management, participatory/open space design, conditions and consequences of media technologies, human-computer interaction, social theory, and philosophy. Natalie has worked in Singapore, Malaysia, Australia, China, and Italy. She has served as an Honorary Research Associate of Museum Victoria and the Victorian Association for Tertiary Libraries in Australia. Natalie is also a contributing member of the Foundation for Peer to Peer Alternatives, with interests in Web 2.0, social networks, and the application of open content licenses.

Balasubramanian Raman is an Assistant Professor in the Department of Mathematics at Indian Institute of Technology Roorkee since February 2006. He received his PhD in Mathematics from Indian Institute of Technology, Madras, India in 2001. He received his BSc and MSc in Mathematics from University of Madras in 1994 and 1996, respectively. So far he has published 26 international journals, 41 conference proceedings, 4 book chapter and a technical report. His areas of research include computer vision, graphics, satellite image analysis, scientific visualization, imaging geometry, reconstruction problems, biometrics, and watermarking.

Yoshiyasu Takefuji is a tenured Professor on Faculty of Environmental Information at Keio University since April 1992. He was an Editor of the *Journal of Neural Network Computing*, an associate editor of *IEEE Trans. on Neural Networks*, *Neural/parallel/scientific computations,* and *Neurocomputing*, and a guest editor of *Journal Analog Integrated Circuits and Signal Processing* in the special issue on analog VLSI neural networks and also guest editor of *Neurocomputing* in the special issue on neural network optimization.

Kanji Ueda received his B.E. and M.E. degrees in precision engineering and Ph.D. degree (1978) from Osaka University. He is currently a vice president at the National Institute of Advanced Industrial Science and Technology (AIST) and an emeritus professor at RACE (Research into Artifacts, Center for Engineering) at the University of Tokyo, Japan. He has been engaged in research and teaching at Kobe University, Kanazawa University, and the University of Tokyo for more than 30 years since 1972 in the fields of manufacturing systems and computational intelligence. He has published over 400 scientific papers and 15 books. He has also been given many best paper awards and research awards by academic societies and research foundations. He is also serving on editorial boards as a co-editor or a member for many international journals.

Gaia Varese is a Ph.D. student in Computer Science at the University of Milano, where she received her master degree in Computer Science in 2008. Her main research interests include semantic web, ontology matching, and knowledge representation and evolution. On these topics, she has been involved in the EU FP6 BOEMIE project.

Jonathan Wu received the PhD degree in Electrical Engineering from the University of Wales, Cardiff, U.K., in 1990. In 1995, he joined the National Research Council of Canada, Ottawa, ON, Canada, where he was a Senior Research Officer and Group Leader. He is currently a full Professor with the Department of Electrical and Computer Engineering, University of Windsor, Windsor, ON. He is a holder of the Canada Research Chair in automotive sensors and sensing systems. He is the author of over 100 published scientific papers in the areas of computer vision, neural networks, fuzzy systems, robotics, micro sensors and actuators, and integrated microsystems. Dr. Wu is an Associate Editor for the *IEEE Transactions on Systems Man and Cybernetics—PART A: Systems and Humans*. His current research interests include 3-D image analysis, active video object extraction, vision-guided robotics, sensor analysis and fusion, wireless sensor networks, multimedia security, and integrated microsystems.

Stephen J.H. Yang received his PhD degree in Computer Science from the University of Illinois at Chicago in 1995. He is now a professor of the Department of Computer Science and Information Engineering, and is also the Associate Dean of Academic Affairs in National Central University, Taiwan. He is the co-founder and the CEO of T5 Corp, a company providing XML-based Web services. Dr. Yang has published 2 books and over 150 journal articles and conference papers. He is currently the Co-Editor-in-Chief of International Journal of Knowledge Management & E-Learning, an advisory board member of Educational Technology and Society, and an editorial board member of International Journal of Web Services Research and International Journal of Knowledge and Learning. He severed as the Program Co-Chair of IEEE MSE 2003, IEEE CAUL 2006, and IEEE W2ME 2007. His research interests include Web services, Web 2.0, software engineering, knowledge engineering, semantic Web, and context aware ubiquitous computing. He is a member of IEEE.

Index

D

E

F

G

H

I

J

K

L

M

N

O

P

Q

R

S

T

V

W

Z

CPSIA information can be obtained at www.ICGtesting.com
Printed in the USA
BVOW081748030512

289291BV00006B/5/P

9 781613 501351